A Bentham Reader

Edited by Mary Peter Mack

PEGASUS   NEW YORK

A Bentham Reader

Contents

Introduction

Here is an eternal dilemma of human knowledge: we cannot think at all *without* labels and compartments, for the flood of unorganized experience is altogether overwhelming and ungovernable; and we cannot think at all well and truly *with* them, for no men, no ideas are as small, rigid, and bloodless as the labels and compartments thrust upon them. Labels are deadly. They diminish any man, but they murder the giant. Bentham was such a giant, and he has been so prodigally mislabeled, and over so many generations successively forced into so many ever more cramped compartments, that his reputation is now ground to dust. The source and kind are of little account. The highest celebration, the basest denunciation; it is much the same. Disciples are no more just, open, and flexible than enemies. Almost all their labels are mislabels, from god-like veneration to curses, and Bentham has suffered them all. Few men have ever been raised up so high and then pitched so far below, once so deified and then profaned. The response is now often automatic: it is instant contempt.

What are labels, however, but names, and compartments but empty boxes? So Bentham himself explained to the Czar Alexander in 1815:

> Altogether above dispute, are the importance of good arrangement to legislation, and the importance of a set of synoptic tables . . . to good arrangement: good arrangement and good tables are at once *effect* and *cause*. . . . Here are so many *drawers* or *boxes*. But the *contents?*—what will they be? Everything depends upon the contents. . . .[1]

"Reader!" exclaimed the French revolutionary, Brissot, of Bentham, "Has your imagination ever attempted to trace the portraits of those rare beings, whom Heaven sometimes sends down upon earth as a consola-

---

[1] Ed. Bowring, *Bentham's Collected Works,* IV, p. 525, hereafter referred to by volume number.

tion for woes, who in the form of imperfect man, possess a heavenly spirit?"[2] In the stormy early years of the nineteenth century, during the Napoleonic Empire and the age of repression that followed it, Bentham was hailed from St. Petersburg to Lisbon as "the Newton of the moral world," who had laid down for all time the basic universal laws of Utility; of pleasure and pain as the original energy of all human action, and the greatest happiness principle as the end by which all existing institutions could and must be measured and would thereby be found evil. Here in his work for the first time they discovered a genuine science of morals and legislation.

George Borrow was seized as a spy while distributing Bibles in a small Spanish town in the 1830's and hauled before the mayor. When he identified himself as an Englishman, he was then immediately freed with a blessing—not as a missionary of the old Christian religion, but as the compatriot of the founder of a new. "The grand Baintham [*sic*]," the mayor rhapsodized. "He who has invented laws for all the world . . . the most universal genius which the world ever produced—a Solon, a Plato, and a Lope de Vega." "Now, here am I," he added, "a simple alcalde of Galicia. Yet I possess all the writings of Baintham on that shelf, and I study them day and night."[3] Even that sharp-eyed cynic, the Marquis de Talleyrand, was full of praise: "The whole world steals from him—and still he is always rich."

But from these giddy heights Bentham has long since been hurled to the pit of abuse, and there he now remains. Men steal from him no longer. To Emerson, Utilitarianism was "a stinking philosophy"; to Nietzsche, "an impossible literature." Goethe called Bentham himself "that frightfully radical ass," and Marx branded him "the arch-philistine . . . the insipid leather-tongued oracle of the commonplace bourgeois intelligence . . . a genius in the way of bourgeois stupidity." Nor did his style escape odium. "I felt," confessed Augustine Birrell, "as though I had been asked to masticate an icthyosaurus." Hazlitt suggested, "His works have been translated into French—they ought to be translated into English."[4]

Each succeeding generation adds another layer of obloquy, and Lord Keynes' shrill diagnosis of the post-Edwardian era is often still assumed as axiomatic today: Benthamism was "the worm which has been gnawing at the insides of modern civilization and is responsible for its present moral decay." On the other hand, Harold Laski, despite his often slap-dash assessments, was measured and appreciative about Bentham: "If

[2] X, 192.
[3] C. W. Everett, *The Education of Jeremy Bentham,* xvi.
[4] All quotes are from M. P. Mack, *Jeremy Bentham,* pp. 2, 196.

Bentham had possessed Hume's exquisite style, instead of his own system of barbarous convolutions, political science would have been fifty years ahead of its present position."[5]

Here then are two vastly distant, different pictures of Bentham's Utilitarian world: the one an earthly kingdom, a secular heaven of certain, pure deductive science, simple universal laws, practical reform, and unending exhilarating progress; the other, a hell of shallow philistinism, ugly neologisms, rationalism, and mechanical calculation. Which one was Bentham's? The fact is—neither.

The history of ideas is never a clean record of what a man said, but always a palimpsest of what others say he said; and Bentham's writings are hopelessly scribbled over with the rhetoric of Victorian piety. The cliché ogre almost everywhere execrated today is largely a fantasy of the prim, earnest, nineteenth-century, middle-class Evangelical; and our subsequent horror of both. The prurient ascetic Victorian saw Bentham in his own image and remade him accordingly. He foisted his faith in individualism, *laissez faire,* and self-help; his hunger for certainty; his morals of prudence, asceticism, and self-denial on Bentham; and so warped him nearly beyond recognition.

The rise and fall, or the use and abuse of Bentham is in itself a very long, intricate, and still untold story. If relentlessly pursued, such a chronicle alone could easily become a history of nineteenth- and twentieth-century British and European thought. "A great man," said Hegel, "condemns men to explicate him"; he also condemns them to explicate his explicators, to become archaeologists who must dig through layer upon layer of later judgment and interpretation. There is no help for it and no alternative: either we cast aside most preconceptions about Bentham, and unearth and read his work afresh, or he never will be truly understood.

Thus this book. It is the first comprehensive edition of selections, the first effort to trace the full development of Bentham's thought in his own words, from his earliest memoranda when he was in his twenties in the early 1770's to his last epigrams at the age of eighty-four in 1832, since his own lifetime nearly a century and a half ago. A serious effort has here been made to identify and offer every one of his most important ideas. Almost all that has hitherto been easily available have been the early *A Fragment on Government* (1776) and *An Introduction to the Principles of Morals and Legislation* (1780–81). Both of these, it is most important to insist, are fragments only; the first, of a full running critique of Blackstone's *Commentaries;* and the second, of a general preface to a

[5] *Ibid.*

complete code of law. From neither is it possible to gather a full picture of the structure, breadth, and development of Bentham's thought. This book is intended to supply it, to offer what has been dug up from the huge buried masses of Bentham MSS as evidence for a new evaluation. What lost and buried world will be discovered there? Not one, but two—a hell and a heaven: the world as it is and as it ought to be; on the one hand, the Technical System, as he called it,[6] or the entire English Establishment as it was, the whole institutional structure, in his eyes so many dens of evil in a labyrinth of arbitrary cruelty, nepotism, venality, corruption, and uncertainty, all under the reign of Chaos, all of which he attacked with unflagging, irrepressible enthusiasm;[7] and, on the other hand, the Natural System, *his* system, the world as it ought to be, based on genuine human feelings of pleasure and pain, his own self-styled vision of a New Jerusalem which drove him enthralled and undaunted on a pilgrim's progress that spanned sixty dedicated years and hundreds of thousands of manuscript pages. To the last day of his life he was still "codifying" exultantly, with the fiery zeal "of any dragon." In his last work, the monumental, unfinished *Constitutional Code,* he still pursued "the degree of supposed perfection which has, like a *New Jerusalem,* been always in view."[8]

This was no rationalist laying down rigid mechanical laws, but a self-styled Romantic frankly chasing an admitted mirage. What were the characteristics of his Natural System? Every philosopher has his key words and phrases; he may or may not be aware of them, but they are nevertheless most revealing. Among Bentham's favorites, which to consider may at least begin to unlock the true nature of his scientific method, are "possibilities," "probabilities," "preponderance," "approximation," and especially "degrees" of more or less, ranging as he often said from zero to infinity. All these he applied continually to perhaps the key of all key phrases, the hyphenated "art-and-science."

He was never at any time entranced with that *ignis fatuus,* the almost universal fascination and faith until modern indeterminacy physics began to snuff it out, in the substantial existence of absolute, perfect certainty. The only "certainty" he recognized was purely formal, the tautologous propositions of deductive logic. But in the entire realm of human feeling and action, no such substantive entities existed, and he declared again and again that any description of any species of human behavior as "per-

---

[6] This as well as the following terms—Establishment, Natural System, codifying—all are Bentham's. He was an indefatigable word-monger.

[7] Though disproportionately little criticism is offered in this book, which is largely concerned to portray his own substantive system.

[8] IX, 146.

fect," "pure," or "certain," was "a term of perfection which it is not possible to reach," though, as a guide or standard, "it is well to have it before our eyes."[9] The Bentham who was so long acclaimed as "the Newton of the moral world" and then dismissed on that very account never existed. With our present feeble knowledge it is impossible, as most of the standard texts truly say, to lay down universal certain laws of human behavior, to create a pure science of morals and legislation strictly analogous to classical physics—any more than it is possible to create a "pure" or "certain" physics. It is also abundantly clear to all who care to read him that Bentham unfailingly said the same. Not even mathematics, he insisted, was any more than highly probable. Uncertainty is "an imperfection no less undeniable than it is believed to be irremediable. . . . Approximation is, throughout, the utmost that can be hoped for."[10]

What do the hyphens between Bentham's favorite phrase, "art-and-science," signify? That the now cliché problem of the "two cultures" had no meaning for him. Neither art nor science is ever pure; neither exists without the other. There is no knowing without doing, theory without practice, science without art. He well knew, as every genuinely creative artist and scientist does know, that they are inseparable. It was all a matter of degree, and the balance, the "preponderance" or "probability" was always on the side of art. He often asked: without practice, action, that is, art, what are all of theory and knowledge and science worth? And he always answered: just nothing.

It is not therefore Newton with whom Bentham should properly be compared. His entire Natural System of Utility was always proudly, gloriously, a composite impure "art-and-science." In his art, therefore, in his passionate moral imagination, he was rather the William Blake or the Martin Luther of the moral world; and in his science, the Francis Bacon, struggling deliberately to create not a *Principia Mathematica* but a *Novum Organum,* a new method.

Already in his earliest book, *A Fragment on Government,* in 1776, he insisted upon the radical distinction between what *is* and what *ought to be,* that is, between the empirical facts, the foundation of his new science, and the value judgments that are its end or justification. In a vast system whose entire formal structure was "exhaustive bifurcation," that is, the ancient Aristotelian classification by exclusive alternatives (X is either A or not A, etc., based on the law of the excluded middle), this division was fundamental. It cut decisively through everything he ever wrote and in his formal analyses he never once blurred it.

[9] C. K. Ogden, ed., *Bentham's Theory of Legislation,* p. 102.
[10] VIII, 100, *Chrestomathia.*

It provided him with one of his fundamental problems, just as it still remains a fundamental problem of value theory today: how can the two levels of discourse be reconciled? How can what *is* and what *ought to be* be tied together? To find his answer, Bentham invented a *Novum Organum,* a "Natural System,"—no less than a new logic, a logic of the will. From the time of Aristotle, he said, there had been only one logic, classical deductive logic whose propositions were assertive sentences merely: "The tickets have been bought." But what about commands and questions? Do they not follow a logic of their own? "Buy the tickets." "Have the tickets been bought?" Bentham's subject was always the law; his audience was always the legislator; and the legislator's discourse always began with a question, that is, with the collection of evidence, and ended with a command, that is, a substantive law, an act of legislation. The logic of the will is therefore the fundamental structure, the very architecture of Bentham's system, and it has four levels.

Working from the bottom up, he began with pleasures and pains, the basic elements of human feeling. They are initially neutral in his analysis. *All* human responses of whatever kinds are either pleasures or pains. They are like Hobbes's desires and aversions, toward or from; whatever we are attracted to or respond toward is a pleasure; whatever we shun or move from is a pain. Every man's constellation of pleasures and pains will of course be different but, as Bentham explained in *An Introduction,* it will be shaped and modified by a great variety of observable, even measurable circumstances—age, sex, profession, education, etc. Looking at human behavior as he always did from the point of view of a judge in court, Bentham saw that he was willy-nilly forced to become a psychologist, forced every day to make dozens of rapid-fire judgments about motives, tastes, passions, actions. Looking at eighteenth-century common and statute law as it was in fact practiced, then, Bentham asked, what kind of psychology is implicit in it? And he was stunned to discover its puerility and crudity. The law, he found, acknowledged no motive, no passion but money. Everyone, everything had a price and could be bought. The love of power, of reputation, the passion of sex did not, as far as the law admitted, exist; and yet these were, so far as Bentham could see, among the most powerful of all human motives.

He knew perfectly well and said again and again that the depths of the mind are possibly infinite; we all hide our actions with covering motives; none of us truly knows our own minds, much less those of others; no motive is *a priori* good or bad; none so rare, so seemingly feeble that it cannot rise up at any time in any man to overwhelm all others. Given a little sympathy, it should be clear how humbly Bentham offered his lists: as a miner's first exploratory inventories, admittedly, inevitably rough and incomplete where few or none had dug before. "O Orthodox!" he implored:

> ... show me where I am mistaken and I will recant. ...
> Is there any one of . . . my pages in which the love of human kind has for a moment been forgotten? Show it to me, and this hand shall be the first to tear it out. ...
> Cast off the prejudices that blind you, drive away the phantoms that affright you; take the line and plummet in your hands, and with firm and cautious steps descend with me into the heart of man.[11]

It was therefore one of the judges' first duties—and all the more so Bentham's, as the judges' guide and teacher—to begin making psychological generalizations, hypothetical empirical rules about human behavior, to be constantly tested and corrected in use. They were by no means rigid, iron-clad, *a priori* "laws"; indeed in Bentham's sense they could not be, for he reserved the term "law" strictly for legislators' commands. Thus the second story of Bentham's new structure, that is, what he often called "Axioms of Mental (or Moral) Pathology."

Rising above these tentative generalizations were four subordinate Principles of Utility, or convenient categories under which these "Axioms" might be grouped: subsistence, abundance, security, and equality. They rose in their own hierarchy from the lowest in the order of importance, equality, to the highest, subsistence and security. It is obvious that subsistence is a precondition of life itself and therefore of the other three principles; but Bentham also insisted on the importance, even urgency, of security, for it alone of the four depends upon time, a guarantee that what exists today will exist tomorrow.

Finally, soaring above the whole edifice, was the legislators' Golden Rule, the Greatest Happiness Principle, the principle that states that the sole foundation, the end and aim of all good government, should be the greatest happiness of the greatest number. Did Bentham mean the greatest amount of happiness altogether, regardless of number; or did number count above amount? Emphatically, numbers counted. This Bentham justified on empirical grounds, that the law of diminishing returns is at work in moral economy as elsewhere; and that any amount of pain is more painful than pleasure is pleasurable. One of his important standing principles was the Orders of Evil: that evil is directly proportionate to the radius of consequences and sufferers. The greatest of all evils is therefore revolution under which potentially everyone suffers.

This is the barest sketch merely of Bentham's overall system; the texts in this book and the prefaces to them are efforts to fill in the details, of

[11] X, 142, 178.

quintessential importance to him whose test of the validity of his method depended altogether on the meticulousness of observed detail.

We have now come to perhaps the thorniest of all Bentham problems. On what grounds can this principle be justified? What is its status? It is obviously a sweeping value judgment: by what means are we to leap from lesser empirical psychological generalizations to such a vast normative judgment? Bentham himself did not see the problem; he merely laid the principle down as fundamental, as an ethical resolution analogous to the doctors' Hippocratic oath. Indeed, he suggested that legislators take such an oath upon inauguration:

> Never . . . will I suffer myself to be guided by any other wish or rule, than that by which a surgeon is guided in the treatment given to his patients. . . . Never will I concur in administering, to any . . . patient . . . pain . . . exceeding the least, that, in my eyes, is sufficient, for preserving the whole community, himself included, from pain in some greater quantity.[12]

How can the legislator know what constitutes the greatest happiness of the greatest number? Bentham would have used the same medical analogy; in legislation as in medicine, good judgment proceeds by calm observation, trial and error, sometimes by negative analogy. When the legislator is faced with reforms, he can as yet have little idea of the workings of unprecedented new cases, but he will have behind him a host of evil consequences of non-reform. Gradually, little by little, as law became a valid, empirically tested, psychological science, based on Bentham's new methods, the gap between the empirical lower levels of the system and the normative greatest happiness principle would narrow. In due course, the body of reliable generalizations would have become so large that a judge might turn to his case books with as much confidence as a physicist turns to the laws of thermodynamics.

Once again Bentham's teacher was Sir Francis Bacon, "that resplendent genius." "*Fiat lux,* were the words of the Almighty:—*Fiat experimentum,* were the words of the brightest genius he ever made."[13] He borrowed the fundamental principle of utility from Priestley, but he took his ambition—to bridge the gap between what *is* and what *ought to be*—from Bacon. He was inspired above all by one particularly illuminating passage from *The Advancement of Learning:*

> . . . all those which have written of laws, have written either as Philosophers or as Lawyers, and not as Statesmen. As for the philosophers, they make imaginary laws for imaginary commonwealths, and their discourses are as the stars, which give little light because they are so high. For the lawyers, they write according to the States where they live, what *is* received law, and not what ought to be law. . . .[14]

[12] IX, 201.
[13] VIII, 99, 437.
[14] Bk. II, *Works,* ed. Mallet, V, II, p. 539.

They write, he added, "as in fetters." Who then shall order and rule the world between? Who then shall span the distance between the eagle and the mole, the philosophers' celestial flights and the lawyers' earth-bound burrowings? "This doctrine," he concluded, "doubtless, properly belongs to statesmen, who best understand civil society, [and] the good of the people." . . .[15]

Indeed, Bentham was so inspired by these words that he paid them an honor unique in his writings: he placed them as an epigraph on his title page. It was his first book, *Elements of Critical Jurisprudence,* a yet unpublished, gigantic, enthusiastic, encyclopedic outburst of hundreds upon hundreds of manuscript pages, a celebration of his great discoveries of the principles of utility in the late 1760's. In the text he expanded in his own way on Bacon's words.

> Between us two might the philosopher and the lawyer say, there is a great gulph. I have endeavoured to throw a bridge over this gulph: so that on it, as on Jacob's Ladder, if not Angels, man, however, may continually be henceforth seen ascending and descending.
>
> The Lawyer immersed in the muddy ditch of his *particulars,* scarce dares to think of mounting to the regions of Philosophy. The philosopher delighted and captivated by his *generals,* deigns not to sink into the gross world of law. . . .
>
> Philosophy for want of more substantial stuff spinning with Cobwebs—Jurisprudence piling up in wide confusion a huge heap of odds and ends for want of spinning. Should I be found so happy as to succeed in bridging these celestial artizans into a more close acquaintance, what a rich and serviceable manufacture may not be hoped for from their united labours.[16]

In a second version Bentham varied the image from "gulph" to mountainside, with Philosophy above and Law below. "Between these two lies a dreary.waste: trackless. . . . I propose to take [it] in hand for cultivation: and in so doing to open a communication [between them]. . . ."[17]

He had no doubt whatever that he could do no more noble and important work, for even in these early fragments he said, "Other Arts and Sciences take in hand each a particular and narrow division of human actions. Jurisprudence extends its views over every species of arts whatever."[18] Forty-five years later his message was still the same:

> Exercising dominion over almost every branch of art and science . . . more necessarily in furtherance of the interests of the whole community, the legislator, on pain of acting blindfold, has need of an insight,—the more clear, correct, and extensive the better,—into the matter of every such branch of art and science.

[15] *Ibid.*
[16] Box 27, pp. 14–16, University College Collection, London.
[17] *Ibid.*
[18] *Ibid.*

Therefore Bentham considered a universal Map of Jurisprudence, a logic of the will, including not only a "Table of *logical relations,*" but also a "Table of relation of *dependence* or *subservience*" as "an essential accompaniment"[19] for the sovereign legislator. And it was Bentham's own duty, as he saw it, to be the legislators' guide or scout, the geographer or map-maker who laid out in exhaustive detail the tight network of interrelationships between every human interest and action, every feeling of pleasure and pain, and the central master art-and-science of legislation based on the supreme principle of utility.

But so far Bentham had devised so many boxes merely, formal structures empty of content, the tentative beginnings of a science as yet without art. He had next to fill up the boxes by infinitely detailed empirical observations about the way men actually do behave. Then finally he had to assess the evidence and remake evil institutions accordingly, a job for generations of men, not one young boy in 1770. But Bentham was nothing if not ambitious. In the 1780's when he first began to study constitutional law, that branch which "in difficulty, so in importance . . . far surpasses every other,"[20] he explained, "My way is first to represent what is *possible,* next what is *eligible,* and lastly what is established."[21] He cast himself, therefore, in two roles, critic and creator, and actually worked the other way around. First he had to demolish the corrupt and corrupting, decaying structure of the old Establishment, or in his angry vituperation, the "Augean stable," a "sink," "swamp," "jungle," "pit," "cesspool" of misery. First he played the critic and then the creator, or as he announced in *A Fragment:*

> There are two characters, one or other of which every man who finds anything to say on the subject of Law, may be said to take upon him;—that of Expositor, and that of Censor. To the province of the Expositor it belongs to explain to us what, as he supposes, the Law *is:* to that of the Censor, to observe to us what he thinks it *ought to be.*[22]

Like all great artists, therefore, Bentham sought to order disorder, and to do it objectively for all men, choked and fettered as they were in archaic bonds of organization. He struggled to bring a present reign of chaos and uncertainty under a new Utilitarian, highly probable, and at best, nearly certain rule of law; as Expositor and Censor, to describe and then transform what is into what ought to be. As he explained as late as 1831, he had always made it an absolute point of honor "be the institution what it might, never to engage in any such attempt as that of

[19] VIII, 102.
[20] II, 270–71.
[21] Box 169, p. 133, University College Collection.
[22] I, 229.

pulling it down, but for the purpose, and with the endeavour, to raise up something that to me seemed better, in the room of it. . . ."[23]

As a Censor Bentham was always a great builder, an inventor. It was his most inspired gift and his true measure as an artist. Certainly he was the greatest social inventor England and perhaps all of Western civilization has ever produced. "Less is more" or elegant simplicity was for him as for Mies van der Rohe one chief test of aesthetic and scientific value; and he sought throughout his life to give his fundamental principles the terse concision of mathematical formulae. One of the fundamental Axioms or Instruments of Invention was "Aspice finem": Look to the end in view; for he was sure that as the balance of value lay all on the side of art over science, he could not stress his dedication to practical reform often enough.

Only by attention to the end . . . can improvement in any shape be made. Only with reference to use—understood always as the attainment of happiness . . . has knowledge . . . any claim to attention: only with reference to practise has knowledge any use; only by its subservience to art is science of any use.[24]

To his early disciples no less than to his critics, Bentham was the quintessential English embodiment of the French classical Enlightenment, the great thinking machine who had re-imported and finally summarized and synthesized the moral and political insights developed throughout the eighteenth century by the French heirs of the Newtonian and Lockean traditions. As presumably Newton stood, so he gratefully acknowledged, "upon the shoulders of giants," upon Tycho Brahe's laborious, massive collection of astronomical observations, Copernicus' first limited challenge of the Ptolemaic theory, Kepler's celestial laws of planetary ellipses, and Galileo's further laws of terrestrial gravity, so presumably did Bentham stand upon the shoulders of Voltaire for his scathing blasts against the established order, Beccaria for his theory of crime and punishments, and Helvétius for his hedonics of pleasure and pain.

Certainly Bentham was under these obligations and he, too, gratefully acknowledged them; but the claim mistakes his ambitions. He was no Newtonian. His most general principles were never offered as objective "laws" of nature but always rather humbly as private opinions, his own feelings based upon "reasons" why X or Y ought to be done. There is much misunderstanding over Bentham's use of the word "reasons." What did he mean by it?

To him they were always empirical matters of fact, but inasmuch as experimental social laboratories were Utopian fantasies, his principles were necessarily often prophecies of hope as yet unexampled, and he

---

[23] X, 26.
[24] Box 101, p. 199, 24 Oct. 1826, University College Collection.

had to use the only available facts the case afforded: historical analogies. John Stuart Mill was perhaps the first to deride him as "anti-historical," and the label has stuck; but Bentham always—perhaps inevitably—began as an historian, certainly a highly selective, often vituperative, but nevertheless a most knowledgeable one. As an Expositor, he was always either a preserver or destroyer, arguing that what *is* and therefore *was* causes measurable pain or pleasure. The Censor and inventor, the architect and builder, then took over, creating what ought to be upon the redesigned foundations, eliminating past evils and strengthening the good. But most of his historical analogies were negative, whose causes must be demolished and avoided in the future;—and such "facts" as these are not what physics is made of. But furthermore and obviously, his principles were entirely psychological and social, altogether human and not Newtonian syntheses of terrestrial and celestial.

The source of Bentham's inspiration was not only scientific, but moral and aesthetic; not so much the scientist's joy in elegant simplicity and the beauty of formal theory as a still greater sensitivity to all suffering, animal and human alike—the passionate protest of a Romantic poet. Indeed, bizarre as it may seem initially, William Blake is Bentham in verse. They both cursed the state as it was and had visions of a New Jerusalem. These verses have a true Benthamic ring.

> A dog starv'd at his master's gate
> Predicts the ruin of the State,
> A Horse misus'd upon the road
> Calls to heaven for human blood. . . .
>
> I wander thro' each charter'd street,
> Near where the charter'd Thames does flow,
> And mark in every face I meet
> Marks of weakness, marks of woe.

Here is hedonism:

> Abstinence sows sand all over
> The ruddy limbs and flaming hair,
> But Desire gratified
> Plants fruits of life and beauty there.

Blake even defined Bentham's formal method in an epigram: "Art and science cannot exist but in minutely organized particulars"; and seen as a whole, Bentham's work is an almost overwhelming, boundless, dynamic, structural system of minutely organized particulars, a spectacular prodigality of meticulous critical analysis and creative social invention. Every great artist creates his own new world from the heights and depths of his private moral and intellectual vision, and gives it shape; he lends to "airy nothing a local habitation and a name." Bentham did no less. Certainly he was an artist and so he saw himself, not of course as a poet, for his prose is often notorious rather for its indigestibility than its lyricism, but as an architect of legislation and therefore, because legislation is the all-encompassing art-and-science, of a whole new social order. It was an avowed New Jerusalem, perhaps an unattainable Utopia that would nevertheless draw men by education and new habit ever closer to it and ultimately transform their minds and hearts.

In any case, Bentham's loving attention to minute particulars, to the unique quality and value of every individual is one hallmark of Romanticism, and certainly in this way as well as others he was a romantic visionary like Blake. "Romance . . . the Utopia . . . Romance—," he exclaimed of his work. "How should it be anything less?"[25] On the other hand, he was an optimist, and intended his new Jerusalem to be a workable Utopia, a promised land that could be reached, for he dedicated his life to creating the needed arts-and-sciences himself. He fully expected that, in time, the whole vast chasm separating the two worlds of is and ought, of Chaos and Utility, could be filled in by infinitely laborious, detailed, empirical "experience, observation, and experiment."[26] "In the *Utopia of the sixteenth century*," he said, "effects present themselves without any appropriate causes, in this of the nineteenth century, *appropriate causes* are presented waiting for their *effects.*"[27]

One example, perhaps the most comprehensive, that poured so prodigally from his teeming mind was his scheme for Panopticon Hill Villages.[28] It evolved in the late 1790's from his earlier prison plans, after some eight or nine years of further thought, and was intended as a grand laboratory of social and economic invention, a self-sufficient and subordinate social and economic system self-contained within the larger British economy as a whole, yet without threatening it or disturbing its equilibrium, but on the contrary, systematically adding to its wealth and resources. It was to set an example to the nation at large in somewhat the same way as Israeli kibbutzes do to the surrounding Arab territories, as centers of the latest experimental techniques in agriculture, manufacturing, and social welfare. Bentham's villages would have looked rather like Ebenezer Howard's garden villages, urban centers surrounded by green belts, large stands of trees for future shipbuilding use, and then beyond that, outlying experimental farms. His division of labor was to

[25] VIII, 362.
[26] His phrase for the scientific method in brief.
[27] My italics, quoted in Graham Wallas, *Men and Ideas*, p. 43.
[28] See below, pp. 189*ff.*

have been one-third manufacturing and two-thirds agricultural, and he hoped to find at least two skilled suitable jobs for every able and semi-able inhabitant.

Who were these inhabitants to have been? The lame, the halt, the blind, the helpless—criminals, orphans, the unemployed and their families, retired soldiers and sailors. The villages, spaced about thirty miles or one good day's walking distance apart, were to have credit banks for the poor, and unemployment offices and gazettes covering the whole nation so that a laborer thrown out of work in the northwest, hearing of work in the southeast, might work his way down day by day at no cost to himself. Bentham hoped to have an army of inventors at work producing the most modern and efficient tools and machines for industrial mass production, designed for the most part so that even the most unskilled and crippled might find some interesting, socially useful work to do. He had a number of intuitions about work loads and the learning process that he hoped to test—for example, that too much repetitive work is boring and ultimately inefficient. He therefore hoped to train everyone in several skills, at least one indoors, in manufacturing, and one outdoors in agriculture. His people, except the criminals of course, were free to come and go, as soon as they had, on the profit-sharing plan, saved enough, or found a better job in the outside world.

A main feature of his communities was schools of every kind—music, merchant marine, nurses' and governess' schools, agricultural academies. Free education was to be available to all, young and old alike; and he wanted also to test another intuition, that sexual appetite reaches its highest peak in the late 'teens. He therefore would have encouraged early marriages and observed the results. In this way, he said, beggars might be happier than kings, who sometimes had to wait for years to find suitable alliances.

These plans were never more than the scrappiest fragments, largely mere ruled lists of suggestions on scattered pages. The nineties were a reactionary age, no time for innovation; and the failure of Panopticon, even after so much official sanction, was sobering; but they do show Bentham's extraordinary fertility of imagination, and were the furthest steps he ever marched toward a New Jerusalem.

He made dozens of minor inventions: Frigidariums for storing foods out of season; conversation tubes, a primitive kind of telephone; a plan for digging a canal through Venezuela; a device for multiple music printing. But all of these were mere *jeux d'esprit* compared to the supreme dedication of his life—a complete code of law, complete in every detail from the most particular provisions of procedure to the highest, most general principles of the constitutional code and international law. He called it a "Pannomion," and it was both the grammar and substance, the form and content, of his new logic of the will, the law as it ought to be, an anatomy and physiology of his body politic. As a grammar, it was divided into two parts: adjective, or the law of procedure and evidence, and substantive, that is, civil, penal, and constitutional law. He began, as we have seen, with a general *Introduction* in 1780–81, then continued steadily from penal to civil law to procedure, then briefly to international law. Then the French Revolution erupted and he busied himself for some dozen years with Panopticon. In 1802 he returned to law, to evidence, and he worked on it until about 1824, when he entrusted the great mass of accumulated manuscripts to the eighteen-year-old John Stuart Mill. Finally, for about the last fifteen years of his life, he devoted himself to constitutional law, and he was still at work on it when he died in 1832.

Grandiose and encyclopedic as Bentham's ambition may seem initially, he really had only this one subject, law or ethics (for ethics is the general art-and-science, divided under his bifurcate system into private ethics or morals, and public, or legislation), the all-comprehensive art-and-science of morals and legislation; one audience, the legislature; one set of values, the greatest happiness of the greatest number; and one overriding ambition, the design and building of a "Pannomion," a complete Utilitarian code of law. Many subjects he knew little about, and these he merely placed on the general map, as a guide for the legislator. Again and again he rang changes on the same metaphors. He tried to do exhaustively what Helvétius had barely begun, "who at every stage when he has seen a branching of the road has thought of setting up a waymark, a direction post,"[29] so that the legislator might "raise his contemplation to that elevated point from which the whole map of human interest and situations lies extended to his view."[30]

But it was only the law that he claimed to know well, that "trackless wild," that "wilderness of sophistry,"[31] which "how often so ever traversed has never hitherto been surveyed by rule,"[32] a labyrinth that need be so no longer, for the principle of utility at last gave the clue; indeed, when "accurately apprehended and steadily applied . . . the only clew to guide a man through these streights."[33] Now at last "Legislators may travel with their eyes open over a plain and level road: instead of groping their way blindfold through a wood."[34]

[29] Box 24, pp. 14–16, University College Collection.
[30] I, 193.
[31] I, 289.
[32] *Limits,* 329.
[33] I, 289.
[34] *Limits, op. cit.,* 329.

But even limited to morals and legislation, Bentham's attempted art-and-science was still all-encompassing and impossibly ambitious. On every level of theory and practice, from his first attempts at neutral definition or "metaphysics" to the final detailed applications of his inventions, from paraphrasis to Panopticon Hill Villages, Bentham inevitably failed to build his Utopia and left more or less confusing and towering heaps of fragments. He had not one but two systems, a difficult, "metaphysical," formal structure of theory, of what ideally ought to be; and a modified, simpler version designed to be applied, of what is "eligible." This "popular" version of his science had still further to be transformed into appropriate arts, a variety of social inventions.

The miserable encounter with Panopticon, his first major experiment in applied social invention, made even more difficulty.[35] Already chronically in the habit of running from a good thing to a better, this disaster turned a bad habit into a worse. Clearly he never could abandon his struggles to practice what he preached, since practice was what he preached. But after this he was no longer so reckless in his enthusiasms. Swept along by a romantic dream of cause and effect, he had plunged wholeheartedly and naïvely into the Panopticon affair. The cause was his brother's magical circular building designed like a wheel with spokes. It seemed to promise a revolution in social control and economy, because from the central hub a small handful of officials might effectively order the behavior of a thousand or more men. And the effect, so Bentham hoped by the terms of his contract—for he proposed to undertake the management himself—was to have been the restoration of a whole class, of the wretched, hitherto unregenerate, criminal population of England. But his ungoverned enthusiasm blinded his foresight, and he threw his entire fortune into the scheme long before he had ground to build on. In fact he never did find it; his plans collapsed, and it was some twenty years before he got some of his money back.

Bentham learned the lesson and did not make that mistake again. Thereafter he moved more cautiously, step by step, offering at first only sketches, rough proposals, outlines, notes. If at all encouraged by the authorities, he began to fill them in. But of the dozens of projects, schemes, proposals he flung out so prodigally, none of them ever came fully to fruit. He did, however, leave behind a great chaos of manuscript, tens of thousands of pages in a bewildering variety of sizes, shapes, and stages of completeness.

He is therefore difficult. It is wrong and futile to deny it. The sad fact is that the harder he strove to guide the legislator through the labyrinth

---

[35] See below, pp. 189*ff.*

of law, the better he succeeded in creating another tangled maze. He had warned of the inevitable difficulty of his enterprise from the beginning. Even the first stage of definition, the road "to the region of metaphysics . . . is rugged and full of thorns. Few are they who have attempted to gain this height; and of those few, still fewer have succeeded in reaching it. . . ."[36] And he often pleaded for sympathy for his giant's task, that in the nature of the case could never be perfectly achieved. It is impossible to define even one single word completely, for in Bentham's metaphysics, in the Encyclopedical Tree, "Not a branch . . . but what is intertwined with every other. Not a twig can be managed as it should be by him who does not bear in mind a picture of the whole."[37] Therefore, to define one word exhaustively the whole system would have to be simultaneously and exhaustively articulated; a job to be attempted only serially in time, and thus an impossible one; for meanwhile the social order may or would have changed more or less in every one of its parts.

His dilemma was similar to the problem of simultaneous measurement in modern probability physics; it might be called the problem of simultaneity in probability psychics. It was part of his overall irresolvable dilemma: his art-and-science demanded a sympathetic audience, for without it there could be no use, that is, no practice or effective art; but his potential eighteenth- and nineteenth-century British audience demanded certainty and simplicity: yet a genuine art-and-science must begin by acknowledging the fundamental fact that all human affairs are complex and uncertain. There are, therefore, unending, shifting tensions between the possible and the eligible in Bentham's system. This caused him much discomfort and added still further to its complexity. "Patience! patience!" he implored his readers, comparing them to the heroines in distress of popular romantic novels, "Ye, too, before you are comforted, must bear to be tormented."[38]

Bentham can, but he need not, perplex and torment. Labyrinthine, fragmentary, impenetrable as his Pannomion or "Natural" System may often seem to be, there is nevertheless a simple guide throughout: metaphor. Although he has been so generally denounced for his abstract, unevocative, and indigestible style, perhaps no one in the entire literature of political theory and philosophy has been so prodigally lavish of imagery, metaphor, and analogy.

In some measure, surely, a man may be known by his metaphors and analogies. Show us his figures of speech and they may begin to tell us who he is. Does he avoid them altogether? Does he play many themes

[36] III, 285.
[37] IV, 338.
[38] VIII, 362.

or merely the same ones with variations? Drop them rarely, casually by the way, or explore one or more of them thoroughly? In political theory, does he speak of the ship of state, the Golden Age, the social contract, the political family with its sovereign father, the body politic with its head and members, the social organism, botanical and physical? A comparative study might well reveal much about a man's mind and temperament, his radicalism or conservatism, his life and times. That hoary vessel, the ship of state, for example, has been sailed by conservatives for centuries; Lord Salisbury as prime minister at the helm wanted merely "to keep an even keel." These figures of speech may tell much or they may tell little. Of Bentham they are truly revelatory.

There is scarcely one of his pages that is not strewn with figures of speech. As was only natural from so diligent a product of those seminaries of the classics, Westminster School and Queen's College, Oxford, Bentham was liberal in his use of Latin and Greek mythology—Hercules, Augean stables, Hydra's heads, Telemachus, Odysseus, labyrinths, all figure largely. He referred to mathematics often, and it was not with calculus, but rather with algebra that he drew the closest analogies. He hoped that the principle of utility and its corollaries would serve as the same kind of compressed conceptual shorthand saying much in little as the equations of algebra. All his metaphors and analogies were meant to serve this same purpose. They were not intended as exact equivalents but as suggestive possibilities, compact nuggets rather like Proust's Japanese paper flower that expanded in water from tight bud to full bloom.

Above all, Bentham used two sets of metaphors; we have seen them both already. One has to do with surveys, maps, architecture, and building: they were all part of one effort to explore the whole territory of human behavior, from the most general or the most particular, gradually to clear the ground, and then to design and build new institutions on it. This series served him well enough for his more formal structural analyses, but as he shifted his focus ever closer on human beings and feelings, from static abstractions to concrete pleasures and pains, laws, institutions, inventions, and reforms, his system sprang to life and he shifted his metaphors. Medicine, not maps or architecture, became the key analogy; and instead of, but more or less equivalent to, roads, foundations, crumbling walls, he spoke of anatomies, nerves, veins, skeletons, pathology, infections, diseases.

In fact, rising above the system as a whole, we begin to see medicine not only as a part, but as the determining part, *the* relevant art-and-science, whose experimental and exploratory methods must become the methods of the art-and-science of morals and legislation. For all the preliminary work, the mapping and building, was, as we have seen, for one purpose only, the use of the legislator, that is, metaphorically, the physician of the body politic. The laws he promulgates, the institutions he commissions and builds are all prescriptions and hospitals designed now to cure and in future to prevent social maladies of every kind. The medical analogy is truly the best guide through the Bentham labyrinth. It is hoary with age; from Plato to Wittgenstein men have commonly spoken of the health and illness of the body politic and the statesman as physician, but it is commonly also merely surface decoration. Bentham alone tracked it to the bottom, and in his thorough hands it became fresh again, for he saw relevant analogies in specialized branches like anatomy, pharmacology, symptomatology, and pathology that no one had seen before. With this analogy fixed in mind, we may perhaps begin to see more clearly and sympathetically what he was trying to do, and say—his undogmatic flexibility, the enormous difficulty of his task, its awkwardness and limitations, and, to him, its urgent importance. For under the established English Technical System, the whole atmosphere was choked with poisons: corruption, depredation, lies, intellectual debility. Inevitably the whole nation was sick. And as Bentham's vision spread first from the courts to the Church, Parliament, and the schools, he saw the plague raging everywhere.

Not dozens but hundreds of times Bentham described the battered English body politic as crushed and "long-suffering" under an "immeasurable load of torment," [39] as "afflicted" with "ruinous injury," [40] "running sores," [41] "rottenness," [42] "inflammation, swelling, gout, and cholera," "deformity and foul nakedness," [43] a "blasting pestilence," [44] caused in part by "the poison of immorality" and Blackstone's revered "blasphemies" whose "poison [is] still injected into all eyes," [45] while religion "by a perpetual fever" keeps up "a perpetual demand for opiates." [46] But above all, and throughout the whole law, "the pestilential breath of Fiction poisons the sense of every instrument it comes near." [47]

Amid all this suffering what do the state physicians, the legislators and

[39] V, 444.
[40] *Ibid.*, 446.
[41] V, 506.
[42] V, 163.
[43] V, 476.
[44] IX, 87.
[45] I, 249.
[46] V, 210–11.
[47] I, 235. Notice that Marx followed Bentham in condemning religion as an opiate. Notice, too, that the medical analogy was already in heavy duty in his first published *Fragment* and still in his last unfinished *Constitutional Code*.

judges, care? ". . . what a steam engine would care for the condition of a human body pressed or pounded by it."[48] According to Bentham, virtually the whole establishment of legislators, judges, lawyers, clergymen, and teachers was Bolingbroke's Hospital of Incurables, all of whom exude "a species of vital gas,"[49] themselves poisoned and debilitated by the Technical System they administered. They had largely become "a passive and enervate race, ready to swallow anything . . . with intellects incapable of distinguishing right from wrong . . . insensible, short-sighted, obstinate; lethargic, yet liable to be driven into convulsions by false terrors. . . ."[50] Their diagnoses and remedies were barbarous; to them everything was black or white, absolutely true or absolutely false, admissible as evidence or totally inadmissible, with no sense of infinite degrees, of any shading or probability. Their one remedy for everything, money, Bentham compared to primitive leeching and bleeding; or to the diagnoses of women in some countries where doctors were never permitted to inspect them.[51]

"A surgeon, a physician,—what vacations, what holidays, what respite from hard and painful labour . . . have they?"[52] Bentham asked, deploring the very short season of justice in the English higher courts. "By the medical practitioner, the man whose leg has been fractured is not left to die of a mortification,"[53] but by the supposed state-physician the crippled citizen is. Disgusted, he said, "In the scale of morality and beneficence does not the medical man stand highest?—the indiscriminate defender of right and wrong by the indiscriminate utterance of truth and falsehood, lowest down at the bottom, many degrees below zero—even at the point where mercury freezes."[54] As Bentham believed the whole Constitution to be a tissue of falsehoods, inevitably all caught up in it must be more or less weakened or diseased by it.

Amid all this misery and stolid ignorance, Bentham saw but one present relief: trials by jury. At best, however, they were only a small palliative,[55] often themselves suffering "a weakness about the head,"[56] useful occasionally to undo the mischief of bad laws. This was usual enough, for example, under a system where over two hundred felonies including stealing goldfish and pocket handkerchiefs were punishable by death; juries often refused to convict.

[48] V, 496.
[49] VIII, 186.
[50] I, *Fragment.*
[51] VI, 150.
[52] III, 407-8.
[53] *Ibid.*
[54] *Ibid.*
[55] III, 283.
[56] V, 163.

To Bentham the condition of the British body politic was perhaps "already desperate,"[57] and "The time is come when the scalpel must be set to work: state of [the law] . . . much rougher than the anatomist could have wished: . . ." "More than fifty years ago," he wrote in 1829, "I took it up for the first time, with Blackstone lying on the table,"[58]— good evidence not only of the pertinacity of established institutions, but of Bentham's efforts as well.

In his role as physician, therefore, he began not with maps but with an exhaustive anatomy, a complete code of law, and he ended with a vision of large-scale social medicine, whereby the Utilitarian legislator healed not one by one, as the ordinary doctor did, but by hundreds and thousands at a time, according to his legislator's Hippocratic oath.[59] Under his new art-and-science of government, the state would no longer be a vast impersonal manufactory filled with engines of grinding oppression, but a great healing and preventive medical center, with local branches over the face of Great Britain, open day and night.

Is Utilitarianism, therefore, a science? Yes, if medicine is: for on a primitive and elementary level, it was a grand vision of social preventive medicine. Working alone, with an entire new art-and-science to create, it was perhaps inevitable that Bentham should fail; but even had he succeeded, his work would still share the deficiencies of medicine, that even in the hands of its most gifted practitioners it is still a crazy-quilt of more or less educated guesses, which smothers and buries its mistakes. Nevertheless, with practice, experience, research it becomes every day more skilled and sure; and in the hands of trained converts and administrators, Bentham's *Novum Organum* would have done the same. Like medicine, like all science, Utilitarianism sought to forge a new vocabulary, neutral and exact; but even this first necessity of good science has failed to be fulfilled.

Like medicine, Utilitarianism deals with pleasures and pains; in neither has it been possible to invent a thermometer of measurement. Perhaps in the nature of the case it never will be possible. Bentham had few hopes and no illusions. Perhaps in a hundred years, he thought, something might be done; but a hundred years have gone by unavailingly.

Harold Laski was one of the rare few who have seen the close connection between Bentham and Aristotle. In a letter to Justice Holmes he wrote, "Like all that . . . [Aristotle] wrote . . . [the *Rhetoric*] is full of acute observation and those sudden flashes that make him, for me, the final criterion of sagacity—a quality incidentally that I think Bentham

[57] V, 186.
[58] V, 391.
[59] See above, p. xiv.

has next to him." [60] What did Laski mean by "those sudden flashes," "the final criterion of sagacity"? For those who take Bentham in short stretches and on the run, it is a quality perhaps easy enough to miss; but as in Aristotle, those with patience to bear with the system, the dryness, the pedantry, are suddenly—and often—rewarded with startling, penetrating insights, perhaps into deep, unforeseen byways of human character, perhaps into unsuspected social mechanisms.

There may also be something to Laski's suspicion that, had it not been for Bentham's ugly and awkward circumlocutions, political theory might well be fifty years further advanced. Certainly after him Utilitarianism took off in strange "spiritual" flights and it was not until the fourth generation that it was restored to its proper heritage. The mantle passed from Bentham to James Mill, who ruled by insistent right of occupation. Under him it became rationalist, deductive, "mechanical"—indeed, all the pejoratives it is usual to heap upon Bentham. Its narrow, heavy spirit almost crushed John Stuart Mill, who turned this inheritance into a qualitative ethical system, a liberal humanism.

Then John, with no children of his own, deliberately chose an even more liberal humanist heir, John Morley, for fifteen years editor of the *Fortnightly Review* and one of the leading positivists of the late 19th century. Under Morley, Utilitarianism became simply "the religion of humanity," just as though it were no more than an English "spiritual" offshoot of Comtism. Morley called himself a Utilitarian, and always worshiped Mill as "the saint of rationalism," but among his thousands of pages there is, astonishingly, no evidence that he had read Bentham. Certainly what passed for Utilitarianism with him and Bentham's genuine article are very different, the one all high-flown ethical resolutions, the other precise, quantitative, experimental, inventive hypothetical propositions. Only with the Fabians did the original Utilitarianism come into its own again, and its true heirs were not Mill and Morley, but the Fabian triumvirate, Sidney Webb, George Bernard Shaw, and Graham Wallas.

This book offers the first panorama of Bentham's thought, and perhaps in this sweeping view of his work as a whole, it may now more easily become possible to begin to see in him what Laski did. One difficulty remains, and it is irresolvable. His system cannot fairly be judged except *in terminus,* because each part depends so minutely and intimately on every other part; and yet it can never be *in terminus,* for it must include not only a delimited past, but the slithery present from moment to moment and the precisely indefinable future.

---

[60] Holmes-Laski Letters, Vol. I, p. 236.

Once venture out into the system, once offer so much as a single abstraction or "fiction" for definition, there is no adequate stopping-place; we should legitimately go on and on, coming ever closer to the proper end without ever overtaking it. Take words like "right" or "obligation" in law. They will not be fully defined until the last period is put to the last sentence of a "Pannomion," a complete code of law. At any rate, Bentham never stopped; he went on working to the last day of his life, after sixty-odd years of tireless, happy effort.

Seen from the widest perspective, what was Bentham? A philosopher? A law reformer? Yes, he was both of these; but had he been called "lexicographer," he would have been content. Had he been called "metaphysician," he would have liked that even better. To him they were more or less synonymous terms, and he who defined the language ruled the universe. He was the ultimate legislator, as the legislator was the ultimate lexicographer. The larger the scope and operational range of his abstractions, the wider his area of government, of legislative and judicial authority. In this way, the legislator was also the supreme moralist, for the vocabulary of ethics fell within his jurisdiction. To him, he said, "belongs the power of making *wrong* and *right* change nature, and determining what shall be *morality* as well as what shall be *law.*" [61] In this way, as a maker of dictionaries, a legislator of definitions, Bentham ultimately thought and wrote about almost every large subject of human interest, from algebra to zoology.

With what results? Seen from this panoramic view, it does not seem that his principles, that is, his science, changed very much. But his art of application surely changed thoroughly. He had been a young conservative; he became an elderly radical, ever less frightened by popular "zeal" and more assured of popular self-possession. His work falls easily into three parts; I. Early Devotion to Law Studies—the years of *A Fragment on Government* and *An Introduction to the Principles of Morals and Legislation*—*ca.* 1774–1790—years of science, of laying down initial principles; II. Years of Panopticon and writings on economics [which are not included here because they are available in Werner Stark's recent edition]—*ca.* 1790–1802–1812—the years of art, of practice, when he attempted to apply the principles of Utilitarianism to the British penal system, to his ultimate humiliation, horror, and anger; III. Second Age of Devotion to Law—return to the Code and its principles, expansion into education and politics—1802–1832—growing ever more tolerant, liberal, then radical.

A very different view of his style emerges from such an overall perspective. Oppressed by the difficulties and awkwardness of his own neologisms, eager to open up his treasures to a wide public, he tried to develop several popular styles: an early epigrammatic, Voltairean one; and two later efforts, one as public letters, the other as open dialogues. He always sought to sprinkle his pages with metaphors, and on the whole, he used the same characteristic ones throughout: architectural, cartographical, and above all, medical. But the older and more radical he grew, the more belligerent and militant his metaphors and figures of speech became.

Finally, at every opportunity in his old age, he tried to cast his principles into graphs and charts, visual renderings that might make them instantly comprehensible to hurried and perhaps dense readers. His texts then became terse descriptions of items in the charts. Thus one of his most important texts is not in this book: *A Table of the Springs of Action.* It is almost entirely a cursory commentary on a series of charts; unlike the other texts, it is all or nothing. Either the whole work must be given entire to be comprehensible or none of it. Briefly, it was Bentham's Baconian effort, in the manner of the Four Idols, to give a detailed accounting of human motives, in neutral, eulogistic, and dyslogistic terms.

But if Bentham hoped to ease his readers' agonies, he never supposed the difficulties non-existent nor that he could make them disappear. On the contrary. True to his Blakean Romantic vision, he insisted that his was a pilgrim's progress, a path strewn with thorns and pitfalls. "Romance! Romance! True: but it is the romance of real life." [62] [VII, 399] In this art-and-science of Blake's "minutely organized particulars" one must come armed with an "infinite capacity for taking pains." Bentham's truths were stubborn things: "They recoil from the tongue and the pen of the declaimer. They flourish not in the same soil with sentiment. They grow among thorns; and are not to be plucked, like daisies, by infants as they run. Labour, the inevitable lot of humanity, is in no tract more inevitable than here. In vain would an Alexander bespeak a peculiar road for royal vanity, or a Ptolemy a smoother one for royal indolence. There is no *King's Road,* no *Stadtholder's* Gate, to legislative, any more than to mathematic science." [63] And if Blake found the universe in a grain of sand, the artist in Bentham quoted the French dancing master, Marcel, who exclaimed, "Leaning on his elbow, in an attitude of profound and solemn meditation, *'What a multitude of things there are . . . in a minuet!'*—May we now add?—and in a Law!" [64]

---

[62] VII, 399.
[63] Preface, An Intd. to the Prins. of Morals and Legislation, I, v.
[64] Closing sentence of *Ibid.,* I, 154.

All good poets know what Bentham knew. His great work was to bring a powerful poetic insight into the arid reaches of the law, to create an anatomy of the law that matched the minute anatomy of the human mind and heart. For our generation, the poetic truth has perhaps nowhere been better expressed than by Dylan Thomas: "Every idea, intuitive or intellectual, can be imaged and translated in terms of the body, its flesh, skin, blood, sinews, veins, glands, organs, cells, or senses. Through my small, bone-bound island I have learnt all I know, experienced all, and sensed all. . . . As much as possible, therefore, I employ the scenery of the island to describe the scenery of my thoughts, the earthquake of the body to describe the earthquake of the heart."

Notes on the Text

All but two of the texts come from the eleven-volume Collected Edition of 1843, edited by John Bowring (Edinburgh: William Tait), hitherto the only source for most of the Bentham works. It is very good news that the first two volumes of a complete new, definitive edition, published by the Athlone Press of the University of London, have now appeared, ultimately to be followed by thirty-six more. Meanwhile, for the next few years, we must make do with what we have; and this book aims to make more Bentham more easily accessible than he has ever been before.

The selection on *Indirect Legislation* comes from C. K. Ogden's edition of *The Theory of Legislation* (New York: 1931), and that on *The Limits of Jurisprudence Defined* from Charles Warren Everett's edition of that work (New York: 1945). In all cases it was thought better to give one or more important, long, connected passages rather than random assortments of many small snippets. Except for minor changes where the modern reader might be positively misled, the spelling and punctuation have been left just as found in the 1843 edition.

I am most grateful to my student-indexers, Carol La Shine and Jacqueline Earle; and to the Connecticut College History Department for financial aid. I offer most deeply grateful thanks to the Rockefeller and Guggenheim Foundations, for whom one works under ideal condition of freedom.

A Bentham Reader

Early Memoranda, 1773–75

A Note on *Early Memoranda, 1773–75*

Bentham wondered in his old age what had become of his early writings; he wanted to see again what had once been the source of so much pain. "I should like to ask myself now," he said, "if they were well written; for, in those days, composition was inconceivably difficult. I often commenced a sentence which I could not complete. I began to write fragments on blotting paper, and left them to be filled in happier vein. By hard labour I subjugated difficulties; and my example will show what hard labour will accomplish."[1] His great models for style were Voltaire and above all, Sir Francis Bacon, the hero of heroes throughout his life; and Baconian maxims and aphorisms were sprinkled over his last pages as well as his earliest.[2]

So were many of his themes. From first to last he was critical of the English monarchy, though only in his old age, as he became ever more bold and bitter, did he dare to publish his long-standing complaints. From first to last he raged against the tyranny, depredations, and corruption of English law and lawyercraft. His attitude toward religion was the same as his attitude toward monarchy, and went through the same phases: a long underground silence exploding at last in public wrath.

These *pensées* were strictly private jottings. Bentham knew only too well that his England was numb with smug complacency, that if any small fraction of his reforms were to be entertained, he must hide the

---

[1] X, 67–8.
[2] See last epigrams, pp. 362*ff.* below.

larger balance, and discreetly keep his radical opinions to himself. As he admitted in *An Introduction,* he was unavoidably forced to develop two doctrines, a popular and an occult. In eighteenth-century England religion and monarchy were cult objects and, for him, strictly taboo. But by 1815 he broke the tapes of discretion that had bound his mouth, and began to roar dissatisfaction.

Bentham never, however, hid his intellectual debts, and he always happily, gratefully acknowledged his obligations to Locke and Helvétius, along with Bacon, Blackstone, Priestley, Beccaria, D'Alembert, Voltaire, etc. Though J. S. Mill berated him for refusing to honor his intellectual heritage, Bentham did honor it; and though Mill's harsh judgment has long been taken for granted, it is mistaken.

Among other lifelong themes that Bentham introduces here are his celebration of invention and conciseness, of education as education for happiness, and of the uses of antiquity. It always seemed to him absurd to worship the ancient as the source of wisdom and experience, and therefore to condemn any attempted reforms as sacrilegious defilement, when clearly antiquity was the naïve childhood of the race, long since outdated by increased knowledge and experience. Again and again he returned to this paradox.

As Bentham's contempt for monarchy grew, so did his respect for "the people." By the time of his last *pensées* in 1831–32, he had long since been a radical democrat. He cried out in 1774, "The people is my Caesar!" And so he would cry his entire life. But he then continued, "I appeal from the present Caesar to Caesar better informed." It did not take many years of bitter experience with the autocratic, corrupt machinery of British government to teach him that for all purposes of good Utilitarian government, Caesar was well enough informed already.

Bentham was singularly consistent, and it is curious to compare his first and last *pensées.* In 1774 he asked, "Would you appear actuated by generous passion? be so.—You need then but show yourself as you are." In 1831 he said, "The way to be comfortable is to make others comfortable. The way to make others comfortable is to appear to love them. The way to appear to love them—is to love them in reality." Bentham hoped to have some claim to be the most benevolent man who ever lived. "Someone must have been so," he said. "Why not I?" Why not indeed?

Early Memoranda, 1773–75

(Vol. X, pp. 68ff.)

"There is no man that doth a wrong for the wrong's sake, but thereby to purchase himself profit or pleasure." This grand truth was not hidden from Lord Bacon. His was a mind to be struck with the beauty of truth wherever it met him, but his was not an age when to pursue it to the utmost was either practicable or safe.

When will men cease beholding in Almighty Benevolence a cruel tyrant, who (to no assignable end) commands them to be wretched?

Why should the names of Religion and Morality be employed for purposes by which, if accomplished, Religion and Morality must suffer?

Men ought to be cautious ere they represent Religion to be that noxious thing which magistrates should proscribe.

The grand catastrophe of our sacred history is itself an act of the most illustrious suicide.

Préjugés in favour of Antiquity. It is singular that the persons who are most loud in magnifying the pretended advantage in point of wisdom of ancient over modern times, are the very same who are the most loud in proclaiming the superiority in the same respect of old men above young ones. What has governed them in both cases seems to have been the prejudice of names: it is certain that if there be some reasons why the old should have advantage over the young, there are at least the same reasons for times that are called modern having it over times that are called ancient. There are more: for decrepitude as applied to persons is real: as applied to times it is imaginary. Men, as they acquire experience, lose the faculties that might enable them to turn it to account: it is not so with times: the stock of wisdom acquired by ages is a stock transmitted through a vast number of generations, from men in the perfection of their faculties to others also in the perfection of their faculties: the stock of knowledge transmitted from one period of a man's life to another period of the same man's life is a stock from which, after a certain period, large defalcations are every minute making by the scythe of Time.

Vulgar Errors—Political.

1. To make consummate characters, either in depravity or in virtue.
2. To attribute every motion of public men to political motives; to attribute every action to ends and purposes which belong to them as politicians, and none to those which belong to them as men.
3. To attribute every instance of supposed misconduct in public men to the depravity of the heart; and none to the imbecility of the head.
4. To suppose everything *illegal* which appears to them *inexpedient.*

Pensées. There is no pestilence in a state like a zeal for religion, independent of (as contradistinguished from) morality.

As to people at large, I want little of their company, and much of their esteem.

Morality may well say of religion—Wherever it is not for me, it is against me.

No man appears to himself so bad as he is. No man acts against conscience in all that he acts amiss.

Prejudice and imposture always seek obscurity.

What is called legal style is the most execrable way of putting words together that ever was devised.

Ladies, like birds of paradise, have no legs; it is all *feet* with them.

Invention is learning digested: quotation is learning vomited up raw.

The constitutions of the Society of Arts, and of many other societies, are penned with conciseness and perspicuity. How happens this? Either there are no lawyers concerned, or their right hand forgets her cunning. They forget that they are lawyers, and, seduced by example, become gentlemen, scholars, and philosophers.

Conciseness is an apter term than *brevity* for a desirable property of style—conciseness is *relative* brevity.

A monarch is a sort of a creature that unites the properties of the Grand Lama and the Pope of Rome, not to mention an odd attribute or two that remain unclaimed by any other created being. Like the first of these, he is immortal: like the last infallible: as if this were not enough, he is omnipresent: no perfection that is imaginable is wanting to this god of our idolatry. Look at him well; turn him round and round; about and about; examine him limb by limb; a more accomplished deity at all points never trod upon dry ground. . . .

Greedy of incense without caring to deserve it: fond of any principle of awe that could serve to screen his person against attack—regardless whether it rooted there, glad to behold it planted by however ignoble hands; content to draw upon his office for a perpetual tribute of respect, without ever thinking of deserving it. Such is the condition of a king!

Digest of the Law premature before Locke and Helvétius. A digest of the Laws is a work that could not have been executed with advantage before Locke and Helvétius had written: the first establishing a test of perspicuity for ideas; the latter establishing a standard of rectitude for actions. The idea annexed to a word is a perspicuous one, when the simple ideas included under it are assignable. This is what we owe to Locke. A sort of action is a right one, when the tendency of it is to augment the mass of happiness in the community. This is what we are indebted for to Helvétius.

The matter of the Law is to be governed by Helvétius. For the form and expression of it we must resort to Locke.

From Locke it must receive the ruling principles of its form—from Helvétius of its matter.

By the principles laid down by Locke it must be governed, inasmuch as it is a discourse; by those of Helvétius, inasmuch as it is a discourse from authority, predicting punishment for some modes of conduct, and reward for others.

Principles of Education. Education is a series of conduct directed to an end: before any directions can properly be given for the education of any person, the end of his education must be settled.

The common end of every person's education is Happiness. . . .

The only active plan of education the state ought to encourage, is that which tends no otherwise to increase the happiness of the individual than by increasing at the same time, the happiness of the community.

This is done by improving the arts and sciences which produce the instruments of happiness, or directing them in their application.

This, too, is the only plan of active education the preceptor ought to promote by his instructions. The arts of supplanting and competition (where the advancement of one man is the depression of another) ought to be noticed in no other view than that of pointing out the means of frustrating them: they are of that sort of pernicious or unprofitable secrets, which it is right to teach only to make them inefficacious.

From the years 1774–75. Oh, Britain! Oh, my country! the object of my waking and my sleeping thoughts! whose love is my first labour and greatest joy—passing the love of woman, thou shalt bear me witness against these misruling men.

I cannot buy, nor ever will I sell my countrymen. My pretensions to their favour are founded not on promises, but on past endeavours,—not on the having defended the popular side of a question for fat fees, but on the sacrifice of years of the prime of life—from the first dawnings of reflection to the present hour—to the neglect of the graces which adorn a private station; deaf to the calls of present, and to all the temptations of a lucrative profession.

Barristers are so called (a man of spleen might say) *à Barrando,* from barring against reformation the entrances of the law. It would be as good an etymology as many a one of Lord Coke's, and I believe entirely in his taste.

Public Virtue in the Body of the People. The great body of the people can have no other virtue but zeal, no other corruption but indifference. It is impossible they can be zealous against their own political interests; but they may be so immersed in their private interests as to neglect them.

The zeal of the people, which is the virtue of the people, does not depend upon the wisdom with which it chooses its objects: a people may be virtuous, that is, clamorous for very detrimental measures, so as it does but think them right. A people may be virtuous, though warmly attached to one who is nothing less than a friend to his country, so as they do but think him so. . . .

Pensées. The people is my Caesar: I appeal from the present Caesar to Caesar better informed.

Would you appear actuated by generous passion? be so.—You need then but show yourself as you are.

I would have the dearest friend I have to know, that his interests, if they come in competition with that of the public, are as nothing to me. Thus I will serve my friends—thus would I be served by them.

Has a man talents? he owes them to his country in every way in which they can be serviceable.

Independence is not in the fortune, but the mind.

In England the clergy are scorpions which sting us. On the continent they are dragons which devour us.

To trace errors to their source is to refute them.

It is rare to meet with a man disinterested upon reflection.

'Tis here in matters of the law as it is in Roman Catholic countries in matters of religion: to keep clear of mistakes, you must be warned at every turn not to believe your own eyes.

Voluminousness is of itself a poison to perspicuity.

Falsehood is the high-road to (self) contradiction.

The effect of praise is to dispose to imitation.

All the industry of lawyers has been hitherto employed to prevent the grounds of law being canvassed, almost as anxiously as that of divines to prevent the grounds of religion from being examined.

In respect of notoriety, what is wanted is, that people may know the legal consequences of a point of conduct *before*, not *after*, they have pursued it.

It is as impossible for a lawyer to wish men out of litigation, as for a physician to wish them in health. No man (that is of the ordinary race of men) wishes others to be at their ease that he may starve.

There is no way in which the state can be prejudiced unless some individual suffer.

The use of words is not less to fix ideas for a man himself, than to communicate them to others. A man scarce knows he has the *idea* till he has the words.

A Fragment on Government

A Note on *A Fragment on Government*

Next to the Bible and Shakespeare, probably no book was more highly valued and honored in Bentham's 1776 England than Sir William Blackstone's *Commentaries on the Laws of England.* It was bold of Bentham to attack it. That an unknown young law student should deliver so rude a blast against it, full of high invective and Voltairean irony, was a piece of singular insolence, and it was good policy to publish it anonymously. He hoped it would be assigned to well-known authors, and so, for a time, it was: Lord Mansfield, Lord Camden, Lord Ashburton. But Bentham could not resist telling his father, so long disappointed in the insignificant career of his prodigiously gifted son who so deliberately flouted his parental ambition to see him ultimately Lord Chancellor; and his father could not resist telling others.

Once the secret was revealed, Bentham's hopes soared. "No sooner had my farthing candle been taken out of the bushel, than I looked for the descent of torches to it from the highest regions: my imagination presented to my view torches descending in crowds to borrow its fire. . . . Nothing could be more opposite to the truth. Instead of the universal sympathy, of which I had expected to see these graspings after improvement productive in those higher regions, universal antipathy—antipathy on the part of all parties—was the result. . . ."[1]

It took him half a lifetime fully to discover why reform was so universally odious, and when he did, he became a radical democrat, certain at last, as he said in 1822 when he reminisced about the reception given

---

[1] X, 80.

to *A Fragment:* ". . . what is the true [picture of the British constitution?] . . . What there is of purity in the mixture, is to be found, if not absolutely at the bottom, much nearer to it than at the top; what there is of corruption rises to the top: if the lower orders have been called the dregs of the population, the higher may, by a much clearer title, be termed the scum of it."[2]

As Bentham explained in the Preface, his ambition was very limited; merely to analyze, sentence by sentence, a few pages of the most theoretical but highly ambiguous and muddled pages of the celebrated *Commentaries.* He had first heard them as lectures at Oxford, when he was only a boy of sixteen; and even then, long before he had worked out his own beliefs and principles, found them confusing. But by 1776 he had spent a dozen years in his rooms at Lincoln's Inn, studying, reading, thinking, writing tens of thousands of practice pages, and now, fully armed with Utilitarian doctrine, was happy to attack Blackstone head on.

But these pages of *A Fragment* are only a few of the hundreds, perhaps thousands, that he wrote upon Blackstone;[3] fifty years later he was still taking occasional pot shots, for Blackstone was still as much of a god in Regency England as he had been in the age of the American Revolution, and needed more than ever to be knocked from his pedestal. However, Bentham was neither an indiscriminate nor an unappreciative enemy. In at least three ways he paid homage to Blackstone: he celebrated his fine style; and he borrowed and expanded two of the doctrines, the doctrine of sanctions (though Bentham defined and changed them radically, from three ultimately to fourteen) and the doctrine of sovereignty as trust.

Like almost all of Bentham's following work, this essay is literally a fragment. His good friend George Wilson accused him of always running from a good thing to a better; and he seems to have been constitutionally incapable of completing anything. We will see this time and again throughout this book.

If *A Fragment* is itself only a fragment of a fragment, the selections given here are of course still more fragmentary. They are chosen to reveal the most important principles and doctrines of Utilitarianism, and it is remarkable how many he had already fully developed in all their essentials—so much so that he saw no need to revise them at any time in his career. First of all, he forthrightly announced the notorious principle of utility, source of so much misunderstanding even in his own lifetime, so that he later changed it, in order to avoid the ambiguities of "utility," to "the greatest happiness principle." It states that "It is the greatest

[2] X, 82.
[3] See Chas. Warren Everett's *A Comment on the Commentaries* for further examples.

happiness of the greatest number that is the measure of right and wrong";
and happiness he measured in terms of pleasure and pain, the ultimate
sensual elements of human feeling, defined in an all-embracing sense.
He then announced a fundamental distinction between *what is* and
what ought to be, the descriptive and the normative; one the work of
the Expositor; the other, of the Censor. This he borrowed from Hume
and it runs sharply throughout everything he ever wrote. Unfortunately
most critics forget it, and much needless condemnation might have been
spared had it been better heeded.

Immediately Bentham put the distinction to use. He had to reconcile
the normative greatest happiness principle with the descriptive—empirical
elements of pleasure and pain; and this he did by his new system of
definition, paraphrasis. "A word may be said to be expounded by *paraphrasis*, when not that *word* alone is translated into other *words*, but some
whole *sentence*, of which it forms a part, is translated into another sentence; the words of which latter are expressive of such ideas as are *simple* . . . that is, in terms calculated to raise *images* either of *substances*
perceived, or of *emotions;*—sources, one or other of which every idea
must be drawn from, to be a clear one." [4]

Given this first necessity, Bentham's next step was inevitably a dictionary.[5] In a sense, then, he was rather a supreme lexicographer than a
philosopher, a definer of the abstractions of political and moral thought;
in his words, a "metaphysician" or "logician." Almost all his works are
at least partial dictionaries.

As a critic he was from the beginning a violent enemy to abuses of
language, especially to the reification of fictions, assuming the real
existence of abstractions like natural right and social contracts. From
first to last, they were prime targets; and so were the law and lawyers,
"the long-robed Cacus" as he explains in *A Fragment;* nor did he ever
stop bombarding "the imperfections swarming in the frame of government."

In so doing, he made another important all-pervasive distinction—
between technical-mechanical and natural systems. English law was a
technical, mechanical system, choked in an arbitrary chaos of ancient,
irrelevant rules and fictions. His new Utilitarian system was a natural one,
based on human nature, on the universal feelings of all mankind; and
for that reason, *mutatis mutandis*, readily acknowledging the brotherhood
of man.

---

[4] See below, p. 69n.
[5] See pp. 240*ff* below, A Note on *Pannomial Fragments*, where these points are made more
fully.

A Fragment on Government

The age we live in is a busy age; an age in which knowledge is rapidly advancing towards perfection. In the natural world, in particular, every thing teems with discovery and with improvement. The most distant and recondite regions of the earth traversed and explored—the all-vivifying and subtle element of the air so recently analyzed and made known to us, -are striking evidences, were all others wanting, of this pleasing truth.

Correspondent to *discovery* and *improvement* in the natural world, is *reformation* in the moral: if that which seems a common notion be, indeed, a true one, that in the moral world there no longer remains any matter for *discovery*. Perhaps, however, this may not be the case: perhaps among such observations as would be best calculated to serve as grounds for reformation, are some which, being observations of matters of fact hitherto either incompletely noticed, or not at all, would, when produced, appear capable of bearing the name of discoveries: with so little method and precision have the consequences of this fundamental axiom, *It is the greatest happiness of the greatest number that is the measure of right and wrong,* been as yet developed.

Be this as it may, if there be room for making, and if there be use in publishing, *discoveries* in the *natural* world, surely there is not much less room for making, nor much less use in proposing, *reformation* in the *moral.* If it be a matter of importance and of use to us to be made acquainted with *distant* countries, surely it is not a matter of much less importance, nor of much less use to us, to be made better and better acquainted with the chief means of living happily in our *own:* If it be of importance and of use to us to know the principles of the element we breathe, surely it is not of much less importance, nor of much less use, to comprehend the principles, and endeavour at the improvement of those *laws,* by which alone we breathe it in security. If to this endeavour we should fancy any author, especially any author of great

45

name, to *be,* and as far as could in such case be expected, to *avow himself* a determined and persevering enemy, what should we say of him? We should say that the interests of reformation, and through them the welfare of mankind, were inseparably connected with the downfall of his works: of a great part, at least, of the esteem and influence which these works might, under whatever title, have acquired.

Such an enemy it has been my misfortune (and not mine only) to see, or fancy at least I saw, in the Author of the celebrated COMMENTARIES *on the* LAWS *of* ENGLAND: an author whose works have had, beyond comparison, a more extensive circulation, have obtained a greater share of esteem, of applause, and consequently of influence (and that by a title on many grounds so indisputable), than any other writer who on that subject has ever yet appeared.

It is on this account that I conceived, some time since, the design of pointing out some of what appeared to me the capital blemishes of that work, particularly this grand and fundamental one, the antipathy to reformation: or, rather, indeed, of laying open and exposing the universal inaccuracy and confusion which seemed to my apprehension to pervade the whole. For, indeed, such an ungenerous antipathy seemed of itself enough to promise a general vein of obscure and crooked reasoning, from whence no clear and sterling knowledge could be derived: so intimate is the connexion between some of the gifts of the understanding, and some of the affections of the heart.

It is in this view, then, that I took in hand that part of the first volume to which the Author has given the name of INTRODUCTION. It is in this part of the work that is contained whatever comes under the denomination of *general principles.* It is in this part of the work that are contained such preliminary views as it seemed proper to him to give of certain objects, real or imaginary, which he found connected with his subject LAW by identity of name: two or three sorts of LAWS of *Nature,* the *revealed* LAW, and a certain LAW of *Nations.* . . .

There are two characters, one or other of which every man who finds any thing to say on the subject of Law, may be said to take upon him:— that of the *Expositor,* and that of the *Censor.* To the province of the *Expositor* it belongs to explain to us what, as he supposes, the Law *is:* to that of the *Censor,* to observe to us what he thinks it *ought to be.* The former, therefore, is principally occupied in stating, or in inquiring after *facts:* the latter, in discussing *reasons.* The *Expositor,* keeping within his sphere, has no concern with any other faculties of the mind than the *apprehension,* the *memory,* and the *judgment:* the latter, in virtue of those sentiments of pleasure or displeasure which he finds occasion to annex to the objects under his review, holds some intercourse with the *affections.*

That which *is* Law, is, in different countries, widely different: while that which *ought to be,* is in all countries to a great degree the same. The *Expositor,* therefore, is always the citizen of this or that particular country: the *Censor* is, or ought to be, the citizen of the world. To the *Expositor* it belongs to show what the *Legislator* and his underworkman the *Judge* have done *already:* to the *Censor* it belongs to suggest what the *Legislator ought* to do *in future.* To the Censor, in short, it belongs to *teach* that *science,* which, when by change of hands converted into an *art,* the LEGISLATOR *practises.* . . .

It is wonderful how forward some have been to look upon it as a kind of presumption, and ingratitude, and rebellion, and cruelty, and I know not what besides, not to allege only, nor to own, but to suffer any one so much as to imagine, that an old-established law could in any respect be a fit object of condemnation. Whether it has been a kind of *personification* that has been the cause of this, as if the Law were a living creature, or whether it has been the mechanical veneration for antiquity, or what other delusion of the fancy, I shall not here inquire. For my part, I know not for what good reason it is that the merit of justifying a law when right, should have been thought greater than that of censuring it when wrong. Under a government of laws, what is the motto of a good citizen? *To obey punctually: to censure freely.*

Thus much is certain: that a system that is never to be censured, will never be improved: that if nothing is ever to be found fault with, nothing will ever be mended: and that a resolution to justify every thing at any rate, and to disapprove of nothing, is a resolution which, pursued in future, must stand as an effectual bar to all the *additional* happiness we can ever hope for: pursued hitherto, would have robbed us of that share of happiness which we enjoy already.

Nor is a disposition to find "every thing as it should be," less at variance with itself, than with reason and utility. The commonplace arguments in which it vents itself justify not what is established, in effect, any more than they condemn it; since whatever *now* is establishment, *once* was innovation. . . .

Thus destitute of foundation are the terrors, or pretended terrors, of those who shudder at the idea of a free censure of established institutions: so little does the peace of society require the aid of those lessons which teach men to accept of any thing as a reason, and to yield the same abject and indiscriminating homage to the Laws here, which is paid to the despot elsewhere. The fruits of such tuition are visible enough in the character of that race of men who have always occupied too large a space in the circle of the profession; a passive and enervate race, ready to swallow any thing, and to acquiesce in any thing; with intellects incapable of distinguishing right from wrong, and with affections alike indifferent to either; insensible, short-sighted, obstinate; lethargic, yet liable to be driven into convulsions by false terrors; deaf to the voice of reason and public utility; obsequious only to the whisper of interest, and to the beck of power. . . .

Those who duly consider upon what slight and trivial circumstance, even in the happiest times, the adoption or rejection of a Law so often turns; circumstance with which the utility of it has no imaginable connexion—those who consider the desolate and abject state of the human intellect, during the periods in which so great a part of the still subsisting mass of institutions had their birth—those who consider the backwardness there is in most men, unless when spurred by personal interests or resentments, to run a-tilt against the colossus of authority—those, I say, who give these considerations their due weight, will not be quite so zealous, perhaps, as our Author has been, to terrify men from setting up what is now "private judgment," against what once was "public": not to thunder down the harsh epithet of "arrogance" on those, who, with whatever success, are occupied in bringing rude establishments to the test of polished reason. They will rather do what they can to cherish a disposition at once so useful and so rare. . . .

The function of the Expositor may be conceived to divide itself into two branches: that of *history,* and that of simple *demonstration.* The business of history is to represent the Law in the state it *has* been in, in past periods of its existence: the business of simple demonstration, in the sense in which I will take leave to use the word, is to represent the Law in the state it *is* in for the time being.

Again, to the head of demonstration belong the several businesses of *arrangement, narration,* and *conjecture.* Matter of narration it may be called, where the law is supposed to be explicit, clear, and settled: matter of conjecture, or interpretation, where it is obscure, silent, or unsteady. It is matter of arrangement to *distribute* the several real or supposed institutions into different masses, for the purpose of a general survey; to determine the *order* in which those masses shall be brought to view; and to find for each of them a *name.*

The businesses of narration and interpretation are conversant chiefly about particular institutions. Into the details of particular institutions it has not been my purpose to descend. On these topics, then I may say, in the laguage of procedure, *non sum informatus.* Viewing the work in this light, I have nothing to add to, or to except against, the public voice.

History is a branch of instruction which our Author, though not rigidly necessary to his design, called in, not without judgment, to cast light and ornament on the dull work of simple *demonstration:* this part he has executed with an elegance which strikes every one: with what fidelity, having not very particularly examined, I will not take upon me to pronounce.

Among the most difficult and the most important of the functions of *demonstration*, is the business of *arrangement*. In this our Author has been thought, and not, I conceive, without justice, to excel; at least in comparison of any thing that has hitherto appeared. 'Tis to him we owe such an arrangement of the elements of Jurisprudence, as wants little, perhaps, of being the best that a technical nomenclature will admit of. A technical nomenclature, as long as it is admitted to mark out and denominate the principal heads, stands an invincible obstacle to every other than a technical arrangement. For to *denominate* in general terms, what is it but to arrange? and to arrange under heads, what is it but to *denominate* upon a large scale? A technical arrangement, governed then in this manner, by a technical nomenclature, can never be otherwise than *confused* and *unsatisfactory*. The reason will be sufficiently apparent, when we understand what sort of an arrangement that must be, which can be properly termed a *natural* one.

That arrangement of the materials of any science may, I take it, be termed a *natural* one, which takes such properties to characterize them by, as men in general are, by the common constitution of man's *nature*, disposed to attend to: such, in other words, as *naturally*, that is readily, engage, and firmly fix the attention of any one to whom they are pointed out. The materials, or elements here in question, are such actions as are the objects of what we call Laws or Institutions.

Now then, with respect to actions in general, there is no property in them that is calculated so readily to engage, and so firmly to fix the attention of an observer, as the *tendency* they may have *to*, or *divergency* (if one may so say) *from*, that which may be styled the common *end* of all of them. The end I mean is *Happiness*: and this *tendency* in any act is what we style its *utility*: as this *divergency* is that to which we give the name of *mischievousness*. With respect, then, to such actions in particular as are among the objects of the Law, to point out to a man the *utility* of them, or the mischievousness, is the only way to make him see *clearly* that property of them which every man is in search of; the only way, in short, to give him *satisfaction*.

From *utility*, then we may denominate a *principle*, that may serve to preside over and govern, as it were, such arrangement as shall be made of the several institutions, or combinations of institutions, that compose the matter of this science: and it is this principle that, by putting its stamp upon the several names given to those combinations, can alone render *satisfactory* and *clear* any arrangement that can be made of them.

Governed in this manner by a principle that is recognised by all men, the same arrangement that would serve for the jurisprudence of any one country, would serve with little variation for that of any other. Yet more. The mischievousness of a bad law would be detected, at least the utility of it would be rendered suspicious, by the difficulty of finding a place for it in such an arrangement: while, on the other hand, a *technical* arrangement is a sink that with equal facility will swallow any garbage that is thrown into it.

That this advantage may be possessed by a natural arrangement, is not difficult to conceive. Institutions would be characterized by it in the only universal way in which they can be characterized; by the nature of the several *modes of conduct* which, by prohibiting, they constitute *offences.*

These offences would be collected into classes denominated by the various modes of their *divergency* from the common *end;* that is, as we have said, by their various forms and degrees of *mischievousness;* in a word, by those properties which are *reasons* for their being made *offences:* and whether any such mode of conduct possesses any such property, is a question of experience. Now, a bad law is that which prohibits a mode of conduct that is *not* mischievous. Thus would it be found impracticable to place the mode of conduct prohibited by a bad law under any denomination of offence, without asserting such a matter of fact as is contradicted by experience. Thus cultivated, in short, the soil of Jurisprudence would be found to repel, in a manner, every evil institution: like that country which refuses, we are told, to harbour any thing venomous in its bosom.

The *synopsis* of such an arrangement would at once be a compendium of *expository* and of censorial Jurisprudence: nor would it serve more effectually to instruct the *subject,* than it would to justify or reprove the *Legislator.*

Such a synopsis, in short, would be at once a map, and that an universal one, of Jurisprudence as it *is,* and a slight but comprehensive sketch of what it *ought to be.* For, the *reasons* of the several institutions comprised under it would stand expressed, we see, and that uniformly (as in our Author's synopsis they do in scattered instances), by the names given to the several classes under which those institutions are comprised. And what reasons? Not *technical* reasons, such as none but a Lawyer gives, nor any but a Lawyer would put up with:*

[*Technical reasons: so called from the Greek . . . which signifies an art, science, or profession.

Utility is that standard to which men in general (except in here and there an instance where they are deterred by prejudices of the religious class, or hurried away by the force of what is called *sentiment* or *feeling*)—utility, as we have said, is the standard to which they refer a law or institution in judging of its title to approbation or disapprobation. Men of Law, corrupted by interests, or seduced by illusions, which it is not here our business to display, have deviated from it much more frequently, and with much less reserve. Hence it is that such reasons as pass with Lawyers, and with no one else, have got the name of *technical* reasons; reasons peculiar to the art, peculiar to the profession.]

but reasons, such as were they in themselves what they might and ought to be, and expressed too in the manner they might and ought to be, any man might see the force of as well as he.

Nor in this is there any thing that need surprise us. The consequences of any Law, or of any act which is made the object of a Law—the only consequences that men are at all interested in—what are they but *pain* and *pleasure?* By some such words, then, as *pain* and *pleasure,* they may be expressed: and *pain* and *pleasure,* at least, are words which a man has no need, we may hope, to go to a Lawyer to know the meaning of.*

[*The *reason* of a Law, in short, is no other than the *good* produced by the mode of conduct which it enjoins, or (which comes to the same thing) the *mischief* produced by the mode of conduct which it prohibits. This *mischief,* or this *good,* if they be real, cannot but show themselves somewhere or other in the shape of *pain* or *pleasure.*]

In the synopsis, then, of that sort of arrangement which alone deserves the name of a natural one, terms such as these—terms which, if they can be said to belong to any science, belong rather to Ethics than to Jurisprudence, even than to universal Jurisprudence, will engross the most commanding stations.

What, then, is to be done with those names of classes that are purely technical?—with offences, for example, against prerogative, with misprisons, contempts, felonies, praemunires? What relation is it that these mark out between the laws that concern the sorts of acts they are respectively put to signify, and that *common end* we have been speaking of? Not any. In a natural arrangement, what then would become of them? They would either be banished at once to the region of *quiddities* and *substantial forms:* or if, and in deference to attachments too inveterate to be all at once dissolved, they were still to be indulged a place, they would be stationed in the corners and bye-places of the Synopsis: stationed, not as now to *give* light, but to *receive* it. But more of this, perhaps, at some future time.

To return to our Author. Embarrassed, as a man must needs be, by this blind and intractable nomenclature, he will be found, I conceive, to have done as much as could reasonably be expected of a writer so circumstanced: and more and better than was ever done before by any one. . . .

With regard to this Essay itself, I have not much to say. The principal and professed purpose of it is, to expose the errors and insufficiencies of our Author. The business of it is therefore rather to *overthrow* than to *set up:* which latter task can seldom be performed to any great advantage where the former is the principal one. . . .

Among the few positions of my own which I have found occasion to advance, some I observe which promise to be far from popular. These, it is likely, may give rise to very warm objections: objections which in themselves I do not wonder at, and which in their motive I cannot but approve. The people are a set of masters whom it is not in a man's power in every instance fully to please, and at the same time faithfully to serve. He that is resolved to persevere without deviation in the line of truth and utility, must have learnt to prefer the still whisper of enduring approbation, to the short-lived bustle of tumultuous applause. . . .

Historical Preface Intended For the Second Edition

(first printed in 1828)

. . . II. When the Fragment made its appearance, the sensation it produced was for some time not inconsiderable. To the unqualified admiration which the Commentaries had for so many years been in possession of, it constituted the first considerable exception, perhaps the very first exception, bearing any thing like a general aspect, that had ever been seen in print. No name being in the title-page, nor any information concerning the author obtainable from the bookseller, conjecture set itself to work. More than one father was found for it: each of the very first class: no minor one: Lord Mansfield, Lord Camden, and Mr. Dunning: the latter, five years afterward, cabineted and ennobled under the title of Lord Ashburton. . . .

III. Among the effects of the work, such as it was, was a sort of concussion, produced by it in the sort of world it belongs to: in the world of politics, but more particularly in the world of law: more particularly still, in the higher region; the inhabitants of which, in this as in other professions, form a sort of celestial conclave, of the secrets of which, whatsoever observation is endeavoured to be made from the subjacent low grounds, is made through a medium impregnated with awe, admiration, and conjecture.

The peep here given into its mysteries will, perhaps, be found neither uninteresting nor uninstructive: it may be assistant to the grand purposes which the work itself has for its objects—objects which may be seen containing the germ of every thing which, on the same field, has been sown by the same hand since. A more particular object is the throwing light into the den of the long-robed Cacus.—Cacus felt the light, and trembled. The more extensive, and indeed all-comprehensive object is, the pointing attention to the imperfections which even at that time of day were seen swarming in the frame of the government, and to the ricketiness of the only foundations in which, on the ground of argument, it had ever found support. No such imperfection having place but what brought profit, in some shape or other, to those among whom the power was shared, their interest of course was, that those same imperfections should, in their whole mass, remain for ever unremoved, and therefore be at all times as little as possible in view.

As a basis for all such operation as should be directed to this same object, the Fragment, at the same time, Fragment as it was, undertook to set up, and may be seen setting up accordingly, the greatest happiness of the greatest number, in the character of the proper, and only proper and defensible, end of government; as the only standard by which any apt judgment could be formed on the propriety of any measure, or of the conduct of any person, occupied in making opposition, or giving support to it. At that time of day, so far as regards the general frame of the Government, scarcely in any one of those imperfections did the Author of the Fragment see the effect of any worse cause than inattention and prejudice; he saw not in them then, what the experience and observations of nearly fifty years have since taught him to see in them so plainly, the elaborately organized, and anxiously cherished and guarded products of sinister interest and artifice.

Under the name of the *principle of utility,* (for that was the name adopted from David Hume), the Fragment set up, as above, the *greatest happiness* principle in the character of the standard of right and wrong in the field of Morality in general, and of Government in particular. In the field of Government, it found in this country the *original contract* in possession of that character.

The existence of that pretended agreement (need it now be said?) was and is a fable: authors of the fable, the Whig lawyers. The invention, such as it was, had been made by them for their own purposes, and nothing could have been better contrived: for, the existence of the contract being admitted, the terms remained to be settled: and these would of course be, on each occasion, what the interest of the occasion required that they should be. It was in this offspring of falsehood and sinister interest that the Fragment beheld the phantom, on the shoulders of which, the Revolution that substituted Guelphs to Stuarts, and added corruption to force, had till then had its sole declared support. Against this phantom, the Fragment will be seen making declared war: the only war but one that had ever been made against it, on any side, and the only war without exception that had ever been made against it, on the side and in favour of the people. Against this attack, thus made, no defence has, I believe, ever been attempted: scarcely since that time has the chimera been seen to show itself; scarcely, at any rate, under its own name. Such as it was, it was the offspring of Fiction; meaning here by the word *Fiction,* that which is meant by it in law-language.

A fiction of law may be defined—a wilful falsehood, having for its object the stealing legislative power, by and for hands which could not, or durst not, openly claim it,—and, but for the delusion thus produced, could not exercise it.

Thus it was that, by means of mendacity, usurpation was, on each occasion, set up, exercised, and established. . . .

A Fragment on Government

[In his own copy, Bentham made this note: "This was the very first pub-lication by which men at large were invited to break loose from the trammels of authority and ancestor-wisdom on the field of law." —M.P.M.]

Introduction

I. The subject of this examination is a passage contained in that part of Sir W. BLACKSTONE'S COMMENTARIES on the LAWS of ENG-LAND, which the Author has styled the INTRODUCTION. This Intro-duction of his stands divided into four Sections . . .

II. 'Tis in the *second* of these Sections, that we shall find the passage proposed for examination. . . .

V. The digression we are about to examine is, as it happens, not at all involved with the body of the work from which it starts. No mutual references or allusions: no supports or illustrations communicated or received. It may be considered as one small work inserted into a large one; the contain*ing* and the contain*ed*, having scarce any other connexion but what the operations of the press have given them. It is this discon-nexion that will enable us the better to bestow on the latter a separate examination, without breaking in upon any thread of reasoning, or any principle of order. . . .

VIII. . . . the contents of the dissertation before us . . . will furnish us with the matter of five chapters:—one, which I shall entitle "FORMATION OF GOVERNMENT";—a second, "FORMS OF GOVERNMENT";—a third, "BRITISH CONSTITUTION";—a fourth, "RIGHT *of the* SU-PREME POWER *to make* LAWS";—a fifth, "DUTY *of the* SUPREME POWER *to make* LAWS."

Chapter I.

FORMATION OF GOVERNMENT.

I. The first object which our Author seems to have proposed to himself in the dissertation we are about to examine, is to give us an idea of the *manner* in which Governments were formed. . . .

III. When leading terms are made to chop and change their several significations; sometimes meaning one thing, sometimes another, at the upshot perhaps nothing; and this in the compass of a paragraph; one may judge what will be the complexion of the whole context. This, we shall see, is the case with the chief of those . . . [he speaks of]: for instance, with the words "society,"—"state of nature,"—"original contract,"—not to tire the reader with any more. *"Society,"* in one place, means the same thing as *"a state of nature"* does: in another place, it means the same as *"Government."* Here, we are required to believe there *never was* such a state as a state of nature; there, we are given to understand there *has been.* In like manner; with respect to an *original contract,* we are given to understand that such a thing never existed; that the notion of it is even ridiculous: at the same time that there is no speaking nor stirring without supposing that there was one.

IV. First, Society means a *state of nature.* For if, by *"a state of nature,"* a man means any thing, it is the state, I take it, men are in or supposed to be in, before they are under *government:* the state men quit when they enter into a state of government; and in which, were it not for government, they would remain. But by the word *"society"* it is plain at one time that he means that state. First, according to him, comes *society;* then afterwards comes *government.* "For when society," says our Author, "is once formed, government results of course; as necessary to preserve and keep that society in order." And again, immediately afterwards—"A state in which a superior has been constituted, whose commands and decisions all the members are bound to obey," he puts as an explanation (nor is it an inapt one) of a state of *"government":* and "unless" men were in a state of that description, they would still "remain," he says, "as in a *state of nature."* By *society,* therefore, he means, once more, the same as by *"a state of nature":* he *opposes* it to *government.* And he speaks of it as a state which, in this sense, has actually existed.

V. Secondly, This is what he tells us in the beginning of the *second* of the two paragraphs: but all the time the *first* paragraph lasted, *society* meant the same as *government.* In shifting, then, from one paragraph to another, it has changed its nature. 'Tis "the foundations of *society,*" that he first began to speak of; and immediately he goes on to explain to us, after his manner of explaining, the foundations of *government*. 'Tis of a "formal beginning" of "society" that he speaks soon after; and by this formal beginning, he tells us immediately, that he means, "the *original contract* of *society*," which contract entered into, "a *state*," he gives us to understand, is thereby "instituted," and men have undertaken to "submit to Laws." So long, then, as this first paragraph lasts, "*society*," I think, it is plain, cannot but have been meaning the same as "*government.*"

VI. Thirdly, All this while, too, this same "*state of nature*" to which we have seen "*society*" (a state spoken of as existing) put synonymous, and in which, were it not for *government*, men, he informs us, in the next page, would "*remain*," is a state in which they never *were*. . . .

VII. Fourthly, The *original contract* is a thing, we are to understand, that never had existence: perhaps not in *any* state: certainly, therefore, not in *all*. "Perhaps, in no instance," says our Author, "has it ever been formally expressed at the first institution of a state."

VIII. Fifthly, Notwithstanding all this, we must suppose, it seems, that it had in *every* state: "yet in nature and reason," says our Author, "it must always be understood and implied." . . .

IX. Let us try whether it be not possible for something to be done towards drawing the import of these terms out of the mist in which our Author has involved them. The word "SOCIETY," I think, it appears, is used by him, and that without notice, in two senses that are opposite. In the one, SOCIETY, or a STATE OF SOCIETY, is put *synonymous* to a STATE OF NATURE; and stands *opposed* to GOVERNMENT, or a STATE OF GOVERNMENT: in this sense it may be styled, as it commonly is, *natural* SOCIETY. In the other, it is put *synonymous* to GOVERNMENT, or a STATE OF GOVERNMENT; and stands *opposed* to a STATE OF NATURE: in this sense it may be styled, as it commonly is, *political* SOCIETY. Of the difference between these two states, a tolerably distinct idea, I take it, may be given in a word or two.

X. The idea of a natural society is a *negative* one: the idea of a political society is a *positive* one. 'Tis with the latter, therefore, we should begin. When a number of persons (whom we may style *subjects*) are supposed to be in the *habit* of paying *obedience* to a person, or an assemblage of persons, of a known and certain description (whom we may call *governor* or *governors*) such persons altogether (*subjects* and *governors*) are said to be in a state of *political* SOCIETY.

XI. The idea of a state of *natural* SOCIETY is, as we have said, a *negative* one. When a number of persons are supposed to be in the habit of *conversing* with each other, at the same time that they are not in any such habit as mentioned above, they are said to be in a state of *natural* SOCIETY.

XII. If we reflect a little, we shall perceive, that, between these two states, there is not that explicit separation which these names, and these definitions, might teach one, at first sight, to expect. It is with them as with light and darkness: however distinct the ideas may be, that are, at first mention, suggested by those *names*, the *things* themselves have no determinate bound to separate them. The circumstance that has been spoken of as constituting the difference between these two states, is the presence or absence of an *habit of obedience*. This habit, accordingly, has been spoken of simply as *present* (that is, as being *perfectly* present) or, in other words, we have spoken as if there were a *perfect* habit of obedience, in the *one* case: it has been spoken of simply as *absent* (that is, as being *perfectly* absent) or, in other words, we have spoken as if there were no habit of obedience at all, in the *other*. But neither of these manners of speaking, perhaps, is strictly just. Few, in fact, if any, are the instances of this habit being perfectly *absent*: certainly none at all, of its being perfectly *present*. Governments, accordingly, in proportion as the habit of obedience is more perfect, recede from: in proportion as it is less perfect, approach to, a state of nature: and instances may present themselves, in which it shall be difficult to say whether a habit, perfect, in the degree in which, to constitute a government, it is deemed necessary it *should* be perfect, does subsist or not.* . . .

[*1. A *habit* is but an assemblage of *acts:* under which name I would also include, for the present, *voluntary forbearances.*

2. A *habit of obedience,* then, is an assemblage of *acts of obedience.*

3. An *act of obedience* is any act done in pursuance of an *expression of will* on the part of some *superior.*

4. An *act of* POLITICAL obedience (which is what is here meant) is any act done in pursuance of an expression of will on the part of a person governing.

5. An *expression of will* is either *parole* or *tacit.*

6. A *parole expression of will* is that which is conveyed by the *signs* called *words.*

7. A *tacit expression of will* is that which is conveyed by any other *signs* whatsoever: among which none are so efficacious as *acts of punishment,* annexed in time past, to the non-performance of acts of the same sort with those that are the objects of the will that is in question.

8. A *parole* expression of the will of a superior is a *command.*

9. When a *tacit* expression of the will of a superior is supposed to have been uttered, it may be styled a *fictitious command.*

10. Were we at liberty to coin words after the manner of the Roman lawyers, we might say a *quasi*-command.

11. The STATUTE LAW is composed of *commands:* the COMMON LAW, of *quasi*-commands.

12. An act which the object of a command actual or fictitious; such an act, considered before it is performed, is styled a *duty* or a *point of duty.*

13. These definitions premised, we are now in a condition to give such an idea, of what is meant by the *perfection* or *imperfection* of a *habit of obedience* in a society, as may prove tolerable precise.

14. A *period* in the duration of the society; the number of *persons* it is composed of during that period; and the number of *points of duty* incumbent on each person being given;—the habit of obedience will be more or less *perfect,* in the ratio of the number of acts of *obedience* to those of *disobedience.*

15. The habit of obedience in this country appears to have been more perfect in the time of the Saxons than in that of the Britons: unquestionable it is more so now than in the time of the Saxons. It is not yet so perfect, as well contrived and well digested laws in time, it is to be hoped, may render it: but absolutely perfect, till man ceases to be man, it never *can* be. . . .]

XIV. . . . To some ears, the phrases, "state of nature," "state of political society," may carry the appearance of being *absolute* in their signification: as if the condition of a man, or a company of men, in one of these states, or in the other, were a matter that depended altogether upon themselves. But this is not the case. . . . For one party to *obey,* there must be another party that is *obeyed.* But this party who is obeyed, may at different times be different. Hence may one and the same party be conceived to obey and not to obey at the same time. . . . Hence it is, then, that one and the same party may be said to *be* in a state of nature, and *not* to be in a state of nature, and that at one and the same time. . . .

XV. In the same manner we may understand, how the same man, who is *governor* with respect to one man or set of men, may be *subject* with respect to another: how among governors some may be in a *perfect* state of *nature* with respect to each other: as the KINGS of FRANCE and SPAIN: others, again, in a state of *perfect subjection;* as the HOSPODARS of WALLACHIA and MOLDAVIA with respect to the GRAND SIGNIOR: others, again, in a state of manifest but *imperfect subjection;* as the GERMAN States with respect to the EMPEROR: others, again, in such a state in which it may be difficult to determine whether they are in a state of *imperfect subjection* or in a *perfect* state of *nature;* as the KING of NAPLES with respect to the POPE.

XVI. In the same manner, also, it may be conceived, without entering into details, how any single person, born, as all persons are born, into a perfect subjection to his parents, that is, into a state of perfect political society with respect to his parents, may from thence pass into a perfect state of nature; and from thence successively into any number of different states of political society, more or less perfect, by passing into different societies.

XVII. In the same manner, also, it may be conceived how, in any political society, the same man may, with respect to the same individuals, be, at different periods, and on different occasions, alternately in the state of governor and subject: to-day concurring, perhaps active, in the business of issuing a *general* command for the observance of the whole society, amongst the rest of another man in quality of *Judge:* to-morrow, punished, perhaps by a *particular* command of that same Judge, for not obeying the general command which he himself (I mean the person acting in character of governor) had issued. I need scarce remind the reader how happily this alternate state of *authority* and *submission* is exemplified among ourselves. . . .

XXI. One difficulty there is that still sticks by us. It has been stated, indeed, but not solved. This is to find a note of distinction—a characteristic mark—whereby to distinguish a society in which there *is* a habit of obedience, and that at the degree of perfection which is necessary to constitute a state of government, from a society in which there is *not:* a mark, I mean, which shall have a visible determinate commencement; insomuch that the instance of its first appearance shall be distinguishable from the last at which it had not as yet appeared. 'Tis only by the help of such a mark that we can be in a condition to determine, at any given time, whether any given society is in a state of government, or in a state of nature. I can find no such mark, I must confess, any where, unless it be this:—the establishment of names of office: the appearance of a certain man, or set of men, with a certain name, serving to mark them out as objects of obedience; such as King, Sachem, Cacique, Senator, Burgomeister, and the like. This, I think, may serve tolerable well to distinguish a set of men in a state of political union among *themselves,* from the *same* set of men not yet in such a state. . . .

XXV. In general, then, At what precise juncture is it, that persons subject to a government, become, by disobedience, with respect to that government, in a state of nature? When is it, in short, that a *revolt* shall be deemed to have taken place? and when, again, is it, that that revolt shall be deemed to such a degree successful, as to have settled into *independence?*

XXVI. As it is the obedience of individuals that constitutes a state of submission, so is it their disobedience that must constitute a state of revolt. Is it, then, every act of disobedience that will do as much? The affirmative, certainly, is what can never be maintained: for then would there no such thing as government to be found any where. Here, then, a distinction or two obviously presents itself. Disobedience may be distinguished into *conscious,* or *unconscious;* and that with respect as well to the *law* as to the *fact.* Disobedience that is unconscious with respect to either, will readily, I suppose be acknowledged not to be a revolt. Disobedience, again, that is conscious with respect to *both,* may be distinguished into *secret* and *open:* or, in other words, into *fraudulent* and *forcible.* Disobedience that is only fraudulent, will likewise, I suppose be readily acknowledged not to amount to a revolt.

XXVII. The difficulty that will remain, will concern such disobedience only as is both *conscious* (and that as well with respect to *law* as *fact*) and *forcible.* This disobedience, it should seem, is to be determined neither by *numbers* altogether (that is, of the persons supposed to be disobedient) nor by *acts,* nor by *intentions:* all three may be fit to be taken into consideration. But having brought the difficulty to this point, at this point I must be content to leave it. To proceed any farther in the endeavour to solve, would be to enter into a discussion of particular local jurisprudence. It would be entering upon the definition of Treason, as distinguished from Murder, Robbery, Riot, and other such crimes, as, in comparison with Treason, are spoken of as being of a more private nature. Suppose the definition of Treason settled, and the commission of an act of Treason is, as far as regards the person committing it, the characteristic mark we are in search of. . . .

XXXIII. It is time this passage of our Author were dismissed. As among the expressions of it are some of the most striking of those which the vocabulary of the subject furnishes, and these ranged in the most harmonious order, on a distant glance nothing can look fairer: a prettier piece of tinsel-work one should seldom see exhibited from the show-glass of political erudition. Step close to it, and the delusion vanishes. It is then seen to consist partly of self-evident observations, and partly of contradictions; partly of what every one knows already, and partly of what no one can understand.

XXXIV. Throughout the whole of it, what distresses me is, not meeting with any positions, such as, thinking them false, I find a difficulty in proving them so: but the not meeting with any positions, true or false (unless it be here and there a self-evident one), that I can find a meaning for. If I can find nothing positive to accede to, no more can I to contradict. Of this latter kind of work, indeed, there is the less to do for any one else, our Author himself having executed it, as we have seen, so amply.

The whole of it is, I must confess, to me a riddle: more acute by far than I am, must be the Oedipus that can solve it. Happily it is not necessary, on account of any thing that follows, that it should be solved. Nothing is concluded from it. For aught I can find, it has in itself no use, and none is made of it. There it is, and as well might it be any where else, or no where.

XXXV. Were it then possible, there would be no use in its being solved: but being, as I take it, *really* unsolvable, it were of use it should *be seen* to be so. Peace may, by this means, be restored to the breast of many a desponding student, who now, prepossessed with the hopes of a rich harvest of instruction, makes a crime to himself of his inability to reap what, in truth, his Author has not sown.

XXXVI. As to the Original Contract, by turns embraced and ridiculed by our Author, a few pages, perhaps, may not be ill bestowed in endeavouring to come to a precise notion about its reality and use. The stress laid on it formerly, and still, perhaps, by some, is such as renders it an object not undeserving of attention. I was in hopes, however, till I observed the notice taken of it by our Author, that the chimera had been effectually demolished by Mr. HUME.*

[*In the third volume of his TREATISE *on* HUMAN NATURE.

Our Author, one would think, had never so much as opened that celebrated book: of which the criminality in the eyes of some, and the merits in the eyes of others, have since been almost effaced by the splendour of more recent productions of the same pen. The magnanimity of our Author scorned, perhaps, or his circumspection feared, to derive instruction from an enemy: or, what is still more probable, he knew not that the subject had been so much as touched upon by that penetrating and acute metaphysician, whose works lie so much out of the beaten track of Academic reading. But here, as it happens, there is no matter for such fears. Those men who are most alarmed at the dangers of a free inquiry; those who are most intimately convinced that the surest way to truth is by hearing nothing but on one side, will, I dare answer almost, find nothing of that which they deem poison in the third volume. I would not wish to send the reader to any other than this, which, if I recollect aright, stands clear of the objects that have of late been urged, with so much vehemence, against the work in general. . . . But after all retrenchments, there will still remain enough to have laid mankind under indelible obligations. That the foundations of all *virtue* are laid in *utility,* is there demonstrated, after a few exceptions made, with the strongest force of evidence: but I see not, any more than Helvétius saw, what need there was for the exceptions.

For my own part, I well remember, no sooner had I read that part of the work which touches on this subject, than I felt as if scales had fallen from my eyes. I then, for the first time, learned to call the cause of the People the cause of Virtue.

Perhaps a short sketch of the wanderings of a raw but well-intentioned mind, in its researches after moral truth, may, on this occasion, be not unuseful: for the history of one mind is the history of many. The writings of the honest, but prejudiced, Earl of Clarendon . . . and the contagion of a monkish atmosphere: these and other concurrent causes, had listed my infant affections on the side of despotism. The Genius of the place I dwelt in, the authority of the State, the voice of the Church in her solemn offices:

all these taught me to call Charles a Martyr, and his opponents rebels. I saw innovation, where indeed innovation, but a glorious innovation, was, in their efforts to withstand him. I saw falsehood, where indeed falsehood was, in this disavowal of innovation. I saw selfishness, and an obedience to the call of passion, in the efforts of the oppressed to rescue themselves from oppression. I saw strong countenance lent in the sacred writings to Monarchic government; and none to any other. I saw *passive Obedience* deep stamped with the seal of the Christian Virtues of humility and self-denial.

Conversing with lawyers, I found them full of the virtues of their Original Contract, as a recipe of sovereign efficacy for reconciling the accidental necessity of resistance with the general duty of submission. This drug of theirs they administered to me to calm my scruples. But my unpractised stomach revolted against their opiate. I bid them open to me that page of history in which the solemnization of the important contract was recorded. They shrunk from this challenge; nor could they, when thus pressed, do otherwise than our Author has done, confess the whole to be a fiction. This, methought, looked ill. It seemed to me the acknowledgement of a bad cause, the bringing a fiction to support it. "To prove fiction, indeed," said I, "there is need of fiction; but it is the characteristic of truth to need no proof but truth. Have you then really any such privilege as that of coining facts? You are spending argument to no purpose. Indulge yourselves in the license of supposing that to be true which is not, and as well may you suppose that proposition itself to be true, which you wish to prove, as that other whereby you hope to prove it." Thus continued I, unsatisfying and unsatisfied, till I learnt to see that *utility* was the test and measure of all virtue; of loyalty as much as any: and that the obligation to minister to general happiness was an obligation paramount to and inclusive of every other. Having thus got the instruction I stood in need of, I sat down to make my profit of it. I bid adieu to the original contract: and I left it to those to amuse themselves with this rattle, who could think they needed it.]

I think we hear not so much of it now as formerly. The indestructible prerogatives of mankind have no need to be supported upon the sandy foundation of a fiction.

XXXVII. With respect to this, and other fictions, there was once a time, perhaps, when they had their use. With instruments of this temper, I will not deny but that some political work may have been done, and that useful work, which, under the then circumstances of things, could hardly have been done with any other. But the season of *Fiction* is now over: insomuch, that what formerly might have been tolerated and countenanced under that name, would, if not attempted to be set on foot, be censured and stigmatized under the harsher appellations of *encroachment* or *imposture*. To attempt to introduce any *new* one, would be *now* a crime: for which reason there is much danger, without any use, in vaunting and propagating such as have been introduced already. In point of political discernment, the universal spread of learning has raised mankind in a manner to a level with each other, in comparison of what they have been in any former time: nor is any man now so far elevated above his fellows, as that he should be indulged in the dangerous license of cheating them for their good.

XXXVIII. As to the fiction now before us, in the character of an *argumentum ad hominem,* coming when it did, and managed as it was, it succeeded to admiration.

That compacts, by whomsoever entered into, ought to be kept;—that men are *bound* by compacts, are propositions which men, without knowing or inquiring why, were disposed universally to accede to. The observance of promises they had been accustomed to see pretty constantly enforced. They had been accustomed to see Kings, as well as others, behave themselves as if bound by them. This proposition, then, "that men are bound by *compacts*"; and this other, "that, if one party performs not his part, the other is released from his," being propositions which no man disputed, were propositions which no man had any call to prove. In theory they were assumed for axioms; and in practice they were observed as rules. If, on any occasion, it was thought proper to make a show of proving them, it was rather for form's sake than for any thing else; and that, rather in the way of memento or instruction to acquiescing auditors, than in the way of proof against opponents. On such an occasion, the common-place retinue of phrases was at hand: *Justice, Right Reason* required it; the *Law of Nature* commanded it, and so forth: all which are but so many ways of intimating that a man is firmly persuaded of the truth of this or that moral proposition, though he either thinks he *need not,* or finds he *can't,* tell *why.* Men were too obviously and too generally interested in the observance of these rules, to entertain doubts concerning the force of any arguments they saw employed in their support. It is an old observation, how Interest smooths the road to Faith. . . .

XLII. But, after all, for what *reason* is it, that men *ought* to keep their promises? The moment any intelligible reason is given, it is this: that it is for the *advantage* of society they should keep them; and if they do not, that as far as *punishment* will go, they should be *made* to keep them. It is for the advantage of the whole number that the promises of each individual should be kept: and, rather than they should not be kept, that such individuals as fail to keep them should be punished. If it be asked, how this appears? the answer is at hand:—Such is the benefit to gain, and mischief to avoid, by keeping them, as much more than compensates the mischief of so much punishment as is requisite to oblige men to it. Whether the dependence of *benefit* and *mischief* (that is, of *pleasure* and *pain*) upon men's conduct in this behalf, be as here stated, is a question of *fact,* to be decided, in the same manner that all other questions of fact are to be decided, by testimony, observation, and experience.

XLIII. This, then, and no other, being the *reason* why men should be made to keep their promises, viz. that it is for the advantage of society that they should, is a reason that may as well be given at once why *Kings,* on the one hand, in governing, should in general keep within established Laws, and (to speak universally) abstain from all such measures as tend to the unhappiness of their subjects: and, on the other hand, why *subjects* should obey Kings as long as they so conduct themselves, and no longer; why they should obey, in short, *so long as the probable mischiefs of obedience are less than the probable mischiefs of resistance:* why, in a word, taking the whole body together, it is their *duty* to obey just so long as it is their *interest,* and no longer. This being the case, what need of saying of the one, that he PROMISED so to *govern:* of the other, that they PROMISED so to *obey,* when the fact is otherwise?

XLVII. . . . Allow, for argument's sake . . . that the obligation of a promise is independent of every other: allow that a promise is binding *propria vi:* Binding, then, on whom? On him certainly who makes it. Admit this: For what reason is the same individual promise to be binding on those who *never* made it? The King, *fifty years ago,* promised my *Great-Grandfather* to govern him according to Law: my Great-Grandfather, *fifty years ago,* promised the King to obey him according to Law. The King, *just now,* promised my *neighbour* to govern him according to Law: my neighbour, *just now,* promised the King to obey him according to Law. Be it so: What are these promises, all or any of them, to *me?* To make answer to this question, some other principle, it is manifest, must be resorted to, than that of the intrinsic obligation of promises upon those who make them.

XLVIII. Now this other principle that still recurs upon us, what other can it be than the *principle of* UTILITY?*

[*§*Added to the 1828 edition*—M.P.M.§ To this denomination, has of late been added, or substituted, the *greatest-happiness* or *greatest-felicity* principle: this for shortness, instead of saying at length, *that principle* which states the greatest happiness of all those whose interest is in question, as being the right and proper, and only right and proper and universally desirable, *end* of human action: of human action in every situation; and, in particular, in that of a functionary, or set of functionaries, exercising the powers of Government. The word *utility* does not so clearly point to the ideas of *pleasure* and *pain,* as the words *happiness* and *felicity* do: nor does it lead us to the consideration of the *number* of the interests affected; of the *number* as being the circumstance which contributes, in the largest proportion, to the formation of the standard here in question—the *standard of right and wrong,* by which alone the propriety of human conduct, in every situation, can with propriety be tried.

This want of a sufficiently manifest connexion between the ideas of *happiness* and *pleasure* on the one hand, and the idea of *utility* on the other, I have every now and then found operating, and with but too much efficiency, as a bar to the acceptance, that might otherwise have been given, to this principle. . . .]

⌊The principle which furnishes us with that *reason,* which alone depends not upon any higher reason, but which is itself the sole and all-sufficient reason for every point of practice whatsoever.⌉

[In Chapters II and III Bentham easily demolished Blackstone's Aristotelian discussion of forms of government; of monarchy, aristocracy, and democracy as based on mere numbers—the one, the few, and the many; and his conclusion that therefore the British constitution, representing as it did in King, Lords, and Commons all three principles, was the best of all possible constitutions.

Because the aim of these selections is to focus on Bentham's own principles, and these are largely given in the Preface and Chapter I, only a few additional pages from Chapters IV and V are needed to round out this panorama of his early beliefs.—M.P.M.]

Chapter IV.

RIGHT OF THE SUPREME POWER TO MAKE LAWS.

XXVI. Let us avow then, in short, steadily but calmly, what our Author hazards with anxiety and agitation, that the authority of the supreme body cannot, *unless where limited by express convention,* be said to have any assignable, any certain bounds.—That to say there is any act they *cannot* do,—to speak of any thing of their's as being *illegal,*—as being *void:*— to speak of their exceeding their *authority* (whatever be the phrase)—their *power,*—their *right,*—is, however common, an abuse of language. . . .

XXXIV. . . . In denying the existence of any assignable bounds to the supreme power, I added, "unless where limited by express convention"; for this exception I could not but subjoin. Our Author, indeed, in that passage in which, short as it is, he is the most explicit, leaves, we may observe, no room for it. "However they began," says he (speaking of the several forms of government)—"however they began, and by what right soever they subsist, there is and must be in ALL of them an authority that is absolute. . . ." To say this, however, of *all* governments without exception;—to say that *no* assemblage of men can subsist in a state of government, without being subject to some *one* body whose authority stands unlimited so much as by convention;—to say, in short, that not even by convention can any limitation be made to the power of that body in a state which in other respects is supreme, would be saying, I take it, rather too much: it would be saying that there is no such thing as government in the German Empire; nor in the Dutch Province; nor in the Swiss Cantons: nor was of old in the Achaean league. . . .

XXXIX. I cannot look upon this as a mere dispute of words: I cannot help persuading myself, that the dispute between contending parties—between the defenders of a law and the opposers of it, would stand a much better chance of being adjusted than at present, were they but explicitly and constantly referred at once to the principle of UTILITY. The footing on which this principle rests every dispute, is that of matter of fact; that is, future fact—the probability of certain future contingencies. Were the debate, then, conducted under the auspices of this principle, one of two things would happen: either men would come to an agreement concerning that probability, or they would see at length, after due discussion of the real grounds of the dispute, that no agreement was to be hoped for. They would, at any rate, see clearly and explicitly the point on which the *dis*agreement turned. The discontented party would then take their resolution to resist or to submit, upon just grounds, according as it should appear to them worth their while—according to what should appear to them the importance of the matter in dispute—according to what should appear to them the probability or improbability of success—according, in short, *as the mischiefs of submission should appear to bear a less, or a greater ratio to the mischiefs of resistance.* But the door to reconcilement would be much more open, when they saw that it might be, not a mere affair of passion, but a difference of judgment, and that, for any thing they could know to the contrary, a sincere one, that was the ground of quarrel.

XL. All else is but womanish scolding and childish altercation, which is sure to irritate, and which never can persuade.—*I* say, the legislature can*not* do this—*I* say, that it can. *I* say, that to do this, *exceeds* the bounds of its *authority*—*I* say, it does *not*. It is evident, that a pair of disputants setting out in this manner, may go on irritating and perplexing one another for everlasting without the smallest chance of ever coming to an agreement. It is no more than announcing, and that in an obscure and at the same. time a peremptory and captious manner, their opposite persuasions, or rather affections, on a question of which neither of them sets himself to discuss the grounds. The question of utility . . . is never so much as at all brought upon the carpet: if it be, the language in which it is discussed is sure to be warped and clouded to make it match with the obscure and entangled pattern we have seen.

XLI. On the other hand, had the debate been originally and avowedly instituted on the footing of utility, the parties might at length have come to an agreement; or at least to a visible and explicit issue—*I* say, that the mischiefs of the measure in question are to *such* an amount—*I* say, *not* so, but to a *less*.—*I* say, the benefits of it are only to *such* an amount —*I* say, *not* so, but to a *greater*.—This, we see, is a ground of controversy very different from the former. The question is now manifestly a question of conjecture concerning so many future contingent matters of fact: to solve it, both parties then are naturally directed to support their respective persuasions by the only evidence the nature of the case admits of;— the evidence of such *past* matters of fact as appear to be analogous to those contingent *future* ones. Now these *past* facts are almost always numerous: so numerous, that till brought into view for the purpose of the debate, a great proportion of them are what may very fairly have escaped the observation of one of the parties: and it is owing, perhaps, to this and nothing else, that that party is of the persuasion which sets it at variance with the other. Here, then, we have a plain and open road, perhaps, to present reconcilement: at the worst, to an intelligible and explicit issue—that is, to such a ground of difference as may, when thoroughly trodden and explored, be found to lead on to reconcilement at the last. Men, let them but once clearly understand one another, will not be long ere they agree. It is the perplexity of ambiguous and sophistical discourse that, while it distracts and eludes the apprehension, stimulates and inflames the passions.

But it is now high time we should return to our Author, from whose text we have been insensibly led astray, by the nicety and intricacy of the question it seemed to offer to our view.

Chapter V.

DUTY OF THE SUPREME POWER TO MAKE LAWS.

. . . IV. . . . "Thus far," says our Author (recapitulating what he had been saying before) "as to the *right* of the supreme power to make law.—By this *"right,"* we saw, in the preceding chapter, was meant, a right to make law *in all cases whatsoever.* "But further," he now adds, "it is its *duty* likewise." Its *duty,* then, to do—what? to do the same thing that it was before asserted to be its *right* to do—to make laws in all cases whatsoever: or (to use another word, and that our Author's own, and that applied to the same purpose) that it is its duty to be *"absolute."* A sort of duty this, which will probably be thought rather a singular one.

V. Meantime, the observation which, if I conjecture right, he really had in view to make, is one which seems very just indeed, and of no mean importance, but which is very obscurely expressed, and not very obviously connected with the purport of what goes before. The duty he here means is a duty which respects, I take it, not so much the actual *making* of laws, as the taking of proper measures to *spread abroad* the knowledge of whatever laws happen to *have been* made: a duty which (to adopt some of our Author's own words) is conversant, not so much about *issuing* "directions," as about providing that such as *are* issued shall be *"received."*

VI. Meantime, to speak of the *duties* of a supreme power;—of a *legislature,* meaning a *supreme* legislature;—of a set of men acknowledged to be absolute;—is what, I must own, I am not very fond of. Not that I would wish the subordinate part of the community to be a whit less watchful over their governors, or more disposed to unlimited submission in point of *conduct,* than if I were to talk with ever so much peremptoriness of the *"duties"* of these latter, and of the *rights* which the former have against them:*

[*With this note let no man trouble himself, who is not used, or does not intend to use himself, to what are called *metaphysical* speculations; in whose estimation the benefit of understanding clearly what he is speaking of, is not worth the labour.

1. That may be said to be my *duty* to do (understand political duty) which you (or some other person or persons) have a *right* to have me made to do. I have, then, a DUTY *towards* you; you have a RIGHT as *against* me.

2. What you have a right to have me made to do (understand a political right) is that which I am liable, according to law, upon a requisition made on your behalf, to be *punished* for not doing.

3. I say *punished:* for without the notion of punishment (that is, of *pain* annexed to an act, and accruing on a certain *account,* and from a certain *source*) no notion can we have of either *right* or *duty.*

4. Now the idea belonging to the word *pain* is a simple one. To *define,* or rather (to speak more generally) to *expound* a word, is to resolve, or to make a progress towards resolving, the idea belonging to it into simple ones.

5. For expounding the words *duty, right, power, title,* and those other terms of the same stamp that abound so much in ethics and jurisprudence, either I am much deceived, or the only method by which any instruction can be conveyed, is that which is here exemplified. An exposition framed after this method I would term *paraphrasis.*

6. A word may be said to be expounded by *paraphrasis,* when not that *word* alone is translated into other *words,* but some whole *sentence,* of which it forms a part, is translated into another *sentence;* the words of which latter are expressive of such ideas as are *simple,* or are more immediately resolvable into simple ones than those of the former. Such are those expressive of *substances* and *simple modes,* in respect of such *abstract* terms as are expressive of what LOCKE has called *mixed modes.* This, in short, is the only method in which any abstract terms can, at the long run, be expounded to any instructive purpose; that is, in terms calculated to raise *images* either of *substances* perceived, or of *emotions;*—sources, one or other of which every idea must be drawn from, to be a clear one.

7. The common method of defining—the method *per genus et differentiam,* as logicians call it, will, in many cases, not at all answer the purpose. Among abstract terms we soon come to such as have no *superior genus.* A definition *per genus et differentiam,* when applied to these, it is manifest, can

make no advance; it must either stop short, or turn back, as it were, upon itself, in a *circulate* or a *repetend.*

8. "Fortitude is a virtue":—Very well:—but what is a virtue? "A virtue is a disposition":—Good again:—but what is a *disposition?* "A disposition is a . . ."; and there we stop. The fact is, a *disposition* has no *superior genus:* a *disposition* is not a . . . , anything:—this is not the way to give us any notion of what is meant by it. "A *power,*" again, "is a *right*": and what is a *right?* It is a *power.* An *estate* is an *interest,* says our Author somewhere, where he begins defining an estate:—as well might he have said an *interest* was an *estate.* As well, in short, were it to say of the preposition *through,* or of the conjunction *because;* a *through* is a . . . , or a *because* is a . . . , and so go on defining them.

9. Of this stamp, by the bye, are some of his most fundamental definitions; of consequence they must leave the reader where they found him. But of this, perhaps, more fully and methodically on some future occasion. In the mean time, I have thrown out these loose hints for the consideration of the curious.]

What I am afraid of is, running into solecism and confusion in *discourse.*

VII. I understand, I think, pretty well, what is meant by the word *duty* (political duty) when applied to myself; and I could not persuade myself, I think, to apply it in the same sense in a regular didactic discourse to those whom I am speaking of as my supreme governors. That it is my *duty* to do, which I am liable to be *punished,* according to law, if I do not do: this is the original, ordinary, and proper sense of the word duty.*

[*1. One may conceive three sorts of duties: *political, moral,* and *religious;* correspondent to the three sorts of *sanctions* by which they are enforced; or the same point of conduct may be a man's duty on these three several accounts. After speaking of the one of these to put the change upon the reader, and without warning begin speaking of another, or not to let it be seen from the first which of them one is speaking of, cannot but be productive of confusion.

2. Political duty is created by punishment; or at least by the will of persons who have punishment in their hands; persons stated and *certain—* political superiors.

3. Religious duty is also created by punishment: by punishment expected at the hands of a person *certain—*the Supreme Being.

4. Moral duty is created by a kind of motive, which, from the *un*certainty of the *persons* to apply it, and of the *species* and *degree* in which it will be applied, has hardly yet got the name of punishment: by various mortifications resulting from the ill-will of persons *un*certain and variable,—the community in general; that is, such individuals of that community as he, whose duty is in question, shall happen to be connected with.

5. When in any of these three senses a man asserts a point of conduct to be a duty, what he asserts is the existence, actual or probable, of an *external* event; viz. of a punishment issuing from one or other of these sources in consequence of a contravention of the duty: an event *extrinsic* to, and distinct from, as well the conduct of the party spoken of, as the sentiment of him who speaks:—if he persists in asserting it to be a duty,

but without meaning it should be understood that it is on any one of these three accounts that he looks upon it as such; all he then asserts is his own internal *sentiment:* all he means then is, that he feels himself *pleased* or *displeased* at the thoughts of the point of conduct in question, but without being able to tell *why.* In this case, he should e'en say so: and not seek to give an undue influence to his own single suffrage, by delivering it in terms that purport to declare the voice either of God, or of the law, or of the people.

6. Now which of all these senses of the word our Author had in mind; in which of them all he meant to assert that it was the duty of supreme governors to make law, I know not. *Political* duty is what they cannot be subject to: and to say that a duty even of the *moral* or *religious* kind to his effect is incumbent on them, seems rather a precipitate assertion.

In truth, what he meant was neither more nor less, I suppose, than that he should be glad to see them do what he is speaking of: to wit, "*make* laws"; that is, as he explains himself, spread abroad the knowledge of them.—Would he so? So indeed should I; and if asked why, what answer our Author would give I know not; but I, for my part, have no difficulty. I answer,—because I am persuaded that it is for the benefit of the community that they (its governors) should do so. This would be enough to warrant me in my own opinion for saying that they *ought* to do it. . . .]

Have these supreme governors any such duty? No: for if they are at all liable to punishment according to law, whether it be for *not* doing any thing, or for *doing,* then are they not, what they are supposed to be, supreme governors: those are the supreme governors, by whose appointment the former are liable to be punished. . . .

XIII. I now put an end to the tedious and intricate war of words that has subsisted, in a more particular manner during the course of these two last chapters: a logomachy, wearisome enough, perhaps, and insipid to the reader, but beyond description laborious and irksome to the writer. What remedy? Had there been sense, I should have attached myself to the sense: finding nothing but words, to the words I was to attach myself, or to nothing. Had the doctrine been but *false,* the task of exposing it would have been comparatively an easy one: but it was what is worse, *unmeaning;* and thence it came to require all these pains which I have been here bestowing on it: to what profit, let the reader judge.

"Well then," cries an objector, "the task you have set yourself is at an end; and the subject of it, after all, according to your own representation, teaches nothing;—according to your own showing, it is not worth attending to. Why then bestow on it so much attention?"

In this view: To do something to instruct, but more to undeceive, the timid and admiring student:—to excite him to place more confidence in his own strength, and less in the infallibility of great names:—to help him to emancipate his judgment from the shackles of authority:—to let him see that the not understanding a discourse may as well be the writer's fault as the reader's:—to teach him to distinguish between shewy language and sound sense:—to warn him not to pay himself with words:—to show him that what may tickle the ear, or dazzle the imagination, will not always inform the judgment:—to show him what it is our Author can do, and has done; and what it is he has not done, and cannot do:—to dispose him rather to fast on ignorance than feed himself with error:—to let him see, that with regard to an expositor of the law, our Author is not *he that should come,* but that we may be still *looking for another.*—"Who then," says my objector, "shall be that other? Yourself?"—No, verily. My mission is at end, when I have *prepared the way before him.*

An Introduction to the Principles of Morals and Legislation

A Note on *An Introduction to the Principles of Morals and Legislation*

Doubtless *An Introduction to the Principles of Morals and Legislation* was Bentham's most important work, as it was also for him the most tormenting. It began simply enough. In 1778 the city of Berne offered a prize for a specimen penal code and Bentham entered the contest, confident that his set of first principles, the greatest happiness of the greatest number with its subordinate principles of security, subsistence, abundance, and equality, would surely guide him through it. But he soon came to a halt. He saw that there could be no progress without first redefining the entire vocabulary of morals and politics. The terms of law were not enough, for law was a subordinate branch of ethics; and ethics in turn was still not enough, for it was a subordinate branch of *eudaemonics,* his neologism for the art and science of well-being, the universal, all-comprehensive art and science of human existence.

Those were unhappy years as Bentham struggled day after day, without reward, poor and unrecognized in his rooms at Lincoln's Inn. "I had got into a mizmaze," he recalled in the 1820's, "I could not see my way clearly,—it was a dark forest,—for the vast field of law was around me with all its labyrinths. Little by little great principles threw their light upon the field, and the path became clear."[1] *An Introduction* is by no means a balanced and finished work. First he saw light in one area,

---

[1] X, pp. 123–4.

then jumped to another; on the one hand, anxious to fill up all the defini-
tional preliminaries; but on the other, still more anxious to get to work
on the penal code itself. Many of the basic terms of psychology and
ethics he overlooked, but as he said in his 1789 Preface, they were easily
inferable from the principle of utility itself. In a sense the book is a
great work of metaphysics, for the nominalist Bentham defined metaphysics as lexicography.

Among his most important definitions, as they appear successively
throughout the text, are: utility, principle, interest, happiness, ought, right,
wrong, asceticism, sympathy, antipathy, moral sense, common sense,
sanction, value, good, bad, mischief, pleasure, pain, perception, punishment, reward, intention, understanding, consciousness, will, disposition,
motives, crime, offense, duty, prudence, probity, beneficence.

But when he came at last, in Chapter XVII, to the definitions of civil
and penal law and the difference between them—to them and their difference from ethics, constitutional law, and jurisprudence in general—he
was caught in a murky labyrinth and could not find his way out. This
much he ordered printed, and there he floundered, as gradually the unpublished sheets gathered dust and water stains. By 1789 they were half-
eaten by rats as well. Gradually, however, the murk lifted and Chapter
XVII became several hundred pages longer; they were first published in
1945 by Professor Everett as *The Limits of Jurisprudence Defined.*[2] A
Chapter XVIII on Indirect Legislation also followed;[3] this too was several hundred pages long. In its prevision of the welfare state it is a fascinating work; nevertheless, but for a few pages in Dumont's *Traités* and
Hildreth, it has never been published.

By 1789 Bentham's friends had become exasperated. He is often pictured as a lonely recluse; on the contrary, he was surrounded by loving,
admiring friends who considered him a great genius. But he would not
publish any substantial work, and indefatigable worker that he was,
writing at least sixteen folio pages a day, his manuscripts piled up alarm-
ingly, and his friends became ever more pressing. He was after all already
forty-one; some of his work was circulating in manuscript form; how
long would it take before others stole his best ideas? Finally his most
loyal friend, the somewhat stiff and priggish, but eminently helpful and
appreciative Scots barrister, George Wilson, wrote him a strong letter.
"It grieves me to think that so much excellent matter should be either
lost or forestalled—you are not likely at present to complete that Code;
but is it impossible to publish the Introduction by itself? It is not unusual
to publish part of a book; and why not this part, which . . . contains a

²See below, pp. 147*ff.*
³See below, pp. 168*ff.*

system of morals and general jurisprudence superior to any extant? I am convinced it would raise your reputation more than anything you have yet published. . . . I think the best way will be to publish whatever is finished, but not to begin to write anything new; that you can do afterwards if the subject and the success please you. . . . I have really this matter very much at heart, and shall be much mortified if you don't consent."[4]

Bentham did consent, and the unspoiled remains of the 1780 edition were duly published in 1789. They were ignored as he expected. He always doubted that any sizable group of men could be brought to an interest in so dry a subject as metaphysics at any time; but still less was it possible during the exploding years of the French Revolution. The early English welcome to the French upheaval was soon superseded by horror and reaction, and *An Introduction* sank beneath the furor.

It is supremely interesting to see how Bentham's mind changed during those nine years between printing and publication. These changes are mirrored throughout in added footnotes, in the 1789 Preface, and in the final long footnote to Chapter XVII. How did he escape his mizmaze? He discovered what he called a "logic of the will," *i.e.*, that the art and science of jurisprudence is a structure of commands.[5] Under it civil laws are largely expository and penal laws imperative. The constitutional law now became all-important to him, for he saw that by conferring general powers to punish and reward, it included all the other branches of law. With this new insight he saw his planned law codes as so many propositions of a new logic.

Now his entire life's work at last became clear. In the Preface, he outlined his plan,[6] so vastly ambitious that a corps of specialists might well take a lifetime to finish it. The astonishing thing is that Bentham did it single-handedly—and did a great deal else besides. Here he limited his ambition to law and government; he offered a vision of a complete substantive code of law, complete not only in private but public law, civil as well as penal and constitutional; reward as well as punishment; economic as well as political law, and formal structure as well as substantive content. But he was fascinated by the whole mind and life of man; his moral, religious, economic, cultural, educational roles as well as his more strictly political and legal ones. Nothing human was alien to him, and by the end of his life he had investigated, with more or less thoroughness and insight, just about every subject of human interest.

Why did Bentham consider *An Introduction* his most important work? Because he here laid down the fabric of almost all he was to do later,

[4] X, pp. 194–5.
[5] See p. 84 below.
[6] See p. 82 below.

again and again picking up and then dropping threads and weaving them into ever more tightly knit tapestries. His discussion of ethics and psychology was typical. In the Preface he acknowledged that his dictionary was incomplete, that the book was unfinished and badly organized. Later in the text he briefly mentioned what afterward became a fundamentally important distinction between dyslogistic and eulogistic language. As the years went by, he became more and more concerned to fill up the gaps in the ethical and psychological dictionary, and to show not only the full range of synonyms but to divide them up into their full amplitude of neutral terms, dyslogisms, and eulogisms. All this he did in the tersest possible chart form, adamant as always that intelligence, genuine thought, and concision go hand in hand. The final result of his most mature ethical and psychological analyses was *A Table of the Springs of Actions,* published in 1815(?);[7] it is too cryptic and unreadable in its chart form to be usefully included in this book. It is a set of charts with long comparative strings of words and titles in the style of Sir Francis Bacon's four idols. Bentham listed, for example, Interest of the Palate, the Bottle (of taste), Interest of the Purse (pecuniary interest), Interest of the Sceptre (power), Interest of the Spying Glass (curiosity), Interest of the Closet (amity), Interest of the Gall Bladder (antipathy), etc.

Here, in the *Introduction,* most of his major doctrines are laid out, sometimes only as hints and rough sketches, sometimes in fairly full discussions. Among the most important are: the four sanctions, physical, moral, political, and religious, hints which he first borrowed from Blackstone and later expanded to fourteen; the notorious calculus with its seven elements of measurement, intensity, duration, certainty, propinquity, remoteness, purity, and extent; the definition and elaborate classification of offenses; the principles of punishment relative to pain; the orders of evil, one of his most important though largely neglected doctrines, in which evil is measured by the radius of mischievous effects.

Here we find his fullest discussions of psychology and ethics in general, and his explanation of and apology for the unavoidable dilemma of language. Because his system grew out of violent dissatisfaction with the highly ambiguous and confusing fictions of English law, Bentham was unavoidably called upon from the very beginning to create a new, clear vocabulary of his own. Willy-nilly he became a neologist, all the while sadly aware that he had made an evil choice, though the lesser of two evil choices: if he kept to the old terms, he would surely be misunderstood; if he invented new ones, he would surely be abused or ignored. And so he was.

[7] I, pp. 195ff.

Here, too, Bentham hinted at what later became a major work, *The Rationale of Reward*. He claimed to have invented the subject. For centuries, he declared, men wrote upon punishments; but political power took the direction of pleasure as well as pain, so why should there not be a scientific investigation of rewards as well as punishments? Finally, he offered the most complete discussion of his method of "exhaustive bifurcation," which was the old scholastic definition *per genus et differentiam*. It was "unspeakably useful to me," he said, and from first to last formed the structure of his entire system.

An Introduction to the Principles of Morals and Legislation (1780)

Preface (1789)

The following sheets were, as the title-page expresses, printed so long ago as the year 1780. The design, in pursuance of which they were written, was not so extensive as that announced by the present title. They had at that time no other destination than that of serving as an introduction to a plan of a penal code, *in terminis,* designed to follow them, in the same volume.

The body of the work had received its completion according to the then present extent of the author's views, when, in the investigation of some flaws he had discovered, he found himself unexpectedly entangled in an unsuspected corner of the metaphysical maze. A suspension, at first not apprehended to be more than a temporary one, necessarily ensued: suspension brought on coolness; and coolness, aided by other concurrent causes, ripened into disgust.

Imperfections pervading the whole mass had already been pointed out by the sincerity of severe and discerning friends; and conscience had certified the justness of their censure. The inordinate length of some of the chapters, the apparent inutility of others, and the dry and metaphysical turn of the whole, suggested an apprehension, that, if published in its present form, the work would contend under great disadvantages for any chance, it might on other accounts possess, of being read, and consequently of being of use.

But, though in this manner the idea of completing the present work slid insensibly aside, that was not by any means the case with the considerations which had led him to engage in it. Every opening, which promised to afford the lights he stood in need of, was still pursued: as occasion arose, the several departments connected with that in which he had at first engaged, were successively explored; insomuch that, in one branch or other of the pursuit, his researches have nearly embraced the whole field of legislation.

78

Several causes have conspired at present to bring to light, under this new title, a work which under its original one had been imperceptibly, but as it had seemed irrevocably, doomed to oblivion. In the course of eight years, materials for various works, corresponding to the different branches of the subject of legislation, had been produced, and some nearly reduced to shape: and, in every one of those works, the principles exhibited in the present publication had been found so necessary, that, either to transcribe them piecemeal, or to exhibit them somewhere, where they could be referred to in the lump, was found unavoidable. The former course would have occasioned repetitions too bulky to be employed without necessity in the execution of a plan unavoidably so voluminous: the latter was therefore indisputably the preferable one.

To publish the materials in the form in which they were already printed, or to work them up into a new one, was therefore the only alternative: the latter had all along been his wish; and, had time and the requisite degree of alacrity been at command, it would as certainly have been realized. Cogent considerations, however, concur with the irksomeness of the task, in placing the accomplishment of it at present at an unfathomable distance.

Another consideration is, that the suppression of the present work, had it been ever so decidedly wished, is no longer altogether in his power. In the course of so long an interval, various incidents have introduced copies into various hands, from some of which they have been transferred, by deaths and other accidents, into others that are unknown to him. Detached, but considerable extracts, have even been published, without any dishonourable views (for the name of the author was very honestly subjoined to them), but without his privity, and in publications undertaken without his knowledge.

It may perhaps be necessary to add, to complete his excuse for offering to the public a work pervaded by blemishes, which have not escaped even the author's partial eye, that the censure, so justly bestowed upon the form, did not extend itself to the matter.

In sending it thus abroad into the world with all its imperfections upon its head, he thinks it may be of assistance to the few readers he can expect, to receive a short intimation of the chief particulars, in respect of which it fails of corresponding with his maturer views. It will thence be observed how in some respects it fails of quadrating with the design announced by its original title, as in others it does with that announced by the one it bears at present.

An introduction to a work which takes for its subject the totality of any science, ought to contain all such matters, and such matters only, as belong in common to every particular branch of that science, or at least to more branches of it than one. Compared with its present title, the present work fails in both ways of being conformable to that rule.

As an introduction to the principles of *morals,* in addition to the analysis it contains of the extensive ideas signified by the terms *pleasure, pain, motive,* and *disposition,* it ought to have given a similar analysis of the not less extensive, though much less determinate, ideas annexed to the terms *emotion, passion, appetite, virtue, vice,* and some others, including the names of the particular *virtues* and *vices.* But as the true, and, if he conceives right, the only true ground-work for the development of the latter set of terms, has been laid by the explanation of the former, the completion of such a dictionary, so to style it, would, in comparison of the commencement, be little more than a mechanical operation.

Again, as an introduction to the principles of *legislation in general,* it ought rather to have included matters belonging exclusively to the *civil* branch, than matters more particularly applicable to the *penal:* the latter being but a means of compassing the ends proposed by the former. In preference, therefore, or at least in priority, to the several chapters which will be found relative to *punishment,* it ought to have exhibited a set of propositions which have since presented themselves to him as affording a standard for the operations performed by government, in the creation and distribution of proprietary and other civil rights. He means certain axioms of what may be termed *mental pathology,* expressive of the connexion betwixt the feelings of the parties concerned, and the several classes of incidents, which either call for, or are produced by, operations of the nature above mentioned.*

[*For example: *It is worse to lose than simply not to gain. A loss falls the lighter by being divided. The suffering, of a person hurt in gratification of enmity, is greater than the gratification produced by the same cause.* These . . . have the same claim to the appellation of axioms, as those given by mathematicians under that name; since, referring to universal experience as their immediate basis, they are incapable of demonstration, and require only to be developed and illustrated, in order to be recognised as incontestable.]

The consideration of the division of offences, and every thing else that belongs to offences, ought, besides, to have preceded the consideration of punishment: for the idea of *punishment* presupposes the idea of *offence:* punishment, as such, not being inflicted but in consideration of offence.

Lastly, the analytical discussions relative to the classification of offences would, according to his present views, be transferred to a separate treatise, in which the system of legislation is considered solely in respect of its form; in other words, in respect of its *method* and *terminology.*

In these respects, the performance fails of coming up to the author's own ideas of what should have been exhibited in a work, bearing the title he has now given it, viz. that of an *Introduction to the Principles of Morals and Legislation.* He knows however of no other that would be less unsuitable: nor, in particular, would so adequate an intimation of its actual contents have been given, by a title corresponding to the more limited design, with which it was written; viz. that of serving as an *introduction to a penal code.*

Yet more. Dry and tedious as a great part of the discussions it contains must unavoidably be found by the bulk of readers, he knows not how to regret the having written them, nor even the having made them public. Under every head, the practical uses, to which the discussions contained under that head appeared applicable, are indicated: nor is there, he believes, a single proposition that he has not found occasion to build upon in the penning of some article or other of the provisions of detail, of which a body of law, authoritative or unauthoritative, must be composed. He will venture to specify particularly, in this view, the several chapters shortly characterized by the words *Sensibility, Actions, Intentionality, Consciousness, Motives, Disposition, Consequences.* Even in the enormous chapter on the division of offences, which, notwithstanding the forced compression the plan has undergone in several of its parts, in manner there mentioned, occupies no fewer than one hundred and four closely printed quarto pages [in the first edition, 1780—M.P.M.], the ten concluding ones are employed in a statement of the practical advantages that may be reaped from the plan of classification which it exhibits. [*cf.* below pp. 133*ff.*—M.P.M.] . . . To some readers, as a means of helping them to support the fatigue of wading through an analysis of such enormous length, he would almost recommend the beginning with those ten concluding pages.

One good at least may result from the present publication; viz. that the more he has trespassed on the patience of the reader on this occasion, the less need he will have so to do on future ones: so that this may do to those, the office which is done by books of pure mathematics to books of mixed mathematics and natural philosophy. The narrower the circle of readers is, within which the present work may be condemned to confine itself, the less limited may be the number of those to whom the fruits of his succeeding labours may be found accessible. He may therefore, in this respect, find himself in the condition of those philosophers of antiquity, who are represented as having held two bodies of doctrine, a popular and an occult one: but with this difference, that in his instance the occult and the popular will, he hopes, be found as consistent as in those they were contradictory; and that, in his production, whatever there is of occultness has been the pure result of sad necessity, and in no respect of choice.

Having, in the course of this advertisement, had such frequent occasion to allude to different arrangements, as having been suggested by more extensive and maturer views, it may perhaps contribute to the satisfaction of the reader to receive a short intimation of their nature: the rather, as without such explanation, references made here and there to unpublished works might be productive of perplexity and mistake. The following, then, are the titles of the works by the publication of which his present designs would be completed. They are exhibited in the order which seemed to him best fitted for apprehension and in which they would stand disposed, were the whole assemblage ready to come out at once: but the order in which they will eventually appear, may probably enough be influenced in some degree by collateral and temporary considerations.

Part the 1st.—Principles of legislation in matters of *civil,* more distinctively termed *private distributive,* or for shortness, *distributive, law.*

Part the 2d.—Principles of legislation in matters of *penal law.*

Part the 3d.—Principles of legislation in matters of *procedure:* uniting in one view the *criminal* and *civil* branches, between which no line can be drawn, but a very indistinct one, and that continually liable to variation.

Part the 4th.—Principles of legislation in matters of *reward.*

Part the 5th.—Principles of legislation in matters of *public distributive,* more concisely as well as familiarly termed *constitutional,* law.

Part the 6th.—Principles of legislation in matters of *political tactics:* or of the art of maintaining *order* in the proceedings of political assemblies, so as to direct them to the end of their institution; viz. by a system of rules, which are to the constitutional branch, in some respects, what the law of procedure is to the civil and the penal.

Part the 7th.—Principles of legislation in matters betwixt nation and nation, or, to use a new though not inexpressive appellation, in matters of *international* law.

Part the 8th.—Principles of legislation in matters of *finance.*

Part the 9th.—Principles of legislation in matters of *political economy.*

Part the 10th.—Plan of a body of law, complete in all its branches, considered in respect of its *form;* in other words, in respect of its method and terminology; including a view of the origination and connexion of the ideas expressed by the short list of terms, the exposition of which contains all that can be said with propriety to belong to the head of *universal jurisprudence.**

[*Such as obligation, right, power, possession, title, exemption, immunity, franchise, privilege, nullity, validity, and the like.]

The use of the principles laid down under the above several heads is to prepare the way for the body of law itself exhibited *in terminis:* and which, to be complete with reference to any political state, must consequently be calculated for the meridian, and adapted to the circumstances, of some one such state in particular.

Had he an unlimited power of drawing upon *time,* and every other condition necessary, it would be his wish to postpone the publication of each part to the completion of the whole. In particular, the use of the ten parts, which exhibit what appear to him the dictates of utility in every line, being no other than to furnish reasons for the several corresponding provisions contained in the body of law itself, the exact truth of the former can never be precisely ascertained, till the provisions, to which they are destined to apply, are themselves ascertained, and that *in terminis.* But as the infirmity of human nature renders all plans precarious in the execution, in proportion as they are extensive in the design, and as he has already made considerable advances in several branches of the theory, without having made correspondent advances in the practical applications, he deems it more than probable, that the eventual order of publication will not correspond exactly with that which, had it been equally practicable, would have appeared most eligible. . . .

Allusion was made, at the outset of this advertisement, to some unspecified difficulties as the causes of the original suspension, and unfinished complexion, of the present work. Ashamed of his defeat, and unable to dissemble it, he knows not how to refuse himself the benefit of such an apology as a slight sketch of the nature of those difficulties may afford.

The discovery of them was produced by the attempt to solve the questions that will be found at the conclusion of the volume: *Wherein consisted the identity and completeness of a law? What the distinction, and where the separation, between a* penal *and a* civil *law? What the distinction, and where the separation between the* penal *and* other *branches of* the law?

To give a complete and correct answer to these questions, it is but too evident that the relations and dependencies of every part of the legislative system, with respect to every other, must have been comprehended and ascertained. But it is only upon a view of these parts themselves, that such an operation could have been performed. To the accuracy of such a survey one necessary condition would therefore be, the complete existence of the fabric to be surveyed. Of the performance of this condition no example is as yet to be met with any where. *Common* law, as it styles itself in England, *judiciary* law, as it might more aptly be styled every where, that fictitious composition which has no known person for its author, no known assemblage of words for its substance, forms every where the main body of the legal fabric: like that fancied ether, which, in default of sensible matter, fills up the measure of the universe. Shreds and scraps of real law, stuck on upon that imaginary ground, compose the furniture of every national code. What follows? That he who, for the purpose just mentioned, or for any other, wants an example of a complete body of law to refer to, must begin with making one.

There is, or rather there ought to be, a *logic* of the *will,* as well as of the *understanding:* the operations of the former faculty are neither less susceptible, nor less worthy, than those of the latter, of being delineated by rules. Of these two branches of that recondite art, Aristotle saw only the latter: succeeding logicians, treading in the steps of their great founder, have concurred in seeing it with no other eyes. Yet so far as a difference can be assigned between branches so intimately connected, whatever difference there is, in point of importance, is in favour of the logic of the will; since it is only by their capacity of directing this faculty, that the operations of the understanding are of any consequence.

Of this logic of the will, the science of *law,* considered in respect of its *form,* is the most considerable branch,—the most important application. It is, to the art of legislation, what the science of anatomy is to the art of medicine: with this difference, that the subject of it is what the artist has to work *with,* instead of being what he has to operate *upon.* Nor is the body politic less in danger from a want of acquaintance with the one science, than the body natural from ignorance in the other. One example, amongst a thousand that might be adduced in proof of this assertion, may be seen in the note which terminates this volume.

Such, then, were the difficulties: such the preliminaries:—an unexampled work to achieve, and then a new science to create; a new branch to add to one of the most abstruse of sciences.

Yet more: a body of proposed law, how complete soever, would be comparatively useless and uninstructive, unless explained and justified, and that in every tittle, by a continued accompaniment, a perpetual commentary of reasons:*

[*To the aggregate of them a common denomination has since been assigned—the *rationale.*]

which reasons, that the comparative value of such as point in opposite directions may be estimated, and the conjunct force of such as point in the same direction may be felt, must be marshalled, and put under subordination to such extensive and leading ones as are termed principles. There must be therefore, not one system only, but two parallel and connected systems, running on together; the one of legislative provisions, the other of political reasons; each affording to the other correction and support.

Are enterprises like these achievable? He knows not. This only he knows, that they have been undertaken, proceeded in, and that some progress has been made in all of them. He will venture to add, if at all achievable, never at least by one, to whom the fatigue of attending to discussions, as arid as those which occupy the ensuing pages, would either appear useless, or feel intolerable. He will repeat it boldly (for it has been said before him), truths that form the basis of political and moral science are not to be discovered but by investigations as severe as mathematical ones, and beyond all comparison more intricate and extensive. The familiarity of the terms is a presumption, but it is a most fallacious one, of the facility of the matter. Truths in general have been called stubborn things: the truths just mentioned are so in their own way. They are not to be forced into detached and general propositions, unincumbered with explanations and exceptions. They will not compress themselves into epigrams. They recoil from the tongue and the pen of the declaimer. They flourish not in the same soil with sentiment. They grow among thorns; and are not to be plucked, like daisies, by infants as they run. Labour, the inevitable lot of humanity, is in no track more inevitable than here. In vain would an Alexander bespeak a peculiar road for royal vanity, or a Ptolemy a smoother one for royal indolence. There is no *King's Road*, no *Stadtholder's Gate*, to legislative, any more than to mathematic science.

Chapter I.

OF THE PRINCIPLE OF UTILITY.

Nature has placed mankind under the governance of two sovereign masters, *pain* and *pleasure*. It is for them alone to point out what we ought to do, as well as to determine what we shall do. On the one hand the standard of right and wrong, on the other the chain of causes and effects, are fastened to their throne. They govern us in all we do, in all we say, in all we think: every effort we can make to throw off our subjection, will serve but to demonstrate and confirm it. In words a man may pretend to abjure their empire: but in reality he will remain subject to it all the while. The *principle of utility* recognises this subjection, and assumes it for the foundation of that system, the object of which is to rear the fabric of felicity by the hands of reason and of law. Systems which attempt to question it, deal in sounds instead of sense, in caprice instead of reason, in darkness instead of light.

But enough of metaphor and declamation: it is not by such means that moral science is to be improved.

II. The principle of utility is the foundation of the present work: it will be proper therefore at the outset to give an explicit and determinate account of what is meant by it. By the principle*

[*Principle. The word principle is derived from the Latin *principium:* which seems to be compounded of the two words *primus,* first, or chief, and *cipium,* a termination which seems to be derived from *capio,* to take, as in *mancipium, municipium;* to which are analogous *auceps, forceps,* and others. It is a term of very vague and very extensive signification: it is applied to any thing which is conceived to serve as a foundation or beginning to any series of operations: in some cases, of physical operations: but of mental operations in the present case. The principle here in question may be taken for an act of the mind; a sentiment; a sentiment of approbation; a sentiment which, when applied to an action, approves of its utility, as that quality of it by which the measure of approbation or disapprobation bestowed upon it ought to be governed.]

of utility is meant that principle which approves or disapproves of every action whatsoever, according to the tendency which it appears to have to augment or diminish the happiness of the party whose interest is in question: or, what is the same thing in other words, to promote or to oppose that happiness. I say of every action whatsoever; and therefore not only of every action of a private individual, but of every measure of government.

III. By utility is meant that property in any object, whereby it tends to produce benefit, advantage, pleasure, good, or happiness (all this in the present case comes to the same thing), or (what comes again to the same thing) to prevent the happening of mischief, pain, evil, or unhappiness to the party whose interest is considered: if that party be the community in general, then the happiness of the community: if a particular individual, then the happiness of that individual.

IV. The interest of the community is one of the most general expressions that can occur in the phraseology of morals: no wonder that the meaning of it is often lost. When it has a meaning, it is this. The community is a fictitious *body,* composed of the individual persons who are considered as constituting as it were its *members.* The interest of the community then is, what?—the sum of the interests of the several members who compose it.

V. It is in vain to talk of the interest of the community without understanding what is the interest of the individual.*

[*Interest. Interest is one of those words, which not having any superior *genus,* cannot in the ordinary way be defined.]

A thing is said to promote the interest, or to be *for* the interest, of an individual, when it tends to add to the sum total of his pleasures: or, what comes to the same thing, to diminish the sum total of his pains.

VI. An action then may be said to be conformable to the principle of utility, or, for shortness sake, to utility (meaning with respect to the community at large), when the tendency it has to augment the happiness of the community is greater than any it has to diminish it.

VII. A measure of government (which is but a particular kind of action, performed by a particular person or persons) may be said to be conformable to or dictated by the principle of utility, when in like manner the tendency which it has to augment the happiness of the community is greater than any which it has to diminish it.

VIII. When an action, or in particular a measure of government, is supposed by a man to be conformable to the principle of utility, it may be convenient, for the purposes of discourse, to imagine a kind of law or dictate, called a law or dictate of utility: and to speak of the action in question, as being conformable to such law or dictate.

IX. A man may be said to be a partizan of the principle of utility, when the approbation or disapprobation he annexes to any action, or to any measure, is determined, by and proportioned to the tendency which he conceives it to have to augment or to diminish the happiness of the community: or in other words, to its conformity or unconformity to the laws or dictates of utility.

X. Of an action that is conformable to the principle of utility, one may always say either that it is one that ought to be done, or at least that it is not one that ought not to be done. One may say also, that it is right it should be done: that it is a right action: at least that it is not a wrong action. When thus interpreted, the words *ought,* and *right* and *wrong,* and others of that stamp, have a meaning: when otherwise, they have none.

XI. Has the rectitude of this principle been ever formally contested? It should seem that it had, by those who have not known what they have been meaning. Is it susceptible of any direct proof? It should seem not: for that which is used to prove every thing else, cannot itself be proved: a chain of proofs must have their commencement somewhere. To give such proof is as impossible as it is needless.

XII. Not that there is or ever has been that human creature breathing, however stupid or perverse, who has not on many, perhaps on most occasions of his life, deferred to it. By the natural constitution of the human frame, on most occasions of their lives men in general embrace this principle, without thinking of it: if not for the ordering of their own actions, yet for the trying of their own actions, as well as of those of other men. There have been, at the same time, not many, perhaps, even of the most intelligent, who have been disposed to embrace it purely and without reserve. There are even few who have not taken some occasion or other to quarrel with it, either on account of their not understanding always how to apply it, or on account of some prejudice or other which they were afraid to examine into, or could not bear to part with. For such is the stuff that man is made of: in principle and in practice, in a right track and in a wrong one, the rarest of all human qualities is consistency.

XIII. When a man attempts to combat the principle of utility, it is with reasons drawn, without his being aware of it, from that very principle itself.*

> [*"The principle of utility (I have heard it said) is a dangerous principle: it is dangerous on certain occasions to consult it." This is as much as to say, what? that it is not consonant to utility, to consult utility; in short, that it is *not* consulting, to consult it. . . .]

His arguments, if they prove any thing, prove not that the principle is *wrong,* but that, according to the applications he supposed to be made of it, it is *misapplied.* Is it possible for a man to move the earth? Yes; but he must first find out another earth to stand upon.

XIV. To disprove the propriety of it by arguments is impossible; but, from the causes that have been mentioned, or from some confused or partial view of it, a man may happen to be disposed not to relish it. Where this is the case, if he thinks the settling of his opinions on such a subject worth the trouble, let him take the following steps, and at length, perhaps, he may come to reconcile himself to it.

1. Let him settle with himself, whether he would wish to discard this principle altogether; if so, let him consider what it is that all his reasonings (in matters of politics especially) can amount to?

2. If he would, let him settle with himself, whether he would judge and act without any principle, or whether there is any other he would judge and act by?

3. If there be, let him examine and satisfy himself whether the principle he thinks he has found is really any separate intelligible principle: or whether it be not a mere principle in words, a kind of phrase, which at bottom expresses neither more nor less than the mere averment of his own unfounded sentiments: that is, what in another person he might be apt to call caprice?

4. If he is inclined to think that his own approbation or disapprobation, annexed to the idea of an act, without any regard to its consequences, is a sufficient foundation for him to judge and act upon, let him ask himself whether his sentiment is to be a standard of right and wrong, with respect to every other man, or whether every man's sentiment has the same privilege of being a standard in itself?

5. In the first case, let him ask himself whether his principle is not despotical, and hostile to all the rest of [the] human race?

6. In the second case, whether it is not anarchical, and whether at this rate there are not as many different standards of right and wrong as there are men? and whether even in the same man, the same thing, which is right to-day, may not (without the least change in its nature) be wrong to-morrow? and whether the same thing is not right and wrong in the same place at the same time? and in either case, whether all argument is not at an end? and whether, when two men have said, "I like this," and "I don't like it," they can (upon such a principle) have any thing more to say?

7. If he should have said to himself, No: for that the sentiment which he proposes as a standard must be grounded on reflection, let him say on what particulars the reflection is to turn? If on particulars having relation to the utility of the act, then let him say whether this is not deserting his own principle, and borrowing assistance from that very one in opposition to which he sets it up: or if not on those particulars, on what other particulars?

8. If he should be for compounding the matter, and adopting his own principle in part, and the principle of utility in part, let him say how far he will adopt it?

9. When he has settled with himself where he will stop, then let him ask himself how he justifies to himself the adopting it so far? and why he will not adopt it any farther?

10. Admitting any other principle than the principle of utility to be a right principle, a principle that it is right for a man to pursue: admitting (what is not true) that the word *right* can have a meaning without reference to utility, let him say whether there is any such thing as a *motive* that a man can have to pursue the dictates of it: if there is, let him say what that motive is, and how it is to be distinguished from those which enforce the dictates of utility: if not, then lastly let him say what it is this other principle can be good for?

Chapter II.

OF PRINCIPLES ADVERSE TO THAT OF UTILITY.

I. If the principle of utility be a right principle to be governed by, and that in all cases, it follows from what has been just observed, that whatever principle differs from it in any case must necessarily be a wrong one. To prove any other principle, therefore, to be a wrong one, there needs no more than just to show it to be what it is, a principle of which the dictates are in some point or other different from those of the principle of utility: to state it is to confute it.

II. A principle may be different from that of utility in two ways: 1. By being constantly opposed to it: this is the case with a principle which may be termed the principle of *asceticism.* 2. By being sometimes opposed to it, and sometimes not, as it may happen: this is the case with another, which may be termed the principle of *sympathy* and *antipathy.*

III. By the principle of asceticism I mean that principle, which, like the principle of utility, approves or disapproves of any action, according to the tendency which it appears to have to augment or diminish the happiness of the party whose interest is in question; but in an inversive manner: approving of actions in as far as they tend to diminish his happiness: disapproving of them in as far as they tend to augment it. . . .

IX. The principle of asceticism seems originally to have been the reverie of certain hasty speculators, who having perceived, or fancied, that certain pleasures, when reaped in certain circumstances, have, at the long run, been attended with pains more than equivalent to them, took occasion to quarrel with every thing that offered itself under the name of pleasure. Having then got thus far, and having forgot the point which they set out from, they pushed on, and went so much further as to think it meritorious to fall in love with pain. Even this, we see, is at bottom but the principle of utility misapplied. . . .

XI. Among principles adverse to that of utility, that which at this day seems to have most influence in matters of government, is what may be called the principle of sympathy and antipathy.*

[*(Note added 1789) It ought rather to have been styled, more extensively, the principle of *caprice.* Where it applies to the choice of actions to be marked out for injunction or prohibition, for reward or punishment, (to stand, in a word, as subjects for *obligations* to be imposed), it may indeed with propriety be termed, as in the text, the principle of *sympathy* and *antipathy.* But this appellative does not so well apply to it, when occupied in the choice of the *events* which are to serve as sources of *title* with respect to *rights:* where the actions prohibited and allowed, the obligations and rights being already fixed, the only question is, under what circumstances a man is to be invested with the one or subjected to the other? from what incidents occasion is to be taken to invest a man, or to refuse to invest him, with the one, or to subject him to the other? In this latter case it may more appositely be characterized by the name of the *phantastic principle*. Sympathy and antipathy are affections of the *sensible* faculty. But the choice of *titles* with respect to *rights,* especially with respect to proprietary rights, upon grounds unconnected with utility, has been in many instances the work, not of the affections but of the imagination.]

By the principle of sympathy and antipathy, I mean that principle which approves or disapproves of certain actions, not on account of their tending to augment the happiness, nor yet on account of their tending to diminish the happiness of the party whose interest is in question, but merely because a man finds himself disposed to approve or disapprove of them: holding up that approbation or disapprobation as a sufficient reason for itself, and disclaiming the necessity of looking out for any extrinsic ground. Thus far in the general department of morals: and in the particular department of politics, measuring out the quantum (as well as determining the ground) of punishment, by the degree of the disapprobation. . . .

XIV. The various systems that have been formed concerning the standard of right and wrong, may all be reduced to the principle of sympathy and antipathy. One account may serve for all of them. They consist all of them in so many contrivances for avoiding the obligation of appealing to any external standard, and for prevailing upon the reader to accept of the author's sentiment or opinion as a reason, and that a sufficient one, for itself. The phrases different, but the principle the same.*

[*It is curious enough to observe the variety of inventions men have hit upon, and the variety of phrases they have brought forward, in order to conceal from the world, and, if possible, from themselves, this very general and therefore very pardonable self-sufficiency.

1. One man (Lord Shaftesbury, Hutchinson, Hume, etc.) says, he has a thing made on purpose to tell him what is right and what is wrong: and that is called a *moral sense:* and then he goes to work at his case, and says, such a thing is right, and such a thing is wrong—why? "because my moral sense tells me it is."

2. Another man (Dr. Beattie) comes and alters the phrase: leaving out *moral,* and putting in *common,* in the room of it. He then tells you, that his common sense teaches him what is right and wrong, as surely as the other's moral sense did: meaning by common sense, a sense of some kind or other, which, he says, is possessed by all mankind: the sense of those, whose sense is not the same as the author's, being struck out of the account as not worth taking. This contrivance does better than the other; for a moral sense, being a new thing, a man may feel about him a good while without being

able to find it out: but common sense is as old as the creation; and there is no man but would be ashamed to be thought not to have as much of it as his neighbours. It has another great advantage: by appearing to share power, it lessens envy: for when a man gets up upon this ground, in order to anathematize those who differ from him, it is not by a *sic volo sic jubeo,* but by a *velitis jubeatis.*

3. Another man (Dr. Price) comes, and says, that as to a moral sense indeed, he cannot find that he has any such thing: that however he has an *understanding,* which will do quite as well. This understanding, he says, is the standard of right and wrong: it tells him so and so. All good and wise men understand as he does: if other men's understandings differ in any point from his, so much the worse for them: it is a sure sign they are either defective or corrupt.

4. Another man says, that here is an eternal and immutable Rule of Right: that that rule of right dictates so and so: and then he begins giving you his sentiments upon any thing that comes uppermost: and these sentiments (you are to take for granted) are so many branches of the eternal rule of right. . . .

6. A great multitude of people are continually talking of the Law of Nature; and then they go on giving you their sentiments about what is right and what is wrong: and these sentiments, you are to understand, are so many chapters, and sections of the Law of Nature.

7. Instead of the phrase, Law of Nature, you have sometimes Law Of Reason, Right Reason, Natural Justice, Natural Equity, Good Order. Any one of them will do equally well. This latter is most used in politics. The three last are much more tolerable than the others, because they do not very explicitly claim to be any thing more than phrases: they insist but feebly upon the being looked upon as so many positive standards of themselves, and seem content to be taken, upon occasion, for phrases expressive of the conformity of the thing in question to the proper standard, whatever that may be. On most occasions, however, it will be better to say *utility: utility* is clearer, as referring more explicitly to pain and pleasure. . . .

The mischief common to all these ways of thinking and arguing (which, in truth, as we have seen, are but one and the same method, couched in different forms of words) is their serving as a cloke, and pretence, and aliment, to despotism: if not a despotism in practice, a despotism however in disposition: which is but too apt, when pretence and power offer, to show itself in practice. The consequence is, that with intentions very commonly of the purest kind, a man becomes a torment either to himself or his fellow-creatures. If he be of the melancholy cast (Dr. Price), he sits in silent grief, bewailing their blindness and depravity: if of the irascible (Dr. Beattie), he declaims with fury and virulence against all who differ from him; blowing up the coals of fanaticism, and branding with the charge of corruption and insincerity, every man who does not think, or profess to think as he does.

If such a man happens to possess the advantages of style, his book may do a considerable deal of mischief before the nothingness of it is understood. . . .]

Chapter III.

OF THE FOUR* SANCTIONS OR SOURCES OF PAIN AND PLEASURE.

[*The following is an extract from a letter of Bentham's to Dumont, dated Oct. 28, 1821:—

"*Sanctions.* Since the Traites, others have been discovered. There are now,
I. Human: six, viz. 1. Physical; 2. Retributive; 3. Sympathetic; 4. Antipathetic; 5. Popular, or moral; 6. Political, including Legal and Administrative.

II. Superhuman, *vice* Religious: all exemplifiable in the case of drunkenness; viz. the punitory class.

Note—Sanctions *in genere* duae, punitoriae et remuneratoriae; *in serie,* septem ut super; seven multiplied by two, equal fourteen.

The Judicatory of the popular or moral sanction has two Sections: that of the few, and that of the many: Aristocratical and Democratical: their laws, their decisions, are to a vast extent opposite."]

I. It has been shown that the happiness of the individuals, of whom a community is composed, that is, their pleasures and their security, is the end and the sole end which the legislator ought to have in view: the sole standard, in conformity to which each individual ought, as far as depends upon the legislator, to be *made* to fashion his behaviour. But whether it be this or any thing else that is to be *done,* there is nothing by which a man can ultimately be *made* to do it, but either pain or pleasure. Having taken a general view of these two grand objects (viz. pleasure, and what comes to the same thing, immunity from pain) in the character of *final* causes; it will be necessary to take a view of pleasure and pain itself, in the character of *efficient* causes or means.

II. There are four distinguishable sources from which pleasure and pain are in use to flow: considered separately, they may be termed the *physical,* the *political,* the *moral,* and the *religious:* and inasmuch as the pleasures and pains belonging to each of them are capable of giving a binding force to any law or rule of conduct, they may all of them be termed *sanctions.**

[*Sanctio, in Latin, was used to signify the *act of binding,* and, by a common grammatical transition, *any thing which serves to bind a man:* to wit, to the observance of such or such a mode of conduct. According to a Latin grammarian, the import of the word is derived by rather a far-fetched process . . . from the word *sanguis,* blood: . . .

A Sanction then is a source of obligatory powers or *motives:* that is, of *pains* and *pleasures;* which, according as they are connected with such or such modes of conduct, operate, and are indeed the only things which can operate, as *motives.*]

III. If it be in the present life, and from the ordinary course of nature, not purposely modified by the interposition of the will of any human being, nor by any extraordinary interposition of any superior invisible being, that the pleasure or pain takes place or is expected, it may be said to issue from, or to belong to, the *physical sanction.*

IV. If at the hands of a *particular* person or set of persons in the community, who under names correspondent to that of *judge,* are chosen for the particular purpose of dispensing it, according to the will of the sovereign or supreme ruling power in the state, it may be said to issue from the *political sanction.*

V. If at the hands of such *chance* persons in the community, as the party in question may happen in the course of his life to have concerns with, according to each man's spontaneous disposition, and not according to any settled or concerted rule, it may be said to issue from the *moral* or *popular sanction.*

VI. If from the immediate hand of a superior invisible being, either in the present life, or in a future, it may be said to issue from the *religious sanction.*

VII. Pleasures or pains which may be expected to issue from the *physical, political,* or *moral* sanctions, must all of them be expected to be experienced, if ever, in the *present* life: those which may be expected to issue from the religious sanction, may be expected to be experienced either in the *present* life or in a *future.*

VIII. Those which can be experienced in the present life, can of course be no others than such as human nature in the course of the present life is susceptible of: and from each of these sources may flow all the pleasures or pains of which, in the course of the present life, human nature is susceptible. With regard to these, then (with which alone we have in this place any concern), those of them which belong to any one of those sanctions differ not ultimately in mind from those which belong to any one of the other three: the only difference there is among them lies in the circumstances that accompany their production. A suffering which befals a man in the natural and spontaneous course of things, shall be styled, for instance, a *calamity:* in which case, if it be supposed to befal him through any imprudence of his, it may be styled a punishment issuing from the physical sanction. Now this same suffering, if inflicted by the law, will be what is commonly called a *punishment;* if incurred for want of any friendly assistance, which the misconduct, or supposed misconduct, of the sufferer has occasioned to be withholden, a punishment issuing from the *moral* sanction; if through the immediate interposition of a particular providence, a punishment issuing from the religious sanction.

IX. A man's goods, or his person, are consumed by fire. If this happened to him by what is called an accident, it was a calamity: if by reason of his own imprudence (for instance, from his neglecting to put his candle out), it may be styled a punishment of the physical sanction: if it happened to him by the sentence of the political magistrate, a punishment belonging to the political sanction—that is, what is commonly called a punishment: if for want of any assistance which his *neighbour* withheld from him out of some dislike to his *moral* character, a punishment of the *moral* sanction: if by an immediate act of *God's* displeasure, manifested on account of some *sin* committed by him, or through any distraction of mind, occasioned by the dread of such displeasure, a punishment of the *religious sanction.*

X. As to such of the pleasures and pains belonging to the religious sanction, as regard a future life, of what kind these may be, we cannot know. These lie not open to our observation. During the present life they are matter only of expectation: and, whether that expectation be derived from natural or revealed religion, the particular kind of pleasure or pain, if it be different from all those which lie open to our observation, is what we can have no idea of. The best ideas we can obtain of such pains and pleasures are altogether unliquidated in point of reality. In what other respects our ideas of them *may be* liquidated, will be considered in another place.

XI. Of these four sanctions, the physical is altogether, we may observe, the ground-work of the political and the moral: so is it also of the religious, in as far as the latter bears relation to the present life. It is included in each of these other three. This may operate in any case (that is, any of the pains or pleasures belonging to it may operate) independently of *them:* none of *them* can operate but by means of this. In a word, the powers of nature may operate of themselves; but neither the magistrate, nor men at large, *can* operate, nor is God in the case in question *supposed* to operate, but through the powers of nature.

XII. For these four objects, which in their nature have so much in common, it seemed of use to find a common name. It seemed of use, in the first place, for the convenience of giving a name to certain pleasures and pains, for which a name equally characteristic could hardly otherwise have been found: in the second place, for the sake of holding up the efficacy of certain moral forces, the influence of which is apt not to be sufficiently attended to. Does the political sanction exert an influence over the conduct of mankind? The moral, the religious sanctions, do so too. In every inch of his career are the operations of the political magistrate liable to be aided or impeded by these two foreign powers: who, one or other of them, or both, are sure to be either his rivals or his allies. Does it happen to him to leave them out in his calculations? he will be sure almost to find himself mistaken in the result. Of all this we shall find abundant proofs in the sequel of this work. It behoves him, therefore, to have them continually before his eyes; and that under such a name as exhibits the relation they bear to his own purposes and designs.

Chapter IV.

VALUE OF A LOT OF PLEASURE OR PAIN, HOW TO BE MEASURED.

I. Pleasures then, and the avoidance of pains are the *ends* which the legislator has in view: it behoves him therefore to understand their *value*. Pleasures and pains are the *instruments* he has to work with: it behoves him therefore to understand their force, which is again, in another point of view, their value.

II. To a person considered *by himself,* the value of a pleasure or pain considered *by itself,* will be greater or less, according to the four following circumstances:*

[*These circumstances have since been denominated *elements* or *dimensions* of *value* in a pleasure or a pain.

Not long after the publication of the first edition, the following memoriter verses were framed, in the view of lodging more effectually, in the memory, these points, on which the whole fabric of morals and legislation may be seen to rest.

> *Intense, long, certain, speedy, fruitful, pure—*
> Such marks in *pleasures* and in *pains* endure.
> Such pleasures seek, if *private* be thy end:
> If it be *public,* wide let them *extend.*
> Such *pains* avoid, whichever be thy view:
> If pains *must* come, let them *extend* to few.]

1. Its *intensity.*
2. Its *duration.*
3. Its *certainty* or *uncertainty.*
4. Its *propinquity* or *remoteness.*

III. These are the circumstances which are to be considered in estimating a pleasure or a pain considered each of them by itself. But when the value of any pleasure or pain is considered for the purpose of estimating the tendency of any *act* by which it is produced, there are two other circumstances to be taken into the account; these are,

5. Its *fecundity,* or the chance it has of being followed by sensations of the *same* kind: that is, pleasures, if it be a pleasure: pains, if it be a pain.

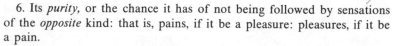

6. Its *purity,* or the chance it has of not being followed by sensations of the *opposite* kind: that is, pains, if it be a pleasure: pleasures, if it be a pain.

These two last, however, are in strictness scarcely to be deemed properties of the pleasure or the pain itself; they are not, therefore, in strictness to be taken into the account of the value of that pleasure or that pain. They are in strictness to be deemed properties only of the act, or other event, by which such pleasure or pain has been produced; and accordingly are only to be taken into the account of the tendency of such act or such event.

IV. To a *number* of persons, with reference to each of whom the value of a pleasure or a pain is considered, it will be greater or less, according to seven circumstances: to wit, the six preceding ones; *viz.*

1. Its *intensity.*

2. Its *duration.*

3. Its *certainty* or *uncertainty.*

4. Its *propinquity* or *remoteness.*

5. Its *fecundity.*

6. Its *purity.*

And one other, to wit:

7. Its *extent;* that is, the number of persons to whom it *extends;* or (in other words) who are affected by it.

V. To take an exact account, then, of the general tendency of any act, by which the interests of a community are affected, proceed as follows. Begin with any one person of those whose interests seem most immediately to be affected by it: and take an account,

1. Of the value of each distinguishable *pleasure* which appears to be produced by it in the *first* instance.

2. Of the value of each *pain* which appears to be produced by it in the *first* instance.

3. Of the value of each pleasure which appears to be produced by it *after* the first. This constitutes the *fecundity* of the first *pleasure* and the *impurity* of the first *pain.*

4. Of the value of each *pain* which appears to be produced by it after the first. This constitutes the *fecundity* of the first *pain,* and *impurity* of the first pleasure.

5. Sum up all the values of all the *pleasures* on the one side, and those of all the pains on the other. The balance, if it be on the side of pleasure, will give the *good* tendency of the act upon the whole, with respect to the interests of that *individual* person; if on the side of pain, the *bad* tendency of it upon the whole.

6. Take an account of the *number* of persons whose interests appear to

be concerned; and repeat the above process with respect to each. *Sum up* the numbers expressive of the degrees of *good* tendency, which the act has, with respect to each individual, in regard to whom the tendency of it is *good* upon the whole: do this again with respect to each individual, in regard to whom the tendency of it is *bad* upon the whole. Take the *balance;* which, if on the side of *pleasure,* will give the general *good tendency* of the act, with respect to the total number or community of individuals concerned; if on the side of pain, the general *evil tendency,* with respect to the same community.

VI. It is not to be expected that this process should be strictly pursued previously to every moral judgment, or to every legislative or judicial operation. It may, however, be always kept in view: and as near as the process actually pursued on these occasions approaches to it, so near will such process approach to the character of an exact one.

VII. The same process is alike applicable to pleasure and pain, in whatever shape they appear; and by whatever denomination they are distinguished: to pleasure, whether it be called *good* (which is properly the cause or instrument of pleasure), or *profit* (which is distant pleasure, or the cause or instrument of distant pleasure), or *convenience,* or *advantage, benefit, emolument, happiness,* and so forth: to pain, whether it be called *evil* (which corresponds to *good*), or *mischief,* or *inconvenience,* or *disadvantage,* or *loss,* or *unhappiness,* and so forth.

VIII. Nor is this a novel and unwarranted, any more than it is a useless theory. In all this there is nothing but what the practice of mankind, wheresoever they have a clear view of their own interest, is perfectly conformable to. An article of property, an estate in land, for instance, is valuable: on what account? On account of the pleasures of all kinds which it enables a man to produce, and, what comes to the same thing, the pains of all kinds which it enables him to avert. But the value of such an article of property is universally understood to rise or fall according to the length or shortness of the time which a man has in it: the certainty or uncertainty of its coming into possession: and the nearness or remoteness of the time at which, if at all, it is to come into possession. As to the *intensity* of the pleasures which a man may derive from it, this is never thought of, because it depends upon the use which each particular person may come to make of it; which cannot be estimated till the particular pleasures he may come to derive from it, or the particular pains he may come to exclude by means of it, are brought to view. For the same reason, neither does he think of the *fecundity* or *purity* of those pleasures.

Thus much for pleasure and pain, happiness and unhappiness, in *gen-*

eral. We come now to consider the several particular kinds of pain and pleasure.

Chapter V.
PLEASURES AND PAINS, THEIR KINDS.

I. Having represented what belongs to all sorts of pleasures and pains alike, we come now to exhibit, each by itself, the several sorts of pains and pleasures. Pains and pleasures may be called by one general word, *interesting perceptions.* [My italics. M.P.M.] Interesting perceptions are either simple or complex. The simple ones are those which cannot any one of them be resolved into more: complex are those which are resolvable into divers simple ones. A complex interesting perception may accordingly be composed either, 1. Of pleasures alone: 2. Of pains alone: or, 3. Of a pleasure or pleasures, and a pain or pains together. What determines a lot of pleasures, for example, to be regarded as one complex pleasure, rather than as divers simple ones, is the nature of the exciting cause. Whatever pleasures are excited all at once by the action of the same cause, are apt to be looked upon as constituting all together but one pleasure.

II. The several simple pleasures of which human nature is susceptible, seem to be as follows: 1. The pleasures of sense. 2. The pleasures of wealth. 3. The pleasures of skill. 4. The pleasures of amity. 5. The pleasures of a good name. 6. The pleasures of power. 7. The pleasures of piety. 8. The pleasures of benevolence. 9. The pleasures of malevolence. 10. The pleasures of imagination. 11. The pleasures of memory. 12. The pleasures of expectation. 13. The pleasures dependent on association. 14. The pleasures of relief.

III. The several simple pains seem to be as follows: 1. The pains of privation. 2. The pains of the senses. 3. The pains of awkwardness. 4. The pains of enmity. 5. The pains of an ill name. 6. The pains of piety. 7. The pains of benevolence. 8. The pains of malevolence. 9. The pains of the memory. 10. The pains of the imagination. 11. The pains of expectation. 12. The pains dependent on association. . . .

[M.P.M.—Bentham then describes each one of these pleasures and pains, and concludes:]

XXXIII. Of all these several sorts of pleasures and pains, there is scarce any one which is not liable, on more accounts than one, to come under the consideration of the law. Is an offence committed? It is the tendency which it has to destroy, in such or such persons, some of these pleasures, or to produce some of these pains, that constitutes the mischief of it, and the ground for punishing it. It is the prospect of some of these pleasures, or of security from some of these pains, that constitutes the motive or temptation: it is the attainment of them that constitutes the profit of the offence. Is the offender to be punished? It can be only by the production of one or more of these pains, that the punishment can be inflicted.*

[*It would be a matter not only of curiosity, but of some use, to exhibit a catalogue of the several complex pleasures and pains, analyzing them at the same time into the several simple ones, of which they are respectively composed. But such a disquisition would take up too much room to be admitted here. A short specimen, however, for the purpose of illustration, can hardly be dispensed with.

The pleasures taken in at the eye and ear are generally very complex. The pleasures of a country scene, for instance, consist commonly, amongst other, of the following pleasures;

I. Pleasures of the senses.

1. The simple pleasure of sight, excited by the perception of agreeable colours and figures, green fields, waving foliage, glistening water, and the like.

2. The simple pleasures of the ear, excited by the perceptions of the chirping of birds, the murmuring of waters, the rustling of the wind among the trees.

3. The pleasures of the smell, excited by the perceptions of the fragrance of flowers, of new-mown hay, or other vegetable substances, in the first stages of fermentation.

4. The agreeable inward sensation, produced by a brisk circulation of the blood, and the ventilation of it in the lungs by a pure air, such as that in the country frequently is in comparison of that which is breathed in towns.

II. Pleasures of the imagination produced by association.

1. The idea of the plenty, resulting from the possession of the objects that are in view, and of the happiness arising from it.

2. The idea of the innocence and happiness of the birds, sheep, cattle, pigs, and other gentle or domestic animals.

3. The idea of the constant flow of health, supposed to be enjoyed by all these creatures: a notion which is apt to result from the occasional flow of health enjoyed by the supposed spectator.

4. The idea of gratitude, excited by the contemplation of the all-powerful and beneficent Being, who is looked up to as the author of these blessings.

These four last are all of them, in some measure at least, pleasures of sympathy.

The depriving a man of this group of pleasures is one of the evils apt to result from imprisonment; whether produced by illegal violence, or in the way of punishment, by appointment of the laws.]

Chapter VI.

OF CIRCUMSTANCES INFLUENCING SENSIBILITY.

I. Pain and pleasure are produced in men's minds by the action of certain causes. But the quantity of pleasure and pain runs not uniformly in proportion to the cause; in other words, to the quantity of force exerted by such cause. The truth of this observation rests not upon any metaphysical nicety in the import given to the terms *cause, quantity,* and *force:* it will be equally true in whatsoever manner such force be measured.

II. The disposition which any one has to feel such or such a quantity of pleasure or pain, upon the application of a cause of given force, is what we term the degree or *quantum* of his sensibility. This may be either *general,* referring to the sum of the causes that act upon him during a given period: or *particular,* referring to the action of any one particular cause, or set of causes.

III. But in the same mind such and such causes of pain or pleasure will produce more pain or pleasure than such or such other causes of pain or pleasure: and this proportion will in different minds be different. The disposition which any one has to have the proportion in which he is affected by two such causes, different from that in which another man is affected by the same two causes, may be termed the quality or *bias* of his sensibility. One man, for instance, may be most affected by the pleasures of the taste; another by those of the ear. So also, if there be a difference in the nature or proportion of two pains or pleasures which they respectively experience from the same cause; a case not so frequent as the former. From the same injury, for instance, one man may feel the same quantity of grief and resentment together as another man: but one of them shall feel a greater share of grief than of resentment: the other, a greater share of resentment than of grief.

IV. Any incident which serves as a cause, either of pleasure or of pain, may be termed an *exciting* cause: if of pleasure, a pleasurable cause: if of pain, a painful, afflictive, or dolorific cause.*

[*The exciting cause, the pleasure or pain produced by it, and the intention produced by such pleasure or pain in the character of a motive, are objects so intimately connected, that, in what follows, I fear I have not, on every occasion, been able to keep them sufficiently distinct. I thought it necessary to give the reader this warning: after which, should there be found any such mistakes, it is to be hoped they will not be productive of much confusion.]

V. Now the quantity of pleasure, or of pain, which a man is liable to experience upon the application of an exciting cause, since they will not depend altogether upon that cause, will depend in some measure upon some other circumstance or circumstances: these circumstances, whatsoever they be, may be termed *circumstances influencing sensibility.**

[*Thus, in physical bodies, the momentum of a ball put in motion by impulse, will be influenced by the circumstance of gravity: being in some direction increased, in others diminished by it. So in a ship, put in motion by the wind, the momentum and direction will be influenced not only by the attraction of gravity, but by the motion and resistance of the water, and several other circumstances.]

VI. These circumstances will apply differently to different exciting causes; insomuch that to a certain exciting cause, a certain circumstance shall not apply at all, which shall apply with great force to another exciting cause. But without entering for the present into these distinctions, it may be of use to sum up all the circumstances which can be found to influence the effect of *any* exciting cause. These, as on a former occasion, it may be as well first to sum up together in the concisest manner possible, and afterwards to allot a few words to the separate explanation of each article. They seem to be as follows: 1. Health. 2. Strength. 3. Hardiness. 4. Bodily imperfection. 5. Quantity and quality of knowledge. 6. Strength of intellectual powers. 7. Firmness of mind. 8. Steadiness of mind. 9. Bent of inclination. 10. Moral sensibility. 11. Moral biases. 12. Religious sensibility. 13. Religious biases. 14. Sympathetic sensibility. 15. Sympathetic biases. 16. Antipathetic sensibility. 17. Antipathetic biases. 18. Insanity. 19. Habitual occupations. 20. Pecuniary circumstances. 21. Connexions in the way of sympathy. 22. Connexions in the way of antipathy. 23. Radical frame of body. 24. Radical frame of mind. 25. Sex. 26. Age. 27. Rank. 28. Education. 29. Climate. 30. Lineage. 31. Government. 32. Religious profession.* . . .

[*. . . To search out the vast variety of exciting or moderating causes, by which the degree or bias of a man's sensibility may be influenced, to define the boundaries of each, to extricate them from the entanglements in which they are involved, to lay the effect of each article distinctly before the reader's eye, is, perhaps, if not absolutely the most difficult task, at least one of the most difficult tasks, within the compass of moral physiology. Disquisitions on this head can never be completely satisfactory without examples. To provide a sufficient collection of such examples, would be a work of great labour as well as nicety: history and biography would need to be ransacked: a vast course of reading would need to be travelled through on purpose. By such a process the present work would doubtless have been rendered more amusing; but in point of bulk so enormous, that this single chapter would have been swelled into a considerable volume. . . . On this therefore, as on so many other occasions, I must confine myself to dry and general instruction: discarding illustration, although sensible that without it instruction cannot manifest half its efficacy. The subject, however, is so difficult, and so new, that I shall think I have not ill succeeded, if, without pretending to exhaust it, I shall have been able to mark out the principal points of view, and to put the matter in such a method as may facilitate the researches of happier inquirers.

The great difficulty lies in the nature of the words; which are not, like pain and pleasures, names of homogeneous real entities, but names of various fictitious entities, for which no common genus is to be found: and which therefore, without a vast and roundabout chain of investigation, can never be brought under any exhaustive plan of arrangement, but must be picked up here and there as they happen to occur.]

[As above, Bentham then describes in detail the complete list of circumstances.—M.P.M.]

XLI. 31. The last circumstance but one, is that of government: the government a man lives under at the time in question: or rather that under which he has been accustomed most to live. This circumstance operates principally through the medium of education: the magistrate operating in the character of a tutor upon all the members of the state, by the direction he gives to their hopes and to their fears. Indeed, under a solicitous and attentive government, the ordinary preceptor, nay even the parent himself, is but a deputy, as it were, to the magistrate: whose controlling influence, different in this respect from that of the ordinary preceptor, dwells with a man to his life's end. The effects of the peculiar power of the magistrate are seen more particularly in the influence it exerts over the quantum and bias of men's moral, religious, sympathetic, and antipathetic sensibilities. Under a well-constituted, or even under a well-administered though ill-constituted government, men's moral sensibility is commonly stronger, and their moral biases more conformable to the dictates of utility: their religious sensibility frequently weaker, but their religious biases less unconformable to the dictates of utility: their sympathetic affections more enlarged, directed to the magistrate more than to small parties or to individuals, and more to the whole community than to either: their antipathetic sensibilities less violent, as being more obsequious to the influence of well-directed moral biases, and less apt to be excited by that of ill-directed religious ones: their antipathetic biases more conformable to well-directed moral ones, more apt (in proportion) to be grounded on enlarged and sympathetic than on narrow and self-regarding affections, and accordingly, upon the whole, more conformable to the dictates of utility. . . .

XLIII. These circumstances, all or many of them, will need to be attended to as often as upon any occasion any account is taken of any quantity of pain or pleasure, as resulting from any cause. Has any person sustained an injury? they will need to be considered in estimating the mischief of the offence. Is satisfaction to be made to him? they will need to be attended to in adjusting the *quantum* of that satisfaction. Is the injurer to be punished? they will need to be attended to in estimating the force of the impression that will be made on him by any given punishment.

XLIV. It is to be observed, that though they seem all of them, on some account or other, to merit a place in the catalogue, they are not all of equal use in practice. Different articles among them are applicable to different exciting causes. Of those that may influence the effect of the same exciting cause, some apply indiscriminately to whole classes of persons together; being applicable to all, without any remarkable difference in degree: these may be directly and pretty fully provided for by the legislator. This is the case, for instance, with the primary circumstances of bodily imperfection, and insanity: with the secondary circumstance of sex: perhaps with that of age: at any rate, with those of rank, of climate, of lineage, and of religious profession. Others, however they may apply to whole classes of persons, yet in their application to different individuals are susceptible of perhaps an indefinite variety of degrees. These cannot be fully provided for by the legislator; but, as the existence of them, in every sort of case, is capable of being ascertained, and the degree in which they take place is capable of being measured, provision may be made for them by the judge, or other executive magistrate, to whom the several individuals that happen to be concerned may be made known. This is the case, 1. With the circumstance of health. 2. In some sort with that of strength. 3. Scarcely with that of hardiness: still less with those of quantity and quality of knowledge, strength of intellectual powers, firmness or steadiness of mind; except in as far as a man's condition, in respect of those circumstances, may be indicated by the secondary circumstances of sex, age, or rank: hardly with that of bent of inclination, except in as far as that latent circumstance is indicated by the more manifest one of habitual occupations: hardly with that of a man's moral sensibility or biases, except in as far as they may be indicated by his sex, age, rank, and education: not at all with his religious sensibility and religious biases, except in as far as they may be indicated by the religious profession he belongs to: not at all with the quantity or quality of his sympathetic or antipathetic sensibilities, except in as far as they may be presumed from his sex, age, rank, education, lineage, or religious profession. It is the case, however, with his habitual occupations, with his pecuniary circumstances, and with his connexions in the way of sympathy. Of others, again, either the existence cannot be ascertained, or the degree cannot be measured. These, therefore, cannot be taken into account, either by the legislator or the executive magistrate. Accordingly, they would have no claim to be taken notice of, were it not for those secondary circumstances by which they are indicated, and whose influence could not well be understood without them. What these are, has been already mentioned.

XLV. It has already been observed, that different articles in this list of circumstances apply to different exciting causes: the circumstances of bodily strength, for instance, has scarcely any influence of itself (whatever it may have in a roundabout way, and by accident) on the effect of an incident which should increase or diminish the quantum of a man's property. It remains to be considered, what the exciting causes are with which the legislator has to do. These may, by some accident or other, be any whatsoever: but those with which he has principally to do, are those of the painful or afflictive kind. With pleasurable ones he has little to do, except now and then by accident: the reasons of which may be easily enough perceived, at the same time that it would take up too much room to unfold them here. The exciting causes with which he has principally to do, are, on the one hand, the mischievous acts, which it is his business to prevent; on the other hand, the punishments, by the terror of which it is his endeavour to prevent them. Now of these two sets of exciting causes, the latter only is of his production: being produced partly by his own special appointment, partly in conformity to his general appointment, by the special appointment of the judge. For the legislator, therefore, as well as for the judge, it is necessary (if they would know what it is they are doing when they are appointing punishment) to have an eye to all these circumstances. For the legislator, lest, meaning to apply a certain quantity of punishment to all persons who shall put themselves in a given predicament, he should unawares apply to some of those persons much more or much less than he himself intended: for the judge, lest, in applying to a particular person a particular measure of punishment, he should apply much more or much less than was intended, perhaps by himself, and at any rate by the legislator. They ought each of them, therefore, to have before him, on the one hand, a list of the several circumstances by which sensibility may be influenced; on the other hand, a list of the several species and degrees of punishment which they purpose to make use of: and then, by making a comparison between the two, to form a detailed estimate of the influence of each of the circumstances in question, upon the effect of each species and degree of punishment.

There are two plans or orders of distribution, either of which might be pursued in the drawing up this estimate. The one is to make the name of the circumstance take the lead, and under it to represent the different influences it exerts over the effects of the several modes of punishment: the other is to make the name of the punishment take the lead, and under it to represent the different influences which are exerted over the effects of it by the several circumstances above mentioned. Now of these two sorts of objects, the punishment is that to which the intention of the legislator is directed in the first instance. This is of his own creation, and will be whatsoever he thinks fit to make it: the influencing circumstance exists independently of him, and is what it is whether he will or no. What he has occasion to do is to establish a certain species and degree of punishment: and it is only with reference to that punishment that he has occasion to make any inquiry concerning any of the circumstances here in question. The latter of the two plans therefore is that which appears by far the most useful and commodious. But neither upon the one or the other plan can any such estimate be delivered here. . . .

Chapter VII.

OF HUMAN ACTIONS IN GENERAL.

I. The business of government is to promote the happiness of the society, by punishing and rewarding. That part of its business which consists in punishing, is more particularly the subject of penal law. In proportion as an act tends to disturb that happiness, in proportion as the tendency of it is pernicious, will be the demand it creates for punishment. What happiness consists of, we have already seen: enjoyment of pleasures, security from pains.

II. The general tendency of an act is more or less pernicious, according to the sum total of its consequences: that is, according to the difference between the sum of such as are good, and the sum of such as are evil. . . .

V. Now the intention, with regard to the consequences of an act, will depend upon two things: 1. The state of the will or intention, with respect to the act itself. And, 2. The state of the understanding, or perceptive faculties, with regard to the circumstances which it is, or may appear to be, accompanied with. Now with respect to these circumstances, the perceptive faculty is susceptible of three states: consciousness, unconsciousness, and false consciousness. Consciousness, when the party believes precisely those circumstances, and no others, to subsist, which really do subsist: unconsciousness, when he fails of perceiving certain circumstances to subsist, which, however, do subsist: false consciousness, when he believes or imagines certain circumstances to subsist, which in truth do not subsist.

VI. In every transaction, therefore, which is examined with a view to punishment, there are four articles to be considered: 1. The *act* itself, which is done. 2. The *circumstances* in which it is done. 3. The *intentionality* that may have accompanied it. 4. The *consciousness,* unconsciousness, or false consciousness, that may have accompanied it.

What regards the act and the circumstances will be the subject of the present chapter: what regards intention and consciousness, that of the two succeeding.

VII. There are also two other articles on which the general tendency of an act depends: and on that, as well as on other accounts, the demand which it creates for punishment. These are, 1. The particular *motive* or motives which gave birth to it. 2. The general *disposition* which it indicates. These articles will be the subject of two other chapters. . . .

[M.P.M.—After a brief and inconclusive discussion of intentions and consciousness, Bentham concludes in Chapter IX:]

XVIII. The above-mentioned definition and distinctions are far from being mere matters of speculation. They are capable of the most extensive and constant application, as well to moral discourse as to legislative practice. Upon the degree and bias of a man's intention, upon the absence or presence or consciousness or mis-supposal, depend a great part of the good and bad, more especially of the bad consequences of an act; and on this, as well as other grounds a great part of the demand for punishment. The presence of intention with regard to such or such a consequence, and of consciousness with regard to such or such a circumstance, of the act, will form so many criminative circumstances, or essential ingredients in the composition of this or that offence: applied to other circumstances, consciousness will form a ground of aggravation, annexable to the like offence. In almost all cases, the absence of intention with regard to certain consequences, and the absence of consciousness, or the presence of mis-supposal, with regard to certain circumstances, will constitute so many grounds of extenuation.

Chapter X.

OF MOTIVES.

1. *Different Senses of the word, Motive.*

I. It is an acknowledged truth, that every kind of act whatever, and consequently every kind of offence, is apt to assume a different character, and be attended with different effects, according to the nature of the motive which gives birth to it. This makes it requisite to take a view of the several motives by which human conduct is liable to be influenced.

II. By a motive, in the most extensive sense in which the word is ever used with reference to a thinking being, is meant any thing that can contribute to give birth to, or even to prevent, any kind of action. Now the action of a thinking being is the act either of the body, or only of the mind: and an act of the mind is an act either of the intellectual faculty, or of the will. Acts of the intellectual faculty will sometimes rest in the understanding merely, without exerting any influence in the production of any acts of the will. Motives, which are not of a nature to influence any other acts than those, may be styled purely *speculative* motives, or motives resting in speculation. But as to these acts, neither do they exercise any influence over external acts, or over their consequences, nor consequently over any pain or any pleasure that may be in the number of such consequences. Now it is only on account of their tendency to produce either pain or pleasure, that any acts can be material. With acts, therefore, that rest purely in the understanding, we have not here any concern: nor therefore with any object, if any such there be, which, in the character of a motive can have no influence on any other acts than those.

III. The motives with which alone we have any concern, are such as are of a nature to act upon the will. By a motive, then, in this sense of the word, is to be understood any thing whatsoever, which, by influencing the will of a sensitive being, is supposed to serve as a means of determining him to act, or voluntarily to forbear to act, upon any occasion. Motives of this sort, in contradistinction to the former, may be styled *practical* motives, or motives applying to practice.

IV. Owing to the poverty and unsettled state of language, the word *motive* is employed indiscriminately to denote two kinds of objects, which, for the better understanding of the subject, it is necessary should be distinguished. On some occasions it is employed to denote any of those really existing incidents from whence the act in question is supposed to take its rise. The sense it bears on these occasions may be styled its literal or *unfigurative* sense. On other occasions it is employed to denote a certain fictitious entity, a passion, an affection of the mind, an ideal being, which upon the happening of any such incident is considered as operating upon the mind, and prompting it to take that course, towards which it is impelled by the influence of such incident. Motives of this class are Avarice, Indolence, Benevolence, and so forth; as we shall see more particularly farther on. This latter may be styled the *figurative* sense of the term *motive*.

V. As to the real incidents to which the name of motive is also given, these too are of two very different kinds. They may be either, 1. The *internal* perception of any individual lot of pleasure or pain, the expectation of which is looked upon as calculated to determine you to act in such or such a manner; as the pleasure of acquiring such a sum of money, the pain of exerting yourself on such an occasion, and so forth: Or, 2. Any *external* event, the happening whereof is regarded as having a tendency to bring about the perception of such pleasure or such pain: for instance, the coming up of a lottery ticket, by which the possession of the money devolves to you: or the breaking out of a fire in the house you are in, which makes it necessary for you to quit it. The former kind of motives may be termed interior, or internal: the latter exterior, or external. . . .

2. *No Motives either constantly good, or constantly bad.*

IX. In all this chain of motives, the principal or original link seems to be the last internal motive in prospect; it is to this that all the other motives in prospect owe their materiality: and the immediately acting motive its existence. This motive in prospect, we see, is always some pleasure, or some pain: some pleasure, which the act in question is expected to be a means of continuing or producing: some pain which it is expected to be a means of discontinuing or preventing. A motive is substantially nothing more than pleasure or pain, operating in a certain manner.

X. Now, pleasure is in *itself* a good; nay, even setting aside immunity from pain, the only good: pain is in itself an evil; and, indeed, without exception, the only evil; or else the words good and evil have no meaning. And this is alike true of every sort of pain, and of every sort of pleasure. It follows, therefore, immediately and incontestibly, that *there is no such thing as any sort of motive that is in itself a bad one.**

[*Let a man's motive be ill-will; call it even malice, envy, cruelty; it is still a kind of pleasure that is his motive: the pleasure he takes at the thought of the pain which he sees, or expects to see, his adversary undergo. Now even this wretched pleasure, taken by itself, is good: it may be faint; it may be short; it must at any rate be impure: yet while it lasts, and before any bad consequences arrive, it is as good as any other that is not more intense. . . .]

XI. It is common, however, to speak of actions as proceeding from *good* or *bad* motives: in which case the motives meant are such as are internal. The expression is far from being an accurate one; and as it is apt to occur in the consideration of almost every kind of offence, it will be requisite to settle the precise meaning of it, and observe, how far it quadrates with the truth of things.

XII. With respect to goodness and badness, as it is with every thing else that is not itself either pain or pleasure, so is it with motives. If they are good or bad, it is only on account of their effects: good, on account of their tendency to produce pleasure, or avert pain: bad, on account of their tendency to produce pain, or avert pleasure. Now the case is, that from one and the same motive, and from every kind of motive, may proceed actions that are good, others that are bad, and others that are indifferent. This we shall proceed to shew with respect to all the different kinds of motives, as determined by the various kinds of pleasures and pains.

XIII. Such an analysis, useful as it is, will be found to be a matter of no small difficulty; owing, in great measure, to a certain perversity of structure which prevails more or less throughout all languages. To speak of motives, as of anything else, one must call them by their names. But the misfortune is, that it is rare to meet with a motive of which the name expresses that and nothing more. Commonly along with the very name of the motive, is tacitly involved a proposition imputing to it a certain quality; a quality which, in many cases, will appear to include that very goodness or badness, concerning which we are here inquiring whether, properly speaking, it be or be not imputable to motives. To use the common phrase, in most cases, the name of the motive is a word which is employed either only in a *good sense,* or else only in a *bad sense.* Now, when a word is spoken of as being used in a good sense, all that is necessarily meant is this: that in conjunction with the idea of the object it is put to signify, it conveys an idea of *approbation;* that is, of a pleasure or satisfaction, entertained by the person who employs the term, at the thoughts of such object. In like manner, when a word is spoken of as being used in a bad sense, all that is necessarily meant is this: that, in conjunction with the idea of the object it is put to signify, it conveys an idea of *disapprobation:* that is, of a displeasure entertained by the person who employs the term at the thoughts of such object. Now, the circumstance on which such approbation is grounded will, as naturally as any other, be the opinion of the *goodness* of the object in question, as above explained: such, at least, it must be, upon the principle of utility: so, on the other hand, the circumstances on which any such disapprobation is grounded, will as naturally as any other, be the opinion of the *badness* of the object: such, at least, it must be, in as far as the principle of utility is taken for the standard.

Now there are certain motives which, unless in a few particular cases, have scarcely any other name to be expressed by but such a word as is used only in a good sense. This is the case, for example, with the motives of piety and honour. The consequence of this is, that if, in speaking of such a motive, a man should have occasion to apply the epithet bad to any actions which he mentions as apt to result from it, he must appear to be guilty of a contradiction in terms. But the names of motives which have scarcely any other name to be expressed by, but such a word as is used only in a bad sense, are many more. This is the case, for example, with the motives of lust and avarice. And accordingly, if, in speaking of any such motive, a man should have occasion to apply the epithets good or indifferent to any actions which he mentions as apt to result from it, he must here also appear to be guilty of a similar contradiction.

This perverse association of ideas cannot, it is evident, but throw great difficulties in the way of the inquiry now before us. Confining himself to the language most in use, a man can scarce avoid running, in appearance, into perpetual contradictions. His propositions will appear, on the one hand, repugnant to truth; and on the other hand, adverse to utility. As paradoxes, they will excite contempt: as mischievous paradoxes, indignation. For the truths he labours to convey, however important, and however salutary, his reader is never the better: and he himself is much the worse. To obviate this inconvenience completely, he has but this one unpleasant remedy: to lay aside the old phraseology and invent a new one. Happy the man whose language is ductile enough to permit him this resource. To palliate the inconvenience, where that method of obviating it is impracticable, he has nothing left for it but to enter into a long discussion, to state the whole matter at large, to confess, that for the sake of promoting the purposes, he has violated the established laws of language, and to throw himself upon the mercy of his readers.* . . .

> [*Happily, language is not always so intractable, but that by making use of two words instead of one, a man may avoid the inconvenience of fabricating words that are absolutely new. Thus instead of the word lust, by putting together two words in common use, he may frame the neutral expression, sexual desire: instead of the word avarice, by putting together two other words also in common use, he may frame the neutral expression, pecuniary interest. This, accordingly, is the course which I have taken. In these instances, indeed, even the combination is not novel: the only novelty there is consists in the steady adherence to the one neutral expression, rejecting altogether the terms, of which the import is infected by adventitious and unsuitable ideas.
>
> In the catalogue of motives, corresponding to the several sorts of pains and pleasures, I have inserted such as have occurred to me. I cannot pretend to warrant it complete. To make sure of rendering it so, the only way would be, to turn over the dictionary from beginning to end; an operation which, in a view to perfection, would be necessary for more purposes than this . . .]

4. *Order of Pre-eminence among Motives.*

XXXVI. Of all these sorts of motives, good-will is that of which the dictates, taken in a general view, are surest of coinciding with those of the principle of utility. For the dictates of utility are neither more nor less than the dictates of the most extensive and enlightened (that is *well-advised*) benevolence. The dictates of the other motives may be conformable to those of utility, or repugnant, as it may happen. . . .

5. *Conflict among Motives.*

XLIII. When a man has it in contemplation to engage in any action, he is frequently acted upon at the same time by the force of divers motives: one motive, or set of motives, acting in one direction; another motive, or set of motives, acting as it were in an opposite direction: the motives on one side disposing him to engage in the action; those on the other, disposing him not to engage in it. Now, any motive the influence of which tends to dispose him to engage in the action in question, may be termed an *impelling* motive: any motive, the influence of which tends to dispose him not to engage in it, a *restraining* motive. But these appellations may of course be interchanged, according as the act is of the positive kind, or the negative.

XLIV. It has been shown, that there is no sort of motive but may give birth to any sort of action. It follows, therefore, that there are no two motives but may come to be opposed to one another. Where the tendency of the act is bad, the most common case is for it to have been dictated by a motive either of the self-regarding, or of the dissocial class. In such case the motive of benevolence has commonly been acting, though ineffectually, in the character of a restraining motive. . . .

XLVI. What is here said about the goodness and badness of motives, is far from being a mere matter of words. There will be occasion to make use of it hereafter for various important purposes. I shall have need of it for the sake of dissipating various prejudices, which are of disservice to the community, sometimes by cherishing the flame of civil dissensions, at other times by obstructing the course of justice. It will be shown, that in the case of many offences, the consideration of the motive is a most material one: for that, in the first place, it makes a very material difference in the magnitude of the mischief: in the next place, that it is easy to be ascertained; and thence may be made a ground for a difference in the demand for punishment: but that in other cases it is altogether incapable of being ascertained: and that, were it capable of being ever so well ascertained, good or bad, it could make no difference in the demand for punishment: that in all cases, the motive that may happen to govern a prosecutor is a consideration totally immaterial: whence may be seen the mischievousness of the prejudice that is so apt to be entertained against informers; and the consequence of it is that the judge, in particular, should be proof against the influence of such delusions.

Lastly, the subject of motives is one with which it is necessary to be acquainted, in order to pass a judgment on any means that may be proposed for combating offences in their source.

But before the theoretical foundation for these practical observations can be completely laid, it is necessary we should say something on the subject of *disposition:* which, accordingly, will furnish matter for the ensuing chapter.

Chapter XI.

OF HUMAN DISPOSITIONS IN GENERAL.

I. In the foregoing chapter it has been shown at large, that goodness or badness cannot, with any propriety, be predicated of motives. Is there nothing, then, about a man that can properly be termed good or bad, when, on such or such an occasion, he suffers himself to be governed by such or such a motive? Yes, certainly: his *disposition.* Now disposition is a kind of fictitious entity, feigned for the convenience of discourse, in order to express what there is supposed to be *permanent* in a man's frame of mind, where, on such or such an occasion, he has been influenced by such or such a motive, to engage in an act, which, as it appeared to him, was of such or such a tendency.

II. It is with disposition as with every thing else: it will be good or bad according to its effects; according to the effects it has in augmenting or diminishing the happiness of the community. A man's disposition may accordingly be considered in two points of view: according to the influence it has, either, 1. On his own happiness: or, 2. On the happiness of others. Viewed in both these lights together, or in either or them indiscriminately, it may be termed, on the one hand, good; on the other, bad; or, in flagrant cases, depraved. . . .

XXVII. It is evident, that the nature of a man's disposition must depend upon the nature of the motives he is apt to be influenced by; in other words, upon the degree of his sensibility to the force of such and such motives. For his disposition is, as it were, the sum of his intentions: the disposition he is of during a certain period, the sum or result of his intentions during that period. If, of the acts he has been intending to engage in during the supposed period, those which are apparently of a mischievous tendency bear a large proportion to those which appear to him to be of the contrary tendency, his disposition will be of the mischievous case: if but a small proportion, of the innocent or upright.

XXVIII. Now intentions, like every thing else, are produced by the things that are their causes: and the causes of intentions are motives. If, on any occasion, a man forms either a good or a bad intention, it must be by the influence of some motive.

XXIX. When the act, which a motive prompts a man to engage in, is of a mischievous nature, it may, for distinction's sake, be termed a *seducing* or corrupting motive: in which case also any motive which, in opposition to the former, acts in the character of a restraining motive, may be styled a *tutelary,* conservatory, preservatory, or preserving motive.

XXX. Tutelary motives may again be distinguished into *standing* or constant, and *occasional.* By standing tutelary motives, I mean such as act with more or less force in all, or at least in most cases, tending to restrain a man from *any* mischievous acts he may be prompted to engage in; and that with a force which depends upon the general nature of the act, rather than upon any accidental circumstance with which any individual act of that sort may happen to be accompanied. By occasional tutelary motives, I mean such motives as may chance to act in this direction or not, according to the nature of the act, and of the particular occasion on which the engaging in it is brought into contemplation.

XXXI. Now it has been shown, that there is no sort of motive by which a man may not be prompted to engage in acts that are of a mischievous nature; that is, which may not come to act in the capacity of a seducing motive. It has been shown, on the other hand, that there are some motives which are remarkably less likely to operate in this way than others. It has also been shown, that the least likely of all is that of benevolence or good-will: the most common tendency of which, it has been shown, is to act in the character of a tutelary motive. . . .

XL. We are now in a condition to determine, with some degree of precision, what is to be understood by the *strength of a temptation,* and what indication it may give of the degree of mischievousness in a man's disposition in the case of any offence. When a man is prompted to engage in any mischievous act, we will say, for shortness, in an offence, the strength of the temptation depends upon the ratio between the force of the seducing motives on the one hand, and such of the occasional tutelary ones, as the circumstances of the case call forth into action, on the other. The temptation, then, may be said to be strong, when the pleasure or advantage to be got from the crime is such as in the eyes of the offender must appear great in comparison of the trouble and danger that appear to him to accompany the enterprise: slight or weak, when that pleasure or advantage is such as must appear small in comparison of such trouble and such danger. It is plain, the strength of the temptation depends not upon the force of the impelling (that is, of the seducing) motives altogether: for let the opportunity be more favourable, that is, let the trouble, or any branch of the danger, be made less than before, it will be acknowledged, that the temptation is made so much the stronger: and on the other hand, let the opportunity become less favourable, or, in other words, let the trouble, or any branch of the danger, be made greater than before, the temptation will be so much the weaker.

Now, after taking account of such tutelary motives as have been styled occasional, the only tutelary motives that can remain are those which have been termed standing ones. But those which have been termed the standing tutelary motives, are the same that we have been styling social. It follows, therefore, that the strength of the temptation, in any case, after deducting the force of the social motives, is as the sum of the forces of the seducing, to the sum of the forces of the occasional tutelary motives.

XLI. It remains to be inquired, what indication concerning the mischievousness or depravity of a man's disposition is afforded by the strength of the temptation, in the case where any offence happens to have been committed. It appears, then, that the weaker the temptation is, by which a man has been overcome, the more depraved and mischievous it shows his disposition to have been. For the goodness of his disposition is measured by the degree of his sensibility to the action of the social motives: in other words, by the strength of the influence which those motives have over him. Now, the less considerable the force is by which their influence on him has been overcome, the more convincing is the proof that has been given of the weakness of that influence.

Again, the degree of a man's sensibility to the force of the social motives being given, it is plain that the force with which these motives tend to restrain him from engaging in any mischievous enterprise will be as the apparent mischievousness of such enterprise, that is, as the degree of mischief with which it appears to *him* likely to be attended. In other words, the less mischievous the offence appears to him to be, the less averse he will be, as far as he is guided by social considerations, to engage in it: the more mischievous, the more averse. If, then, the nature of the offence is such as must appear to him highly mischievous, and yet he engages in it notwithstanding, it shows, that the degree of his sensibility to the force of the social motives is but slight: and consequently that his disposition is proportionately depraved. Moreover, the less the strength of the temptation was, the more pernicious and depraved does it show his disposition to have been. For the less the strength of the temptation was, the less was the force which the influence of those motives had to overcome: the clearer, therefore, is the proof that has been given of the weakness of that influence.

XLII. From what has been said, it seems that, for judging of the indication that is afforded concerning the depravity of a man's disposition by the strength of the temptation, compared with the mischievousness of the enterprise, the following rules may be laid down:

Rule 1. *The strength of the temptation being given, the mischievousness of the disposition manifested by the enterprise, is as the apparent mischievousness of the act.*

Thus, it would show a more depraved disposition, to murder a man for a reward of a guinea, or falsely to charge him with a robbery for the same reward, than to obtain the same sum from him by simple theft: the trouble he would have to take, and the risk he would have to run, being supposed to stand on the same footing in the one case as in the other.

Rule 2. *The apparent mischievousness of the act being given, a man's disposition is the more depraved, the slighter the temptation is by which he has been overcome.*

Thus, it shows a more depraved and dangerous disposition, if a man kill another out of mere sport, as the Emperor of Morocco, Muley Mahomet, is said to have done great numbers; than out of revenge, as Sulla and Marius did thousands; or in the view of self-preservation, as Augustus killed many; or even for lucre, as the same Emperor is said to have killed some. And the effects of such a depravity, on that part of the public which is apprized of it, run in the same proportion. From Augustus, some persons only had to fear, under some particular circumstances: from Muley Mahomet, every man had to fear at all times.

Rule 3. *The apparent mischievousness of the act being given, the evidence which it affords of the depravity of a man's disposition is the less conclusive, the stronger the temptation is by which he has been overcome.*

Thus, if a poor man, who is ready to die with hunger, steal a loaf of bread, it is a less explicit sign of depravity, than if a rich man were to commit a theft to the same amount. It will be observed, that in this rule all that is said is, that the evidence of depravity is in this case the less conclusive: it is not said that the depravity is positively the less. For in this case it is possible, for any thing that appears to the contrary, that the theft might have been committed, even had the temptation been not so strong. In this case, the alleviating circumstance is only a matter of presumption; in the former, the aggravating circumstance is a matter of certainty.

Rule 4. *Where the motive is of the dissocial kind, the apparent mischievousness of the act, and the strength of the temptation, being given, the depravity is as the degree of deliberation with which it is accompanied.*

For in every man, be his disposition ever so depraved, the social motives are those which, wherever the self-regarding ones stand neuter, regulate and determine the general tenor of his life. If the dissocial motives are put in action, it is only in particular circumstances, and on particular occasions: the gentle but constant force of the social motives being for a while subdued. The general and standing bias of every man's nature is, therefore, towards that side to which the force of the social motives would determine him to adhere. This being the case, the force of the social motives tends continually to put an end to that of the dissocial ones: as, in natural bodies, the force of friction tends to put an end to that which is generated by impulse. Time, then, which wears away the force of the dissocial motives, adds to that of the social. The longer, therefore, a man continues, on a given occasion, under the dominion of the dissocial motives, the more convincing is the proof that has been given of his insensibility to the force of the social ones.

Thus, it shows a worse disposition, where a man lays a deliberate plan for beating his antagonist, and beats him accordingly, than if he were to beat him upon the spot, in consequence of a sudden quarrel: and worse again, if, after having had him a long while together in his power, he beats him at intervals, and at his leisure. . . .

Chapter XII.

OF THE CONSEQUENCES OF A MISCHIEVOUS ACT.

1. *Shapes in which the Mischief of an Act may show itself.*

I. Hitherto we have been speaking of the various articles or objects on which the consequences or tendency of an act may depend: of the bare *act* itself: of the *circumstances* it may have been, or may have been supposed to be, accompanied with: of the *consciousness* a man may have had with respect to any such circumstances: of the *intentions* that may have preceded the act: of the *motives* that may have given birth to those intentions: and of the *disposition* that may have been indicated by the connexion between such intentions and such motives. We now come to speak of *consequences* or tendency: an article which forms the concluding link in all this chain of causes and effects, involving in it the materiality of the whole. Now, such part of this tendency as is of a mischievous nature, is all that we have any direct concern with; to that, therefore, we shall here confine ourselfes.

II. The tendency of an act is mischievous when the consequences of it are mischievous; that is to say, either the certain consequences or the probable. The consequences, how many and whatsoever they may be, of an act, of which the tendency is mischievous, may, such of them as are mischievous, be conceived to constitute one aggregate body, which may be termed the mischief of the act.

III. This mischief may frequently be distinguished, as it were, into two shares or parcels: the one containing what may be called the primary mischief; the other, what may be called the secondary. That share may be termed the *primary,* which is sustained by an assignable individual, or a multitude of assignable individuals. That share may be termed the *secondary,* which, taking its origin from the former, extends itself either over the whole community, or over some other multitude of unassignable individuals.

IV. The primary mischief of an act may again be distinguished into two branches: 1. The *original:* and, 2. The *derivative.* By the original branch I mean that which alights upon and is confined to any person who is a sufferer in the first instance, and on his own account; the person, for instance, who is beaten, robbed, or murdered. By the derivative branch, I mean any share of mischief which may befal any other assignable persons in consequence of his being a sufferer, and not otherwise. These persons must, of course, be persons who, in some way or other, are connected with him. Now, the ways in which one person may be connected with another, have been already seen: they may be connected in the way of *interest* (meaning self-regarding interest) or merely in the way of *sympathy.* And again, persons connected with a given person, in the way of interest, may be connected with him either by affording *support* to him, or by deriving it from him.

V. The secondary mischief, again, may frequently be seen to consist of two other shares or parcels: the first consisting of *pain;* the other of *danger.* The pain which it produces is a pain of apprehension; a pain grounded on the apprehension of suffering such mischiefs or inconveniences, whatever they may be, as it is the nature of the primary mischief to produce. It may be styled, in one word, the *alarm.* The danger is the *chance,* whatever it may be, which the multitude it concerns may, in consequence of the primary mischief, stand exposed to, of suffering such mischiefs or inconveniences. For danger is nothing but the chance of pain, or, what comes to the same thing, of loss of pleasure. . . .

[The following passage was taken by Bowring from Dumont's *Traités* and added as part of a new chapter XIV to the *Collected Edition,* cf. p. 81, I.— M.P.M.]

I suppose myself a stranger to all our present denominations of vice or virtue: I am called to consider human actions only with relation to their good or evil effects. I open two accounts; I place on the side of pure profit all pleasures; I place on the side of loss all pains: I faithfully weigh the interests of all parties; the man whom prejudice brands as vicious; he who is accounted virtuous, are, for the moment, equal before me. I wish to judge the prejudice itself, and to weigh in this new balance all actions, with the intention of forming a catalogue of those which ought to be permitted, and of those which ought to be prohibited.

The operation, which at first appears to be complicated, becomes easy, by means of the distinction which we have made between the evil of the *first,* the *second,* and the *third* order.

[My italics. Second and third order evils correspond to the secondary mischiefs of danger and alarm, and are among the most important of all distinctions in Bentham, indicating as they do the social extent of mischief, and thereby making large-scale social and political calculations possible.— M.P.M.]

Have I to examine an act attacking the security of an individual? I compare all the pleasure, or, in other terms, all the profit which arises from this act to its author, with all the evil, or all the loss, which results from it to the party injured. I see at once that the evil of the first order surpasses the good of the first order. But I do not stop there. This action is followed by danger and alarm to society: the evil which was confined at first to a single person, spreads itself over all in the shape of fear. The pleasure resulting from the action is only for one: the pain is for a thousand, for ten thousand, for all. The disproportion, already prodigious, appears almost infinite, if I pass on to the evil of the third order, by considering, that if the act in question were not repressed, there would result from it an universal and durable discouragement, a cessation of labour, and at last the dissolution of society. . . .

XII. The two branches of the secondary mischief of an act, the alarm and the danger, must not be confounded: though intimately connected, they are perfectly distinct: either may subsist without the other. The neighbourhood may be alarmed with the report of a robbery, when, in fact, no robbery either has been committed, or is in a way to be committed: a neighbourhood may be on the point of being disturbed by robberies, without knowing any thing of the matter. Accordingly, we shall soon perceive, that some acts produce alarm without danger: others, danger without alarm. . . .

XIV. The distinction between the primary and the secondary consequences of an act, must be carefully attended to. It is so just, that the latter may often be of a directly opposite nature to the former. In some cases, where the primary consequences of the act are attended with a mischief, the secondary consequences may be beneficial, and that to such a degree, as even greatly to outweigh the mischief of the primary. This is the case, for instance, with all acts of punishment, when properly applied. Of these, the primary mischief being never intended to fall but upon such persons as may happen to have committed some act which it is expedient to prevent; the secondary mischief, that is, the alarm and the danger, extends no farther than to such persons as are under temptation to commit it: in which case, in as far as it tends to restrain them from committing such acts, it is of a beneficial nature. . . .

Chapter XIII.
CASES UNMEET FOR PUNISHMENT.

I. The general object which all laws have, or ought to have, in common, is to augment the total happiness of the community; and therefore, in the first place to exclude, as far as may be, every thing that tends to subtract from that happiness: in other words, to exclude mischief.

II. But all punishment is mischief: all punishment in itself is evil. Upon the principle of utility, if it ought at all to be admitted, it ought only to be admitted in as far as it promises to exclude some greater evil.*

[*What follows, relative to the subject of punishment, ought regularly to be preceded by a distinct chapter on the ends of punishment. But having little to say on that particular branch of the subject, which has not been said before, it seemed better, in a work, which will at any rate be but too voluminous, to omit this title, reserving it for another, hereafter to be published, entitled, *Rationale of Punishment*. . . . A very few words, however, concerning the *ends* of punishment, can scarcely be dispensed with.

The immediate principal end of punishment is to controul action. This action is either that of the offender, or of others: that of the offender it controuls by its influence, either on his will, in which case it is said to operate in the way of *reformation;* or on his physical power, in which case it is said to operate by *disablement:* that of others it can influence no otherwise than by its influence over their wills; in which case it is said to operate in the way of *example.* A kind of collateral end, which it has a natural tendency to answer, is that of affording a pleasure or satisfaction to the party injured, where there is one, and, in general, to parties whose ill-will, whether on a self-regarding account, or on the account of sympathy or antipathy, has been excited by the offence. This purpose, as far as it can be answered *gratis,* is a beneficial one. But no punishment ought to be alloted merely to this purpose, because . . . no such pleasure is ever produced by punishment as can be equivalent to the pain. . . .]

III. It is plain, therefore, that in the following cases, punishment ought not to be inflicted.

1. Where it is *groundless:* where there is no mischief for it to prevent; the act not being mischievous upon the whole.

2. Where it must be *inefficacious;* there it cannot act so as to prevent the mischief.

3. Where it is *unprofitable,* or too *expensive;* where the mischief it would produce would be greater than what it would prevent.

4. Where it is *needless;* where the mischief may be prevented, or cease of itself, without it; that is, at a cheaper rate.

Chapter XIV.

OF THE PROPORTION BETWEEN PUNISHMENTS AND OFFENCES.

I. We have seen that the general object of all laws is to prevent mischief; that is to say, when it is worth while: but that, where there are no other means of doing this than punishment, there are four cases in which it is *not* worth while.

II. When it *is* worth while, there are four subordinate designs or objects, which, in the course of his endeavours to compass, as far as may be, that one general object, a legislator, whose views are governed by the principle of utility, comes naturally to propose to himself.

III. 1. His first, most extensive, and most eligible object, is to prevent, in as far as it is possible, and worth while, all sorts of offences whatsoever: in other words, so to manage that no offence whatsoever may be committed.

IV. 2. But if a man must needs commit an offence of some kind or other, the next object is to induce him to commit an offence *less* mischievous, *rather* than one *more* mischievous: in other words, to choose always the *least* mischievous of two offences that will either of them suit his purpose.

V. 3. When a man has resolved upon a particular offence, the next object is to dispose him to do *no more* mischief than is *necessary* to his purpose: in other words, to do as little mischief as is consistent with the benefit he has in view.

VI. 4. The last object is, whatever the mischief be which it is proposed to prevent, to prevent it at as *cheap* a rate as possible.

VII. Subservient to these four objects, or purposes, must be the rules or canons by which the proportion of punishments to offences is to be governed.

VIII. Rule 1. The first object, it has been seen, is to prevent, in as far as it is worth while, all sorts of offences: therefore,

The value of the punishment must not be less in any case than what is sufficient to outweigh that of the profit of the offence. . . .

X. Rule 2. But whether a given offence shall be prevented in a given degree by a given quantity of punishment, is never any thing better than a chance: for the purchasing of which, whatever punishment is employed, is so much expended in advance. However, for the sake of giving it the better chance of outweighing the profit of the offence,

The greater the mischief of the offence, the greater is the expense, which it may be worth while to be at, in the way of punishment.

XI. Rule 3. The next object is, to induce a man to choose always the least mischievous of two offences: therefore,

Where two offences come in competition, the punishment for the greater offence must be sufficient to induce a man to prefer the less.

XII. Rule 4. When a man has resolved upon a particular offence, the next object is, to induce him to do no more mischief than what is necessary to his purpose: therefore,

The punishment should be adjusted in such manner to each particular offence, that for every part of the mischief there may be a motive to restrain the offender from giving birth to it.

XIII. Rule 5. The last object is, whatever mischief is guarded against, to guard against it at as cheap a rate as possible: therefore,

The punishment ought in no case to be more than what is necessary to bring it into conformity with the rules here given.

XIV. Rule 6. It is further to be observed, that owing to the different manners and degrees in which persons under different circumstances are affected by the same exciting cause, a punishment which is the same in name will not always either really produce, or even so much as appear to others to produce, in two different persons the same degree of pain: therefore,

That the quantity actually inflicted on each individual offender may correspond to the quantity intended for similar offenders in general, the several circumstances influencing sensibility ought always to be taken into account. . . .

XVIII. Rule 7. These things being considered, the three following rules may be laid down by way of supplement and explanation to Rule 1.

To enable the value of the punishment to outweigh that of the profit of the offence, it must be increased, in point of magnitude, in proportion as it falls short in point of certainty.

XIX. Rule 8. *Punishment must be further increased in point of magnitude, in proportion as it falls short in point of proximity.*

XX. Rule 9. *Where the act is conclusively indicative of a habit, such an increase must be given to the punishment as may enable it to outweigh the profit not only of the individual offence, but of such other like offences as are likely to have been committed with impunity by the same offender. . . .*

XXII. Rule 10. *When a punishment, which in point of quality is particularly well calculated to answer its intention, cannot exist in less than a certain quantity, it may sometimes be of use, for the sake of employing it,* to stretch a little beyond that quantity which, on other accounts, would be strictly necessary.

XXIII. Rule 11. *In particular, this may sometimes be the case, where the punishment proposed is of such a nature as to be particularly well calculated to answer the purpose of a moral lesson.*

XXIV. Rule 12. The tendency of the above considerations is to dictate an augmentation in the punishment: the following rule operates in the way of diminution. There are certain cases (it has been seen) in which, by the influence of accidental circumstances, punishment may be rendered unprofitable in the whole: in the same cases it may chance to be rendered unprofitable as to a part only. Accordingly,

In adjusting the quantum of punishment, the circumstances, by which all punishment may be rendered unprofitable, ought to be attended to.

XXV. Rule 13. It is to be observed, that the more various and minute any set of provisions are, the greater the chance is that any given article in them will not be borne in mind: without which, no benefit can ensue from it. Distinctions, which are more complex than what the conceptions of those whose conduct it is designed to influence can take in, will even be worse than useless. The whole system will present a confused appearance: and thus the effect, not only of the proportions established by the articles in question, but of whatever is connected with them, will be destroyed. To draw a precise line of direction in such case seems impossible. However, by way of memento, it may be of some use to subjoin the following rule.

Among provisions designed to perfect the proportion between punishments and offences, if any occur, which, by their own particular good effects, would not make up for the harm they would do by adding to the intricacy of the Code, they should be omitted.

XXVI. It may be remembered, that the political sanction, being that to which the sort of punishment belongs, which in this chapter is all along in view, is but one of four sanctions, which may all of them contribute their share towards producing the same effects. It may be expected, therefore, that in adjusting the quantity of political punishment, allowance should be made for the assistance it may meet with from those other controuling powers. True it is, that from each of these several sources a very powerful assistance may sometimes be derived. But the case is, that (setting aside the moral sanction, in the case where the force of it is expressly adopted into and modified by the political) the force of those other powers is never determinate enough to be depended upon. It can never be reduced, like political punishment, into exact lots, nor meted out in number, quantity, and value. The legislator is therefore obliged to provide the full complement of punishment, as if he were sure of not receiving any assistance whatever from any of those quarters. If he does, so much the better: but lest he should not, it is necessary he should, at all events, make that provision which depends upon himself. . . .

XVIII. There are some, perhaps, who, at first sight, may look upon the nicety employed in the adjustment of such rules, as so much labour lost: for gross ignorance, they will say, never troubles itself about laws, and passion does not calculate. But the evil of ignorance admits of cure: and as to the proposition that passion does not calculate, this, like most of these very general and oracular propositions, is not true. When matters of such importance as pain and pleasure are at stake, and these in the highest degree (the only matter, in short, that can be of importance) who is there that does not calculate? Men calculate, some with less exactness, indeed, some with more: but all men calculate. I would not say, that even a madman does not calculate. Passion calculates, more or less, in every man: in different men, according to the warmth or coolness of their dispositions: according to the firmness or irritability of their minds: according to the nature of the motives by which they are acted upon. Happily, of all passions, that is the most given to calculation, from the excesses of which, by reason of its strength, constance, and universality, society has most to apprehend: I mean that which corresponds to the motive of pecuniary interest: so that these niceties, if such they are to be called, have the best chance of being efficacious, where efficacy is of the most importance.

Chapter XV.

OF THE PROPERTIES TO BE GIVEN TO A
LOT OF PUNISHMENT.

I. It has been shown what the rules are, which ought to be observed in adjusting the proportion between the punishment and the offence. The properties to be given to a lot of punishment, in every instance, will, of course, be such as it stands in need of, in order to be capable of being applied, in conformity to those rules: the *quality* will be regulated by the *quantity*. . . .

XXVI. Upon taking a survey of the various possible modes of punishment, it will appear evidently, that there is not any one of them that possesses all the . . . [proper] properties in perfection. To do the best that can be done in the way of punishment, it will therefore be necessary, upon most occasions, to compound them, and make them into complex lots, each consisting of a number of different modes of punishment put together: the nature and proportions of the constituent parts of each lot being different, according to the nature of the offence which it is designed to combat.

XXVII. It may not be amiss to bring together, and exhibit in one view, the eleven properties above established. They are as follows:—

Two of them are concerned in establishing a proper proportion between a single offence and its punishment; viz.

1. Variability.
2. Equability.

One, in establishing a proportion between more offences than one, and more punishments than one; viz.

3. Commensurability.

A fourth contributes to place the punishment in that situation in which alone it can be efficacious; and at the same time to be bestowing on it the two further properties of exemplarity and popularity; viz.

4. Characteristicalness.

Two others are concerned in excluding all useless punishment; the one indirectly, by heightening the efficacy of what is useful; the other in a direct way; viz.

5. Exemplarity.
6. Frugality.

Three others contribute severally to the three inferior ends of punishment; viz.

7. Subserviency to reformation.
8. Efficacy in disabling.
9. Subserviency to compensation.

Another property tends to exclude a collateral mischief, which a particular mode of punishment is liable accidentally to produce; viz.

10. Popularity.

The remaining property tends to palliate a mischief, which all punishment, as such, is liable accidentally to produce; viz.

11. Remissibility.

The properties of commensurability, characteristicalness, exemplarity, subserviency to reformation, and efficacy in disabling, are more particularly calculated to augment the *profit* which is to be made by punishment: frugality, subserviency to compensation, popularity, and remissibility, to diminish the *expense:* variability and equability are alike subservient to both those purposes.

XXVIII. We now come to take a general survey of the system of *offences;* that is, of such *acts* to which, on account of the mischievous *consequences* they have a *natural* tendency to produce, and in the view of putting a stop to those consequences, it may be proper to annex a certain *artificial* consequence, consisting of punishment, to be inflicted on the authors of such acts, according to the principles just established.

Chapter XVI.

DIVISION OF OFFENCES.

[As this is by far the longest chapter of the book, so is it perhaps the most important, making as it does a panoramic sweep over everything that can be defined and classified by way of human action, and therefore everything that can and ought to be done by way of law. We give only a few excerpts to show Bentham's characteristic method of exhaustive bifurcation, for the importance of the chapter lies not in its substantive assertions but in its technique of definition and Linnaean classification.—M.P.M.]

1.   Classes of Offences.

I. It is necessary, at the outset, to make a distinction between such acts as *are* or *may* be, and such as *ought* to be offences.*

[*This chapter is an attempt to put our ideas of offences into an exact method. The particular uses of *method* are various: but the general one is, to enable men to understand the things that are the subjects of it. To understand a thing, is to be acquainted with its qualities or properties. Of these properties, some are common to it with other things; the rest, peculiar. But the qualities which are peculiar to any one sort of thing are few indeed, in comparison with those which are common to it with other things. To make it known in respect of its *difference,* would therefore be doing little, unless it were made known also by its *genus.* To understand it perfectly, a man must therefore be informed of the points in which it agrees, as well as of those in which it disagrees, with all other things. When a number of objects, composing a logical whole, are to be considered together, all of these possessing with respect to one another a certain congruency or agreement denoted by a certain name, there is but one way of giving a perfect knowledge of their nature; and that is, by distributing them into a system of parcels, each of them a part, either of some other parcel, or, at any rate, of the common whole. This can only be done in the way of *bipartition,* dividing each superior branch into two, and but two, immediately subordinate ones; beginning with the logical whole, dividing that into two parts, then each of those parts into two others; and so on. These first-distinguished parts agree in respect of those properties which belong to the whole; they differ in respect of those properties which are peculiar to each. To divide the whole into more than two parcels at once, for example into three, would not answer the purpose; for, in fact, it is but two objects that the mind can compare together exactly at the same time. Thus, then, let us endeavour to deal with offences; or rather, strictly speaking, with acts which possess such properties as seem to indicate them fit to be constituted offences. The task is arduous; and, as *yet* at least, perhaps *for ever,* above our force. There is no speaking of objects but by their names: but the business of giving them names has always been prior to the true and perfect knowledge of their natures. Objects the most dissimilar have been spoken of and treated as if their properties were the same. Objects the most similar have been spoken of and treated as if they had scarce any thing in common. Whatever discoveries may be made concerning them, how different soever their real congruencies and disagreements may be found to be from those which are indicated by their names, it is not without the utmost difficulty that any means can be found out of expressing those discoveries by other more apposite denominations. Change the import of the old names, and you are in perpetual danger of being misunderstood: introduce an entire new set of names, and you are sure not to be understood at all. Complete success, then, is, as yet at least, unattainable. But an attempt, though imperfect, may have its use: and, at the worst, it may accelerate the arrival of that perfect system, the possession of which will be the happiness of some maturer age. Gross ignorance descries no difficulties, imperfect knowledge finds them out, and struggles with them: it must be perfect knowledge that overcomes them.]

Any act *may* be an offence, which they whom the community are in the habit of obeying shall be pleased to make one: that is, any act which they shall be pleased to prohibit or to punish. But, upon the principle of utility, such acts alone *ought* to be made offences, as the good of the community requires should be made so.

II. The good of the community cannot require that any act should be made an offence, which is not liable, in some way or other, to be detrimental to the community. For in the case of such an act, all punishment is *groundless*.

III. But if the whole assemblage of any number of individuals be considered as constituting an imaginary compound *body*, a community or political state; any act that is detrimental to any one or more of those *members* is, as to so much of its effects, detrimental to the *state*.

IV. An act cannot be detrimental to a *state*, but by being detrimental to some one or more of the *individuals* that compose it. But these individuals may either be *assignable* or *unassignable*.

V. When there is any assignable individual to whom an offence is detrimental, that person may either be a person *other* than the offender, or the offender *himself.*

VI. Offences that are detrimental, in the first instance, to assignable persons other than the offender, may be termed by one common name, *offences against individuals*. And of these may be composed the 1st class of offences. To contrast them with offences of the 2d and 4th classes, it may also sometimes be convenient to style them *private* offences. To contrast them at the same time with offences of the 3d class, they may be styled *private extra-regarding* offences.

VII. When it appears, in general, that there are persons to whom the act in question may be detrimental, but such persons cannot be individually assigned, the circle within which it appears that they may be found, is either of less extent than that which comprises the whole community, or not. If of less, the persons comprised within this lesser circle may be considered for this purpose as composing a body of themselves; comprised within, but distinguishable from, the greater body of the whole community. The circumstance that constitutes the union between the members of this lesser body, may be either their residence within a particular place, or, in short, any other less explicit principle of union, which may serve to distinguish them from the remaining members of the community. In the first case, the act may be styled an *offence against a neighbourhood:* in the second, an offence against a particular class of persons in the community. Offences, then, against a class or neighbourhood, may, together, constitute the 2d class of offences. To contrast them with private offences on the one hand, and public on the other, they may also be styled *semi-public* offences.

VIII. Offences, which in the first instance are detrimental to the offender himself, and to no one else, unless it be by their being detrimental to himself, may serve to compose a third class. To contrast them the better with offences of the first, second, and fourth classes, all which are of a *transitive* nature, they might be styled *intransitive* offences; but better still, *self-regarding.*

IX. The fourth class may be composed of such acts as ought to be made offences, on account of the distant mischief which they threaten to bring upon an unassignable indefinite multitude of the whole number of individuals, of which the community is composed; although no particular individual should appear more likely to be a sufferer by them than another. They may be called *public* offences, or offences against the *state.*

X. A fifth class, or appendix, may be composed of such acts as, according to the circumstances in which they are committed, and more particularly according to the purposes to which they are applied, may be detrimental in any one of the ways in which the act of one man can be detrimental to another. These may be termed *multiform,* or *heterogeneous* offences. Offences that are in this case may be reduced to two great heads: 1. Offences by *falsehood:* and, 2. Offences against *trust.*

[Bentham therefore considered everything that could and ought to be done by way of law as classifiable under one or another of these five classes. In the rest of the chapter he took each class, one by one, and broke it down into ever finer gradations and subdivisions of genera and species. For example, we give part of his analysis of public offences—the most fascinating of all, because he here begins, in this dry, analytic, and seemingly unpromising way, for the first time to concern himself with problems of government and sovereignty, whose interest for him became ever more intense until it became the central focus of his studies.—M.P.M.]

2. Divisions and Sub-divisions.

XI. Let us see by what method these classes may be farther sub-divided. . . .

XVI. Public offences may be distributed under eleven divisions.*

[*In this part of the analysis, I have found it necessary to deviate in some degree from the rigid rules of the exhaustive method I set out with. By me, or by some one else, this method may, perhaps, be more strictly pursued at some maturer period of the science. At present, the benefit that might result from the unrelaxed observance of it, seemed so precarious, that I could not help doubting whether it would pay for the delay and trouble. Doubtless such a method is eminently instructive: but the fatigue of following it out is so great, not only to the author, but probably also to the reader, that if carried to its utmost length at the first attempt, it might perhaps do more disservice in the way of disgust, than service in the way of information. For knowledge, like physic, how salutary soever in itself, becomes no longer of any use, when made too unpalatable to be swallowed. Meantime, it cannot but be a mortifying circumstance to a writer, who is sensible of the importance of his subject, and anxious to do it justice, to find himself obliged to exhibit what he perceives to be faulty, with any view, how indistinct soever, of something more perfect before his eyes. If there be any thing new and original in this work it is to the exhaustive method, so often aimed at, that I am indebted for it. It will, therefore, be no great wonder if I should not be able to quit it without reluctance. On the other hand, the marks of stiffness which will doubtless be perceived in a multitude of places, are chiefly owing to a solicitous, and not perfectly successful, pursuit of this same method. New instruments are seldom handled at first with perfect ease.]

1. Offences against external *security*. 2. Offences against *justice*. 3. Offences against the *preventive* branch of the *police*. 4. Offences against the public *force*. 5. Offences against the *positive* increase of the national *felicity*. 6. Offences against the public *wealth*. 7. Offences against *population*. 8. Offences against the national *wealth*. 9. Offences against the *sovereignty*. 10. Offences against *religion*. 11. Offences against the national *interest* in general. The way in which these several sorts of offences connect with one another, and with the interest of the public, that is, of an unassignable multitude of the individuals of which that body is composed, may be thus conceived.

XVII. Mischief, by which the interest of the public, as above defined, may be affected, must, if produced at all, be produced either by means of an influence exerted on the operations of government, or by other means, without the exertion of such influence.*

[*The idea of government, it may be observed, is introduced here without any preparation. The fact of its being established, I assume as notorious, and the necessity of it as alike obvious and incontestible. . . .]

To begin with the latter case: mischief, be it what it will, and let it happen to whom it will, must be produced either by the unassisted powers of the agent in question, or by the instrumentality of some other agents. In the latter case, these agents will be either persons or things. Persons, again, must be either not members of the community in question, or members. Mischief produced by the instrumentality of persons, may accordingly be produced by the instrumentality either of *external* or of *internal* adversaries. . . . The only mischief, of any considerable account, which can be made to impend indiscriminately over the whole number of members in the community, is that complex kind of mischief which results from a state of war, and is produced by the instrumentality of external adversaries: by their being provoked, for instance, or invited, or encouraged to invasion. In this way may a man very well bring down a mischief, and that a very heavy one, upon the whole community in general, and that without taking a part in any of the injuries which came in consequence to be offered to particular individuals.

Next with regard to the mischief which an offence may bring upon the public by its influence on the operations of the government. This it may occasion either, 1. In a more immediate way, by its influence on those *operations* themselves: 2. In a more remote way, by its influence on the *instruments* by, or by the help of which those operations should be performed: or, 3. In a more remote way still, by its influence on the *sources* from whence such instruments are to be derived. First, then, as to the operations of government, the tendency of these, in as far as it is conformable to what on the principle of utility it ought to be, is in every case either to avert mischief from the community, or to make an addition to the sum of positive good.*

[*§This and the following note mark crucial states in Bentham's development. When he began as here to analyse the functions of government into positive good and preventive legislation, *i.e.*, the functions of the police—in his odd use of the word—he began to move away from the *laissez-faire* state into the realm of government intervention and social welfare. It was by way of analyses such as these that Bentham became if not an out-and-out socialist certainly more of one than John Stuart Mill. Bentham believed that the major handicaps to active government were ignorance and the lack of a trained civil service; but that when these should be supplied, there were few foreseeable limits to active government intervention.—M.P.M.§ This branch of the business of government, a sort of work of supererogation, as it may be called, in the calendar of political duty, is comparatively but of recent date. It is not for this that the untutored many could have originally submitted themselves to the dominion of the few. It was the dread of evil, not the hope of good, that first cemented societies together. Necessaries come always before luxuries. The state of language marks the progress of ideas. Time out of mind, the military department has had a name: so has that of justice: the power which occupies itself in preventing mischief, not till lately, and that but a loose one, the police: for the power which takes for its object the introduction of positive good, no peculiar name, however inadequate, seems yet to have been devised.]

Now mischief, we have seen, must come either from external adversaries, from internal adversaries, or from calamities. With regard to mischief from external adversaries, there requires no further division. As to mischief from internal adversaries, the expedients employed for averting it may be distinguished into such as may be applied *before* the discovery of any mischievous design in particular, and such as can not be employed but in consequence of the discovery of some such design: the former of these are commonly referred to a branch which may be styled the *prevention* branch of the *police:* the latter to that of justice.*

[*The functions of justice, and those of the police, must be apt, in many points, to run one into another, especially as the business would be very badly managed if the same persons, whose more particular duty it is to act as officers of the police, were not upon occasion to act in the capacity of officers of justice. The ideas, however, of the two functions may still be kept distinct: and I see not where the line of separation can be drawn, unless it be as above.

As to the word *police,* though of Greek extraction, it seems to be of French growth: it is from France, at least, that it has been imported into Great Britain, where it still retains its foreign garb: . . . Want of words obliged me to reduce the two branches here specified into one. Who would have endured, in this place, to have seen two such words as the *phthano-paranomic* or *crime-preventing* and the *phthano-symphoric* or *calamity-preventing,* branches of the police? The inconvenience of uniting the two branches under the same denomination, are, however, the less, inasmuch as the operations requisite to be performed for the two purposes will in many cases be the same. . . . §Here we have an excellent example of Bentham's life-long dilemma: to use old words for new ideas and be misunderstood, or to coin new ones and be ignored. In these early years he kept largely to the old terms; later on, especially in the *Chrestomathia* (1815), he gave way entirely to his neologist passion.—M.P.M.§]

Second, as to the instruments which government, whether in the averting of evil or in the producing of positive good, can have to work with, these must be either *persons* or *things.* . . . It is here to be observed, that if the influence exerted on any occasion by an individual over the operations of the government be pernicious, it must be in one or other of two ways: 1. By causing, or tending to cause, operations *not* to be performed which *ought* to be performed; in other words, by *impeding* the operations of government: or, 2. By causing operations to *be* performed which ought *not* to be performed; in other words, by *misdirecting* them. Last, to the total assemblage of the persons by whom the several political operations above mentioned come to be performed, we set out with applying the collective appellation of *the government.* Among these persons there *commonly* is some one person, or body of persons, whose office it is to assign and distribute to the rest their several departments, to determine the conduct to be pursued by each in the performance of the particular set of operations that belongs to him, and even upon occasion to exercise his function in his stead. Where there is any such person, or body of persons, *he* or *it* may, according as the turn of the phrase requires, be termed *the sovereign,* or *the sovereignty.* Now it is evident, that to impede or misdirect the operations of the sovereign . . . may be to impede or misdirect the operations of the several departments of government, as described above.

From this analysis, by which the connection between the several above-mentioned heads of offences is exhibited, we may now collect a definition for each article. By *offences against external security,* we may understand such offences whereof the tendency is to bring upon the public a mischief resulting from the hostilities of foreign adversaries. By *offences against justice,* such offences whereof the tendency is to impede or misdirect the operations of that power, which is employed in the business of guarding the public against the mischiefs resulting from the delinquency of internal adversaries, as far as it is to be done by expedients, which do not come to be applied in any case till *after* the discovery of some particular design of the sort of those which they are calculated to prevent. By *offences against the preventive branch of the police,* such offences whereof the tendency is to impede or misdirect the operations of that power, which is employed in guarding against mischiefs resulting from the delinquency of internal adversaries, by expedients that come to be applied *beforehand;* or of that which is employed in guarding against the mischiefs that might be occasioned by physical calamities. By *offences against the public force,* such offences whereof the tendency is to impede or misdirect the operations of that power which is destined to guard the public from the mischiefs which may result from the hostility of foreign adversaries, and, in case of necessity, in the capacity of ministers of justice, from mischiefs of the number of those which result from the delinquency of internal adversaries. By *offences against the increase of the national felicity,* such offences whereof the tendency is to impede or misapply the operations of those powers that are employed in conducting of various establishments, which are calculated to make, in so many different ways, a positive addition to the stock of public happiness. By *offences against the public wealth,* such offences whereof the tendency is to diminish the amount, or misdirect the application, of the money and other articles of wealth, which the government reserves as a fund, out of which the stock of instruments employed in the service above mentioned may be kept up. By *offences against population,* such offences whereof the tendency is to diminish the numbers, or impair the political value, of the sum total of the members of the community. By *offences against the national wealth,* such offences whereof the tendency is to diminish the quantity or impair the value, of the things which compose the separate properties or estates of the several members of the community. . . .

Chapter XVII.

OF THE LIMITS OF THE PENAL BRANCH OF JURISPRUDENCE.

1. *Limits between Private Ethics and the Art of Legislation.*

I. So much for the division of offences in general. Now an offence is an act prohibited or (what comes to the same thing) an act of which the contrary is commanded by the law: and what is it that the law can be employed in doing, besides prohibiting and commanding? It should seem, then, according to this view of the matter, that were we to have settled what may be proper to be done with relation to offences, we should thereby have settled every thing that may be proper to be done in the way of law. Yet that branch which concerns the method of dealing with offences, and which is termed sometimes the *criminal,* sometimes the *penal,* branch, is universally understood to be but one out of two branches which compose the whole subject of the art of legislation; that which is termed the *civil* being the other.*

[*And the *constitutional* branch, what is become of it? Such is the question which many a reader will be apt to put. An answer that might be given is, that the matter of it might without much violence be distributed under the other two heads. But, as far as recollection serves, that branch, notwithstanding its importance, and its capacity of being lodged separately from the other matter, had at that time scarcely presented itself to my view in the character of a distinct one: the thread of my inquiries had not as yet reached it. But in the concluding note of this same chapter . . . the omission may be seen in some measure supplied. §This is one of the most significant of all Bentham's footnotes which, as we have seen, are often more profoundly important than the text itself. From this time forward he began to consider constitutional law the most important of all subjects, and he was still working on his great *Constitutional Code* when he died.— M.P.M.§]

Between these two branches, then, it is evident enough there cannot but be a very intimate connection; so intimate is it indeed, that the limits between them are by no means easy to mark out. The case is the same in some degree between the whole business of legislation (civil and penal branches taken together) and that of private ethics. Of these several limits, however, it will be in a manner necessary to exhibit some idea: lest, on the one hand, we should seem to leave any part of the subject that *does* belong to us untouched, or, on the other hand, to deviate on any side into a track which does *not* belong to us.

In the course of this inquiry, that part of it I mean which concerns the limits between the civil and penal branch of law, it will be necessary to settle a number of points, of which the connection with the main question might not at first sight be suspected. To ascertain what sort of a thing *a* law is; what the *parts* are, that are to be found in it; what it must contain in order to be *complete;* what the connection is between that part of a body of laws which belongs to the subject of *procedure,* and the rest of the law at large:—All these, it will be seen, are so many problems, which must be solved before any satisfactory answer can be given to the main question above mentioned.

Nor is this their only use, for it is evident enough, that the notion of a complete law must first be fixed, before the legislator can in any case know what it is he has to do, or when his work is done.

II. Ethics at large may be defined, the art of directing men's actions to the production of the greatest possible quantity of happiness, on the part of those whose interest is in view.

III. What, then, are the actions which it can be in a man's power to direct? They must be either his own actions, or those of other agents. Ethics, in as far as it is the art of directing a man's own actions, may be styled the *art of self-government,* or *private ethics.*

IV. What other agents, then, are there, which, at the same time that they are under the influence of man's direction, are susceptible of happiness? They are of two sorts: 1. Other human beings, who are styled persons. 2. Other animals, which on account of their interests having been neglected by the insensibility of the ancient jurists, stand degraded into the class of *things.* As to other human beings, the art of directing their actions to the above end is what we mean, or at least the only thing which, upon the principle of utility, we *ought* to mean, by the art of government: which, in as far as the measures it displays itself in are of a permanent nature, is generally distinguished by the name of *legislation:* as it is by that of *administration,* when they are of a temporary nature, determined by the occurrences of the day.

V. Now human creatures, considered with respect to the maturity of their faculties, are either in an *adult,* or in a *non-adult* state. The art of government, in as far as it concerns the direction of the actions of persons in a non-adult state, may be termed the art of *education.* In as far as this business is entrusted with those who, in virtue of some private relationship, are in the main the best disposed to take upon them, and the best able to discharge, this office, it may be termed the art of *private education:* in as far as it is exercised by those whose province it is to superintend the conduct of the whole community, it may be termed the art of *public education.*

VI. As to ethics in general, a man's happiness will depend, in the first place, upon such parts of his behaviour as none but himself are interested in; in the next place, upon such parts of it as may affect the happiness of those about him. In as far as his happiness depends upon the first-mentioned part of his behaviour, it is said to depend upon his *duty to himself.* Ethics, then, in as far as it is the art of directing a man's actions in this respect, may be termed the art of discharging one's duty to one's self: and the quality which a man manifests by the discharge of this branch of duty (if duty it is to be called), is that of *prudence.* In as far as his happiness, and that of any other person or persons whose interests are considered, depends upon such parts of his behaviour as may affect the interests of those about him, it may be said to depend upon his *duty to others;* or, to use a phrase now somewhat antiquated, his *duty to his neighbour.* Ethics, then, in as far as it is the art of directing a man's actions in this respect, may be termed the art of discharging one's duty to one's neighbour. Now the happiness of one's neighbour may be consulted in two ways: 1. In a negative way, by forbearing to diminish it. 2. In a positive way, by studying to increase it. A man's duty to his neighbour is accordingly partly negative and partly positive: to discharge the negative branch of it, is *probity:* to discharge the positive branch, *beneficence.*

VII. It may here be asked, how it is that upon the principle of private ethics, legislation and religion out of the question, a man's happiness depends upon such parts of his conduct as affect, immediately at least, the happiness of no one but himself: this is as much as to ask, What motives (independent of such as legislation and religion may chance to furnish) can one man have to consult the happiness of another? by what motives, or (which comes to the same thing) by what obligations, can he be bound to obey the dictates of *probity* and *beneficence?* In answer to this, it cannot but be admitted, that the only interests which a man at all times and upon all occasions is sure to find *adequate* motives for consulting, are his own. Notwithstanding this, there are no occasions in which a man has not some motives for consulting the happiness of other men. In the first place, he has, on all occasions, the purely social motive of sympathy or benevolence: in the next place, he has, on most occasions, the semi-social motives of love of amity and love of reputation. The motive of sympathy will act upon him with more or less effect, according to the *bias* of his sensibility: the two other motives, according to a variety of circumstances, principally according to the strength of his intellectual powers, the firmness and steadiness of his mind, the quantum of his moral sensibility, and the characters of the people he has to deal with.

VIII. Now private ethics has happiness for its end: and legislation can have no other. Private ethics concerns every member; that is, the happiness and the actions of every member of any community that can be proposed: and legislation can concern no more. Thus far, then, private ethics and the art of legislation go hand in hand. The end they have, or ought to have, in view, is of the same nature. The persons whose happiness they ought to have in view, as also the persons whose conduct they ought to be occupied in directing, are precisely the same. The very acts they ought to be conversant about, are even in a *great measure* the same. Where, then, lies the difference? In that the acts which they ought to be conversant about, though in a great measure, are not *perfectly and throughout* the same. There is no case in which a private man ought not to direct his own conduct to the production of his own happiness, and of that of his fellow-creatures: but there are cases in which the legislator ought not (in a direct way at least, and by means of punishment applied immediately to particular *individual* acts) to attempt to direct the conduct of the several other members of the community. Every act which promises to be beneficial upon the whole to the community (himself included), each individual ought to perform of himself: but it is not every such act that the legislator ought to compel him to perform. Every act which promises to be pernicious upon the whole to the community (himself included), each individual ought to abstain from of himself; but it is not every such act that the legislator ought to compel him to abstain from.

IX. Where, then, is the line to be drawn?—We shall not have far to seek for it. The business is to give an idea of the cases in which ethics ought, and in which legislation ought not (in a direct manner at least) to interfere. If legislation interferes in a direct manner, it must be by punishment. Now the cases in which punishment, meaning the punishment of the political sanction, ought not to be inflicted, have been already stated. If, then, there be any of these cases in which, although legislation ought not, private ethics does or ought to interfere, these cases will serve to point out the limits between the two arts or branches of science. These cases, it may be remembered, are of four sorts: 1. Where punishment would be groundless. 2. Where it would be inefficacious. 3. Where it would be unprofitable. 4. Where it would be needless. Let us look over all these cases, and see whether in any of them there is room for the interference of private ethics, at the same time that there is none for the direct interference of legislation.

X. 1. First, then, as to the cases where punishment would be *groundless*. In these cases it is evident, that the restrictive interference of ethics would be groundless too. It is because, upon the whole, there is no evil in the act, that legislation ought not to endeavour to prevent it. No more, for the same reason, ought private ethics.

XI. 2. As to the cases in which punishment would be *inefficacious*. These, we may observe, may be divided into two sets or classes. The first do not depend at all upon the nature of the act: they turn only upon a defect in the timing of the punishment. . . . These are the cases of an *ex-post facto* law; of a judicial sentence beyond the law; and of a law not sufficiently promulgated. . . . As to the other set of cases, in which punishment would be inefficacious; neither do these depend upon the nature of the act, that is, of the *sort* of act: they turn only upon some extraneous *circumstances,* with which an act of *any* sort may chance to be accompanied. These, however, are of such a nature as not only to exclude the application of legal punishment, but in general to leave little room for the influence of private ethics. These are the cases where the will could not be deterred from any act, even by the extraordinary force of artificial punishment; as in the cases of extreme infancy, insanity, and perfect intoxication: of course, therefore, it could not by such slender and precarious force as could be applied by private ethics. . . .

XII. 3. As to the cases where punishment would be *unprofitable.* These are the cases which constitute the great field for the exclusive interference of private ethics. When a punishment is unprofitable, or in other words too expensive, it is because the evil of the punishment exceeds that of the offence.

XIII. Punishment, then, as applied to delinquency, may be unprofitable in both or either of two ways: 1. By the expense it would amount to, even supposing the application of it to be confined altogether to delinquency: 2. By the danger there may be of its involving the innocent in the fate designed only for the guilty. . . . Thus it is wherever the danger of detection is, (or what comes to the same thing,) is likely to appear to be, so small, as to make the punishment appear in a high degree uncertain. . . . Let the *seducing* motives be strong, the offence then will at any rate be frequently committed. Now and then indeed, owing to a coincidence of circumstances more or less extraordinary, it will be detected and by that means punished. But for the purpose of example, which is the principal one, an act of punishment, considered in itself, is of no use: what use it can be of, depends altogether upon the expectation it raises of similar punishment in future cases of similar delinquency. But this future punishment, it is evident, must always depend upon detection. If then the want of detection is such as must in general (especially to eyes fascinated by the force of the seducing motives) appear too improbable to be reckoned upon, the punishment, though it should be inflicted, may come to be of no use. Here, then, will be two opposite evils running on at the same time, yet neither of them reducing the quantum of the other: the evil of the disease and the evil of the painful and inefficacious remedy. It seems to be partly owing to some such considerations, that fornication for example, or the illicit commerce between the sexes, has commonly either gone altogether unpunished, or been punished in a degree inferior to that in which, on other accounts, legislators might have been disposed to punish it. . . .

XV. For the sake of obtaining the clearer idea of the limits between the art of legislation and private ethics, it may now be time to call to mind the distinctions above established with regard to ethics in general. The degree in which private ethics stands in need of the assistance of legislation, is different in the three branches of duty above distinguished. Of the rules of moral duty, those which seem to stand least in need of the assistance of legislation, are the rules of *prudence*. It can only be through some defect on the part of the understanding, if a man be ever deficient in point of duty to himself. If he does wrong, there is nothing else that it can be owing to, but either some *inadvertence* or some *missupposal,* with regard to the circumstances on which his happiness depends. It is a standing topic of complaint, that a man knows too little of himself. Be it so: but is it so certain that the legislator must know more? It is plain, that of individuals the legislator can know nothing: concerning those points of conduct which depend upon the particular circumstances of each individual, it is plain, therefore, that he can determine nothing to advantage. It is only with respect to those broad lines of conduct in which all persons, or very large and permanent descriptions of persons, may be in a way to engage, that he can have any pretence for interfering; and even here the propriety of his interference will, in most instances, lie very open to dispute. At any rate, he must never expect to produce a perfect compliance by the mere force of the sanction of which he is himself the author. All he can hope to do, is to increase the efficacy of private ethics, by giving strength and direction to the influence of the moral sanction. With what chance of success, for example, would a legislator go about to extirpate drunkenness and fornication, by dint of legal punishment? Not all the tortures which ingenuity could invent would compass it: and, before he had made any progress worth regarding, such a mass of evil would be produced by the punishment, as would exceed, a thousand-fold, the utmost possible mischief of the offence. The great difficulty would be in the procuring evidence; an object which could not be attempted, with any probability of success, without spreading dismay through every family, tearing the bonds of sympathy asunder, and rooting out the influence of all the social motives. All that he can do, then, against offences of this nature, with any prospect of advantage, in the way of direct legislation, is to subject them, in cases of notoriety, to a slight censure, so as thereby to cover them with a slight shade of artificial disrepute.

XVI. It may be observed, that with regard to this branch of duty, legislators have, in general, been disposed to carry their interference full as far as is expedient. The great difficulty here is, to persuade them to confine themselves within bounds. A thousand little passions and prejudices have led them to narrow the liberty of the subject in this line, in cases in which the punishment is either attended with no profit at all, or with none that will make up for the expense. . . .

XIX. As to the rules of beneficence, these, as far as concerns matters of detail, must necessarily be abandoned in great measure to the jurisdiction of private ethics. In many cases the beneficial quality of the act depends essentially upon the disposition of the agent: that is, upon the motives by which he appears to have been prompted to perform it: upon their belonging to the head of sympathy, love of amity, or love of reputation; and not to any head of self-regarding motives, brought into play by the force of political constraint: in a word, upon their being such as denominate his conduct *free* and *voluntary*, according to one of the many senses given to those ambiguous expressions. The limits of the law on this head seem, however, to be capable of being extended a good deal farther than they seem ever to have been extended hitherto. In particular, in cases where the person is in danger, why should it not be made the duty of every man to save another from mischief, when it can be done without prejudicing himself, as well as to abstain from bringing it on him? This, accordingly, is the idea pursued in the body of the work.

XX. To conclude this section, let us recapitulate and bring to a point the difference between private ethics, considered as an art or science, on the one hand, and that branch of jurisprudence which contains the art or science of legislation, on the other. Private ethics teaches how each man may dispose himself to pursue the course most conducive to his own happiness, by means of such motives as offer of themselves: the art of legislation (which may be considered as one branch of the science of jurisprudence) teaches how a multitude of men, composing a community, may be disposed to pursue that course which upon the whole is the most conducive to the happiness of the whole community, by means of motives to be applied by the legislator.

We come now to exhibit the limits between penal and civil jurisprudence. For this purpose it may be of use to give a distinct though
summary view of the principal branches into which jurisprudence, considered in its utmost extent, is wont to be divided.

2.   *Jurisprudence, its Branches*

XXI. Jurisprudence is a fictitious entity: nor can any meaning be found
for the word, but by placing it in company with some word that shall
be significative of a real entity. To know what is meant by jurisprudence,
we must know, for example, what is meant by a book of jurisprudence.
A book of jurisprudence can have but one or the other of two objects:
1. To ascertain what the *law* is: 2. To ascertain what it ought to be. In
the former case, it may be styled a book of *expository* jurisprudence:
in the latter, a book of *censorial* jurisprudence, or, in other words, a
book on the *art of legislation.*

XXII. A book of expository jurisprudence is either *authoritative* or
unauthoritative. It is styled authoritative, when it is composed by him
who, by representing the state of the law to be so and so, causeth it so
to be; that is, of the legislator himself: unauthoritative, when it is the
work of any other person at large. . . .

XXIV. In the first place, in point of extent, what is delivered concerning the laws in question, may have reference either to the laws of such
or such a nation or nations in particular, or to the laws of all nations
whatsoever: in the first case, the book may be said to relate to *local;* in
the other, to *universal, jurisprudence.* . . .

XXV. In the second place, with regard to the *political quality* of the
persons whose conduct is the object of the law. These may, on any given
occasion, be considered either as members of the same state, or as members
of different states: in the first case, the law may be referred to the head
of *internal;* in the second case, to that of *international* [Bentham's own
coinage.—M.P.M.] jurisprudence. . . .

[Thus Bentham continues with his method of exhaustive bifurcation, distinguishing further between national and provincial law; ancient and present
or living jurisprudence; statute and customary law.—M.P.M.]

XXIX. Last, the most intricate distinction of all, and that which comes
most frequently on the carpet, is that which is made between the *civil*
branch of jurisprudence and the *penal;* which latter is wont, in certain
circumstances, to receive the name of *criminal.*

What is a penal code of laws? What a civil code? Of what nature are
their contents? Is it that there are two sorts of laws, the one penal and
the other civil, so that the laws in a penal code are all penal laws, while
the laws in a civil code are all civil laws? Or is it, that in every law there

is some matter which is of a penal nature, and which therefore belongs to the penal code; and at the same time other matter which is of a civil nature, and which therefore belongs to the civil code. Or is it, that some laws belong to one code or the other exclusively, while others are divided between the two? To answer these questions in any manner that shall be tolerably satisfactory, it will be necessary to ascertain what *a law* is; meaning one entire but single law: and what are the parts into which a law, as such, is capable of being distinguished: or, in other words, to ascertain what the properties are that are to be found in every object which can with propriety receive the appellation of a law. This, then, will be the business of the third and fourth sections: what concerns the import of the word criminal, as applied to law, will be discussed separately in the fifth.*

[*Here ends the original work, in the state into which it was brought in November 1780. What follows is now added in January 1789.

1. The third, fourth, and fifth sections, intended, as expressed in the text, to have been added to this chapter, will not here, nor now, be given; because to give them in a manner tolerably complete and satisfactory, might require a considerable volume. This volume will form a work of itself. §And so it did; *cf.* the excerpts from *The Limits of Jurisprudence Defined,* pp. 147*ff.* below—M.P.M.§. . . .

What follows here may serve to give a slight intimation of the nature of the task, which such a work will have to achieve: it will at the same time furnish, not any thing like a satisfactory answer to the questions mentioned, but a slight and general indication of the course to be taken for giving them such an answer.

2. What is a law? what the parts of a law? The subject of these questions, it is to be observed, is the *logical,* the *ideal,* the *intellectual* whole, not the *physical* one: the *law,* and not the *statute.* An inquiry, directed to the latter sort of object, could neither admit of difficulty nor afford instruction. In this sense, whatever is given for law by the person or persons recognised as possessing the power of making laws, is *law.* The Metamorphoses of Ovid, if thus given, would be law. So much as was embraced by one and the same act of authentication, so much as received the touch of the sceptre at one stroke, is one law: a whole law, and nothing more. . . . By the word *law,* then, as often as it occurs in the succeeding pages, is meant that ideal object, of which the part, the whole, or the multiple, or an assemblage of parts, whole, and multiples mixed together, is exhibited by a statute; not the statute which exhibits them.

3. Every law, when complete, is either of a *coercive* or *uncoercive* nature. A coercive law is a *command.* . . .

5. Every coercive law creates an *offence;* that is, converts an act of some sort or other into an offence. It is only by so doing that it can *impose obligation,* that it can *produce coercion.* . . .

15. After this explanation, a general proposition or two, that may be laid down, may help to afford some little insight into the structure and

contents of a complete body of laws.—So many different sorts of *offences* created, so many different laws of the *coercive* kind: so many *exceptions* taken out of the descriptions of these offences, so many laws of the *discoercive* kind.

To class *offences,* as hath been attempted to be done in the preceding chapter, is therefore to class *laws:* to exhibit a complete catalogue of all the offences created by law, including the whole mass of expository matter necessary for fixing and exhibiting the import of the terms contained in the several laws, by which those offences are respectively created, would be to exhibit a complete collection of the laws in force: in a word, a complete body of law, a *pannomion,* if so it might be termed. §Another of Bentham's neologisms; an absolutely fundamental term in the system, the name of his life-long ambition.—M.P.M.§ . . .

The question, *What parts of the total mass of legislative matter belong to the civil branch, and what to the penal?* supposes that divers political states, or at least that some one such state, are to be found, having as well a civil code as a penal code, each of them complete in its kind, and marked out by certain limits. But no one such state has ever yet existed.

To put a question to which a true answer can be given, we must substitute to the foregoing question some such one as that which follows:

Suppose two masses of legislative matter to be drawn up at this time of day, the one under the name of a civil code, the other of a penal code, each meant to be complete in its kind: in what general way is it nature to suppose that the different sorts of matter, as above distinguished, would be distributed between them?

To this question the following answer seems likely to come as near as any other to the truth.

The *civil* code would not consist of a collection of civil laws each complete in itself, as well as clear of all penal ones.

Neither would the *penal* code (since we have seen that it *could* not) consist of a collection of punitive laws, each not only complete in itself, but clear of all civil ones. But

17. The civil code would consist chiefly of mere masses of expository matter. The imperative matter, to which those masses of expository matter respectively appertained, would be found—not in that same code—not in the civil code—nor in a pure state, free from all admixture of punitory laws; but in the penal code—in a state of combination—involved, in manner as above explained, in so many correspondent punitory laws.

18. The penal code then would consist principally of punitive laws, involving the imperative matter of the whole number of civil laws: along with which would probably also be found various masses of expository matter, appertaining, not to the civil, but to the punitory laws. The body of penal law, enacted by the Empress-Queen Maria Theresa, agrees pretty well with this account. . . .

22. Besides the civil and the penal, every complete body of law must contain a third branch, the *constitutional.*

The constitutional branch is chiefly employed in conferring, on particular classes of persons, *powers,* to be exercised for the good of the whole society, or of considerable parts of it, and prescribing *duties* to the persons invested with those powers. . . .

23. Thus it is, that one and the same law, one and the same command,

will have its matter divided, not only between two great codes, or main branches of the whole body of the laws, the civil and the penal; but amongst three such branches, the civil, the penal, and the constitutional. . . .

25. Had the science of architecture no fixed nomenclature belonging to it—were there no settled names for distinguishing the different sorts of buildings, nor the different parts of the same building from each other—what would it be? It would be what the science of legislation, considered with respect to its *form,* remains at present.

Were there no architects who could distinguish a dwelling-house from a barn, or a side wall from a ceiling, what would architects be? They would be what all legislators are at present.

26. From this very slight and imperfect sketch may be collected, not an answer to the questions in the text, but an intimation, and that but an imperfect one, of the course to be taken for giving such an answer; and, at any rate, some idea of the difficulty, as well as of the necessity of the task.

If it were thought necessary to recur to experience for proofs of this difficulty, and this necessity, they need not be long wanting.

Take, for instance, so many well-meant endeavours on the part of popular bodies, and so many well-meant recommendations in ingenious books, to restrain supreme representative assemblies from making laws in such and such cases, to such and such an effect. Such laws, to answer the intended purpose, require a perfect mastery in the science of law, considered in respect of its form—in the sort of anatomy spoken of in the preface to this work: but a perfect, even a moderate insight into that science, would prevent their being couched in those loose and inadequate terms, in which they may be observed so frequently to be conceived; as a perfect acquaintance with the dictates of utility on that head would, in many, if not in most, of those instances, discounsel the attempt. Keep to the letter, and in attempting to prevent the making of bad laws you will find them prohibiting the making of the most necessary laws, perhaps even of all law: quit the letter, and they express no more than if each man were to say, *Your laws shall become ipso facto void, as often as they contain any thing which is not to my mind.*

Of such unhappy attempts, examples may be met with in the legislation of many nations: but in none more frequently than in that newly-created nation §the United States§, one of the most enlightened, if not the most enlightened, at this day on the globe.

27. Take for instance, the *Declaration of Rights,* enacted by the state of North-Carolina, in convention, in or about the month of September 1788, and said to be copied, with a small exception from one in like manner by the state of Virginia.

The following, to go no farther, is the first and fundamental article:—

"That there are certain natural rights, of which men, when they form a social compact, cannot deprive or divest their posterity, among which are the enjoyment of life and liberty, with the means of acquiring, possessing, and protecting property, and pursuing and obtaining happiness and safety."

Not to dwell on the oversight of confining to posterity the benefit of the rights thus declared, what follows? That—as against those whome the protection, thus meant to be afforded, included—every law, or other order, *divesting* a man of *the enjoyment of life or liberty* is voide.

Therefore this is the case, amongst other, with every coercive law.

Therefore, as against the persons thus protected, every order, for example, to pay money on the score of taxation, or of debt from individual to individual, or otherwise, is void: for the effect of it, if complied with, is "to *deprive* and *divest him,*" *pro tanto,* of the enjoyment of liberty, viz. the liberty of paying or not paying as he thinks proper: not to mention the species opposed to imprisonment, in the event of such a mode of coercion being resorted to: likewise of property, which is itself a *"means of acquiring, possessing, and protecting property, and of pursuing and obtaining happiness and safety."*

Therefore also, as against such persons, every order to attack an armed enemy, in time of war, is also void: for, the necessary effect of such an order is *"to deprive* some of them *of the enjoyment of life."*

The above-mentioned consequences may suffice for examples, amongst an endless train of similar ones.

Leaning on his elbow, in an attitude of profound and solem meditation, *"What a multitude of things there are,"* exclaimed the dancing-master Marcel, *"in a minuet!"*—May we now add?—*and in a law!*]

The Limits of Jurisprudence
Defined

A Note on *The Limits of Jurisprudence Defined*

The Limits of Jurisprudence Defined was a maze when Bentham wrote it; it is no less a maze today. It is very dry and difficult, perhaps the least graceful of all his works; and almost strictly a bare dictionary. In *An Introduction* he was largely concerned with the vocabulary of ethics and psychology; here he was largely concerned with the vocabulary of law and government: civil and penal law, law generally, command, duty, punishment, power, right, prohibition, obligation, burden, immunity, exemption, privilege, property, security, liberty.

This is a book of paraphrasis, an attempt to define all these fictions of law in terms of ultimate sense impressions, the final words or phrases that refer directly to immediate experience, to pleasures and pains; and for Bentham one such ultimate term is law, which is not a fiction. Law is a command, a command that creates duties, which in turn delimit rights. And neither of these is meaningful without the power to implement them—and so on through the entire dictionary. Here he considers duty as the first fiction from which all the others follow.

Just as in school grammar, then, Bentham offered these terms as propositions that could be parsed or broken down; and the entire structure of the dictionary and the propositions he called "the logic of the will"—an entirely new logic, and his proudest invention. He explained it at greater length in *The Limits* than anywhere else. "The subject we are now enter-

145

ing upon belongs to a particular branch of logic, untouched by Aristotle. The main and ultimate business of the school-logic of which that philosopher was the father, is to exhibit the several forms of *argumentation:* the business of the branch now before us is to exhibit the several forms of *imperation:* or (to take the subject in its utmost extent) of sentences expressive of volition: a leaf which seems to be yet wanting in the book of science."[1] Bentham dreamed a great vision, that one day the law would be completely codified as a logic of the will, and that great schools of law would be crowded with students, eagerly parsing the commands of the new volitional logic.

It is almost impossible to imagine a book less designed for gay, charming, intimate boudoir reading than the stubbornly gritty *Limits,* and yet these intractable pages found their first audience among the shy, lovely ladies of Lord Shelburne's family in their boudoir over the teacups at Bowood. The equally shy and charming Bentham was their great favorite, and Lord Shelburne, convinced of and "awestruck"[2] by his great genius, read them pages from the work in progress. Bentham sat by, ready to explain the knottier passages. During his first long visit, he was struggling with *The Limits;* one wonders what the ladies made of it. They cannot have been too repelled, for he remained a favorite and, indeed, was the only friend outside the family whom Lady Shelburne permitted at her deathbed.

Technically these pages are not a separate book, but the enormously unwieldy Chapter XVII of *An Introduction.*[3] It was here that Bentham spun himself unexpectedly into a metaphysical mizmaze, and here that he groped his way out by means of paraphrasis and the logic of the will. Here again, as in almost every work he ever wrote, he drew analogies between mathematics and medicine, and legislation.

Here, too, he drew attention to his next major work, the even longer Chapter XVIII on *Indirect Legislation.*[4]

---

[1] See p. 156, below.
[2] X. p. 122.
[3] See above, p. 73.
[4] See below. p. 168.

The Limits of Jurisprudence Defined

Being Part Two of *An Introduction to the Principles of Morals and Legislation*

Chapter 1. *Distinction between Penal Law and Civil.*

So much for private ethics on the one hand and jurisprudence on the other. We come now to speak of what is called a civil law or jurisprudence on the one hand and penal law or jurisprudence on the other: or more properly to the art of legislation in civil matters on the one hand, and the art of legislation in penal matters on the other. Between these two branches which are so often set in opposition to one another where then lies the distinction? Nowhere. They are inextricably interwoven. What individual law is civil and not penal? There is no such thing. What law is penal and not civil? There is no such thing. In every law must be comprised two things: 1. a specification of the cases in which the punishment is to attach; 2. a specification of the punishment itself: without punishment, no such thing as law: without a motive no such thing as action.

The individuation of a law, I mean the description of that which is to be looked upon as neither more nor less than one entire law, is as yet a matter altogether unsettled and obscure: nor is this a place for entering into those details which would be necessary to clear it up. But be it settled anyhow, still it will be equally impossible to draw any precise line between the penal branch as shall discriminate effectively what is delivered concerning the art of treating one of those branches from that of treating the other. Let every assemblage of words that forms a sentence and composes a part of the body of a law be looked upon as constituting an entire law: the proposition would not be the less true. On this supposition every such sentence in which no mention was made of punishment should belong to the civil branch of the law: every sentence in which punishment was mentioned, to the penal branch. Would this be admissible? Certainly not. For never was there a code called a penal

147

one which did not contain abundance of sentences in which there was not the least mention of such a thing as punishment.

Is law to be deemed a species of command? and is that to be deemed one law which constitutes one command? Neither in this way could we find any distinction between what is called the civil branch and the penal. In this case if every law must have a punishment to back it, part of every law would belong to the civil branch, while the other part belonged to the penal.

Suppose even a law to which no punishment was annexed by the legislator; still however a punishment it must have. It might derive it from the moral sanction: it might derive it from the religious sanction: but some punishment at any rate it must have; else it would not be a law; else obtain obedience: it would not have any of the effect of what is really a law.

In the law itself then there is no such distinction to be met with. What distinction there is respects the books that happen to be written on the subject of the law. That book belongs to the subject of penal jurisprudence which has most in it about punishment: that book belongs to the civil branch which has least in it about punishment itself, and most about the cases in which punishment is or is not to be applied. . . .

Whatever business the law may be conversant about, may be reduced to one sort of operation, viz: that of creating duties. To make duties, in the first place it must define them: in the next place it must mark out the punishments to be inflicted for the breach of them.*

[*It is by creating duties and by nothing else that the law can create rights. When the law gives you a right, what does it do? it makes me liable to punishment in case of my doing any of those acts which would have the effect of disturbing you in the exercise of that right.]

Here then are two operations distinguishable in themselves, though for use they must always be conjoined. In point of expression it may take more words to perform them or it may take fewer.

After a manner, they may be performed, both of them together in a single sentence: in which case they will shew as if in substance they were but one.

"Whosoever stealeth, shall be hanged." That might do, after a certain sort, for a law against Theft. In saying thus much an inexperienced or negligent legislator might think he had done enough. In this style accordingly were conceived the first crude attempts at legislation. But what is meant by stealing? for the ideas meant to be represented by this word are certainly not so obvious to present themselves to every man alike without difficulty or danger of mistake. To explain this sufficiently will at any rate take up another sentence: It may take up a paragraph, a page, a volume.

Were a man to put together all that has ever been written in this view, it might perhaps take up a multitude of volumes. Suppose a single one: it is plain that in this whole volume there need not be a syllable about punishment. Yet to punishment it must have reference: and before it amounts to much as any one single law it must be enjoined with some clause by which punishment is appointed. It is a part however of the mass of jurisprudence: that which has been written with or without authority upon the subject of the laws in general. Is it then a part of the penal branch of jurisprudence? But it contains not a syllable about punishment. Is it a part of the civil branch? But it has a necessary reference to punishment, without which it would be nugatory and unavailing. Will this necessary reference then which it has to punishment serve to conjoin it to the penal branch? Not so neither: for the same necessary reference has everything that comes under the head of law. A regulation belonging to the constitutional branch of law has it as much as any other. What then after all is the difference, such as it is, between the penal branch of the law and the civil? or rather between a book written on the subject of penal law and a book written on the subject of civil law? That book belongs to the penal branch which dwells most upon the subject of punishment: that to the civil which without making any mention or at least without making much mention of the article of punishment, dwells most upon the cases in which punishment is or is not to be applied.

Chapter 2.   Analysis and Exposition.

Analysis: Power, right, prohibition, duty, obligation, burthen, immunity, exemption, privilege, property, security, liberty—all these with a multitude of others that might be named are so many fictitious entities which the law upon one occasion or another' is spoken of in common speech as creating or disposing of. Not an operation does it ever perform, but it is considered as creating or in some manner or other disposing of these its imaginary productions. All this it is plain is the mere work of the fancy: a kind of allegory: a riddle of which the solution is not otherwise to be given than by giving the history of the operations which the law performs in that case with regard to certain real entities. Would a man know what it is that the law really does in any case, and in what condition it leaves the parties that are concerned? He must know in such case the acts which it takes into contemplation, and the aspect which it bears to them. He must know who the persons, and what the things, if any, which are in question: what the acts are of those persons, whether for their termination they look to other persons or to things: and in what circumstances if in any the act is prohibited or permitted, commanded or left uncommanded. Knowing thus much, we shall have ideas to our words: not knowing it, we shall have none. The ingenuity of the first masters of language compelled by necessity has thrown a kind of veil of mystery over the face of every science, and over none a thicker than over that of jurisprudence. This however it will not be practicable perhaps not even expedient altogether to remove. We must however have learned upon every occasion how to pierce through it at pleasure before we can obtain a clear perception of the real state of things. These phantastic denominations are a sort of paper currency: if we know how at any time to change them and get sterling in their room, it is well: if not, we are deceived, and instead of being master of such much real knowledge as by the help of them we mean to supply ourselves with, we possess nothing but nonsense.

Exposition: The ideas annexed to the words person and thing are ideas copied immediately from the impressions made by real entities. The ideas annexed to the words and phrases, acts of the will, sign of an act of the will, physical act or act of the body, event, circumstance, etc. are either ideas like the former, ideas copied immediately from the impressions made by real entities or copies of the sensible affections of determinable real entities. The ideas annexed to the words command and prohibition are resolvable immediately into ideas of the number of those just mentioned. Now there can be no such thing as an act which is not the act of some person or of some sentient thing: nor can there be any act of law which is not either a command or a prohibition, of the reverse of the one or the other of those operations: nor lastly, can there be any command or prohibition which has not for its object some sort of act. It follows that whatever words besides these may be made use of in expressing the matter of a law or body of laws and that are not names of real entities or of the sensible affections of determinable real entities, the import of the words just mentioned will serve as a key to the import of such other words: and while it lays open the import of each will lay open the connection between every one of them and that of every other. By this means alone can the import of such words as duty, obligation, power, right and other means of fictitious moral entities be laid open: by these means alone can a regular analysis of the contents of a body of laws be exhibited. I may be excused for announcing in so peremptory a manner the necessity for the ensuing disquisitions, since nothing less than necessity would have excused the exhibition of so uninviting a detail.

We have already had occasion to shew that the division of offences is in fact the division of the whole law: and that a complete analysis of all the offences that can be created includes a complete account of everything that can be done in the way of law. [See Chapter XVI of *Morals and Legislation.*—M.P.M.] It follows that whatever number of these fictitious entities may be created or brought into play, it must all be done in the course of some or other of those operations by which the several sorts of offences are created. They are a sort of vapours which during the course of the legislative process are as it were generated and sublimed. By every operation which the law performs some one of them at least is exhibited or produced: By most operations two or even three: according to the number of persons or rather of the parties whose interest is concerned, and to whom the law during the process bears a different relation. On the one hand whatever the law does in any case, somebody or other there must be (if it has any views at all) somebody or other there must be whom it is meant to favour: on the other hand, whatever it does, if in a positive way it does any thing, to somebody or other it must issue prohibition or command: somebody or other in a word it must be intended to coerce. If the party whom it is meant to favour be the same whom it coerces, there may be but one interest concerned: if different, there must at least be two: and if at the same time that it favours one party it coerces a second party in one way and a third party in the opposite way (which we shall see is frequently the case) there may and indeed must be three. . . .

On Possession and Property. Possession, we see, is after all neither more nor less than a ground of expectation: the expectation of deriving certain advantages from the thing in future in consequence of being already so situated with relation to it. To be in possession of the thing is the being with relation to that thing in a situation of that sort. This situation is purely ideal, not physical, not corporeal: no one image, no one painting can in any case express it. The word possession is equally applicable and it is equally applied to a thousand situations: situations which were they capable of being depicted would require a thousand pictures as different from one another as any thousand that could be imagined: what they have in common, is that and this only, the faculty of raising and keeping up in the mind of the person said to be possessed, the expectation of deriving such or such advantages from the thing according to the nature of the case: the persuasion of the possessing the faculty of reaping those advantages.

Vicinity, contact, act of handling, habit of handling, nothing of that sort will come up to the idea: all those are but single cases out of a thousand: a handkerchief which is in the East Indies may be mine, of the number of my possessions: the handkerchief which is in my hand may be not mine but yours of whom I have borrowed it, and to whom I am going to return it. Different persons in different places may to different purposes be in possession of the same thing: one as carrying it, another as watching it, a third as using it, a fourth as being about to use it, a fifth as being to have the price of it when sold, or the benefit of the making use of it when consumed.

To search out all these cases and decide accordingly is a business of detail which may be, and ought to be completely executed in the text of the civil code.

The error against which these observations are leveled is at least a general one among jurists, not to say an universal one. It is by no means an innocent one: from speculation it creeps into practice, producing obstinacy, ill humour, blindness, turbulence, and in the end disobedience to law. The right I have to my property, to my possessions is derived from physical, from natural acts: being derived from natural acts it is a natural right: being derived from nature it is not derived from law: its origin, its existence was antecedent to law: for nature existed before law. Being antecedent to law, it was not created by law: not being created by law it cannot be taken away by law. Law was instituted to protect a man in the enjoyment of such his rights, not to deprive him of them, or of any part of them: these rights like all other natural rights are sacred and indefeasible. So far as it protects him accordingly, it is comformable to natural justice: so far as it deprives him of such his rights or any part of them it is repugnant to natural justice. Laws conformable to natural justice are valid, and ought to be observed: laws repugnant to natural justice are ipso facto void, and instead of being observed ought to be resisted. Those who make them are tyrants, those who attempt to enforce them are the tools of tyrants: both the one and the other ought to be resisted, made war upon, and destroyed.

When any of the natural rights of man are invaded, a man if he has the spirit of a man, and in proportion to the share he has of that spirit will be vigilant to detect and eager to repel the invasion.

Of rights thus self-evident the existence requires not to be proved but only to be declared: to prove it is impossible because the demonstration of that which is self-evident is impossible: to doubt of it argues of want of sense: to express a doubt of it argues not only a want of sense but a want of honesty.

All this talk about nature, natural rights, natural justice and injustice proves two things and two things only, the heat of the passions, and the darkness of the understanding. Persuaded in his own mind, but unable to develop the grounds of his persuasion, a man falls into uneasiness, and vents it in terms of latent invective upon those whom he conceives to differ from him, upon those whose fancied opposition has engaged him in the difficulty. It is the old intolerance venting itself in new names: instead of saying you are a heretic if you differ from me, you are a tyrant, or the tool of a tyrant, or a slave. It is reproach in the garb of argument, reproach and nothing else, for when you have taken away the idea of reproach, you have taken away all there is of it.

Property the creature of law?—Oh, no—Why not? because if it were the law that gave everything, the law might take away everything: if every thing were given by law, so might every thing be taken away.

The case is that in a society in any degree civilized, all the rights a man can have, all the expectation he can entertain of enjoying any thing that is said to be his is derived solely from the law. Even the expectation which a thief may entertain of enjoying the thing which he has stolen forms no exception: for till it is known to have been stolen the law will as fully protect him in the enjoyment of it, as much as if he had bought or made it.

But what it may be said was the ground the law went upon at first in choosing whom it should take for the object of its protection, and for what things? a time there must always have been in which men were entertaining a *natural* expectation of enjoying certain things, an expectation derived from sources anterior to law.—Certainly occasions there must have originally been, and will have been still in which one man must have found a greater facility in securing to himself the enjoyment of certain things than any other man: but how narrow and how fleeting the security! Without the aid of law a savage, it is true, who has hid in a cave some fruits he has gathered or some animals which he has killed may keep them to himself so long as the cave remains undiscovered, without the aid of law: but if he has any intercourse with his species how long will his haunt remain undiscovered? He may carry his acquisition about with him and still conceal or otherwise protect it—Yes—so long as he is awake: but has not the savage as well as the monarch need of sleep? In the rudest and earliest state therefore of society whatever property a man possesses, whatever articles of property he expects to have the enjoyment of, his possession if derived from any source more permanent than the casual forbearance of those in whose presence he has occasion to find himself, must be derived from a principle which can be called by no other name than *law*. Relations purely physical might then as now generate an expectation of this kind for a moment and in a weak degree: but an expectation in any degree strong and permanent can only be derived from law. Till law existed, property could scarcely be said to exist. Property and law were born and die together. Till there was law there was no such thing as property: take away law and property is at an end. . . .

Chapter 5. Ends which a Law May Have in View.
Of the Principle of Utility. Wherein then consists the good of the community? A question this which is to be answered not by vague declamation, not by point and metaphor, but by minute analysis and sober estimation. We shall endeavour then to travel on slowly and circumspectly, not with Rhetoric, but rather with Metaphysics and Mathematics for our guides. We shall endeavour to catch, as much as possible, the spirit of the two last-named sciences, and, as much as possible, to avoid the language.

Those who cry out against pleasure, as such, know not what it is they say. They swerve manifestly from the principle of utility. Upon that principle the most sordid pleasure which the vilest malefactor ever reaped from his crime (suppose it but pleasure) would not be to be reprobated, *if it stood alone.* This impregnable truth has been recognized by one of the severest of moralists. [Maupertuis.–M.P.M.]

This then I assume as a *postulatum:* and this, in matter of censure and approbation, is the only *postulatum* I do assume. Whatever matter of that nature occurs during the course of this work is but a development of this principle. These then are the two standards to one or other of which I refer in everything I advance. For matter of fact I appeal to the experience or observation of those within whose cognizance it lies. For matter of censure or approbation I appeal solely to this principle. The principle such as it is, is not of my own invention. The merit of discovering it is none of mine. The legitimate consequences of it, should any of them prove obnoxious are not chargeable upon me. I had it from Epicurus, from Carneades, from Horace, from Helvétius, from Beccaria. All that remains for me is only to apply it to particular cases as they come under review. This then I assume as a *postulatum.* If it be denied me, I confess I shall be altogether at a loss to prove it. Nor will I go about to prove it in this essay: which is but a small part detached from an entire system of legal policy of which, were it finished, this axiom would form the bases. I will not, I say, in this place go about to prove it: nor shall I easily be brought to think it necessary. I could not easily have thought it had been new to anyone, if I did not remember that before I had read Helvétius it was new even to myself. I could not have thought it possible when once announced to contravert it; if I had not seen those by whom it has been contraverted. Two short questions may in this place answer the purpose of all argument: Supposing (without any foundation) that any other than his own happiness ought to be the end of any individual policy, what motive has he to pursue it? Supposing (without any foundation) that any other than the happiness of the community ought to be the end of legislative policy, what motive has the community to pursue it?

This then is the postulatum I set out with. To enable me to apply it with advantage it will be necessary before I enter upon the particular subject of Punishment, to go through the following operations:

1st, to distinguish the several sources from whence Pain and Pleasure are in use to flow:

2d, to mark out and describe the several species of pains and pleasures I shall have occasion to distinguish:

3dly, to shew how the value of a pain or pleasure is to be measured:

4thly, to point out how such value may in every case be expressed:

5thly, to shew the various proportions in which pain or pleasure, according as they are applied are apt to follow from the operations which are their causes: by enumerating the causes of the different degrees of *sensibility* that are observeable among men.

6thly, I shall mark out the station occupied by the business of Punishment in the general map or Plan of Jurisprudence. These several operations will form the business of as many chapters.

A reader who comes fresh to the subject and untinctured with any technical prejudices would be apt I imagine to wonder how a principle like this should ever have lain unobserved: how when once observed it should ever after have been neglected, much more how it should ever have been opposed: how any other should ever have been set up: and of what nature such other could possibly have been. He would conceive it impossible that any writer either on morals or what is called Natural Jurisprudence should ever have neglected or opposed it: and if compelled by the evidence of his eyes to acknowledge that such writers have existed, his next wonder would be what it is their speculations could consist of.

Of moralists it does not fall in the way of the present design to take any special notice any further than just to observe that it is to the open opposition or neglect with which the generality of them have treated this principle, that their works are held in such general and deserved neglect, and are acknowledged to be of so little use for the guidance of men in either their political or domestic conduct. . . .

Chapter 19. Distinction between Civil Law and Penal.

Note on Logic. To anyone who should come new to the subject the questions mentioned in the text will naturally appear to be the very A B C of Jurisprudence: they must long ago, he would think, have met with a full and satisfactory solution: to say anything new, impossible. So many ages as have been spent in the study of the laws, so many libraries-full as have been written on them, not know yet what a law is? So many laws as have been made, now know the ingredients they are made of?

Incredible—And yet nothing is more true. To write to any purpose a man must begin *ab ovo:* I see no fund open that he can draw from: what he makes use of he must make.

The wonder will cease when it comes to be perceived that the idea of a law, meaning one single but entire law, is in a manner inseparably connected with that of a complete body of laws: so that what is a law and what are the contents of a complete body of the laws are questions of which neither can well be answered without the other. A body of laws is a vast and complicated piece of mechanism, of which no part can be fully explained without the rest. To understand the functions of a balance-wheel you must take to pieces the whole watch: to understand the nature of a law you must take to pieces the whole code.

The subject we are now entering upon belongs to a particular branch of logic, untouched by Aristotle. The main and ultimate business of the school-logic of which that philosopher was the father, is to exhibit the several forms of *argumentation:* the business of the branch now before us is to exhibit the several forms of *imperation:* or (to take the subject in its utmost extent) of sentences expressive of volition: a leaf which seems to be yet wanting in the book of science.

All language whatsoever, every sentence whatsoever, inasmuch as it *expresses* something must *assert* something: something expressive of the state and condition, real or pretended, of the mind of him whose language it is: that is either of his understanding or his will: for at bottom, whatever is said even of external events resolves itself into this. In the first case the sentence expressive of it has been styled exclusively a *sentence of assertion:* in the other case, a *sentence of volition:* of which latter, a *sentence of interrogation* is a particular species. "The robber is killed":—"Kill the robber":—"Is the robber killed?"—This is as much as to say, "I *understand* or I believe that the robber is killed."—"My *will* is that you kill the robber": "My *will* is that you tell me whether the robber be killed or no": that is, that if the robber is killed, you tell me he is killed: if not, that he is not killed. Now it is to sentences of the assertive kind that the logic of the schools has confined itself: those which concern volition it has left untouched. The demesnes of the logical branch of science appear then to be more extensive than has commonly been suspected: the language of the will being a new and unexplored province which, neglected as it has been hitherto, might be cultivated, it is probably to at least as good a purpose as the old. It is the branch here in question that is more particularly applicable to the business of government: that subdivision which concerns the forms of imperation at large having a more particular regard to legislation; that which concerns the forms of interrogation, to the less dignified but not less necessary business of collecting verbal information:

a process subservient to the business as well of the legislative as of the executive departments. Had Aristotle happened to turn his view this way, as many pens might perhaps have been employed on this branch of logic as on the other: like that it might have had its algebraical method of notation, its graphical schemes, and its mnemonic verses: "Assent A *nugat* B" . . . : *"Barbara, celarent, darii, ferioque"* of the school men, might here have found their parodies: and every piece of intellectual machinery which the ingenuity of those subtle speculatists has even invented for the accommodation or affrightment of beginners might here have been imitated and improved.

Had this happened to be the case the subject we are entering upon would it is to be presumed by this time have stood in a much clearer light than that in which in the course of a cursory review, I have been able to place it: the business of a great part of the following pages might in that case have been dispatched by a few references. As it is I mean not to descend any deeper into the subject than is absolutely necessary in order to find the requisite materials for the task actually in hand: content with opening the mine, I leave the working of it out to others. . . .

That no settled line can be drawn between the civil branch and the penal is most manifest. Suppose a line to be drawn between them anywhere: an act of a general description having no punishment annexed to it or none above the ordinary, falls without the penal branch and belongs only to the civil. But now let the legislator make a law against such act, annexing to it a severe punishment. It is plain that the same act which before belonged to the civil branch, belongs now to the penal; and the boundary set up between them is broke down.

The law can do nothing without exercising power somehow or other, power of some sort or other then must be concerned in every act which it proposes. Now it cannot exercise power over one man but by means of power which it confers or has conferred upon another. Power is either over things or persons: and in either case it is either beneficial or fiduciary. When fiduciary it is coupled with trust. What concerns beneficial power, whether over things or over persons, and fiduciary where the benefitee is an individual, or an assemblage of individuals, belongs to the Private Law: what concerns fiduciary power where the benefitee is the whole community or a class of unassignable individuals, belongs to the public or Constitutional branch.

But power can no other wise be constituted than by means of punishment. This punishment is either ordinary or extraordinary. Where either the means of enforcing the command or variety in the means of enforcing the command does not come in question, but the provision of the law turns upon the question concerning the acts which a man is to perform or abstain from, or the person by whom, or the circumstances in which they are to be abstained from or performed, it comes under the head of the civil branch: where the nature of the punishment is the principal object that strikes the eye, and the business is to mark out the different cases where different punishments are to take place, then that matter belongs to the penal branch.

To Ethics it belongs to ascertain the cases in which on the one hand the punishment, and on the other the reward of the moral sanction ought to apply: and to instruct a man how to avoid the one and obtain the other, there also ought to apply that of the moral: in this respect therefore this whole work belongs still to Ethics. On the other hand there are divers cases in which although the punishment of the political ought not at any rate to apply, howsoever it may be with the moral, there are others in which neither the one ought to apply nor the other, nor in short any punishment at all. These cases have already been marked out. Where any punishment is groundless, there all punishment is groundless: there neither that of the political nor that of the moral ought to apply. So also if the punishment of the political sanction is inefficacious, the feebler punishment of the moral sanction must be so likewise: but it may very well happen that all punishment on the part of the political sanction may be unprofitable or needless, where that of the moral shall be both requisite and profitable. . . .

Chapter 21. Analysis, and Uses of the Preceding Chapters.

Thus inextricably is the penal branch of the law interwoven with the civil: that which we are here immediately concerned, with that with which here we have no such immediate concern: in order to settle and arrange the former, it became therefore unavoidably necessary to look through all the latter: so toilsome and so arduous when pursued with care and industry is the business of arrangement. Before we conclude it may not be amiss to gather up in the way of recapitulation the broken hints that have been given in the course of this chapter and thereby to give a sort of analytical sketch of the whole business of the art of legislation.

The art of legislation has two general objects or purposes in view: the one direct and positive, to add to the happiness of the community: the other indirect and negative, to avoid doing anything by which that happiness may be diminished. To enable it to compass the former of these purposes it has two great instruments or engines: 1. coercion and 2. remuneration. Coercion is either 1. physical or 2. moral, viz: by punishment. Physical coercion, by which a human being is treated upon the footing of an inanimate machine, it is evident enough can be made but little use of, by reason of the vast and incessant expense it would cost in labour and attention on the part of those whose business it must be made to apply it. Remuneration is also in comparison employ'd but little, for various reasons, one of which is the boundless expense it would require, and the absolute want of a fund from which that expense could be supplied.

Having these instruments to work with, the way in which the law promotes the happiness of men, is by influencing *actions*. Take any individual for example. The actions which it influences must be either his *own* or those of *other* individuals. His own actions it cannot influence in any material degree by reward, on account of the expense. In what instances it can be consistent with the above mentioned *collateral* purpose of legislation, in other words, whether it can be worthwhile to attempt to influence them by coercive methods, is a matter that in most cases lies very open to dispute. As to the actions of other men, the way in which it may promote his happiness by influencing those actions is either by causing such as would be productive of *inconvenience* to him to be *abstained from,* or by causing such as are productive of *advantage* to him to be *performed.* In as far as by coercive methods it causes or endeavours to cause an action to be abstained from or performed it thereby creates a duty. Duties accordingly are either duties of *abstinence,* i.e. negative duties, or duties of *performance,* i.e. positive duties.

Now the objects in which the actions are capable of *terminating* are either *things* or persons. It is by causing certain actions to be abstained from on the suit of other men which would lessen the advantage you are capable of reaping either for your self or others from certain things, at the same time that you, or such and such persons of your appointment, are not caused to abstain from certain actions by which that happiness may be promoted, that you have *power* given you over those things. This power according to the amplitude of it is termed either the *property* of, or a property or *interest* in, the thing in question. Power over things is constituted then by the imposing of duties of abstinence on other persons. This power then either you are left free to exercise or not according as may contribute most to your own advantage, in which case it may be styled a beneficial power, or it is coupled with a duty, in other words you are bound to exercise it for the sake of some other party, in which case it is called a *trust.*

When the acts you are left free to perform are such whereby the interests of other individuals is liable to be affected, you are thereby said to have a power over those individuals. In this case in as far as you possess the power in question you possess an exemption from the duty of *abstinence* as far as concerns the acts to the performance of which your power extends. This exemption then on your part may either stand single or it may be coupled with an assistant duty (subservient to the same design) on the part of other men. In the first case it may be styled a *naked* or *uncorroborated* power: in the other case it may be styled a *corroborated* power. This assistant duty will either be a duty of forbearance, viz: the duty of abstaining from all such acts as may tend to prevent you from exercising the power in question, or 2. a duty of performance, viz: the duty of performing such acts as may enable you to overcome any obstacle that may oppose itself to the exercise of that power. Power over persons may accordingly be consider'd as susceptible of three degrees of perfection. Power in the first, lowest, or least perfect degree, is where it is not made any body's duty to oppose you, in case of your going about to exercise it. Power in the second or middle degree is where not only it is not made any body's duty to oppose you in case of your going about to exercise it, but it is made every body's duty not to oppose you in case of your going about to exercise it. Power in the third, highest, or most perfect degree is where not only it is made every body's duty not to oppose you in case of your going about to exercise it, but in case of your meeting with any obstacle to the exercise of it whether from the party over whom it is to be exercised or any other person or in short from any other cause, it is made the duty of such or such persons to enable you to overcome such obstacles.

The law prohibits in me and others all such acts as it thinks fit to prohibit on account of the prejudice it conceives them liable to import to you in respect of your person, your property, your reputation, or your condition in life: by every such act which it prohibits it gives you a certain right: a right of being protected against any enterprise that may prejudice you in any of those respects: this right of being protected is also called in one word, *protection.*

If the legislator goes further and in the view of preventing you from suffering any such prejudice as you might be exposed to suffer in any of those respects from any other cause, such as the agency of irrational or unsentient beings, commands me in certain cases to exert my endeavors for that purpose, he thereby for every act so commanded gives you a distinct sort of right and one which has a different name, viz: a right to a certain service on my part.

I have been speaking of the manner in which the legislator acts in order to give you protection for your property and your condition in life. But in thus speaking I have been obliged to consider your property and your condition as objects already established and subsisting. But to establish you in possession of those privileges requires a distinct and various series of operations. . . .

With regard to fiduciary power, whether it be power over things or power over persons, the party to be benefited may consist either of a single individual, or of divers individuals. When it consists of divers individuals, these individuals may be either assignable or unassignable. When unassignable, the number of them may either be limitable to a multitude less than the whole multitude of individuals in the state, or it may not. First then, where the party to be benefited consists of a single assignable individual or a number of assignable individuals, in either case the trust may be termed a private one. 2. Where it consists of an unassignable number of persons limitable to a multitude less than the multitude which compose the state, it may be termed a semi-public trust. 3. Where the number of persons to be benefited is not limitable to a multitude less than that which composes the state, it may be termed a *public* trust.

But power, we may remember, whether it be beneficial or fiduciary, depends upon duty. It is constituted by prescribing duties, that is again by commanding acts, to wit on the part of persons other than him to whom the power is given. That branch of the law which prescribes those duties to which correspond power of the beneficial kind and private trust may be termed Private Law: that which prescribes those duties to which correspond semi-public and public trust, Constitutional Law. Private Law then we see is naturally divisible into two great branches [i.e. civil and penal.—M.P.M.]. . . .

An act is a real entity: a law is another. A duty or obligation is a fictitious entity conceived as resulting from the union of the two former. A law commanding or forbidding an act thereby creates a duty or obligation. A right is another fictitious entity, a kind of secondary fictitious entity, resulting out of a duty. Let any given duty be proposed, either somebody is the better for it or nobody. If nobody, no such duty ought to be created: neither is there any right that corresponds to it. If somebody, this somebody is either the party bound, or some other. If it be he himself, then the duty, if such it may be called, is a duty he owes to himself: neither in this case is there any *right* that corresponds to it. If it be any other party then is it a duty owing to some other party: and then that other party has at any rate a right: a right to have this duty performed: perhaps also a *power:* a power to compel the performance of such duty.

What is it that every article of law has in common with the rest? it issues commands and by so doing it creates *duties,* or, what is another word for the same thing, *obligations.* The notion of duty is a common measure for every article of law. It is from hence that the differences and resemblances of the various branches of law are to be traced as from this common source.

The notion of command leads to that of duty: that of duty to that of right: and that of right to that of power. Right is either naked or armed with power. That of exemption to that of privilege: power and duty together that of trust. . . .

Of all the words that occur in language there are few that are more familiar, that is occur more frequently, than those of which I have been giving an explanation: at the same time I think it may be observed with confidence that there are few that are so far from being clearly understood. If it be true that our ideas are derived all of them from our senses and that the only way of rendering any of our ideas clear and determinate is to trace it up to the sensible objects in which it originates, the only method that can be taken for explaining them to the purpose is the method I have just been taking here. This method is that of defining these and other names of fictitious entities not *per genus* and *differentia,* nor by an other of the methods which are applicable to real entities, but by a method which I have ventured to style that of paraphrases: a method new in itself and which therefore if mentioned at all must be mentioned by a new name. Now this method is one that most assuredly has never been taken hitherto: if therefore they are now properly explained this is the first time they have ever been so. These explanations then, dry and tedious as they are, seemed indispensable: since without them no part of what follows could have been clearly and perfectly understood. No wonder that legislators should not any where have done precisely what they ought to do when they have never hitherto had a clear understanding of what it is they themselves have actually been doing. No wonder they have so often handled their instruments improperly when as yet they have not so much as learnt to distinguish one of them from another. . . .

It is with language in general as with mathematical language in particular. Algebraical notation may on many occasions be made use of with advantage for the sake of expedition: but it never is clearly understood until it be translated into the language of geometry or plain arithmetic. In like manner abstract phraseology must on many occasions be tolerated for the same reason: but on no occasion can it be clearly understood unless it can be translated into such expressions as have a direct reference to the sensible objects that are in question. . . .

When once an improvement has been made in any science and the utility of it ascertained, when it stands confirmed by the suffrages of the experienced in that line, the next care is to facilitate the communication of it to the rising generation. In its turn every intellectual production undergoes this course of husbandry. If while in the nursery of invention it is found to bear the blasts of criticism, it is taken up by somebody, pruned into form, and transplanted into the garden of science.

In that department of logical science which goes by the name of grammar (for between what is commonly called logic and what is commonly called grammar there seems to be no clear line of separation) many helps are made use of for the purpose of teaching the rules of speech in general, which might be transferred and adapted upon occasion if it were worth while to any particular branch of discourse in particular. Such is that exercise which consists in ranging particular words and combinations of words under general classes and uses, and which when applied to words in the light in which they are considered by grammar goes commonly under the name of *parsing*.

The most general propositions or grammatical rules as they are called, however abstract and abstruse as they are in themselves, being repeatedly exemplified over and over again upon different models, the purport of them may as experience testifies be enabled by degrees to make a lasting impression upon the least susceptible conceptions. A word being proposed to the scholar, he is required to point out the classes to which it is conformable. Each word and combination of words is thus referred to a particular class invented and named for the purposes of discourse in general. This process is equally applicable to every other branch of logic as to the elementary branch which is called grammar.

As words of any sort may be *parsed* by referring them to the classes entitled a *verb*, a *noun*, a *verb in the infinitive mood*, a *noun in the accusative case* and so forth, so words of a particular stamp considered in a particular point of view may be parsed by referring then to the classes entitled by the words *genus, species, subject, predicate*, and the like: as may also entire propositions of the argumentative stamp by referring them to the classes entitled by the words *Barbara, celarent, darii*, and so on. In the same manner may propositions of the legislative stamp be parsed by referring them to the classes entitled law against simple personal injuries, law against semi-public offences, law against public offences: imperative provision, qualificative, limitative, exceptive, justificative, substantive law, adjective law, remedial law, punitive law; and so on through all the variety of appellatives above exhibited, as well as of such others as upon a maturer and more particular examination it might be found advisable to add or substitute to the foregoing.

When these rules and exercises were prepared and brought into order, a sort of school might be established: a school, of which the business should be to teach, not the art of forensic disputation for the emolument of individuals, but the art of legislation for the benefit of empires.

If a model of a complete code, applied for exemplification's sake to the circumstances of some one nation in particular, were once formed, and students of various nations were to meet together under one roof (as hath so often been the case in the schools of medicine, of botany, of chemistry, and other branches of the physical department of science) a harmony of the laws actually in force upon the plan above mentioned might form one part of the business of such a school, each student taking in hand the jurisprudence of his own state. By this work the old laws of each country would be arranged upon a new plan. This being accomplished the next and finishing achievement would be to frame for each nation a complete code new in point of substance as well as form, copied from the general model above mentioned with such alterations as shall be deemed requisite to adapt it to the particular manners, sentiments, and exterior circumstances of each respective state. If the time when an institution of such a sort could be proposed with any probability of its adoption is yet at a great distance, the idea of it however can not be thrown out too soon: the sooner it is exposed to public view, the sooner it takes rank among those embryo projects which chance will sometimes bring into life and a happy concurrence of talents and resolution sooner or later brings onward to maturity.

As grammar is taught by sentences thrown on purpose out of regimen, and geography by dissected maps, in like manner might the art of legislation, particularly what may be styled the mechanical branch of it, be taught by means of shapeless laws, to be taken to pieces and put together again after the manner of the model. As to making examples on purpose it is what there could be no need of here: since enough and enough might be found ready made among the laws that are anywhere in being.

But to pursue these visions any farther, would be to wander too far from the proper track of this design. It is time we should resume the regular thread of the discourse which leads in the next place into the examination of the different plans which the legislator may form to himself for the attack of the mischiefs which he has to combat, and the steps which it may be in his way to take for bringing the whole of the force he has at his disposal to cooperate together and act in subservience to the principal design.

Legislation is a state of warfare: political mischief is the enemy: the legislator is the commander: the moral and religious sanctions his allies: punishments and rewards (raised some of them out of his own resources, others borrowed from those allies) the forces he has under his command: punishments his regular standing force, rewards an occasional subsidiary force too weak to act alone: the mechanical branch of legislation, the branch we have been treating of in the present chapter, the art of tactics: direct legislation a formal attack made with the main body of his forces in the open field: indirect legislation a secret plan of connected and long-concerted operations to be executed in the way of stratagem or *petite guerre*. All these heads except this last have been discussed already. It remains that we should say something of this irregular system of warfare: a 'system which on account of the economy with which it may be used and the ingenuity which it is thought to require and which it often gives Beccaria to display stands in much higher favour with men in general than that which is carried on by open force. [Therefore, the next "chapter" he wrote—also the size of a full-length book—, number eighteen, is devoted to indirect legislation; see the following selection.—M.P.M.]

A school boy is thought to have made but a small proficiency in grammar, if when a grammatical sentence is set before him, there be a word which he is unable to refer to the place that belongs to it in that sentence. If the science of legislation were as far advanced as that of grammar, and it were the custom for legislators to be as well acquainted with that science as it is for school boys to be with grammar, a statesman would be thought to have made but a small proficiency in legislation, if in any book of law that were set before him there were a word which he knew not how to refer to the place that it occupies in some mandate. But to love power is one thing: and to love the labour which alone can qualify a man to exercise it as he should do, is another.

Laws that are hasty have often been cited in proof of the necessity of interpretation: but methinks it might also have been well at the same time to have observed that they are indications equally strong of imbecility and short sightedness on the part of the legislator: that they bespeak the infancy of the science: and that when once it shall have been brought to a state of tolerable maturity the demand for interpretation will have been in great measure if not altogether taken away.

Now the mischief in cases of this sort being manifest, it was necessary to apply a remedy. Such a remedy if applied by the legislature itself would at any rate be attended with some of the inconveniences of an *ex post facto* law if extensive of the obligation, none if limitative of it. But perhaps the legislative power is vested in a body: and that body is not or cannot be assembled: or it is so constituted that it is next to impossible to consult it: or cases which call for an interpretation of this sort are so frequent and many of them so trifling that there would be no end of consultations: for these reasons or for others not so good, properly or improperly this power has always been assumed and exercised by the Judge. As fast as it has been exercised the cases in which it has been exercised have been noted down: general rules have been formed from the observation of those cases: and thus the customary law breaking through its original barriers has spread itself like a plague over the surface of the statute law, infecting it with its own characteristic obscurity, uncertainty and confusion.

To a mischief thus flagrant it is impossible to turn our thoughts without looking eagerly after a remedy. Let us not despair. Let us look round a little. A cure and that a pretty effectual, need not be despaired of. Such an one unless I am much mistaken, might be extracted from the principle of utility. To demonstrate that this may be done and to shew *how* it may be done is part of the object of the present work. Let the legislator have carried his views over the whole field of human action, let him have given a certain degree of perfection to his method, of regularity and consistency to his laws, he may bring them to such a degree of perfection, that they shall need no more interpretation than he himself is equal to supply.

In a system thus constructed upon this plan, a man need but open the book in order to inform himself what the aspect borne by the law bears to every imaginable act that can come within the possible sphere of human agency: what acts it is his duty to perform for the sake of himself, his neighbour or the public: what acts he has a right to do, what other acts he has a right to have others perform for his advantage: whatever he has either to fear or to hope from the law. In this one repository the whole system of the obligations which either he or any one else is subject to are recorded and displayed to view: delineated either actually by the commands it pronounces contained in it, or potentially by the powers it confers: powers of manual governance, or powers of issuing commands either permanent in the shape of laws or transient in the shape of executive mandates.

The acts to the performance of which a man is actually obliged are embraced by the commands that are delineated upon the fact of the law itself: the acts to the performance of which a man may *come* to be obliged are embraced by the powers of imperation which are conferred by the law. The commands issued in virtue of these powers will be either of the permanent or of the transient kind: those which are of the former kind go to augment the body of the laws: the latter quit the stage one after another and vanish altogether in proportion as the purposes they are designed to answer come to an end.

In a map of the law executed upon such a plan there are no terrae incognitae, no blank spaces: nothing is at least omitted, no thing unprovided for, the vast and hitherto shapeless expanse of Jurisprudence is collected and condensed into a compact sphere which the eye at a moment's warning can traverse in all imaginable directions.

Such are the fruits of a method planned under the auspices of the principle of utility, in which the laws are ranged according to the ends they have in view.

Indirect Legislation

A Note on *Indirect Legislation*

As Bentham's pages on Indirect Legislation are among the most neglected of all his work, so too are they among the most important. What
did he mean by "indirect legislation"? "Legislation is a state of warfare,"
he said in another favorite metaphor: "Direct legislation a formal attack
made with the main body of [the legislator's] . . . forces in the open field:
indirect legislation a secret plan of connected and long-concerted operations to be executed in the way of stratagem or *petite guerre.*" [1] Using his
standard medical analogy, indirect legislation is preventive or therapeutic
medicine applied to the body politic. His vision was remarkably Con-
fucian. "But the thing is," Confucius said in the *Analects,* "to aim so that
there should not be any lawsuits at all." [2]

In 1794 Bentham explained, "Vulgar legislation drags men to its purpose in chains, from which, thanks to the bungling clumsiness of the
grimgribber man at the anvil who forges them, the captives break loose in
crowds: transcendental [or indirect] legislation leads men by silken threads,
entwined round their affections, and makes them its own forever." [3]

Bentham wrote the history of civilization in different ways at different
times, but he usually tied it to the relative strength of a given sanction
at a given moment in history. In the most barbarous ages, the physical
sanction predominated; men did little but hunt, fight, eat, and sleep.

[1] See above, p. 164. *Limits.*
[2] Mack, p. 293.
[3] *Ibid.*

Gradually the religious, then the political sanction became uppermost, and revenge gave way to justice. But in the future age of indirect legislation, the moral sanction will have largely replaced the political. There will no longer be government by force, but government by inclination, the private voluntary choice of Utilitarian actions. These pages are so many efforts to lead the nation to that distant time. They answer the question, what can the government do *now* to strengthen the moral sanction? Here as always Bentham insisted on the removal of censorship and complete liberty of the press. His more strictly legal aims were to substitute money payments for physical punishment and again, as always, to eliminate capital punishment.

He dreamed of moral as well as legal codes. Why should not each profession, each class, have its own logic of the will, drawn up and taught in schools? What the logic of the will came to under indirect legislation was the harmonization of contrary motives. Bentham loved to quote a favorite maxim from Ovid:

> I see the better and approve it;
> And do the worse.

But under the new transcendental logic of the will this disharmony would disappear; men would *do* what they *saw* to be better, and all without coercion. Like the logic of the will, Bentham saw Indirect Legislation as a new subject, and he was proud to have invented it. As usual, though his pages ran into the hundreds, they were mere fragments of his grandiose design to encompass all of human behavior.

There is a remarkable difference in style between Chapter XVII and Chapter XVIII—as well there might be, for *The Limits* passed through no other hands but Bentham's, whereas *Indirect Legislation* went from hand to hand. So far we have had him directly, with all his apologies for dryness and difficulty; in this and the next two selections we have him at second remove, softened and ameliorated by two other sets of hands, those of his devoted Genevan disciple, Etienne Dumont, who first translated Bentham's massive piles of fragment and notes into smoothly flowing French, and then those of his later American disciple, Robert Hildreth, who retranslated them into English. In this way his chronic dilemma of language resolved itself. If he could not himself temper his style to fit his audience, others could and did do it for him. He was that rare phenomenon: a writer with little pride of authorship. Knowing his own weaknesses, he positively welcomed editorial meddling and rewriting. With what results? there was a new naïvete: Bentham himself approached everything analytically, with no waste of words giving concrete examples. Dumont, on the other hand, never made a point without giving one or more historical illustrations or graphic stories. Nevertheless, despite the radical change in style from gnarled to fluent, Bentham's thought is faithfully represented, and these pages can be taken as authentic.

This and the following two selections come from Hildreth's book, *The Theory of Legislation* (1864), reprinted by C. K. Ogden in 1931; this in turn comes from Dumont's three-volume *Traités des Législations* (1802), which was in its turn a popularized abridgment of the tens of thousands of loose, unsorted MS pages, including *An Introduction,* that Bentham gratefully relinquished to him in the 1790's. Most of these pages can also be found in an earlier, stiffer English version in Volume I of Bowring's edition.

Indirect Legislation

Indirect Means of Preventing Offences. Introduction. In all the sciences there are branches which have been cultivated more tardily than others, because they demand a longer series of observations and meditations more profound. It is thus that mathematics have their transcendental or higher branch—that is, a new science, as it were, above ordinary science.

The same distinction, to a certain extent, may be applied to the art of legislation. What means shall be adopted to prevent injurious actions? The first answer, which presents itself to everybody, is this: "Forbid those actions; punish them." This method of combatting offences being the most simple and the first adopted, every other method of arriving at the same end is, so to speak, a refinement of the art, and its transcendental branch.

That branch consists in devising a course of legislative acts adapted to *prevent* offences—in acting principally upon the inclinations of men, in order to turn them from evil and to impress upon them the direction most useful to themselves and to others.

The first method—that on combatting offences by punishments—constitutes *direct legislation.*

The second method—that of combatting offences by *preventive means*—constitutes a branch of legislation which may be called *indirect.*

The sovereign acts *directly* against offences when he prohibits them individually under special penalties. He acts *indirectly* when he takes precautions to prevent them.

By direct legislation the evil is attacked in front. Indirect legislation attacks it obliquely. In the first case, the legislator declares open war against the enemy, points him out, pursues him, meets him foot to foot, and carries his defences sword in hand. In the second case, he does not announce his whole design; he works underground, he procures intelligence, he seeks to prevent hostile enterprises, and to keep still in his alliance those who may have formed secret intentions against him.

Speculative writers upon politics have had glimpses of this art; but in speaking of this second branch of legislation they do not evince any clear idea of it. The first branch has been a long time reduced to system, the good part of it as well as the bad. The second branch has never been thoroughly examined; nobody has undertaken to treat it with method, to arrange it, to classify it—in one word, to master it in its whole extent. It is yet a new subject. . . .

To distinguish exactly what appertains to these two branches, it is necessary to begin by forming a just idea of direct legislation. It proceeds, or ought to proceed, in this way:—

1st. The choice of acts to be erected into offences.

2nd. The description of each offence, as murder, theft, peculation, etc.

3rd. An exposition of the reasons for attributing to these acts the quality of offences—reasons which ought to be deduced from the single principle of utility, and consequently to be consistent with themselves.

4th. The assigning of a competent punishment for each offence.

5th. An exposition of the reasons which justify these punishments.

The penal system, though it be made as perfect as possible, is defective in several respects:—1st. The evil must exist before the remedy can be applied. The remedy consists in the application of punishment, and punishment cannot be applied till offence is committed. Every new instance of punishment inflicted is an additional proof that punishment lacks efficacy and leaves behind it a certain degree of danger and alarm. 2nd. Punishment itself is an evil, though necessary to prevent greater evils. Penal justice, in the whole course of its operation, can only be a series of evils—evils arising from the threats and constraint of the law, evils arising from the prosecution of the accused before it is possible to distinguish innocence from guilt, evils growing out of the infliction of judicial sentences, evils from the unavoidable consequences which result to the innocent. 3rd. The penal system is not able to reach many injurious actions, which escape justice either by their frequency, the facility of concealing them, by the difficulty of defining them, or finally by some vicious turn of public opinion by which they are favoured. Penal law can operate only within certain limits, and its power extends only to palpable acts, susceptible of manifest proof.

This imperfection of the penal system has caused new expedients to be sought for to supply its deficiences. These expedients have for their object the prevention of offences, either by preventing the acquisition of the *knowledge* necessary to their commission or by taking away the *power* or the *will* to commit them. The most numerous class of these means relates to the art of directing the inclinations by weakening the seductive motives which excite to evil, and by strengthening the tutelary motives which impel to good.

Indirect means, then, are those which, without having the character of punishments, act upon man physically or morally, to dispose him to obey the laws, to shield him from temptations, to govern him by his inclinations and his knowledge.

These indirect means not only have a great advantage on the side of mildness, but they succeed in a multitude of cases in which direct means will not answer. All modern historians have remarked how much the abuses of the Catholic Church have diminished since the establishment of the Protestant religion. What popes and councils could not do by their decrees a fortunate rivalry has accomplished without difficulty; and scandals which would afford to hostile sects a matter of triumph have been carefully avoided. The indirect means of free competition among religions has more power to restrain and reform the clergy than all positive laws. . . .

Chapter I. Means of taking away the Physical Power to do Harm. When the will, the knowledge, and the power necessary to the performance of an act concur, that act is of necessity performed. *Inclination, knowledge, power,*—these, then, are the three points at which it is necessary to apply the influence of law, in order to determine the conduct of men. These three words contain in the abstract the sum and substance of all that can be done by legislation, direct or indirect.

I begin with *power,* because means in this respect are more simple and more limited, and because, in those cases in which we can succeed in taking away the power to do harm, we have accomplished everything. Success is certain.

Power may be distinguished into two kinds: 1st. *Internal* power, that which depends upon the intrinsic faculties of the individual; 2nd. *External* power, that which depends upon persons and things external to the individual, but the aid of which he must have, in order to act.

As to internal power, that which depends upon the faculties of the individual, it is scarcely possible to deprive a man of it with advantage. The power of doing evil is inseparable from the power of doing good. With his hands cut off, a man cannot steal, but neither can he work.

Besides, these privative means are so severe that they cannot be employed except upon criminals already convicted. Imprisonment is the only one of them that can be justified, in certain cases, to prevent an apprehended offence.

The legislator will find greater resources for the prevention of offences by turning his attention to the material objects which aid their commission. There are cases in which the power of doing harm may be taken away, by excluding what Tacitus calls *irritamenta malorum,* irritations to evil,— the subjects, the instruments of offence. In such cases, the policy of the legislator may be compared to that of a nurse; iron bars at the windows, grates around the fire, the care of keeping sharp and dangerous instruments from the hands of children, are means of the same kind as the prohibition to sell and to make tools for the fabrication of false money, venerific drugs, arms easy to be concealed, dice, or other instruments of prohibited games, and the prohibition to make or to have certain nets for the chase, or other instruments for trapping wild game. . . .

Among the expedients of this sort, I know none more happy or more simple than that commonly used in England to render difficult the theft of bank-notes. When it is necessary to send them by a messenger or the post, they are cut into two parts, which are sent separately. The theft of half a bank-note would be useless, and the difficulty of stealing the two parts, one after the other, is so great that the offence is almost impossible.

Persons who contract with the administration for the supply of commissary stores, and the provisioning of the fleet, cannot have a seat in parliament. These persons may be defaulters, and be subject to parliamentary investigation; it is not proper, therefore, that they should be members. But there are stronger reasons yet for this exclusion, derived from the danger of increasing ministerial influence.

Chapter II. Prohibition of acquiring Knowledge which may be turned to a bad purpose. I mention this kind of policy only to condemn it. It has produced the censorship of the press; it has produced the inquisition; and wherever it is employed it will always produce the brutalization of mankind.

I propose here to show,—1st, that the diffusion of knowledge is not injurious on the whole, the offences of refinement being less fatal than those of ignorance; 2nd, that the most advantageous method of combatting the evil which may result from a limited degree of knowledge is to augment its quantity.

In the first place, the diffusion of knowledge is not injurious on the whole. Some writers have thought, or seemed to think, that the less men know the better off they will be: that the less enlightened they are, the less acquaintance they will have with the objects that serve as motives to evil, or as means of committing it. It is not surprising that fanatics have entertained this opinion, since there is a natural and constant rivalry between the knowledge of things real, useful, and intelligible, and the knowledge of things unintelligible, imaginary, and useless. But these notions about the dangers of knowledge are sufficiently common among the mass of mankind. The age of gold,—that is, the age of ignorance,— is spoken of with regret. To put in a clear light the error upon which these notions rest, there needs a more precise method of estimating the evil of an offence than any hitherto employed. . . .

The greatest offences are those for which the smallest degree of knowledge is sufficient; the most ignorant individual always knows enough to commit them. Inundation is a graver crime than arson, arson than homicide; homicide than robbery; robbery than pilfering. This proposition may be demonstrated by an arithmetical process, by an inventory of the items of evil in each case, by a comparison of the greatness of each individual suffering, and of the number of individuals who are made to suffer. But how much knowledge is required to enable a man to commit these offences? The most atrocious of all demands only a degree of intelligence possessed by the most barbarous, the most savage of men.

Rape is worse than seduction or adultery; but rape is more frequent in times of barbarism, seduction and adultery in those of refinement.

The dissemination of knowledge has not increased the number of offences, nor even the facility of committing them; it has only diversified the means of their perpetration. And how? By gradually substituting less injurious means in the place of those which are more injurious.

Is a new method of theft invented? The inventor profits for a time by his discovery; but presently his secret is found out, and people are on their guard. It then becomes necessary to have recourse to some new means, which has its turn, like the first, and passes by in the same way. All this is still but theft, not so bad as highway robbery, which itself is not so bad as plundering committed by armed bands. Why? Because the confidence every one has in his own prudence and his own sagacity prevents him from being so much alarmed by theft as by robbery.

Let it be granted, however, that bad men abuse everything; that the more they know, the more means they have of doing evil; what follows?

If the good and the bad composed two distinct races, like the white and the black, the one might be enlightened and the other kept in ignorance. But since it is impossible to discriminate between them, and especially when we consider the frequent alternation of good and evil in the same individual, all must be subjected to the same rule. General light, or general darkness; there is no middle course.

However, the very evil complained of carries with it its own cure. Knowledge cannot give advantage to the bad, except so far as they have the exclusive possession of it. A snare which is known ceases to be a snare. The most ignorant tribes have known how to poison the tips of their arrows; but it is only nations well instructed who have become acquainted with all poisons, and have known how to oppose them by antidotes.

All men have the capacity to commit offences; but only enlightened men are able to discover laws which can prevent them. The more ignorant a man is, the more he is inclined to separate his private interest from the interest of his fellows. The more enlightened he is, the more clearly will he perceive the connection between his private interest and the interest of the whole. . . .

Compare the results in states in which the publication of ideas has been restrained, and in those where freedom of thought and of speech has been permitted. You have, on the one side, Spain, Portugal, Italy; on the other, England, Holland, North America. Where is the most happiness? Where the best morals? Where the most crimes? Where is society most agreeable and most secure? . . .

But it is said we do not pretend to keep men in ignorance; all governments perceive the necessity of knowledge; what they are afraid of is the liberty of the press. They do not oppose the publication of scientific treatises; but is it not reasonable that they should oppose the spread of immoral or seditious writings, the evil effects of which cannot be prevented if they are once allowed to circulate? Punishing a guilty author may act as a preventive to those who might incline to imitate him; but to prevent the publication of bad books by the institution of the censorship, is to check the evil at its source.

The liberty of the press has its inconveniences; nevertheless, the evils which result from it are not to be compared to those of a censorship. Where will you find that rare genius, that superior intelligence, that mortal, accessible to all truths, and inaccessible to any passion, to whom can be intrusted this supreme dictatorship over all the productions of the human mind? Do you suppose that a Locke, a Leibnitz, or a Newton, would have had the presumption to undertake it? And what is this power which you are forced to confer upon inferior men? It is a power which by a singular necessity combines in its exercises all the causes of partiality, and all the characteristics of injustice. What is a censor? He is an interested judge, a sole judge, an arbitrary judge, who proceeds in secret, condemns without a hearing, and decides without appeal. Secrecy of procedure, that greatest of abuses, is absolutely essential. If a book were publicly examined, it would be publishing the book, in order to know if it ought to be published.

As to the evil which results from a censorship, it is impossible to measure it, because it is impossible to tell where it ends. It is nothing less than the danger of stopping the whole progress of the human mind in all its paths. Every new and important truth must of necessity have many enemies, for the single reason that it is new and important. Is it to be presumed that the censor will belong to that class, infinitely the smaller, which elevates itself above established prejudices? And though he should have that uncommon strength of mind, will he have the courage to endanger himself on account of discoveries of which he will not share the glory? There is but one sure course for him to take; to proscribe everything which rises above common ideas, to draw his pen through everything elevated. He risks nothing by prohibition, but everything by permission. In doubtful cases, it will not be he that suffers; it will be Truth.

If the advance of the human mind had depended upon the good will of those in authority, where should we be to-day? Religion, legislation, morals, the physical sciences, all would be in darkness. But it is not necessary to dwell upon so common an argument.

The true censorship is that of an enlightened public, which discountenances false and dangerous opinions, and encourages useful discoveries. In a free country, the audacity of a libel does not save it from general contempt; but by a contradiction easy to be explained, the indulgence of the public in this respect is always in proportion to the rigour of the government.

Chapter III. Indirect Means of preventing the Wish to commit Offences.
We have seen that legislation can only operate by influencing the power, the knowledge, and the will. We have spoken of the indirect means of taking away the power to do injury; we have shown that the policy of preventing men from acquiring information, does more harm than good. All the indirect means, then, which we can use with advantage, must be employed in directing the inclinations of men, in putting into operation the rules of a logic hitherto but little known, *the logic of the will—* a logic which, as Ovid has so well expressed it, seems often to be in opposition to that of the *understanding:—*

> *Video meliora proboque*
> *Deteriora sequor.*

> I see the better and approve it;
> the worse I follow.

The means about to be presented are of a nature to put a stop in many cases to this interior discord; to diminish that contrariety among motives, which often owes its existence to want of address on the part of the legislator, to an opposition which he has himself created between the natural sanction and the political sanction, between the moral sanction and the religious sanction. If he could make all these powers concur towards the same end, all the faculties of man would be in harmony, and the will to do evil would not exist. In cases where this end cannot be attained, it is necessary, at all events, that the force of the tutelary motives should exceed that of the seductive motives.

The indirect means by which the will can be influenced, may be illustrated under the form of political or moral problems, of which the solution may be shown by various examples:

Problem First.—To change the course of dangerous desires, and to direct the inclinations towards amusements conformable to the public interest.

Second.—To arrange so that a given desire may be satisfied without injury, or with the least possible injury.

Third.—To avoid furnishing encouragements to crime.

Fourth.—To increase responsibility in proportion as temptation increases.

Fifth.—To diminish the sensibility to temptation.

Sixth.—To strengthen the impression of punishments upon the imagination.

Seventh.—To facilitate knowledge of the fact of an offence.

Eighth.—To prevent an offence by giving to many persons an immediate interest to prevent it.

Ninth.—To facilitate the means of recognizing and finding individuals.

Tenth.—To increase the difficulty of escape.

Eleventh.—To diminish the uncertainty of prosecutions and punishments.

Twelfth.—To prohibit accessory offences, in order to prevent the principal offence.

After these means, of which the object is special, others more general will be pointed out, such as the culture of benevolence, the culture of honour, the employment of the impulse of religion, and the use to be made of the power of instruction, and of education.

Chapter IV. To change the Course of Dangerous Desires, and to direct the Inclinations towards Amusements conformable to the Public Interest.
The object of direct legislation is to combat pernicious desires, by prohibitions and punishments directed against the injurious acts to which those desires give birth. The object of indirect legislation is to counteract their influence by increasing the force, of less dangerous desires, capable of entering into rivalry with them.

There are two objects to be considered—What are the desires which it is an object to weaken? By what means can that end be obtained?

Pernicious desires are of three classes.—1st, Malevolent passions; 2nd, The appetite for strong drinks; 3rd, Idleness.

The means of weakening these desires may be reduced to three heads:—1st, To encourage honest inclinations; 2nd, To avoid forcing men into idleness; 3rd, To favour the consumption of non-inebriating liquors, in preference to those of an intoxicating quality.

Some persons may be surprised that the catalogue of vicious inclinations is so limited; but they should recollect that the human heart has no passions absolutely bad. There is none which does not stand in need of guidance; and at the same time none which ought to be eradicated. When the angel Gabriel prepared the prophet Mahomet for his divine mission, he plucked from his heart a black spot, which contained the seed of evil. Unfortunately, this operation cannot be practised upon the hearts of ordinary men. The seeds of good and the seeds of evil are inseparably mixed. The inclinations are governed by motives; but all pains and all pleasures are motives; pains to be avoided, pleasures to be pursued. Now, all these motives may produce all sort of effects, from the best to the worst. They are trees which bear wholesome fruits or poisons, according to exposure, according to the care of the gardener, according to the wind that blows, or the temperature of the day. The purest benevolence, confining itself too exclusively to a single subject, or mistaken in its means, may produce great evils. Attachment to one's self, though occasionally it becomes hurtful, is constantly necessary; and in spite of their deformity, the malevolent passions are at least useful as means of defence, as safeguards against the invasion of personal interest. We ought not, then, to attempt rooting out any affections of the human heart, since there is none which does not play its part in the system of utility. We should confine ourselves to the operation of these affections in detail, according to the direction which they take, and the effects which they are likely to produce. A useful balance may be established between these inclinations, by strengthening those which are too strong. It is thus that the cultivator directs the course of waters in such a manner that ·his grounds suffer neither from overflow nor from drought. . . .

The first expedient, as I have said, is to encourage innocent amusements. It is a branch of that science, so complicated and so ill-defined, which consists in advancing civilization. The state of barbarism differs from civilization by two characteristic traits:—1st, The force of the *irascible* appetites; 2nd, The small number of objects of enjoyment offered to the *concupiscent* appetites.

The occupations of a savage after he has supplied himself with physical necessaries, the only ones he knows, are soon described. The pursuit of revenge; the pleasure of drunkenness if he has the means; sleep; or perfect indolence; such is the sum total of his resources. Each of these inclinations is favourable to the development and to the action of the other. Resentments find easy access to a mind unoccupied; idleness leads to drunkenness; and drunkenness produces quarrels, which nourish and multiply resentments. The pleasures of love, not being mingled with the sentimental refinements which embellish and increase them, seem not to play a great part in the life of the savage, and go but a little way towards filling up the intervals of exertion.

Under a regular government the necessity of vengeance is suppressed by legal protection, and the pleasure of giving one's self up to it is counteracted by the fear of punishment; the power of indolence is enfeebled; but the love of strong liquors is not diminished. A nation of savages and a nation of hunters are convertible expressions. The life of the hunter, as well as that of the fisherman, provided they know how to preserve the game they take, affords long intervals of idleness; while in a civilized state, the mass of the community is composed of labourers and artisans, who have scarcely the leisure necessary for sleep and relaxation. But the misfortune is, that the passion for strong drink can be satisfied in the midst of a most laborious life, and that it trenches upon the hours allotted to repose. In the lowest conditions poverty is a restraint upon it; but artisans, whose labour is better paid, can make great sacrifices to this fatal taste, and the opulent classes may devote all their time to it. Thus we see, in ages of barbarism, that the upper classes have divided their whole life between war; the chase, which is the image of war; the animal functions; and long repasts, of which drunkenness was the greatest attraction. Such is the whole history of a great proprietor, a great feudal lord of the Middle Ages. The privilege of this noble warrior, or of this noble hunter, extended into the midst of a more civilized society the occupations and the character of a savage.

This being so, every innocent amusement which human art can invent, is useful under a double point of view:—1st, For the very pleasure which results from it; 2nd, From its tendency to weaken the dangerous inclinations above described. By innocent amusements must be understood all those which cannot be proved to be injurious. Their introduction being favourable to the happiness of society, it is the duty of the legislator to encourage them, or, at least, to put no obstacle in their way. They will be enumerated here; first, those which are esteemed the most gross, and afterwards those which suppose more refinement.

1st, The introduction of a variety of aliments, and the progress of the art of gardening, applied to the production of nutritious vegetables.

2nd. The introduction of non-inebriating liquors, of which tea and coffee are the principal. These two articles, which superficial minds will be astonished to see figuring in a catalogue of moral objects, are so much the more useful, since they come into direct competition with inebriating liquors.

3rd. Progress in all that constitutes elegance, whether in dress, furniture, the embellishment of grounds, etc.

4th. The invention of plays and pastimes, whether athletic or sedentary, among which games of cards hold a distinguished rank. Games of hazard should alone be excluded. These tranquil sports have brought the sexes together, have diminished *ennui,* that malady peculiar to the human race, especially to the opulent class and to the old.

5th. The cultivation of music.

6th. Theatres, assemblies, public amusements.

7th. The cultivation of the arts and sciences, and of literature.

When these different means of enjoyment are placed in opposition to the means necessary to provide for subsistence, they are called objects of luxury; but if their tendency be such as is above suggested, luxury, singular as it may appear, is rather a source of virtue than of vice.

This branch of policy has not been entirely neglected; but it has been cultivated rather with political than with moral views. The object has rather been to render the people tranquil and submissive to the government, than to render the citizens more united among themselves, more happy, more industrious, more virtuous. . . .

The rigid observation of Sunday, such as prevails in Scotland, in England, and in some parts of Germany, is a violation of this policy. The Act of Parliament upon this subject, passed in 1781, seems more appropriate to the times of Cromwell than our own. It prohibits people from every kind of Sunday amusement, except sensual pleasures, drunkenness, and debauchery. It was in the name of good morals that a law so contrary to good morals was enacted. Sunday becomes by this kind of rigour an institution in honour of idleness, and profitable to all the vices.

Two suppositions are necessary to justify such a law: one, that amusements, innocent six days in the week, change their nature, and become mischievous on the seventh; the other, that idleness, the mother of all the vices, is the safeguard of religion. I do not know what to make of these ideas; let the theologians expound them. . . .

To deprive the people one day in the week of pleasures acknowledged to be innocent, is to take away a portion of their happiness; for if happiness is not composed of pleasures, of what is it composed? How is it possible to justify the severity of the legislator, who, without necessity, takes away from the labouring classes those little enjoyments which soften their hard lot, and who forces them into gloominess or vice, under pretext of religion?

There are two ways of doing injury to mankind: one, the introduction of pains; the other, the exclusion of pleasures. If one of these ways deserves to be condemned, how can the other be worthy of praise? Both are acts of tyranny; for in what does tyranny consist, if not in this? It is only effects which are here spoken of; no doubt good is intended; but it is easier to reason vaguely, than to go to the bottom of a matter; to float here and there between folly and wisdom, than to persevere in one or the other; to follow the current of prejudice, than to resist its torrent. However good the intention may be, it is certain that the tendency of this ascetic practice is hurtful and immoral.

Happy the people which is seen to elevate itself above gross and brutal vices, to cultivate elegance of manner, the pleasures of society, the embellishment of gardens, the fine arts, the sciences, public amusements, the exercises of the understanding! Religions which inspire gloom, governments which render men distrustful and which keep them apart, contain the germ of the greatest vices, and the most injurious passions. . . .

Chapter XIX. Use to be made of the Power of Instruction. . . . Government ought not to do everything by force; it is only the body which submits to that; nothing but wisdom can extend its empire over the mind. When a government orders, it but gives its subjects an artificial interest to obey; when it enlightens, it gives them an interior motive, the influence of which they cannot evade. The best method of instruction is the simple publication of facts, but sometimes it is advisable to aid the public in forming a judgment upon those facts.

When measures of government, excellent in themselves, are seen to fail through the opposition of an ignorant people, we feel an immediate irritation against the stupidity of the multitude, and a disinclination to trouble ourselfes further with the promotion of the public good. But when we come to reflect, when we observe that this opposition was easy to be foreseen, and that government, with the habitual pride of authority, had taken no precautions to prepare the minds of the people, to dissipate prejudices, to conciliate confidence, our indignation ought to be transferred from a people ignorant and deceived, to its disdainful and despotic rulers.

Experience has proved, contrary to the general anticipation, that newspapers are one of the best means of directing opinion, of quieting its feverish movements, and of dissipating those falsehoods and concocted rumours by which the enemies of government aim to accomplish their evil designs. By means of these papers, instruction descends from the government to the people, and remounts from the people to the government; the more liberty the press enjoys the easier it is to ascertain the current of opinion, so as to act with certainty.

To form an adequate idea of their utility, it is necessary to go back to the times when newspapers did not exist, and to consider the scenes of imposture, political and religious, which were played off with success, in countries where the people could not read. The last of these personators of royalty was Pugatcheff. Would it have been possible in our times to play such a part in France or in England? Would not the imposture be unmasked as soon as it was announced? There are offences which are not even attempted among enlightened nations; the ease of detecting imposture prevents their existence.

There are many other snares from which the government can protect the people, by public instructions. How many frauds are practised in commerce, in the arts, in the price or quality of goods, which it would be easy to put an end to by exposing them! How many dangerous remedies, or rather true poisons, are impudently sold by empirics, as marvellous secrets, as to which it would be easy to disabuse the most credulous, by making known their composition! How many mischievous opinions, errors fatal or absurd, which might be extinguished at their birth, by enlightening public opinion! . . .

The principal sort of instruction which governments owe to the people, is knowledge of the laws. How can we require laws to be obeyed, when they are not even known? How can they be known, unless they are published under the simplest forms, so that each individual may read for himself, the enactments which are to regulate his conduct?

The legislator may exercise an influence over public opinion, by causing to be compiled a body of political morals, analogous to the body of laws, and divided in the same manner into a general and particular codes. The most delicate questions relative to each profession might be explained. It would not be necessary to confine the work to mere didactic lessons; by intermingling a judicious selection of historical anecdotes, it might be made a book of amusement for persons of all ages.

To compose such moral codes, would be dictating, as it were, the judgments of public opinion upon these different questions of politics and morals. In the same spirit, there might be added to these moral codes a list of popular prejudices, to which should be subjoined the considerations which prove their fallacy.

If sovereign power has ever appeared before men with dignity, it was in the *Instructions,* published by Catherine II, for a code of laws. Let us consider for a moment this unique example, distinct from the remembrance of an ambitious reign. It is impossible to see without admiration a woman descending from the car of victory to civilize so many semi-barbarous tribes, and to offer them the finest maxims of philosophy, sanctioned by the approval of an empress. Superior to the vanity of composing this work herself, she borrowed the best that could be found in the writings of the wise men of the age; but by adding the weight of her authority, she lent to those writers more than she borrowed. . . .

Chapter XX. Use to be made of the Power of Education. Education may be considered as the government of a domestic magistrate.

The analogies between a family and a state are of a nature to strike at the first glance; but the *differences* are not less obvious, and are equally deserving of attention.

1st. Domestic government needs to be more active, more vigilant, more occupied with details, than civil government. Without an attention always vigilant families could not subsist. Civil authority cannot do better than to trust the management of personal interests to the prudence of individuals who always understand them better than the magistrate; but the head of a family must be constantly aiding the inexperience of those submitted to his care.

Here it is that the censorship can be exercised,—a policy which we have condemned in civil government. The domestic governor may protect those subject to his authority from knowledge which may do them harm; he can watch over their social intercourse and their studies; he can accelerate or retard the progress of their enlightenment, according to circumstances.

2nd. This continual exercise of power, which would be liable to so many abuses in a state, is much less so in a family; for the father and mother have a natural affection for their children, far stronger than that of the civil magistrate for those whom he governs. On their part, indulgence is generally the prompting of nature, while severity is the effect of reflection. . . .

4th. It is especially as regards the power of rewarding, that these two governments differ. All the amusements, all the wants of the young, may be made to assume a remuneratory character by granting them on certain conditions, after certain performances. In the Isle of Minorca, the dinner of the boys depended upon their skill in shooting the bow; and the honour of eating at the public table was the prize alloted at Lacedemon to the warlike virtues of the young. No civil government is rich enough to do much by rewards; no father is so poor as not to possess an inexhaustible fund of them.

The legislator ought nevertheless to pay particular attention to youth, that season of lively and durable impressions, in order to direct the course of the inclinations towards those tastes most conformable to the public interest. . . .

But when education is considered as an indirect means of preventing offences, an essential reform is evidently needed. The class most neglected ought to become the principal object of its cares. The less the parents are capable of discharging their duty in this respect, the more necessary it is that the government should make up for their deficiencies. Not only should attention be given to orphans left in indigence, but also to children whose parents are not of a character to be trusted; to those who have already committed some offence; and to those who, being destitute of protectors and resources, are a prey to all the seductions of want. These classes, so absolutely neglected in the greater number of states, become, in consequence, the pupils of crime.

A man of rare beneficence, the Chevalier Paulet, created at Paris an institution for more than two hundred children whom he took from among the very poorest class. His plan rested upon four principles: To offer the pupils many objects of study and of labour, and to leave them the greatest possible latitude of taste; to employ them in mutual instruction, by offering to the scholar, as the highest reward of proficiency, the honour of becoming in his turn a master; to employ them in all the domestic services of the establishment, for the double purpose of instruction and economy; to govern them by means of themselves, by putting each pupil under the inspection of an older one, in a way to render them securities for each other. In this establishment, everything breathed an appearance of freedom and gaiety; there was no punishment except compulsive idleness, and a change of dress. The more advanced pupils were as much interested in the general success as the founder himself; and the whole was going on prosperously, when the revolution, amid the general overthrow, swallowed up also this little colony.

A greater extent might be given to institutions of this kind, and their expensiveness might be diminished, either by teaching a great number of trades, or by retaining the pupils till the age of eighteen or twenty, so that their labour might contribute to discharge the expense of their education, and to aid in that of the younger pupils. Schools upon this plan, instead of being an expense to the state, might become lucrative enterprises. But the pupils themselves should be interested in the labour, by allowing them a fair rate of wages, to be paid them at leaving the school. . . .

Chapter XXII. Means of Diminishing the Bad Effect of Offences. General Result and Conclusion. The general result of the principles laid down in this treatise upon the subject of penal legislation, offers a happy perspective, and well-founded hopes of diminishing offences and of diminishing punishments. At first, this subject presents to the mind only sombre ideas, images of suffering and of terror. But while occupied with this class of evils painful feelings soon give place to agreeable and consoling sentiments, when it is discovered that the human heart is not corrupted by any inherent and incurable perversity; that the multiplicity of offences is principally owing to errors of legislation easy to be reformed; and that even the evil that results from them is susceptible of being repaired in various ways.

This is the great problem of penal legislation:—1st. To reduce all the evil of offences, as far as possible, to that kind which can be cured by a pecuniary compensation. 2nd, To throw the expense of this cure upon the authors of the evil, or, in their default, upon the public. What can be done in this respect is much more than is generally imagined.

The word *cure* is employed in order to present the party injured, whether it be an individual or the community, under the character of a patient suffering from a disorder. The comparison is just, and it points out the procedure best adapted to the end in view, without the intermixture of popular passions, and of antipathies, which ideas of crime are but too apt to awaken, even in legislators themselves. . . .

Do not forget that all penal police is but a choice of evils. Let the wise administrator of punishments always keep the balance in his hand, and in his zeal to prevent trifling evils let him avoid the imprudence of himself producing great ones. Death is almost always a remedy which is unnecessary or inefficacious. It is not necessary as to those whom an inferior punishment might deter from crime, or whom imprisonment might restrain; it has no efficacy as to those who throw themselves, so to speak, in its way as a refuge against despair. The policy of a legislator who punishes every offence with death, is like the pusillanimous terror of a child who crushes the insect he does not dare to look at. But if the circumstances of society, if the frequency of a great offence demand this terrible means, be careful, without aggravating the torments of death, to give it an aspect more dreadful than nature gives it; surround it with mournful accessories, with emblems of crime, and the tragic pomp of ceremony.

But be slow to believe in this necessity for death. By disusing it as a punishment you will prevent it as a crime; for when men are placed between two offences it is desirable to give them a sensible interest not to commit the greater. It is desirable to convert the assassin into a thief; and to give him a reason for preferring a reparable to an irreparable offence.

That which can be repaired is comparatively trifling. Everything that can be made up for by a pecuniary indemnity, may soon become as if it had never been; for if the injured individual always receives an equivalent compensation, the alarm caused by the offence ceases altogether, or is reduced to its lowest term.

It is an object highly desirable that the fund of compensation due for offences should be amassed from among the delinquents themselves, either by being levied upon their property, or obtained from the profits of their compulsory labour. If this were so, security would be the inseparable companion of innocence; and grief and anguish would fall exclusively to the lot of the disturbers of social order. Such is the point of perfection to which we ought to aspire, though we can only expect to reach it slowly and by continuous efforts. It is enough for me to have pointed out the end. The happiness of attaining it will be the reward of persevering and enlightened governments.

This means failing, it is necessary to provide compensation either from the public treasury, or by means of *private insurances*.

The imperfections of our laws, in this behalf, are very flagrant. If an offence is committed, those who have suffered from it, either in their persons or their fortune, are abandoned to their fate. But society, which they have contributed to uphold, and which has undertaken to protect them, owes them an indemnity.

When an individual, even in his own case, prosecutes a criminal at his own expense, he is not less the defender of the state than he who fights its foreign enemies; the losses which he sustains in defending the public ought to be made up for at the public expense.

But when an innocent person has suffered by mistake of the courts, when he has been arrested, detained, subjected to suspicion, condemned to all the misery of a trial and a long confinement, it is not only for his sake, but for her own, that Justice should grant him compensation. Established to repair injuries, does she desire an exclusive privilege to injure?

Governments have made no provision for any of these indemnities. In England, some voluntary associations have been formed to supply this deficiency. If the institution of insurance is good in one case, it is good in all, with the precautions necessary to prevent negligence and fraud. . . .

Insurances against offences may have two objects:—1st, To create a fund to indemnify the parties injured, in case the delinquent is unknown or insolvent; 2nd, To defray, in the first instance, the expense of judicial prosecutions in favour of the poor. This payment might be extended to cases purely civil.

But the method of these indemnities would be foreign to the subject of this treatise; its principles have been explained elsewhere, and I must here confine myself to the announcement of the general result of this work. It is this: *That by good laws almost all offences may be reduced to acts which can be repaired by a simple pecuniary compensation, and thus the evil of offences may be almost wholly done away.*

At first, this result, simply announced, does not strike the imagination; it must be meditated upon before its importance can be perceived, and its weight be felt. It is not the brilliant society of fashion that can be interested by a formula almost arithmetic in expression. It is offered, statesmen, to you! It is yours to judge it!

The science of which the basis has been investigated in this work can be pleasing only to elevated souls who are warmed with a passion for the public good. It has no connection with that trickish and subversive kind of politics which prides itself upon clandestine projects, which acquires a glory composed wholly of human misery, which sees the prosperity of one nation in the abasement of another, and which mistakes convulsions of government for conceptions of genius. We are here employed upon the greatest interests of humanity; the art of forming the manners and the character of nations; of raising to its highest point the security of individuals; and of deriving results equally beneficial from different forms of government. Such is the object of this science; frank and generous; asking only for light; wishing nothing exclusive; and finding no means so sure to perpetuate the benefits it confers as to share them with the whole family of nations.

Panopticon Papers

A Note on *Panopticon Papers*

Panopticon was the central event of Bentham's life. He devoted nearly a quarter of a century, from 1789 to 1812, to it, and he suffered the tortures of the damned. How could it be otherwise than central? All his life he preached on the text, theory without practice is worthless; and he rejoiced to discover his brother's architectural drawings for a rotunda-shaped workshop and their possibilities as reform prisons slowly opened up to him. His vision gradually encompassed all of England, then Europe, and the world. In the early days of the enterprise, when he still felt hopeful about it, he playfully described a dream of the Great Dragon who exclaimed, "Be of good cheer: thou shalt build the Panopticon: and thy fame shall go forth amongst the nations." [1]

Panopticon has at least two histories, and they are both of them tragicomical, in the style of Dickens' Circumlocution Office. There is Bentham's personal story, as he was buffeted from office to office, plunged in and out of bankruptcy, taunted, reviled, ignored, defended, and at last, exhausted and broken-hearted. Its importance lies not so much in its immediate as its long-range emotional and intellectual impact: how did this adventure in despair affect his thought? How did his ideas change under this siege of torments? At the bottom of his wretchedness he wrote to his stepbrother, Charles Abbot, in 1802, "Mr. Addington's hope is—what Mr. Pitt's was—to see me die broken-hearted, like a rat

[1] X, p. 274.

in a hole."[2] He rose to a crescendo of avenging eloquence. "I may die any day: but so long as perfidy, and treachery, and oppression, and corruption, and arbitrary power, and contempt of Parliament, and the persevering propagation of immorality and misery are the order of the day with him, so long as I live he will find me living to his annoyance. Living did I say? Yes: and even when I am dead, he will not be rid of me."

The great anti-slavery reformer, Wilberforce, was then one of Bentham's strongest supporters in Parliament, and he wrote, "Never was any one worse used than Bentham. I have seen the tears run down the cheeks of that strong-minded man through vexation, at the pressing importunity of creditors, and the insolence of official underlings, when, day after day, he was begging at the Treasury for what was indeed a mere matter of right. How indignant did I often feel when I saw him thus treated by men infinitely his inferiors! I could have extinguished them. He was quite soured by it; and I have no doubt that many of his harsh opinions afterwards, were the fruits of this ill-treatment."[3]

But were they? This is the important question, and it is still open, despite the fact that Wilberforce's judgment has always been taken for granted. Here is early Bentham, men say: Tory, conservative, *before* Panopticon; then come the years of miserable misadventure; here then follows the late Bentham, bitter, ever more vituperative, democratic, and radical, the enemy of government. It is too easy. Bentham's responses were not nearly so primitive. Certainly the £23,000 reimbursement paid to him in 1813 went a long way to mollify his anguish, and he was thereafter enabled to underwrite a number of favorite social inventions.[4] To his intense delight and the joy of the whole Mill family, who were his regular guests, he rented for some years the princely Ford Abbey and played the gentleman-farmer, proudly showing off his peacocks and deer, and the Renaissance tapestries in the grand halls.

But long before 1813 he had come to terms with his misfortune. From the beginning he had had several other important projects going; during the '90's he also wrote over 4,000 pages on the Elizabethan Poor Laws and their intended amendment under Pitt. He saw no reason why Panopticons were not equally adaptable to housing paupers as well as prisoners. These, too, were the years of his writings on economics; he wrote thousands of pages in the manner of Adam Smith, but specifically de-

[2] XI, p. 139. Addington had recently replaced Pitt as Prime Minister.
[3] X, p. 390 note.
[4] *E.g.,* Robert Owen's New Lanark mills and a Chrestomathic progressive school in his own backyard. Though this last was never built, it put him to considerable architectural costs.

signed to cope with the crises of the French Wars.[5] Suddenly in 1802 he gave up writing on economics entirely; it flashed into his mind that he really had nothing new to say, and therefore he thereafter said nothing. But that did not mean sitting back indolently to brood; he could no more have done that than stem the tides. Instead, he turned once again to English law, and began in 1802 his monumental *Rationale of Judicial Evidence*. As the years went by he became more and more involved in the more theoretical and arcane parts of his system—logic, language, epistomology; and by 1815 he had also written *Chrestomathia* and *A Table of the Springs of Action*.

The fact is, almost all of Bentham's ideas had been stored in embryo in his mind ever since "that wonderful year," 1768–69, when he had first discovered Beccaria, Priestley, Locke, Helvétius, and the other *philosophes*. He had been an active democrat at least since the French Revolution, whose spirit he entered with the highest enthusiasm; it did not take the failure of Panopticon to make him one. It did not even change his ideas on monarchy, though it certainly made them more intense and eccentric. He began to think of it as George III's personal conspiracy against him. As we see in the text below, titled, "History of the War Between Jeremy Bentham and George III, By One of the Belligerents," Bentham believed that George III refused to sign the paper of transfer of the final £1,000 payment because Lord Spencer, who was most reluctant to see a prison arise on his land, which presumably would devalue the rest of his neighboring property, was a good friend of his.

This may or may not have been the case; we do not know. But it led Bentham into curious misapprehensions about the effective sovereign power of monarchy. In fact, it was becoming less and less powerful as Parliament became more so; Bentham was mistaken. Probably this led him further in the direction of republicanism than he had originally been prepared to go. At any rate, the great *Constitutional Code*[6] was designed for the uses of a republic.

Why did Bentham's Panopticon plan fail, despite the fact that special parliamentary legislation had been enacted to authorize it? Why did year after year drag by with nothing accomplished? Why was George III not persuaded to sign the final paper? Bentham's dear friend, the brilliant, astute barrister Sir Samuel Romilly, probably gave him the correct an-

---

[5] None of these writings are included here, partly because they are neo-Smithian; partly because Bentham himself set little store by them; and partly because they were not long ago published in an excellent three-volume edition edited by Werner Stark, *Jeremy Bentham's Economic Writings*.

[6] See Volume IX of the Collected Edition.

swer. The public, he tried to explain to the over-wrought and exasperated Bentham, does not care tuppence for prisons and prisoners at any time; but during these years of critical emergency, during the French Wars, they care nothing at all, and Parliament, the Home Office, and the Treasury took their cues accordingly.

The second history of Panopticon is sociological and is a chapter in penology. Here again Bentham's views are taken for granted. He is written off as a narrow-minded, heartless eccentric who called for retrograde measures like solitary confinement; and once again, this is mistaken. Taken by themselves, his reforms do not perhaps seem so advanced; but measured, as they must be in any fair judgment, against the brutality, the bestiality rampant in the hulks and prisons of eighteenth-century England, they were amazingly progressive. The fundamental injunction in those days was, let the men rot! They were pitched into the fetid hulks, three or four to a berth; left often to starve unless they could pay for food; left shivering in the dark, without medical care, left defenseless among every kind of malefactor, young children with hardened prostitutes, thieves, murderers; the well with the diseased. If they were not corrupt when they went in, they were surely corrupt when they left. These foul conditions had been exposed all over England and Europe by Bentham's favorite reformer, John Howard, the great prison inspector. Bentham hoped to take up where he left off, and actually to transform the entire institutional structure by setting up Panopticons all over England, about one day's walking distance or thirty miles apart. He undertook to feed the inmates all they could eat of substantial wholesome food, to dress them warmly and comfortably, to issue them each a separate bed, to heat the building, and keep it well lit, always to have a doctor and nurses at hand, to train each man for suitable work in one or more money-making skills, to provide him with work and pocket money during imprisonment and a lump sum on leaving, to build "post-liberation houses" or way stations for those who found civilian adjustment difficult, and, indeed, dozens of other thoughtful provisions designed never to let the prisoners forget that they were men—even useful and respected men.

During the many years that Bentham was so deeply involved with Panopticon, his ideas on prison reform became ever more imaginative, liberal, and benevolent. Keeping his medical analogy, he began to consider criminals as ill children, who needed not harsh and vindictive punishment but sympathetic prescriptions. He always deplored solitary confinement, although his first drafts necessarily included provisions for it, because the Blackstone-Eden Hard Labour Bill which formed its legislative foundation demanded it. But as time went by he discarded it altogether and in his delightful, visionary schemes for "Panopticon Hill Villages," his most trusted prisoners were almost free to come and go; they were to live in their own cottages and farm the open fields surrounding the villages. These villages were intended to be grand social hospitals, unique experiments in wholesale social engineering, where every kind of misfit or outcast, the poor, the unemployed, the elderly, orphans, criminals, pensioned soldiers and sailors, etc., were to find comfortable homes and work. Exercising his prodigious gift of invention, Bentham designed bars with fountains spraying scented, colored waters, swimming pools, bands and orchestras, child care centers, progressive schools for adults as well as children, experimental breeding farms, a national system of savings banks and hotels. Criminals were not to be ostracized; they were full-time members of the community. To be sure, they had fewer rights and were more strictly guarded; but the choice was open to them to win freedom and full honor in the community.

Panopticon Papers

Outline of the Plan of Construction of a Panopticon Penitentiary House: as designed by Jeremy Bentham, of Lincoln's Jun. Esq.

"Thou art about my path, and about my bed:
and spiest out all my ways
If I say, peradventure the darkness shall cover me,
then shall my night be turned into day.
Even there also shall thy hand lead me; and thy right hand
shall hold me.

PSALM CXXXIX (XI, 96)

The building *circular*—the cells occupying the circumference—the keepers, etc.—the centre—an *intermediate annular well,* all the way up, crowned by a *sky-light* usually open, answering the purpose of a *ditch* in *fortification,* and of a *chimney* in *ventilation*—the cells, laid *open* to it by an iron *grating.*

The *yards* without, laid out upon the same principle:—as also the *communication* between the building and the yards.

By *blinds* and other contrivances, the keeper concealed from the observation of the prisoners, unless where he thinks fit to show himself: hence, on their part, the sentiment of an invisible omnipresence.—The whole circuit reviewable with little, or, if necessary, without any, change of place.

One station in the inspection part affording the most perfect view of the *two* stories of cells, and a considerable view of another:—the result of a difference of level.

The same cell serving for *all* purposes: *work, sleep, meals, punishment, devotion:* The unexampled airiness of construction conciliating this economy with the most scrupulous regard to health. The minister, with a numerous, but mostly concealed auditory of visitors, in a regular *chapel* in the *centre,* visible to half the cells, which on this occasion may double their complement.

The *sexes,* if both are admitted, *invisible* to each other.

194

Solitude, or *limited seclusion, ad libitum.*—But, unless for punishment, limited seclusion in assorted companies of two, three, and four, is preferred: an arrangement, upon this plan alone exempt from danger. The degree of *seclusion* fixed upon may be preserved, in all places, and at all time, *inviolate.* Hitherto, where solitude has been aimed at, some of its chief purposes have been frustrated by occasional associations.

The *approach, one* only—*gates* opening into a walled *avenue* cut through the area. Hence, no strangers near the building without *leave,* nor without being surveyed from it as they pass, nor without being known to come on *purpose.* The gates, of *open* work, to *expose hostile* mobs: on the other side of the road, a wall with a branch of the road behind, to *shelter peaceable* passengers from the fire of the building. A mode of fortification like this, if practicable in a city, would have saved the *London prisons,* and prevented the unpopular accidents in *St. George's Fields.*

The *surrounding wall,* itself surrounded by an open palisade, which serves as a fence to the grounds on the other side.—Except on the side of the approach, *no public path* by that fence.—A *sentinel's walk* between: on which no one else can set foot, without forcing the fence, and declaring himself a trespasser at least, if not an enemy. To the four walls, four such walks *flanking* and *crossing* each other at the ends. Thus each sentinel has two to check him.

Thus simple are the leading principles.—The application and preservation of them in the detail, required, as may be supposed, some variety of contrivance.

N.B.—The expense of this mode might, it is supposed, be brought *within half* that of the late ingenious Mr. Blackburn's, which was £120 a man.

History of the War Between Jeremy Bentham and George the Third. By One of the Belligerents

(1830, XI, 96)

But for George the Third, all the prisoners in England would, years ago, have been under my management. But for George the Third, all the paupers in the country would, long ago, have been under my management.

The work entitled "Pauper Management," the work to which this brief, and, it is hoped, not altogether uninstructive nor uninteresting history, is designed to serve as an introduction,—would have become law. But for George the Third, one of the joint wishes and endeavours of Pitt the Second and Lord Melville the First [Home Secretary in Pitt's admin-istration.—M.P.M.], to which no just condemnation can be attached, (would they had been more numerous,) would have been fulfilled. It was with me the war commenced. I confess it. I feel no need of being ashamed of it: it is for the reader to say to himself whether I have or no. Yes, I was the first aggressor,—meaning in the character of a subject mak-ing in a certain way war upon his sovereign. But whether that sovereign had not been intentionally an aggressor in endeavouring to plunge his subjects into a groundless war against a foreign sovereign, the reader will judge.

[In his *Anti-Machiavel Letters*, Bentham attacked the government for its Anti-Russian belligerency, 1789.—M.P.M.]

I paralysed his hand. I saved the two countries, perhaps others likewise, from this calamity. He vowed revenge; and to effect it he wounded me through the sides of this his country, not to speak of so many others.

No muse shall I invoke: no muse would listen to me. A plain tale is all I have to tell: let others, if any, who may feel disposed and able, stick flowers in it.

Catharine the Second had celebrity, nor that altogether undeserved. In a female body she had a masculine mind. She laid the foundation of a code,—an all-comprehensive code.

My brother, whose loss I had to lament not many years ago,—my only brother, of whose education, he being nine years my junior, the super-intendence fell into my hands, when on a traveller's visit to that country, was found possessed of rare talents, was arrested, put into office, and succeeded.

In the year 1786, or 1787, I being on a visit to my brother, of a year and a half, or thereabouts, at Crichoff in White Russia, where he was stationed with a battalion of a thousand men under his command, on an estate then lately purchased by Prince Potemkin, Prime Minister of Rus-sia, under Catharine the Second, the idea presented itself to him of a mode of architecture, to which I gave the name of Panopticon, from the two Greek words,—one of which signified everything, the other a place of sight. A Mr Pinchbeck, a sort of artist, who enjoyed more or less of the personal favour of George the Third, had either anticipated me, or afterwards followed me, in the employment given to that name.

The purpose to which this rotunda-form was destined to be employed by my brother, was that of a large workshop, in which, with or without the benefit of steam-engine power, occupations capable of being in any degree diversified, might be carried on; partitions in the form and posi-tion of radii of the circle being employed in separating from each other such as required to be so separated: in the centre was the apartment, styled, from its destination, the Inspector's Lodge: from thence by turning round his axis, a functionary, standing or sitting on the central point, had it in his power to commence and conclude a survey of the whole establishment in the twinkling of an eye, to use a proverbial phrase. But forasmuch as men had not in these days,—whatsoever may have been the case in the days of Pliny and the traveller Mandeville,—any visual organs seated in the back part of the human frame, it was considered accordingly, that it was material to good order, that the workmen, whose operations were designed to be thus watched, should not be able to know each of them respectively at any time, whether he was or was not at that moment in a state in which the eyes of the inspector were directed to his person in such manner as to take a view of it: accordingly, for the production of this effect, provision was made of an annular screen, pierced in such a manner with slits or holes, that by any person it might be seen whether a person, whom, in this or that other part of the building, he was taking a view of, was knowing whether he was viewed or not.

Taking in hand this idea, I made application of it for the purpose of the case in which the persons subjected to inspection, were placed in that situation, and not only for the purpose of being subjected to direction, but also for the purpose of being made to suffer in the way of punishment: in a word, as a place of labour and confinement for convicts.

To the carrying this design into effect, two requisites were necessary:— The first an appropriate form of architecture as above, and an appropriate plan of management, so organized as to draw from that mode of architecture, as far as practicable, all the advantages it was capable of affording. In the course of my reflections on this latter subject, I came to my conclusion, that the customary plan pursued in works instituted by Government, and carried on, on account of Government, was, in an eminent degree, ill adapted to the purpose: though to this general rule, particular exceptions there might be; but to the particular purpose then in hand, they had no application. Accordingly, management by contract, I became convinced, was the only plan that afforded a probability of good success.

In pursuance of the labours of Howard [John Howard (1726–90), the celebrated prison reformer, one of Bentham's heroes.—M.P.M.], who died a martyr to benevolence, Sir William Blackstone, the illustrious Commentator on the Law of England,—Sir William Blackstone, in connexion with Mr Eden, Afterwards coroneted by the title of Lord Auckland, devised a plan of architecture and management of a prison for the confinement of convicts, and accordingly drew up for that purpose a Bill which received the official denomination of the *Hard-Labour Bill.* Their plan was in some form or other laid before the public, with such explanations as were thought requisite. The plan of management was—not contract-management, as above, but trust-management: the managing hands, whether one or more, not having any interest in the success: gaining nothing in case of profit, losing nothing in case of loss: in a word, their interest was not to be coincident with their duty. On the contrary, the one was destined to operate in constant opposition to the other: for where a man has nothing to gain by labour, it is his interest to be idle or do anything but labour.

Actuated by these conceptions, I published, anno 1789, a tract, entitled, "View of the Hard-Labour Bill." In this work I took in hand the plan of the two illustrious statesmen, applied to it the above principle, examined it in all its details, and the result was what appeared to me to be a complete demonstration of its inaptitude. Blackstone, notwithstanding the war I had made upon him in my "Fragment on Government," in answer to the present I made him of a copy of that little work sent me a civil note, acknowledging that he and his cooperator had derived assistance from it: they went to work notwithstanding, and obtained an Act of Parliament, under and by virtue of which they fixed upon a site for the erection. It was a spot of about fourscore acres, in the vicinity of Battersea, and distinguished by the name of Battersea Rise. For ascertaining the sum to be paid for it by Government, a jury, according to custom, was summoned, and assessed the value at a sum between six and seven thousand pounds. On payment of that sum it was in the power of Government at any time to take possession of it, and transfer it into any hands at pleasure.

From causes not necessary to bring on this occasion to view, the undertaking lingered, and the verdict of the appraising jury remained without effect. Meantime, my brother remaining still in Russia, I was unable, for want of his assistance, to determine upon the exact form of the edifice, and through want of means, to make a proposal for the performance of the function in question by contract. In the year 1790, the return of my brother to England, furnished me with the requisite architectural skill; and the death of my father, which took place in March 1792, with the addition of assistance from without, supplied the pecuniary means. Accordingly, in March 1792, I sent in to Mr Pitt, then First Lord of the Treasury; and Mr Dundas, then Secretary of State, afterwards created Lord Melville, a proposal for the taking charge of convicts to the number of a thousand, according to the above-mentioned plan of construction and management upon the terms therein mentioned. This proposal, in the terms in which it was sent in, is here subjoined at the bottom of the page.*

[*Outline of a Plan for the Management of a Panopticon Penitentiary-House
I would undertake,—

1st. To furnish the prisoners with a constant supply of wholesome food,
to the extent of their desires; such privations excepted as may be inflicted
in the way of punishment, or in case of necessity, as a spur to industry.
A state of constant famine, and that under every modification of behaviour,
as in some establishments, is what I cannot approve.

2d. To keep them *clad* in a state of tightness and neatness superior to
what is usual among the lower classes, or even in the improved prisons.

3d. To keep them supplied with *beds* and bedding competent to their
situation, and in a state of cleanliness, scarce anywhere conjoined with
liberty.

4th. To ensure to them a sufficient supply of artificial *warmth* and *light,*
whenever the season renders it necessary, and thereby preserve them from
being obliged, as in other places, to desist from or relax in their work, as
well as from suffering, by the inclemency of the weather.

5th. To keep constantly from them, in conformity to the practice so happily received, every kind of *strong* or spirituous *liquors,* unless where ordered
in the way of medicine.

6th. To provide them with *spiritual* and *medical* assistance constantly on
the spot.

7th. To make and maintain such a distribution of their time, as, deduction made of what is necessary for meals and repose, and on Sundays for
devotions, shall fill up the whole measure of it with either productive labour
or profitable *instruction.* To allow them the *sex horas sommo,* the time Lord
Coke allows to his student, and no more: not to leave them stewing or
shivering in bed for sixteen hours out of the four-and-twenty, as in other
improved prisons, to save candles.

8th. To give them an *interest* in their work, by allowing them a share in
the produce.

9th. To convert the prison into a *school,* and by an extended application
of the principle of the *Sunday* schools, to return its inhabitants into the
world instructed, at least as well as in an ordinary school, and the common
and most useful branches of vulgar learning. Extraordinary culture of
extraordinary talents is not in this point of view worth mentioning: it would
be my private amusement: in the account of public benefit,—I should take
no credit for it.

10th. To ensure to them the means of *livelihood* at the *expiration* of their
terms; by giving, to every one of them who wanted it, a trade not requiring
confidence on the part of the employer, and for the produce of which I
could engage to furnish them a demand.

11th. To lay for them the foundation-stone of a *provision* for old *age,*
upon the plan of the Annuity Societies.

12th. To pay a *penal sum* for every *escape,* with or without any default
of mine, irresistible violence from without excepted.

13th. To take upon me the *insurance* of their *lives* for an under premium,
at a rate grounded on an average of the number of deaths among imprisoned criminals.

14th. To take up my ordinary *residence* in the midst of them, and, in
point of health, to share whatever might be their fate.

15th. To present to the Court of King's Bench on a certain day of every

Term, and afterwards print and publish at my own expense, a *Report*, exhibiting in detail, the state, not only *moral* and *medical*, but *economical*, of the Establishment; and then and there to make *answer* to all such *questions* as shall be put to me relative thereto, not only on the part of the Court or Officer of the Crown, but, by leave of the Court, on the part of any person whatsoever: questions, the answer to which might tend to subject me to conviction for any *capital* or other *crime* not excepted: treading under foot a maxim invented by the guilty for the benefit of the guilty, and from which none but the guilty ever derived any advantage.

By neatness and cleanliness, by diversity of employment, by variety of contrivance, and above all, by that peculiarity of construction, which, without any unpleasant or hazardous vicinity, enables the whole establishment to be inspected almost at a view, it should be my study to render it a spectacle, such as persons of all classes would, in the way of amusement, be curious to partake of; and that not only on Sundays at the time of Divine service, but on ordinary days at meal times or times of work: providing thereby a system of inspection, universal, free, and gratuitous, the most effectual and permanent of all securities against abuse.

To any one who should be apprehensive of seeing the condition of convicts made too desirable, I have only this answer—Art lies in meliorating man's lot: any bungler may make it worse. At any rate, what you take from severity you might add to duration.

You see the use of a rent, and that a high one, payable by me, for a building not yet erected, but under my direction, to be erected. The interest of the public is completely mine. Every penny spent beyond necessity lays a tax upon me.

I should require no new confidence. Give the convicts to me as they have been given to the hulks. Capital I should want little or none: the subsistence-money is capital: *that* you would have security for. The hulks are and must be impenetrable to the public eye. They need more than human goodness to ensure them from abuse.

My prison is transparent: my management, no less so. The hulk-masters have, from year to year, to do as they please. A summons from the King's Bench might oust me the same day. I am no Nabob. I want no Jury. I would have none. The best friend to innocence I know of, is open and speedy justice.

Of the dispositions I should bring with me to such an enterprise, or the motives that have urged me on to it, I shall say nothing.—You would inquire, What is public I will mention. The books I send will show, by their dates, that the subject had occupied a warm place in my thoughts, *four* years and *thirteen* years, before any personal views had mixed with it. Those views are but of yesterday. I began with planning, for A and B to execute—you will see that I did.—Every page of the tract just printed (four years ago sent over in manuscript) will show it you: views rising upon views drew my affections after them: till at last I said to myself—Alas! where is the stranger who will enter as deeply as the contriver into the spirit of the contrivance?

On my part, I should wish to stipulate—

1. To have the office assured to the contractor *during good behaviour:* a phrase which, in the ordinary terms, means, for life; but which, on terms like the above, would mean simply what it says.

2. The station of jailor is not, in common account, a very elevated one. The addition of contractor has not much tendency to raise it. Education, profession, connexions, occupations, and objects considered, I hope I should not be thought unreasonable in wishing to be preserved from being altogether confounded with those by whom those situations have been hitherto filled, and from finding myself a sufferer in estimation by having performed a public service. In this view, two expedients present themselves:—one is, the assurance of your assistance towards obtaining a Parliamentary sanction for the offer of standing examination in manner above-mentioned: the other is an eventual assurance, that, if after a fair trial the success of the undertaking, and the propriety of my conduct in it, should appear to have been fully ascertained, I shall be recommended to his Majesty for a mark of distinction not pecuniary, such as may testify that I have incurred no ultimate loss of honour by the service, and afford me some compensation for the intervening risk.]

For giving the requisite powers to the executive authority, an Act of Parliament was necessary. Somehow or other the business lingered: nobody but the King and Prime Minister Pitt knew why. Even Lord Melville, I have some reason to think, remained in a state of ignorance; for, as I still remember, Mr Nepean, then Under-Secretary of State under Mr Dundas, showed me a short note from Mr Dundas to Mr Pitt reproaching him with the delay. What I also remember is, Mr Douglas, created then or afterwards Lord Glenbervie, telling me of something which, on the occasion of an interview of his with Mr Pitt, he had said in the view of expediting it. At length came the day, in 1794, on which the act was passed, by which the doing the business by contract was authorized. And the spot at Battersea Rise, which, as above, had been destined to the reception of a penitentiary establishment on the plan of Sir William Blackstone and Mr Eden, was made to change its destiny, and was transferred to the intended penitentiary to be erected and managed upon my plan. The lingering continued: nobody knew why. Mr Pitt was shy in speaking of it. After three or four years' interval, the business came upon the carpet in another form. In the year 1797 was instituted the important and influential Finance Committee,—the first by which a report approaching to any such length as that which this Committee gave birth to was produced. Mr Abbot having distinguished himself at Christ Church College, Oxford, where, through the medium of Westminster School, he had succeeded to a studentship, had been received into favour by the Duke of Leeds of that day, and through his means had been sent by a rotten borough to the House of Commons, having been called to the Bar. He was nominated Chairman to that committee by Mr Pitt, at the recommendation of Mr Pepper Arden, afterwards made Lord Chief-Justice of the Common Pleas.

Mr Abbot was related to me by marriage. When he was between five and six years old, his mother took for her second husband my father, and became his second wife. He and his elder brother were bred up together with my brother in the house which I now inhabit: they going at the same time for instruction to Westminster School. Between the ages of the Abbots there was an interval of two years,—my brother's was at a nearly equal distance between the two.

In those days Mr Colquhoun, who, upon the institution of the Metropolitan Police Magistracy in the year 1792, was appointed one of the three police magistrates sitting at the Queen Square Westminster Office, had distinguished himself by his work on the Police. By the above-mentioned Finance Committee, he was brought before them with my proposal, the same by which the above-mentioned Act of Parliament had been procured, in his hand. How this happened I never knew,—whether it was of his own accord, or at the suggestion of the Prime Minister, or some other member of the Government. Among the members of the committee was Mr, now the Right Honourable Reginald Pole Carew. He had become my friend, and a warm partisan of the Panopticon system, through the medium of my brother, with whom he had become acquainted at Petersburg. The task of making a Report on the Panopticon plan was committed to his hands. The Report he drew up accordingly in favour of the plan was couched in such strong terms, that prudence suggested and produced the suppression of it. It went into other hands,—whose they were I do not at present recollect, if I ever knew—whether those of Mr Abbot, chairman of the entire committee, or any one else. Of a speech which, on that occasion, Mr Abbot made in the Committee, the substance was at that time reported to me. Referring to some of the most noted instances of cruelty that history records: "We do not sit here," said he, "to try causes; but the cruelty of the cruelest of those cases was not comparable to that which this man has been suffering." On this occasion the Lords of the Treasury were called upon to say whether or no they were prepared to go on with the plan; and if not, why not?—they answered, in cold terms, in the affirmative.

At this time, however, or before, I was informed that the spot at Battersea Rise, which had formed the basis of the proposal made by me, and acceded to as above, could not be given to me. Two personages [were the parties interested,]—the then Archbishop of York, Dr Markham, in right of the see, the paramount proprietor; Earl Spencer, as lessee under a long lease from that same see. The Archbishop had been headmaster of Westminster School during the five or six years which I had passed in that seminary: he submitted without reluctance: a civil letter which he wrote to me on that occasion, intimating his consent, is still in my possession. Lord Spencer demurred: he refused to cede the spot to me:

but he gave me reason to hope that another part of his estate, called, I believe, Battersea Fields, might be conceded to me. His steward, he said, had informed him that the setting up of an institution of that sort, threatened to be detrimental to other parts of his vast property in that neighbourhood. The spot destined to the institution by Parliament, was an elevated one,—the highest part of it at the same height above the water, by which one boundary of it was bathed,—namely, about ninety-two feet,—as the top of the roof of Westminster Abbey. The spot which I had been led to expect in lieu of it, was also contiguous to the river, but was little, if anything, better than a marsh. By the noble earl I was kept from the cold, in hot water, for about a twelvemonth; at the end of which time I was informed that it never had been his intention that I should have either the one spot or the other: but that should he be compelled to give up part of his estate for the purpose, the choice between the two being at the same time allowed to him, it should be the low, and not the elevated ground.

I was thereupon turned adrift, dislodged from this spot, and sent abroad in quest of another spot: like our first parents, "the world before me,"—but if Providence was my guide, she proved for this time but a blind one. Many were the spots thought of, several visited, and two or three provisionally approved of. Of one of them, about seven or eight miles to the south or south-east of London, I remember nothing more at present than that it was elevated,—this property being originally recommended, and always wished for, and to such a degree stony as to be barren. Another is that which is called "Hanging Wood,"—an elevated and beautiful spot on this side of Woolwich.

By what means, in these several cases, the door, after having been opened, was finally shut against me, is not worth recollecting: at length an opportunity that seemed favourable presented itself; the Earl of Salisbury, of that day, happened to be in want of a sum in ready money,—he had a freehold estate at Millbank,—it had for one of its boundaries a line of about half-a-mile in length, and washed all the way by the Thames.

At length the time was come for putting a final extinguisher upon all hopes. The Millbank estate was now in my possession, all but the one piece of garden-ground, for the buying out of the lease of which £1000 was necessary. The mornings, as usual, were passed in the Treasury Chambers, either in a waiting room, not unfrequently the board room itself,—or the passages. I had become familiar with three of the chief clerks: one day said one of them to me, "Well, now you will not have long to wait,—the warrant for the £1000 is gone to the king,—his majesty is a man of business,—seldom does a document wait more than twenty-four hours for his signature." The next day came, and the next to that, and so on for three weeks,—a day or two more or less,—all the while the same familiarity and favour in all faces, but the surprise on both parts continually on the increase. On the day that followed, on repairing to the usual haunt, I found everything converted into ice. Upon my putting some question or other, "Mr Bentham," said the clerk to whom I addressed myself, "you must be sensible that this is a sort of information that is never given, and as seldom asked for." If these were not the very words, this, at any rate, was the very substance. Here ended all hopes of setting up the prison institution. Still, however, the Millbank estate remained in my hands, part and parcel in the occupation of tenants holding of me at will,—other part, at first in the hands out of which it should have been purchased, and at length the lease having expired, in the occupation of a tenant at will as before. Not only the land itself was thus in my possession, but the deeds by which it had been conveyed to me. Until those deeds could be got out of my hands, and transferred to certain others, it was not thought advisable to dispose of the land in any other manner. Various were the stratagems employed for the acquisition of these same documents. The recital would be not only instructive but amusing, could time be spared for it.

I come now to another campaign of the war.

In 1797, Pitt the First, [*sic*] then Prime Minister, brought in his Poor Bill.

Universal was the sensation produced by a measure so important and extensive. It had for its leading idea and groundwork a plan that had been proposed by Mr Ruggles, a country gentleman of Essex.

I took in hand this bill. I dissected it. I proposed a succedaneum to it: of letters, addressed to Arthur Young, for proposed insertion into the Annals of Agriculture, [*sic*] which had been brought into existence a short time before. They appeared, accordingly, in four successive numbers, in the form of letters, addressed to the editor of these same Annals: the matter of them is that which forms the matter of the body of Pauper Management.

It may be seen to contain a complete system of provision for the helpless and indigent portion of the community of England and Wales included: Local field the same as that of Minister Pitt's above-mentioned Poor Bill. *Mutatis mutandis* plan of architecture the same as that of Panopticon plan—devised for the lodgement, maintenance, and employment of prisoners. Note,—that it was for persons of the unoffending class that this new plan of architecture was originally devised. Principle of universal and constant inspectability the same in both cases: inspectability of the inspectors by the eye of the public opinion tribunal the same in both cases: but actual subjection to inspection in no cases except those in which it was required by the different purposes, or objects in view, of the different, or, in some respects, coincident institutions.

Arthur Young was in a state of rapture: he presented me with 250 copies of those Nos. of his Annals in which the matter was contained. By me they were distributed, at different time, among such persons in whose hands they presented to my conception a promise of being of use: whether any of the copies was ever on sale, is more than I can remember: among those presented, were one to Minister Pitt, the other to Senior Secretary of State, George—afterwards Sir George Rose, and one I take for granted, but from inference rather than remembrance, to Secretary Dundas.

All this while Panopticon for Prison Management remained upon the carpet. One day I received from Mr Rose an invitation to call upon him— not at his office, but at his house. Days are, on this occasion, of more importance than months, or even years. Notwithstanding the unequivocal and repeated tokens of approbation that had been given to the Panopticon plan by the Planner-General of all the arrangements of the Prime Minister, my intercourse with him had as yet been no otherwise than at arm's length. In demeanour, master and man, *proportions gardées,* were alike cold and haughty: the man was passionate, rough, and coarse. Imagine my astonishment who can, when, after giving me to understand that those on whom the issue depended had read the work [*i.e., Pauper Management*—M.P.M.] and read it with approbation, he concluded with saying, "Come and dine with me here one day the beginning of next week,—Mr Pitt and Mr Dundas will meet you,—and we will settle about this plan of yours." The day of the week on which this announcement was made was Friday: I was in the seventh heaven. The Monday passed away—the Tuesday in like manner—the Wednesday eke also. There ended the beginning of the week: on the Thursday I heard, as it were, by accident, by whose mouth I did not long remember, that on the Wednesday, instead of myself, Mr Ruggles had been the guest: but that the entertainment had closed with mutual dissatisfaction. From the above-mentioned seventh heaven this intelligence cast me down, if not to the bottom of the abyss of despair, at any rate but a little distance from it—a bush of thorns having caught hold of the skirts of my clothing and saved me from absolute destruction.

Before this time I had received intimation from Mr Rose, that strong as had been the approbation bestowed upon my plan by all those to whose department the business belonged, other persons were there by whom it had been viewed with an eye not altogether favourable: who these persons were was not mentioned, nor any description given of them less mysterious than this. What the power was that thus stood in the way was more than at that time I had any suspicion of. There was an end to my situation of Sub-Regulus of the Poor; but my claim to be Sub-Regulus of the imprisoned part of the population still lingered.

To contract-management was to be substituted trust-management,—in other words, the trustees being constituted authorities, nominees of other superior constituted authorities, management by functionaries in whose instance interest coincided with duty—trustees whose interest was at daggers-drawn with duty.

That everything might be done in due, that is to say, in accustomed form, a committee of Honourable House was duly organized,—number of members, twenty-one, appropriately packed for the purpose. On this occasion what other persons were examined I cannot recollect,—the votes of the time would of course show. I was of course of the number.

This formality being gone through, an act was passed in 1811.

Never does the current of my thoughts alight upon the Panopticon and its fate, but my heart sinks within me: upon the Panopticon in both its branches,—the prisoner branch and the pauper branch: upon what they are now, and what they ought to have been, and would have been, had any other king than this same George the Third been in those days on the throne. According to the calculations which had then been, with close attention, made, the pecuniary value of a child at its birth,—that value which at present is not merely equal 0, but equal to an oppressively large negative quantity, would, under that system of maintenance and education which I had prepared for it, expense of conveyance to the distant site allowed for, have been a positive quantity to no inconsiderable amount.

So much for unoffending indigence. As to the criminally-offending part of the population, no tamer of elephants had a better grounded anticipation of the success of his management than I had of mine, as applied to the offending school of my scholars. Learned and Right Honourable judges I would not then have undertaken,—I would not now undertake to tame: learned gentlemen in full practice I would not have undertaken to tame: noble lords I would not have undertaken to tame: honourable gentlemen I would not have undertaken to tame. As to learned judges under the existing system, I have shown to demonstration, nor has that demonstration ever been contested, nor will it ever be contested, that (not to speak of malevolence and benevolence) the most maleficent of the men whom they consign to the gallows is, in comparison with those by whom this disposition is made of them, not maleficent, but beneficent.

Various were my adventures when, year after year, I was sent or encouraged to go upon a place . . .—a land-hunting—hunting after *terra firma,* which I so oftentimes found slippery as ice,—slipping through my fingers: analogous in some sort was my unhappy chase to that of Fenelon's Telemachus when rambling in quest of his father Ulysses: as often as he thought himself on the point of receiving the paternal embrace, consigned by some delusion or other to final disappointment. But how sadly different the catastrophe,—how opposite in my case to what is called poetical justice! . . .

[Finally, after 19 years of heartbreaking searches and negotiations, of endless delays waiting in ante-chambers, a Committee was appointed in 1811 to settle the prison question along conventional non-Panopticon lines, and to investigate Bentham's claims for compensation. A Bill was consequently drawn up, enacted in 1812, and under its terms Bentham was finally awarded some £23,000 in 1813.

Certainly these long years were the most impoverished and tormented of Bentham's life, but as always he put them to practical use and learned a great many strong lessons about the nature and techniques of British administration and "justice." He wrote at least four book-length exposés of the administrative anarchy he found in the Treasury and the Home Office, the "illegal" traffic in convicts to Australia, etc. In many an intimate letter to Dumont or his stepbrother Charles Abbot he vented his fury in passionate rhetorical outbursts. . . .

To Charles Abbot: Friday, 3d September, 1802. . . . "In the agony of their distress, the late Treasury, when called upon to show in their 'Proceedings,' why nothing was done about Panopticon, were desperate enough to speak of a pretended 'increase of terms' as the cause. It was not a misconception: it was a studied, long-premeditated, elaborately-prepared falsehood: a grosser, a more transparent one, was never uttered. It was so gross, that the man, whoever it was, that first broached it, was afraid to put his name to it. It stands in the printed 'Proceedings,' in the form of an *anonymous* communication! . . ." What infuriated Bentham especially were the arbitrary changes made or charged to him regarding the numbers of inmates in his planned Panopticon: he had always insisted upon neither more nor less than 1,000 as the best manageable size, and his formal contract with government so provided; but by 1802 government officials were charging him with shifting to 2,000 and then charging him with greed for an underhanded attempt to increase his profits by increasing the number of prisoners. Of course he denied it indignantly: ". . . You have no more forgotten than I have, your opinion of Mr Pitt's treatment of me, as declared for his edification before Mr Rider at the Committee §*i.e.* in June, 1798, Abbot, as chairman of the Committee had made a most sympathetic speech in Bentham's behalf§. The 'barbarity' was then not more than a barbarity of four years. It has since been doubled: in duration I mean: but in multiplicity of acts and variety of engines it has been swollen and improved to a degree that would astonish you. The underhand practices,—the system of long-spun and elaborate, yet always transparent treachery, concerted,— sometimes between the two floors of the Treasury, sometimes between the Treasury and subordinate offices,—form such a history, as I cannot think would be altogether without interest to the public, or even to Parliament. It cannot, if there be any the smallest spark of regard in either, for probity and good faith, in the headquarters of the state. . . .

"Being no longer *hare* but *hunter,* the spirit that animates hunters is come upon me. By leaving me nothing to do, of that which I ought to have had to do so many years ago, he leaves me no other mode of serving the public so efficient or impressive, as the reading of that moral lesson which will be read to it by the uncovering of his shame.

"My demand is an extremely simple one:—that an engagement of one-and-a-half year's standing, entered into after seven months taken to consider of it, may be trampled upon no longer:—that, according to that engagement, prison-room be given me for the 2000:—terms to be grounded on it, as per Memorial settled by Mr Nepean—principles assented to, over and over, in conversation with *him*—by Mr Long. The number to be secured to me, no more than the original number, 1000: for anything beyond that number I neither asked any engagement, nor would have accepted it, had it been offered."—XI, 132*fb*—M.P.M.].

Rationale of Judicial Evidence

A Note on *Rationale of Judicial Evidence*

Was Bentham a philosopher? Many have doubted is. He lacked the gift of contemplation, of speculation, they say; he was too overwhelmingly practical, too immediately concerned with results. He had no metaphysics, no epistemology; at most he was a moralist. Like Dr. Johnson, to prove existence, he kicked a stone. And indeed, Bentham did little to disabuse the doubters. *"Entre nous,"* he said, "I don't care two straws about liberty and necessity at any time."[1]

The question is complex. It can be answered in two ways, in the world's terms—conventionally, professionally—or in Bentham's—personally, idiosyncratically. In either case, however, the answer is yes; certainly he was a philosopher. Yet the orthodox, the professional philosophers have good reason to doubt his comradeship, for his most profound epistemological discussions were well hidden and disguised. They appear in his monumental *Rationale of Judicial Evidence,*[2] under such unlikely headings as "On the Exclusion of Evidence" or "Instructions to be Delivered from the Legislator to the Judge, for the Estimation of the Probative Force of Evidence." Who would think of looking for them here? And indeed, they have been wholly neglected.

From a professional point of view, perhaps the most interesting Chapter is XVI in Book V, "Of Improbability and Impossibility,"[3] where Ben-

---

[1] X, p. 216.
[2] It takes up volumes VI and VII of the eleven-volume collected edition.
[3] See pp. 212*ff* below.

tham gives his most extended discussions of causation, belief, and freedom of the will. Here he successively defines probability, improbability, necessity, possibility, impossibility, certainty, uncertainty, law of nature, cause, credibility, incredibility, will, and freedom of the will.

At the same time, in these and the following pages, he proves himself among the most scrupulous analysts of all time and a remarkably profound psychological observer. For example, in his discussion of physically incredible facts, he lists "Cure of diseases by supposed inadequate means" and offers seven contending facts or possibilities, among them the fact of psychosomatic imagination. There is no such disease; nevertheless the patient is really ill. His symptoms exist, though their supposed cause does not. What other eighteenth- or nineteenth-century epistemologist spoke in such terms? Bentham's language was willy-nilly the language of the then fashionable and now long since outmoded faculty psychology, but many of his insights, *mutatis mutandis,* are strikingly fresh and original.

If it is sometimes doubted that Bentham was a philosopher, it is almost always taken for granted that he was the crudest of psychologists, reductive and mechanistic in the extreme. The very opposite is the case, and these pages serve to show it. They are, among other things, a powerful plea to the judge to be on the lookout for the more or less intense operation of every conceivable motive. There can be no motive or interest, Bentham insisted, so obscure, so seemingly powerless, that it cannot rise up and overwhelm all the more obvious and conventional ones.

In a sense, the entire *Rationale* is a textbook of psychology; it originated, as almost all his work did, in his violent dissatisfaction with English law; here, with its primitive psychological assumptions. English law, he protested, understood one motive only: money. All men were motivated by one passion only, the love of money, be it a farthing, be it £1,000. Of course, money was important, and whenever he could, Bentham tried to translate his rules and axioms into financial terms; but that was because money was conveniently mensurable. It could be added, divided, subtracted, proportioned into subtle degrees of more or less in a better, more accurate way than any other human value. But it was absurdly reductionist to suppose that convenience of this kind determined the facts of human nature, so infinitely complex and mysterious.

In Bentham's own terms, did he consider himself a "philosopher"? Of course he did, as we see everywhere in this book of selections. Philosophy was metaphysics, and metaphysics was definition, or lexicography. A maker of dictionaries was necessarily therefore a philosopher. The essential fact, though, is that Bentham was a strict nominalist: there was no substantial *a priori* universe behind any of his abstractions. They referred, each and every one of them, *ultimately* to immediate sense impressions, to pleasures and pains.

It was this huge and complex work that led to John Stuart Mill's famous breakdown in 1826. Happily seizing every opportunity to unload his disorganized jumble of MSS, Bentham entrusted them to the nineteen-year-old boy in 1825. He had been working on them since 1802, and they had since risen to so chaotically mountainous a pile that even so gifted and brilliant an editor as Mill turned out to be must have collapsed under them. Bentham invited Mill to make his own corrections and comments, to give graphic examples *à la* Dumont; and young Mill did this throughout. It showed remarkable good faith and judgment on Bentham's part, and an almost incredible industry on Mill's, that he could have come cold to so technically abstruse a field and finished the work within a year.

The *Rationale* plays an essential role in Bentham's system, the logic of the will. In Aristotelian classical logic, the standard proposition is the assertive sentence: "The robber is killed." In the new logic there are also two other types of proposition, volitional and interrogative, or the command and the question: "Kill the robber!" "Is the robber killed?" Translated into legal terms, as part of the structure or grammar of legal thought, they become substantive and adjective law. Obviously, the facts of a case must first be determined and assembled before a substantive judgment can properly be made; and therefore the law of evidence was for Bentham of the first importance, as logically prior to the commands of justice. Few if any subjects fascinated him more deeply; and next to *An Introduction,* the *Rationale* is probably his most important work.

Rationale of Judicial Evidence—I

Book V. Ch. XVI. Of Improbability and Impossibility

(Vol. VII, pp. 76ff.)

1. *Improbability and impossibility are names, not for any qualities of the facts themselves, but for our persuasion of their non-existence.* Impossibility and improbability are words that serve to bring to view a particular, though very extensive, modification of circumstantial evidence. The occasion on which they are employed,—the occasion, at least, on which, under the present head, I shall consider them as employed,—is this:—on one side, a fact is deposed to by a witness; on the other side, the truth of it is denied—denied, not on the ground of any specific cause of untrustworthiness on the part of the witness, but because the fact is in its own nature *impossible:* impossible, or (what in practice comes to the same thing) too improbable to be believed on the strength of such testimony as is adduced in proof of it.

What is the nature and probative force of this modification of circumstantial evidence? Is there any, and what criterion, by which impossible facts, or facts which are to such a degree improbable, as to be, for practical purposes, equivalent to impossible ones, may be distinguished from all others?

If any such criterion existed, its use in judicature would be great indeed. By the help of it, a list of such impossible and quasi-impossible facts might in that case be made out—made out by the legislator, and put into the hands of the judge. To know whether the probative force of the testimony in question were or were not destroyed by this modification of circumstantial disprobative evidence, the judge would have nothing more to do than to look into the list, and see whether the species of fact in question were to be found in it.

Unfortunately, there exists no such criterion—no *possibility* (if the word may here be employed without self-contradiction) of making up any such list. Not only would one man's list contain articles which another man would not admit into his; but the same article which would be found in one man's list of impossibilities, would be found in another man's list of certainties.

From a man who sets out with this observation, no such list, nor any attempt to form one, can of course be expected. Yet, on the following questions, some light, however faint, may be, and will here be endeavoured to be, reflected.

1. What it is men mean, when they speak of a fact as being impossible—intrinsically impossible?

2. To what causes it is owing that one man's list of impossible facts will be so different from another's?

3. Different modifications of impossibility: different classes of facts which men in general—well-informed men in general, may be expected to concur in regarding as impossible.

4. Among facts likely to be, in general, considered as impossible, what classes are of a nature to be adduced in evidence?

When, upon consideration given to a supposed matter of fact, a man, feeling in himself a persuasion of its non-existence, comes to give expression to that persuasion,—he pronounces the matter of fact, according to the strength of such his persuasion, either more or less *improbable*, or *impossible*.

In and by the form of words thus employed for giving expression to that which is in truth nothing more than a psychological matter of fact, the scene of which lies in, and is confined to, his own breast,—a sort of quality is thus ascribed to the external phenomenon, or supposed phenomenon; viz. the matter of fact, or supposed matter of fact itself. Upon examination, this quality, it will be seen, is purely a fictitious one, a mere figment of the imagination; and neither improbability and impossibility on the one hand, nor their opposites, probability and certainty, on the other, have any real place in the nature of the things themselves.

So far as concerns probability and improbability, the fictitiousness of this group of qualities will scarcely, when once suggested, appear exposed to doubt.

Take any supposed past matter of fact whatever, giving to it its situation in respect of place and time. At the time in question, in the place in question, either it had existence, or it had not: there is no medium. Between existence and non-existence there is no medium, no other alternative. By probability—by improbability,—by each of these a medium is supposed—an indefinite number of alternatives is supposed.

At the same time, the same matter of fact which to one man is probable, or (if such be his confidence) certain, is to another man improbable, or, if such be his confidence, impossible.

Often and often, even to one and the same man, at different times, all this group of fictitious and mutually incompatible qualities have manifested themselves.

If his persuasion be felt to be of such a strength, that no circumstance capable of being added to the supposed matter of fact could, in his view of the matter, make any addition to that strength; or if, on looking round for other conceivable matters of fact, he fails of finding any one, in relation to which his persuasion of its non-existence could be more intense,—*impossible* is the epithet he attaches to the supposed matter of fact—impossibility is the quality which he ascribes to it.

If, on the other hand, a circumstance presents itself, by which, in his view of the matter, an addition might be made to the intensity of such disaffirmative persuasion; or if the supposed matter of fact presents itself as one in relation to which his persuasion of its non-existence might be more intense; in such case, not *impossible,* but *improbable,* is the epithet,—not *impossibility,* but *improbability* is the quality ascribed.

Certainty, which is the opposite to impossibility, or rather of which impossibility is the opposite, is applied to the persuasion, and from thence to the supposed matter of fact. It is not, any more than impossibility, applied or applicable to testimony.

As certainty, so uncertainty, applies itself to the persuasion and the fact, and not to the testimony. In the scale of persuasion, it embraces all degrees except the two extremes. The existence of a fact is not a matter of uncertainty to me, if the fact be regarded by me as impossible.

Certainty, therefore, has for its opposite, *uncertainty* in one way—*impossibility* in another. Uncertainty, in the language of logicians, is its contradictory opposite—impossibility, its contrary opposite.

The fiction by which (in considering the strength of a man's *persuasion* in relation to this or that fact, and the probative force of any other matter of fact when viewed in the character of an evidentiary fact in relation to it) occasion is taken to ascribe a correspondent quality, indicated by some such words as *certainty* and *probability,* to the principal fact itself,— appears to be like so many other figments, among the offspring of the affections and passions incident to human nature. It is among the contrivances a man employs to force other men to entertain, or appear to entertain, a persuasion which he himself entertains or appears to entertain, and to make a pretence or apparent justification for the pain which he would find a pleasure in inflicting on those on whom a force so applied should have failed to be productive of such its intended effect.

Were it once to be allowed, that, as applied to the facts themselves which are in question, probability and certainty are mere fictions and modes of speaking; that all of which, on any such occasion, a man can be assured, is his own persuasion in relation to it; that that persuasion

will have had for its cause some article or articles of evidence, direct or
circumstantial, real or personal, and will be the result of, and in its degree
and magnitude proportioned to, the probative force of that evidence;
that, of such evidence, neither the probative force, nor consequently the
strength of his persuasion, are at his command; that it is not in the power
of any article of evidence to have acted with any degree of probative
force upon, nor consequently to have given existence to any persuasion
in a mind to which it has not been applied, and that therefore it is not
in the power of any evidence to give either certainty or probability to
any matter of fact (the matter of fact being, at the time in question,
either in existence or not in existence, and neither the evidence nor the
persuasion being capable of making any the slightest change in it); that
it depends in a considerable degree upon the mental constitutions of A
and B respectively, what sort of persuasion, if any, shall be produced in
their minds by the application of any given article of evidence; and that
it is no more in the power of evidence applied to the mind of A, and
not to that of B, to produce in the mind of B a persuasion of any kind,
than it is in the power of evidence applied to the mind of B, and not
of A, to produce a persuasion in the mind of A;—were all this to be duly
considered and allowed, neither the existence nor the non-existence of
a persuasion concerning a matter of fact of any sort, would have the
effect of presenting to any person any other person as a proper object
of punishment, or so much as resentment.

But the certainty of this or that fact is assumed as perfect and indisputable; and thus he of whom it is conceived that he fails of regarding,
or of representing himself as regarding, that same fact in such its true
light, is on no better foundation considered and treated as being either
mendacious, or perverse and obstinate: perverse and obstinate, if he fails
of regarding it in that light—mendacious, if, it being impossible to him
to fail of regarding it in that light, he speaks of himself as if he did not.

When a man is himself persuaded—or though he does but, under the
impulse of some interest by which he is actuated, appear to be, or profess
to be, persuaded—of the existence of a fact,—it is matter of pain and
vexation to him to suppose that this same persuasion fails of being
entertained, still more to observe that it is professed not to be entertained, by those with whom, on the occasion of it, he has to deal.

Hence it is that, in his mind and in his discourse, to entertain it is
made matter of merit—to fail to entertain it, matter of demerit and blame,
on the part of others with whom he has to do; and, to cause them to
pursue that supposed meritorious line of conduct, the power of reward,
if within his reach, is employed; and to deter them from the opposite
conduct, even the power of punishment: of both which powers, in the

application thus made of them, mankind have been unhappily accustomed to see and to feel the exercise, carried to a pitch so repugnant to the dictates of humanity and reason. . . .

4. *Improbability and impossibility resolvable into disconformity to the established course of nature.*

An incredible fact, as contradistinguished from a verbal contradiction (whether improbable or impossible be the epithet by which the particular strength of the belief in its non-existence is designated), owes its incredibility to one cause, and to one cause only.

This cause admits of a variety of appellations. On the part of the matter of fact deposed to by the affirmative evidence, disconformity (as supposed) to the established course*

[*In ordinary language, the phrase would be, disconformity to some one or more of the *laws* of nature.

The expression *law of nature* is figurative, metaphorical: it is a metaphor taken from the use given to the same word *law* in the case of a political law: it is to that source, consequently, that we must resort for an explanation of it.

When a political law, the expression of an act of human will, is issued, that law emanating from recognised authority, and backed with the usual sanctions,—a correspondent degree of conformity in human actions—in the conduct of such individuals as are subject to the law—is the customary and manifest consequence: and (human actions being events) a law—a political law—is thus a cause of conformity among events.

In regard to events of a physical nature, the grand and constant object of curiosity and inquiry, is that which respects the *cause:* and on a subject so interesting, when men cannot come at facts, rather than have nothing, they are eager to catch at, and content themselves with, words. Between this and that group of facts, a certain conformity is observed: what is the cause of that conformity? becomes then the question. Cause of the conformity?— none at all: the conformity is itself nothing: it is nothing but a word expressive of the state our minds are put into by the contemplation of those facts. There are the facts: they do exist: but the conformity, as taken for a fact distinct from the facts themselves, has no existence.

Like so many other truths, this being no more than a confession of ignorance—and that invincible ignorance—is not satisfactory to the human mind. Nothing but words being on this occasion to be had—words, the counterfeit representatives of facts,—them men are determined to have, rather than have nothing. The conformity being (like every other fact, real or supposed) susceptible of the denomination of an effect, this proves the existence of a cause: what name, then, shall be given to that cause? What name?—what word?—for when men have got words, they have got that with which (on this, as on so many other occasions) they are content to pay themselves. What cause?—A *law of nature.* Here are events: these events are conformable to one another: here we have conformity amongst events. But, for that sort of thing which is a cause of conformity among events, we have a known name already: it is a *law.* The sort of events, the conformity among which this term hath been hitherto employed to designate, are human actions. The sort of events of which we are now looking out for the cause, are not human actions, but natural events. Law in this sense must, therefore, have something to distinguish it from law in that sense. In that sense it is termed *law* simply, without an adjunct: to distinguish this from that, let us give the word law an adjunct, and say *law of nature.*

If it were fully understood, that a *law of nature* signifies not an occult cause of conformity among facts, but merely the conformity itself, the phrase might be employed in this sense without danger of confusion.]

of nature: thus may be expressed what seems to be the most apposite and the clearest designation, of which, in any such small number of words, it is susceptible.

From the course of nature at large, that of the mental part of man's nature requires to be distinguished; hence disconformity in a *physical* respect, and disconformity in a *psychological* respect.

The remarks which follow, will, in the first instance, refer more particularly to physical, as contradistinguished from psychological facts. But they will, for the most part, be found applicable equally to both.

As it is only from evidence, coming under one or other of the descriptions already brought to view, that any notion whatever concerning the established course of nature can be derived; and consequently any notion concerning what is conformable to that course; so neither from any other source can any notion be derived respecting the disconformity of any supposed matter of fact to that same course.

The evidence thus characterized will, therefore, be composed of an indeterminate and indefinite multitude of matters of fact, drawn from all the evidence of every description that to the mind of the person in question (viz. the judge), have happened to present themselves during the whole course of his life; and composed of all such facts as present themselves to him as bearing the sort of relation in question, to the matter of fact in question.

To produce disbelief of the existence of the matter of fact in question, this disconformity must be such as (in his judgment) to render its existence *incompatible* with a certain portion, at least, of those other numberless matters of fact, of the existence of which he has been persuaded by the indeterminate but ample mass of evidence above indicated.

When the improbability (that is, the apparent, the relative, improbability) of an alleged fact, is set in the balance against testimony, it is still at bottom little more than testimony against testimony. Of the facts of the existence of which a man is persuaded, the knowledge, the persuasion, is derived partly from his own perceptions, partly from the alleged perceptions of others. But, in the unmeasurable mass of facts which (at least in a country where civilization is tolerably diffused) the most ignorant man is said to *know*, the number of those of which his knowledge is derived from his own immediate perceptions—from his own individual experience, is small, in comparison with those, for the knowledge or supposed knowledge of which, he stands indebted to the experience or supposed experience of others.

Concerning individual facts,—so far as mere perception, exclusively of inference drawn from perception by judgment, is concerned,—no force of exterior evidence can either increase or diminish the degree of persuasion of which such perceptions cannot but have been productive. But in regard to *species* of facts, there is not one, perhaps, concerning which the persuasion derived by a man from his own experience, would not be capable of being overborne by allegations of contrary experience on the part of other men. What makes our confidence so entire as it is in regard to the existence of those species or classes of individual facts, the existence of which is announced by the phrase which exhibits as the cause of it this or that law of nature, is,—that, so often as it falls in his way to make the trial, a man finds his own perceptions in relation to them confirmed by the reputed perceptions of all other men without exception. . . .

10. *Motives tending to produce affirmation of, and belief in, facts disconformable to the course of nature.*

In the case of a fact in regard to which its apparent anti-physicality, its apparent incompatibility with the laws of nature, operates as a disprobative circumstance,—the probative force of the evidence on the other side—the probative force of the testimony deposing in affirmance of the fact—is, on various occasions, apt to be subject to diminution from the same cause. In determining whether any degree of credence ought to be given to an apparently anti-physical fact, regard must be had not only to the circumstantial evidence afforded by its apparent anti-physicality, but also to the probability of seductive motives acting upon the witnesses by whom the fact is affirmed.

Various are the occasions on which, by the inordinate and seductive influence of this or that species of motive, men are led to represent as true, facts which if they were true would be anti-physical, but which are not true. Various are the classes of anti-physical facts, to the truth of which men are, on those occasions, led to depose. Coupling together the nature of the fact and the nature of the occasion, I proceed to bring to view some of the principal instances in which this cause of deception has been observed to operate.

In all these several cases, it may be of use here to premise that the seductive power of the species of motive in question, applying as it were to two different quarters of the mind at once, the understanding and the will, operates upon it with a double influence. What is not true, it prompts a man to regard as true: and what is neither true, nor so much as by him regarded as being so, it prompts him to report as if it were true.

I. Facts promising wealth. Transmutation of less valuable metals into gold. Seductive motive, in the character of a cause of delusion applying to the understanding of the person addressed—the person to whom the report is made,—the love of the matter of wealth. Seductive motive applying to the understanding of the original reporter (the supposed operator) in case of delusion (simple incorrectness, without mendacity),—the same; also, the pleasure of curiosity, the pleasure of reputation, and of the power attending it. Seductive motive applying, in case of mendacity, to the will,—love of the matter of wealth: viz. the wealth to be gained by the sale of the false secret.

Transmutation of a less valuable metal into gold, is in itself neither more nor less credible—a fact neither more nor less anti-physical, nor devious *in specie*—than transmutation of gold into a less valuable metal. Yet, the probative force of a testimony asserting the transmutation of another metal into gold, would be less than that of a testimony asserting the reverse. Why? Because the aggregate force of the seductive motives above mentioned is so much greater in the latter case than in the former. In the latter case, the most powerful of all, the desire of wealth does not apply.

II. Cure of diseases by supposed inadequate means. Seductive motives applying in the character of a cause of delusion to the understanding of the person addressed,—aversion to the pains of sickness: love of life. Seductive motive applying, in the case of delusion to the understanding of the original reporter (the supposed operator,)—the same as in the case of the transmutation of metals. Seductive motive applying, in the case of mendacity, to his will,—the same as in the case of delusion.

In this case, the fact of the cure of the disease in question by the operation of the supposed remedy in question, is one of seven contending facts, of all which the comparative probability requires to be weighed.

1. No real, or at least such, disease: the symptoms really existing, but the result of the imagination.

2. No real disease: the symptoms mendaciously reported.

3. The disease cured, but by the mere influence of the imagination, not by the operation of the supposed remedy,—or by some other remedy.

4. The disease gone off of itself: cured, without the assistance of the imagination, by the unknown healing power of nature, or by the cessation of the action of the morbific cause.

5. The disease not completely cured, *i.e.* not ultimately cured, but the symptoms mollified or removed for a time; viz. by either of the two preceding causes, Nos. 3 and 4.

6. The disease not cured in any degree: the cessation of the symptoms

being falsely reported, whether through delusion of mendacity, and whether on the part of the patient or of the medical practitioner.

7. Or, lastly, the disease cured, and by the operation of the supposed remedy.

Of the delusive influence of the imagination, exemplifications may be found in the choice made formerly of medicines. Gold, it was thought, must be a sovereign remedy: and all the efforts of industry were employed to make it potable. A remedy for diseases? Why? Because it was so valuable—because it was so rare. Diamonds are still more valuable: happily they were never employed for the cure of diseases: partly, perhaps, because they were so much more difficult to come at than gold; partly, because there was no hope of rendering them potable.

III. Facts promising happiness, threatening unhappiness, both in the extreme. The fact in question, spoken of as evidentiary of a commission given by a supernatural being to a man, to issue commands to any or all other men; those commands converted into laws, by threats as well as promises; by prediction of pains to be endured in this or a future life, in case of disobedience—of pleasures, in case of obedience. Take even the promises alone, without the threats—the seductive force is already beyond comparison greater than in the case of the making of gold, or the supernatural cure of diseases: add the threats, it receives a further and prodigiously greater increase.

Prudence suggests and requires the yielding to the probative force of this fact,—the giving credence to it, without staying to inquire into the intrinsic credibility of it—into its coincidence or deviousness, in degree or specie, with reference to the usual course of nature—into its conformity or repugnancy to the obvious laws of nature.

In this way,—by the help of an instrument of seduction which seems to be ready made, courting the hand of whoever has confidence enough to take it up and use it,—any man (it might seem) would have it in his power to impose laws, and those irresistible ones, upon any and every other. Such, accordingly, might have been the result, if the operation had been confined to one person, or if the operators, in whatever number, had agreed among themselves. Happily for human liberty at least (not to speak of happiness and virtue), no such concord has existed. In different nations, sometimes even in the same nation, legislators seeking to rule men by this instrument have come forward, opposing and combating one another with this instrument, no less decidedly and strenuously than others with the sword. Each has proclaimed to the world,—These of mine are the true wonders; all others—all those others that you hear of, are false: these that I promulgate to you are the genuine commands; all others, all those others that you hear of, are spurious. Divided thus, and opposed to itself, the seductive force, how seldom soever effectually resisted, ceased to be absolutely irresistible.

Such are the motives by which a man may be urged to give credit to untrue facts. But how comes it to be in his power? Such is the force by which the will of man is subdued; but by what means is the understanding itself brought into subjection by the will?

I answer,—Judgment, opinion, persuasion, is in a very considerable degree under the dominion of the will; discourse, declared opinion, altogether. But it is the nature of opinion declared, truly or falsely declared, by one man, to produce real opinion on the part of another.

Judgment in the power of the will? By what means? By these means:— To bestow attention on one consideration, to refuse it to another, is altogether in the power of the will. It is in the power of a judge to hear one man speak in the character of a witness, to refuse to hear another; to hear one paper read in the character of an evidentiary document, to refuse to hear another. The power which, in the station of a judge, a man thus exercises in relation to persons and papers, the mind of every man, sitting in the tribunal established in his own bosom, exercises at pleasure over arguments and ideas: over the contents of evidentiary discourses, in the state in which, through the medium of the perceptive faculty, they have been introduced into the memory. An idea to which a man's attention refuses itself, is, to every practical purpose, during the continuance of such refusal, as completely excluded, and thence rendered as completely inoperative, as the testimony of a witness, whom, before he has begun to speak, the judge has sent out of court; or a paper which he has disposed of in the same way, before any part of it has been read.

That discourse of all kinds, more especially discourse declarative of opinion, is completely in the power of the will, is manifest enough. But he who is completely master of men's discourses, is little less than completely master of men's opinions. It is by the discourse of A, that the opinion of B is governed, much more than by any reflections of his own. To take upon trust from others (that is, from the discourses of others) his own opinions, is, on by far the greater part of the subjects that come under his cognizance and call upon him in one way or other for his decision, the lot, the inevitable lot, of the wisest and most cautious among mankind: how much more frequently so, that of the ignorant, the rash, the headstrong, the unthinking multitude!

How wicked (it is frequently said)—how absurd and hopeless the enterprise, to make war upon opinions! Alas! would it were as absurd and hopeless, as it is wicked and pernicious! Upon opinions, in an immediate way, yes. To crush the idea in the mind, to act upon it by mechanical pressure or impulse, is not in the power of the sword or of the rod. In an unimmediate, though, for efficacy, not too remote way, through the medium of discourses, no: for what, in the case of opinions (unhappily for mankind) is but too much in the power of the sword and of the rod, is, to crush the enunciating and offending pen or tongue: to cut asunder the muscles by which they are moved.

Unhappily, the power of the will over opinion, through the medium of discourse, is but too well understood by men in power. Meantime, thus much is plain enough: the more credible the facts in themselves are, the less need has a man to seek to gain credence for them by such means. By such means, credit may be given to facts the most absurd, currency to opinions the most pernicious. Facts which are true, opinions which in their influence are beneficial to society, have no need of such support. If this is to be admitted, the consequence seems undeniable. To employ such means for the securing credence to any fact, is to confess its falsehood and absurdity; to employ such means for the support of any opinion, is to confess its erroneousness and mischievousness. To pursue such ends by such means, is to betray, and virtually to confess, the practice of imposture, the consciousness of guilt. . . .

    12. *Of improbability, as regards psychological facts.*

On passing from physical facts to psychological facts, a change of language becomes necessary. Where physical facts are concerned, the repugnancy between the alleged fact and the facts corresponding to the law of nature from which it is considered as deviating, or of which it is considered as a violation, is sometimes considered as existing in a degree which attaches to the alleged fact in question the character of improbability in this or that degree, sometimes in that superlative degree which stamps the alleged fact as *impossible.* In the case of the psychological class of facts, this highest degree is not considered as having any place in the scale. In such and such circumstances it is *improbable* that a man should have acted or thought so and so,—thus much is said continually: but, that in any such case the improbability should have risen to the height of impossibility, is a degree of intensity to which the assertion has seldom been raised by the utmost heat of altercation. For expressing the conformity, the uniformity, observable amongst physical facts, laws of nature have been long ago laid down, as above observed. To the purpose of denoting conformity among psychological facts, the application of that fictitious mode of speech appears not to have been ever yet extended. The cause of this difference is obvious and simple. Amongst psychological facts, no such close conformity is commonly observed as amongst physical facts. They are not alike open to our observation: nor, in so far as they have happened actually to be observed, has the result of the observation been such as to warrant the supposition of a degree of conformity equally close.

The sort of internal perception or consciousness we all feel of what is called the freedom of our will, is of itself sufficient to put a negative upon the application of any such term as *impossibility* to any of the facts which present themselves as flowing from that source. To assert the impossibility of any given act, is to assert the necessity of the opposite act: and, in a proposition asserting the necessity of this or that act on the part of any human agent, a denial of the freedom of his will is generally understood to be involved.

Examined to the bottom, this consciousness of the freedom of our will would, it is true, be found to amount to neither more nor less than our blindness as to a part, more or less considerable, of the whole number of joint causes or concurrent circumstances, on which the act of the will, and with it the consequent physical acts, depend: nor is this the only instance of a false conception of power, growing out of impotence. But the question is, not as to what sort of expression might be best adapted to the case, but what the expression is, that is in actual use. And here too we see a further confirmation of the observation already made, viz. that it is only by a sort of misconception and verbal illusion, that such attributes as necessity, impossibility, probability, improbability, are considered and spoken of as if they were attributes and properties of the events themselves. The only sort of fact of which they are really and truly indicative, is the disposition of our mind, of our own judgment, to be persuaded, with a greater or less degree of assurance, concerning their existence or non-existence: to entertain an assurance, more or less intense, that, at the place in question, at the time in question, the fact in question was or was not in existence.

Physical improbabilities—facts rendered incredible to enlightened minds by their deviation from the course of irrational nature, have seldom of late years come upon the carpet in any court of judicature. The alleged improbabilities, which, on that theatre, are so much more frequently brought forward and opposed to direct evidence, are of the psychological or mental kind. Alleged or supposed acts or states of the mind:—consciousness or non-consciousness of this or that fact; recollection or non-recollection; intention or non-intention; operation or non-operation of the idea of this or that pain or pleasure, in the character of a motive: conduct of such or such a description, under the influence of such or such an intention:—any of these acts or modes of being are alleged as having exhibited themselves in the mind of some individual, in circumstances in which, to an unbiassed mind, judging from the known constitution of human nature, the existence of such alleged phenomena would present itself as incredible. *Inconsistencies*—inconsistencies in thought or action— is the denomination in common use, under which these psychological improbabilities may perhaps with sufficient propriety be comprised. By the improbabilities of this description with which a narrative appears pregnant, it will frequently lose its credit—if not as to the entire substance of it, at least as to the particular points to which the improbability appears to extend: the credibility of it will in this case be said to be overthrown by its own internal evidence, without its being capable of being supported, or requiring to be opposed, by any external evidence.

In cases of this description, the apparent improbability, as in the above-mentioned physical cases, will be susceptible of an indefinable multitude of gradations. Insanity may be considered as marking the highest point in this scale. According to the degree in each case, will be the force with which it acts against the direct evidence—the persuasive force with which it operates upon the mind of the judge. Such as its relative force is in each instance, such, in that instance, will be its effect. In one instance, it will prevail over the direct evidence, and the direct evidence will be effectually discredited by it: in another instance, the decision will be governed by the direct evidence; though, in proportion to the apparent improbability, it is but natural that the persuasion on which the decision is grounded should be lowered and weakened by it.

To class these cases of psychological improbability under heads, each head being illustrated by apposite examples taken from the most remarkable causes that have been determined, on questions of fact, among the most enlightened nations, would be a work of considerable curiosity; and, notwithstanding the impossibility of marking out and distinguishing the different degrees and shades of improbability, would be of no inconsiderable use. But the task would be a work of itself, too laborious, as well as voluminous, to be comprised within the limits of the present work.

The advances that, within the few last centuries, have been made in the study of these psychological laws of nature,—these advances, though not so describable, nor perhaps so considerable, as those made in relation to the physical laws of nature, have, however, been by no means undiscernible in their effects. To weigh evidence against evidence—to weigh particular evidence against general probability—requires a proportionable skill in the science of psychology. It is to a deficiency of skill in this useful science, accompanied with a consciousness of this deficiency, that the system of procedure may ascribe so many altogether inapposite or imperfect and now exploded contrivances for the investigation of legal truth: trial by ordeal, trial by battle, wager of law, oaths expurgatory and suppletory.

To the same cause may moreover be ascribed those defects which may still be observed in such abundance in the system pursued with respect to evidence among the most enlightened nations. To investigate these defects, step by step, is the direct object of the present work: but, in the meantime, a presumptive only, but not unimpressive, proof of their existence, is the diversity of the courses pursued on this ground, as between nation and nation, in the pursuit of the same end; and not only as between nation and nation, but between province and province; nay, between court and court, in the same nation and the same province.

The Rationale of Judicial Evidence—II

Book IX. On the Exclusion of Evidence

(Vol. VII, pp. 393ff.)

Chapter III. Impropriety of exclusion on the Ground of Interest. . . . To begin with the article of interest. I say here, not sinister interest, but *interest* without addition: for such is the expression employed in the books of English jurisprudence.

On this occasion, as on every other, to understand what *interest* means, we must look to pain and pleasure, to fear and hope; fear, the expectation of pain or of loss of pleasure—hope, the expectation of pleasure or of exemption from pain. The causes of physical motion and rest, are attraction, impulse, and so forth: the causes of psychological motion and rest, are motives. Action, or (in opposition to action) rest,—action, whether positive or negative,—action without motive, without interest, is an effect without a cause.

It is not out of every sort of pleasure, out of every sort of pain, that a motive, an interest, is (at least in a sense applicable to the present purpose) capable of arising. Some pleasures, some pains, are of too ethereal and perishable a nature to excite an interest, to operate in the character of a motive. . . .

With minds of every class the mind of the lawyer has to deal. Of the structure of the human mind what does the lawyer know? Exactly what the grub knows of the bud it preys upon. By tradition, by a blind and rickety kind of experience, by something resembling instinct, he knows by what sophisms the minds of jurymen are poisoned; by what jargon their understandings are bewildered; how, by a name of reproach, the man who asks for the execution of the laws, and the formation of good ones, is painted as an enemy,—the judge who by quibbles paralyzes the laws which exist, and strains every nerve to prevent their improvement, is pointed out as an idol to be stuffed with adoration and with offerings.

In the view taken of the subject by the man of law,—to judge of trustworthiness, or at least, of fitness to be heard, *interest* or *no interest* is (flagrant and stigmatized improbity apart) the only question. Men at large are not under the action of anything that can with propriety be expressed by the name of interest; therefore they are to be admitted. Is a man exposed to the action of anything that can be designated by that invidious name? So sure as he is, so sure will his testimony be false. Enough: all scrutiny is unnecessary: shut the door in his face.

Sinister interest—the term and the distinction are alike unknown to them. Sinister interest? Everything that can be called interest is to their eyes sinister.

Sinister interest, a term so well known to moralists and politicians, is altogether unknown to lawyers, who have at least equal need of it.

What, then? Is it that there are certain sorts of interest that are always sinister interests, while there are other sorts, which, if language, like heraldry, were made by analogy instead of by accident, would be called dexter interests? No, truly. No sort of interest that is not capable of being a sinister interest—no sort of interest that is not capable of being a dexter interest. Acting in a direction to draw a man's conduct aside from the path of probity, any sort of interest may be a sinister interest: acting in a direction to confine a man's conduct within the path of probity, every sort of interest is a dexter interest. The modification of probity here in question is veracity. Any interest acting in a direction to draw his conduct aside from the line of veracity, is a sinister interest,—say, in this case, a mendacity-prompting or instigating interest: every interest acting in a direction to confine his discourse, his conduct, his deportment, within the path of truth, of verity, of veracity, is a dexter interest,—say, in this case, a veracity-securing interest.

Man in general not interested, devoid of interest? His testimony not exposed to the action of interest? Say rather (for so you must say if you would say true), no man, no man's testimony, that is not exposed to the action of interest.

Well: and that interest a sinister one? Not it, indeed. So far from it, there is no man whose testimony is not exposed to the action of, is not acted upon by, at least *three* regular and standing, commonly *four*, forces of this kind—all tending to confine his conduct within the path of probity, his discourse and deportment within the path of veracity and truth.

1. Motive belonging to the physical sanction:—Aversion to labour: love of ease: trouble of inventing and uttering a false statement, which, to answer its purpose, must be so elaborated and dished up as to pass for true.

2. Motive belonging to the political sanction:—Fear of legal punishment; viz. if it be a case in which (as in general) punishment stands annexed by the legislator or the judge to false and mendacious testimony.

3. Motive belonging to the moral, or say popular, sanction:—Fear of shame, in case of detection or unremoved suspicion.

4. Motive belonging to the religious sanction:—Fear of supernatural punishment, in this world or in the world to come.

Of these four motives, the three first have more or less influence on every human mind; the last, probably, on most minds.

On most minds, did I say? On all without exception, if the English lawyer is to be believed: for, by a contrivance of his own, he has shut the door against all witnesses on whose hearts motives of this class fail of exerting their due influence.

In the above list we may see the regular forces which are upon duty on all occasions to guard the heart and the tongue against the seductions to mendacity. But, in addition to these, there may be, by accident, any number of others, acting as auxiliaries in their support. No sort of motive (even these tutelary ones not excepted) to which it may not happen to act in the direction of a seductive one—no motive, over and above these tutelary ones, to which it may not happen to act also in the direction of a tutelary one. For what motive is there to which it has not happened, does not continually happen, to be employed in stimulating men to actions of all sorts, good and bad, in the way of reward? in restraining them from actions of all sorts, in the way of punishment?

Between two opposite propositions, both of them absurd in theory, because both of them notoriously false in fact, the choice is not an easy one. But if a choice were unavoidable, the absurdity would be less gross to say, No man who is exposed to the action of interest will speak false,—than to say, No man who is exposed to the action of interest will speak true. Of a man's, of every man's, being subjected to the action of divers mendacity-restraining motives, you may be always sure: of his being subjected to the action of any mendacity-promoting motives, you cannot be always sure.

But suppose you were sure. Does it follow, because there is a motive of some sort prompting a man to lie, that for that reason he will lie? That there is danger in such a case, is not to be disputed: but does the danger approach to certainty? This will not be contended. If it did, instead of shutting the door against some witnesses, you ought not to open it to any. An interest of a certain kind acts upon a man in a direction opposite to the path of duty: but will he obey the impulse? That will depend upon the forces tending to confine him to that path—upon the prevalence of the one set of opposite forces or the other. All bodies on or about the earth tend to the centre of the earth; yet all bodies are not there. All mountains have a tendency to fall into a level with the plains; yet, notwithstanding, there are mountains. All waters seek a level; yet, notwithstanding, there are waves.

In a machine, motion or rest will depend upon the proportion between the sum of the impelling and the sum of the restraining forces: in the human mind the result will be the same. Everything depends upon proportions; and of any proportions in the case, the man of law takes no more thought than the machine does.

Upon the proportion between the impelling and the restraining forces it depends, whether the waggon moves or no, and at what rate it moves: upon the proportion between the mendacity-promoting and the mendacity-restraining forces it depends, whether any mendacity be produced or no, and in what degree and quantity. Any interest, interest of any sort and quantity, sufficient to produce mendacity? As rational would it be to say, any horse or dog, or flea, put to a waggon, is sufficient to move it: to move it, and set it a-running at the pace of a mail-coach.

In the human mind there is a force to which there is nothing exactly correspondent in the machine—the force of *sensibility:* of sensibility with reference to the action of the various sorts of pains and pleasures, and their respective sources, in the character of motives.

Take what everybody understands, money: for precision's sake, take at once £10; the £10 of the day, whatever be the ratio of it to the £10 of yesterday: to the present purpose, depreciation will not affect it. This £10, will its action be the same in the bosom of Croesus as of Irus? in the bosom of Diogenes, as in that of Catiline? No man will fancy any such thing for a moment: no man, unless, peradventure, it have happened to him to have been stultified by legal science.

In each individual instance, whether mendacity (temptation presenting itself) shall be produced or no, will depend upon four distinguishable quantities: quantities above indicated. On the one side—1. Sum of the mendacity-promoting motives; 2. The patient's sensibility to ditto. On the other side 3. Sum of the mendacity-restraining motives, regularly acting and occasional; 4. Patient's sensibility to ditto. Upon these several quantities; consequently upon the ratio or proportion of the sum of the quantities on the one side to that of the quantities on the other. Of the proportion, the exclusionist knows not anything: he knows not any of the quantities; he will not suffer himself to know anything: he regards mendacity as certain; he excludes the evidence.

Of none of these several quantities can anything be known or conjectured, without examination and sifting of the evidence. Nothing can be known without experiment: and he will not suffer experiment to be made.

It is in psychology as in ship-building and navigation. Suppose the ship's way to depend upon the joint action of six influencing circumstances—six jointly acting, but mutually conflicting, causes: and these, each of them, say (for supposition's sake) of equal force. If, in the investigations and reasonings on this subject, so much as one of the six be omitted, error is the inevitable consequence: the forms of mathematical language, instead of a check to the error, will operate but as a cloak to it. The vessel will be in one part of the world, while the Lagranges and the Eulers are proving it to be in another.

In this respect, what course of ratiocination has been pursued by lawyers, debating on the ground of established systems? Of the whole catalogue of motives, each capable of acting upon the will with the most efficient—all consequently with a practically equal, force, they have taken observation of perhaps one, perhaps two; while on each side, or (what is worse) on one side only, the will of the patient has been acted upon by perhaps twice or thrice the number. What, in consequence, has been the justness of the conclusion? Much about what it would be in navigation, if calculations made for a submarine vessel, or an air-balloon, were to be applied to a ship of ordinary make and size: or as if, in calculating the course of an ordinary vessel, no account were taken of the depth of water drawn by her, or of the position of her sails.

In this state of the progress made by lawyers in the theory of psychology, no wonder if we should find the theory and practice on the subject of evidence in no better plight than navigation was among the most polished nations of Europe, when the scene of it was confined to the Mediterranean, and when, dreading to lose sight of land, the navigator crept along the shore.

Between these two otherwise resembling cases, there is, however, one very material and lamentable difference. In navigation, ignorance, deficient in adequate power, erred by over-caution and timidity: in jurisprudence, ignorance, supersaturated with power, is driven aground continually by hastiness and rashness.

It would be tedious, and surely by this time superfluous, to pursue absurdity on this ground through all its mazes.

No presumption so slender, which is not, under some established system, taken for conclusive: if fact, notorious or proveable fact, run counter, it makes no difference. Mendacity is presumed from affection—from bare wishes: wishes themselves are presumed from situations, from relations. Brother will be for brother, master for servant, servant for master, and so on. What? when you see them fighting with one another every day? Is it for his excessive fondness for Abel, that Cain would have been excluded by you? No matter: it makes no difference. . . .

If, on the ground of interest generally considered—if, on the ground of any other species of interest in particular—the unreasonableness of exclusion is demonstrable,—it is in the instance of pecuniary interest that it is most palpable. In the case of any other species of interest—the interest not having any palpable physical cause, the quantity of which might serve as an index and measure of its force,—the strength of it where it is strong, the weakness of it where it is weak, is not so universally manifest and incontestable. Suppose, for example, it be contended that enmity, known enmity, is a reasonable ground of exclusion. Enmity, like any other passion, is variable *ad infinitum* in degree; capable of existing in any the lowest degree, as well as in the highest. But the force of enmity, as of almost every other passion except the love of money, can no otherwise be measured than by its effects: so that if in this or that instance no visible effects have followed from it, the only proof of which the existence and action of it is susceptible is wanting to the case. In the instance of pecuniary interest, the argument stands upon a very different footing. Without reckoning the variations in degree, resulting from the variations in the degree of opulence of which the pecuniary circumstances of the party are susceptible,—the degrees of which the force of pecuniary interest is susceptible are not only prodigiously numerous, but also, in the lowest degrees, susceptible of an existence as palpable and ponderable as in the highest. As a thousand pounds, applied in the shape of reward, will be recognised as acting on the mind in the character of a lot of pecuniary interest, with a force proportioned to its amount,—so in like manner will a shilling, a penny, or a farthing. The legislator, and the administrator, the great dealers in this species of ware, can as well cut out in pennyworths' and farthings' worths the portion or pecuniary interest which they may be minded to create, as in hundred pounds' worths and thousand pounds' worths; and how questionable soever, or even hopeless, the influence of this species of interest may be, when broken down into these minute and almost impalpable lots, yet the existence of it in this case is not less manifest and indisputable than in the other.

Thus it is that, in the instance of pecuniary interest, the impropriety of the exclusion is exposed to view by a circumstance which has no place in any other. Generally speaking, no other species of interest appears so much as to exist, but in cases in which it acts, not with considerable force only, but with effect. It is not seen to exist, but where it is seen to act; nor is seen to act, but where it is seen to triumph. Far otherwise is it with pecuniary interest. The portions in which it is seen to exist are in many instances so minute, that in those instances the notion of its prevalence is too palpably absurd to be embraced, or so much as pretended to be embraced, by anybody. Who, for instance, speaking of the people of England, would take upon himself to maintain, with a grave face, that the majority of them would be ready, upon all occasions, each of them to perjure himself for the value of a farthing? Propositions, however, far beyond this in extravagance, have been implicitly assumed by many a decision that, on this ground, has issued from English benches. An interest, corresponding to some minute fraction of a farthing, has in many instances been assumed as a legitimate cause for the exclusion of a witness, on the sole ground of the pecuniary interest generated by that cause.

In vain would it be to say, that this is among the cases in which we cannot draw the line; and that, therefore, in order to shut out the evidence in the cases in which the sinister influence exerted on it by this species of interest would be operative, and productive of the apprehended ill effect, we must be content to shut it out in many instances in which, manifestly enough, it cannot be operative. The very impossibility of drawing a line, a proper line, anywhere, is an argument, and that of itself a conclusive one, against the exclusionary principle. A line of this sort (it must be confessed) would, in whatsoever place drawn, be an improper one. But, by the principle of exclusion, a line of this sort is not only drawn, but drawn at the very worst place possible. There is an impropriety in drawing the line, for example, at the sum of forty shillings; and in laying down any such proposition as that which is implicitly contained in the Court of Conscience Acts, that a man is not to be trusted to give his evidence in a case where he has a sum of money to that amount at stake upon the result of it. There is an impropriety. Why? In the first place, because (setting aside all such inscrutable circumstances as those which consist of psychological idiosyncrasies, affecting the sensibility of the individual in question to the respective action of the improbity- and mendacity-restraining motives), there are some incomes to which four hundred pounds are not more than forty shillings to others. In the next place, because, even supposing it clear, in the instance of any particular individual, antecedently to experience, that forty shillings would constitute a temptation sufficiently strong to engage him in the path of perjury,— supposing it possible, I say, to find sufficient reason for predicating this of a sum of forty shillings,—it would not be possible to find sufficient reason for refusing to predicate it of a sum of thirty-nine shillings. But, by the line of exclusion drawn where it is drawn, this effect is predicated, not only of a sum of forty shillings or of a sum of thirty-nine shillings, but of a sum less, and much less, than the thirty-ninth or fortieth part of the smallest piece of base metal that ever came out of a mint: and this by a sweeping and unbending rule, by which people of all degrees of opulence as well as indigence, the Croesuses as well as the Iruses, the Diveses as well as the Lazaruses, are excluded in the lump.

The force with which a motive of a pecuniary kind acts upon the mind of a given individual, will be in the ratio of the sum in question to his pecuniary circumstances. In England, two individuals may be found, one of them belonging to the most numerous class, the income of one of whom is to that of the other as 500 to 1. All other circumstances set aside, the force with which a given sum acts upon the mind of one of these individuals, will be but one five hundredth part of the force with which it acts upon the mind of the other. Yet (supposing this rule to be observed) if, on account of his being acted upon by the prospect of gaining in this way a given sum, the testimony of the poorer of the two individuals in question is to be rejected, so must that of the richer. The same effect, and that a certain one, is to be ascribed for this purpose to two forces, of which the one is in truth but the five hundredth part of the other.

In Great Britain, an estate of the value of 20,000 guineas a-year, or thereabouts, has been known to be at stake upon the event of a single cause: value, at thirty years' purchase, 600,000 guineas. A guinea contains a little more than 1000 farthings: this same sum, then, applied to persons whose incomes stand at different points in the scale, from the highest to the lowest, is capable of acting on them respectively with 1000 different degrees of force: 600,000 being the number of guineas, multiplying the 600,000 by the 1000, here then are 600,000,000 different degrees of force with which the mind of man is capable of being acted upon by this one motive called pecuniary interest, to which by this rule one and the same degree of force (and that in every case an irresistible one) is ascribed.

Thus different are the degrees of force with which this one, among so many causes of falsehood (checked by the action of so many counter causes—of so many causes of truth), tends to the production of its effect:

degrees, which, by the identity of the denomination given to them, viz. *pecuniary interest,* are represented as being the same. From the mere consideration of this diversity, it must be sufficiently evident, that, in a vast number of the instances in which this cause of falsehood has place, its influence must, practically speaking, be equal to 0—not capable of surmounting the mere *vis inertiae* of the human mind, supposing this cause of action to stand alone, unopposed by any other: whereas the whole force of the standing causes of truth is what it has to encounter in every instance, without reckoning the force of such of the causes of truth, the action of which is but occasional. Yet this is the cause, and indeed stands at the head of the list of the causes, the force of which is, by the rule which assumes it for a ground of peremptory exclusion, regarded as being in every instance infinite and irresistible: certain, at least, of preponderating over the sum of all other forces—of all causes of truth—to which it can happen to stand opposed to it.

If there were any sort of witnesses imaginable, against whom it were prudence to shut the door, the sort of witnesses against which the law is so decided to shut the door, are precisely those to whom it may be thrown open with least danger. All witnesses being exposed to seductive influence, all witnesses being dangerous, those will be least dangerous against whom men are most upon their guard: such are those, on whose foreheads the force of the seduction is written down in figures. A cloud involves the workings of friendship, a cloud involves the workings of enmity, a cloud involves the workings of love: the existence of the passion, the force of its action, everything is involved in darkness. No juryman, no stranger, scarcely even the closest intimate, can form any estimate of the degree of the enmity, the friendship, or the love: experience may have shown him no such enmity, no such friendship, no such love. But every man knows what ten shillings is, what twenty shillings is, and what is the difference: every man knows the value—every man feels the power, of money. Every man knows that allowances are to be made for it. Few men are disposed to make less allowance than truth requires, for the force of its action on other people. Few men are disposed to set the incorruptibility of other men at too high a rate, or the force of corruption at too low a one: few men there are in whom suspicions thus grounded are in any danger of not being carried up to the full limits of the truth; few in whom they are not much more apt to be carried beyond the truth than to fall short of it.

Of the force of money, on whatever occasion acting, the judge sitting on his bench is fully aware and acutely sensible. Agreed: but is there any other human being to whom that force is a secret? Sits there that old woman anywhere (not to confine ourselves to benches) who, on hearing a report made to her by another old woman, forgets to ask herself in what way and degree (if in any) the reporting old woman may have to gain or lose by the credit given or not given to her report?

What? can the man of law be sincere in thinking that no sort of men understand either the value of money, or the influence of it upon testimony, but himself?

In this case, therefore, the advantage expected from exclusion of evidence in the character of a security against deception and consequent misdecision, is more plainly ideal than in any other: the reason in favour of the exclusion more palpably frivolous. And yet it is to this modification of interest, that exclusion on the score of interest is in a manner confined by English jurisprudence.

In the eyes of the English lawyer, one thing, and one thing only, has a value: that thing is money.

On the will of man, if you believe the English lawyer, one thing, and one thing only, has influence: that thing is money. Such is his system of psychological dynamics.

If you will believe the man of law, there is no such thing as the fear of God; no such thing as regard for reputation, no such thing as fear of legal punishment; no such thing as ambition; no such thing as filial, no such thing as parental, affection; no such thing as party attachment; no such thing as party enmity, no such thing as public spirit, patriotism, or general benevolence; no such thing as compassion; no such thing as gratitude; no such thing as revenge. Or (what comes to the same thing),— weighed against the interest produced by the value of a farthing, the utmost mass of interest producible from the action of all those affections put together, vanishes in the scale.

Add self-preservation, if you please—self-preservation from whatever be the worst of evils, death not excepted,—the farthing will still be heaviest. "A pin a day is a groat a year." Instead of the farthing, put in a pin, the result will still be the same.

Romance! romance! True; but it is the romance of real life. The picture here drawn of the human mind is romantic enough, no doubt; but, as to the account here given of that picture, nothing was ever more strictly true. Such are the decisions of the sage of law; such his every day's practice; such his opinions, such his thoughts: unless, on learned benches, decision and practice run on without thought.

For a farthing—for the chance of gaining the incommensurable fraction of a farthing, no man upon earth, no Englishman at least, that would not perjure himself. This in Westminster Hall is science: this in Westminster Hall is law. According to the prints of the day, £180,000 was the value of the property left by the late Duke of Bridgewater. For a fraction of a farthing, Aristides, with the duke's property in his pocket, would have perjured himself. . . .

The Rationale of Judicial Evidence—III

Book X. Recapitulation. Instructions to be Delivered from the Legislator to the Judge, for the Estimation of the Probative Force of Evidence

(Vol. VII, p. 597)

Against the following errors it concerns the judge to be upon his guard:—

1. The supposing that there is any man, of whose testimony it is certain that it will throughout be true: true to the purpose of warranting the judge to treat it as conclusive, *i.e.* exclusive of all counter-evidence.

2. The supposing that there is any man, of whose testimony it is certain that it will throughout be untrue; viz. to the purpose of warranting the judge in refusing to hear it. Not that the certainty of its being throughout untrue, would induce anything like a certainty of its being throughout uninstructive.

3. The supposing that there exists any one sort of interest, which, on the occasion in question, can be sure so to overpower the force of the standing tutelary interests, as to render untruth on the part of the testimony certain in any part, much less in the whole.

4. —or any *number* of interests acting in a mendacity-promoting direction.

5. The supposing that because, as to this or that fact, the testimony in question if incontestably false, and even mendacious,—that therefore there is a certainty of its being false as to this or that *other* fact; much more as to all the other facts.

6. The supposing that, where there are divers interests, to the action

of which the testimony is exposed on either side, there is any one of them that ought to be neglected, as if destitute of force.

7. The supposing that, where there are divers interests acting on the same side, the aggregate force with which they act is to be learnt by counting them, without regard to the separate force of each.

The above propositions are the general result of this work.

The anatomical view (shall we say) above given of the human mind,— does it quadrate with the truth? No person by whom this work can ever be taken in hand—no person, male or female, high or low, rich or poor, but is competent to judge.

But if it be, what must we say of the picture given of it in the books of jurisprudence? of the picture of it, as referred to, and wrought from, on every jurisprudential bench?

Judging of it from those books and those benches, is this branch of practical science (if science it is to be called) in any better state than the science of anatomy, when the circulation of the blood was unknown, and nerves and tendons were confounded under one name? or than chemical science, when the great Plowden, no less profound in chemistry than in jurisprudence, gave in his pedigree of the metals, certifying them to be the issue in tail lawfully begotten by Stephen Sulphur upon the body of Mary Mercury?

By way of contrast to the above proposed mementos, and that the reader in whose understanding there is any predilection for reason, or in whose heart there is any concern for the welfare of mankind, might take his choice,—it had been in my intention to subjoin a view of those documents to which English judges are at present in the habit of resorting for their guidance, and which (in addition to, or in explanation of, the particular decision, the supposed purport of which has been preserved by chance), the advocates on each side are wont to present them with in that view.

These documents would range themselves naturally into two classes:— 1. Considerations purely technical, *i.e.* having no reference to anything that will bear the name of reason: 2. *Fragmenta rationalia;* considerations containing in them more or less of the matter of reason. Fragments they cannot but be called; inasmuch as, containing, almost without exception, no reason but on one side, nor of that anything better than a loose and broken hint, they can never, in any instance, be considered as amounting to an entire reason, but only to a quantity of rough matter, by the help of which, with due management, a reason might be made.

Of this research, what, it may be asked, would be the use?

Illustration—illustration merely. Amusement, and nothing more: or, if anything beyond amusement, this:—that the portentous worthlessness and depravity of the technical system, and of that sort of trash which among lawyers goes by the name of science, may be placed in yet another point of view: that, of the mountain of their nonsense, the relative as well as absolute magnitude may be measured by the molehill dimensions of such part of their productions as, without abuse of language, may be capable of passing under the name of sense.

To engage in any such research, in the hope of any instruction, which in any other point of view could afford payment for the labour, would be to scrutinize the contents of the first great dunghill that presented itself, for the possible pearls or diamonds that might be to be found in it. It would at the best be like the reading over and studying the Bibliotheca of Alchemy, in the expectation of meeting with instruction applicable to the advancement of modern chemistry. In the course of a twelvemonth, it is not impossible but here and there a result might be found presenting a fact of which no modern chemist is apprized. But, in less than a thousandth part of the time thus spent in the purlieus of folly and imposture, facts of more use and importance might be brought to certainty, and for the first time, by following the track already opened by genuine and unpolluted science. . . .

CONCLUSION. We are now arrived at the conclusion of this work: a few leading considerations have been pressing upon our minds throughout the whole course of it. At present I speak particularly to Englishmen; the application to other countries will not be difficult.

1. So far as evidence is concerned (and the limitation need not be anxiously insisted on), the existing system of procedure has been framed, not in pursuit of the ends of justice, but in pursuit of private sinister ends—in direct hostility to the public ends. It is time that a new system be framed, really directed to the attainment of the ends of justice.

2. The models, the standards, the exemplifications of the proposed improved system—nay, of a perfect system, are not objects of a Utopian theory;—they are within every man's observation and experience—within the range of every man's view—within the circle of every private man's family.

3. To find these models of perfection, an Englishman has no need to go out of his own country: for invention there is little work—for importation, scarce any. English practice needs no improvement but from its own stores: consistency—consistency is the one thing needful: preserve consistency, and perfection is accomplished.

4. No new powers, no tamperings with the constitution, no revolutions in power, no new authorities, much less any foreign aid, are necessary. All that is necessary (and this is necessary) is, that the laws made for the purpose should be made by the lawful legislator—not by a power sub-

ordinate to that of the legislator, taking advantage of his negligence, usurping his authority, legislating with inadequate means, in pursuit of sinister ends, on false pretences.

5. Nothing more is required, than the extending, in all causes and cases, to rich and poor without distinction, that relief which in certain causes and cases, and in certain districts, has been afforded to the poor: torn (by the appointed guardians and friends of the people) from the rapacity, or abandoned by the negligence, of their natural enemies.

6. It requires, indeed, the establishment of local judicatures: but even this is not innovation (not that even innovation, where necessary, should ever be declined)—not innovation, but restoration and extension. *Restoration*—of powers once in existence,*

[*The Saxon County Courts.]

before they were swallowed up by the framers of the existing system of abuse, under favour of their own resistless power, working by their own frauds, covered by their own disguises, in pursuit of their own sinister ends. *Extension*—the restoring, though with some increase of amplitude, to one half of the island, the fountains of justice so happily retained by the other.*

[*The Sheriffs' Courts and Borough Courts in Scotland.]

An aphorism not unfrequently quoted, and seldom without approbation, is that of Machiavel, in which the taking the constitution of the country to pieces, for the purpose of bringing it back to its first principles, is spoken of as a wise and desirable course. In the character of a general principle extending to all states, and to every branch of the constitution of every state, it is founded on vulgar prejudice, and leads to mischief. It supposes a constitution formed all at once: a supposition scarce anywhere realized. It supposes experience worth nothing; and herein lies the great and mischievous absurdity. It supposes men in the savage state endued with perfect wisdom, but growing less and less wise as experience accumulates, and progress is made in the track of civilization. It supposes that, to make the British constitution better than it is, we ought to bring it back to what it was in the time of William III, or Charles I, or Edward I, or John, or William the Conqueror, or Alfred, or Egbert, or Vortigern, or Cassibelaumus; in whose reign it would still have exhibited a picture of degeneracy, if compared with the primeval golden constitution of New Holland or New Zealand.

In the case at present on the carpet, the supposed wisdom of the maxim may find an apparent confirmation. By doing away the work of five or six hundred years, and throwing back the system of procedure, as to the most fundamental parts, into the state in which it was at the time of Edward I and much earlier, a mountain of abuse might be removed, and even a near approach to perfection made. Why? Because in principle there is but one mode of searching out the truth: and (bating the corruptions introduced by superstition, or fraud, or folly, under the mask of science) this mode, in so far as truth has been searched out and brought to light, is, and ever has been, and ever will be, the same, in all times, and in all places—in all cottages, and in all palaces—in every family, and in every court of justice. Be the dispute what it may,—see everything that is to be seen; hear everybody who is likely to know anything about the matter: hear everybody, but most attentively of all, and first of all, those who are likely to know most about it—the parties.

Under the first Normans, as under the Saxons, the parties were always present in court, whoever else was present. Each was allowed to appear for his own benefit; each was compelled to appear for the benefit of his adversary.

Under the first Normans, as under the Saxons, justice was within the reach of every man: he might have it, in many cases, without travelling out of his own hundred;—in almost all cases, without travelling out of his own county. With, or even without, the assistance of a horse, most commonly he might betake himself to the seat of judicature, and return, without sleeping out of his own bed: at the worst, he might go one day, and return the next.

With minds of a certain texture, many points might perhaps be gained by quoting, as if it were an authority, this conceit of Machiavel. But to rest the cause of utility and truth upon prejudices and wild conceits, would be to give a foundation of chaff to an edifice of granite. In a work which, if true or useful for a moment, will be so as long as men are men, the humour of the day is not worth catching at any such price.

In point of fact, then, I mention it as mere matter of accident, and in point of argument as no better than an argument *ad hominem,* that the system of procedure here proposed, happens to be, in its fundamental principles, not a novel, but an old one: and I give it for good, not *because* it is old, but *although* it happens to be so. Parties meeting face to face, in courts near to their own homes: in county courts, and, where population is thick enough, in hundred-courts or town-courts.

Pannomial Fragments

A Note on *Pannomial Fragments*

This manuscript has all the hall-marks of sterling importance in the Bentham canon: above all, in its mathematics-axiomatic structure. It was a first principle with him that the more important a subject, the more nearly axiomatic he must try to shape and leave it. He worked to create a moral geometry in the same way that Euclid had invented a mathematical one; and in this essay he came closest to his ideal. He always worked toward the tersest, most graphic picture; to simplify, purify, make more and more concise; to offer the verbal equivalent of algebra: *multum in parvo*. Ideally, he would have offered not only axioms, but a chart.

Its intended location in the canon was critical. It was meant to be the Introduction to a Pannomion or complete code of laws, the single-minded object of his entire career; and he was still working on these fragmentary pages, perfecting them, trying to make them still more precise and concise, as late as 1831.

This is in parts a difficult work, as so many of Bentham's later texts are; there is no point in dissembling it. His later style was designed for perfect clarity. Unfortunately, it is like one of those trick knots: the more you struggle to unravel it, the tighter, the more involuted it gets. His method was to announce the main subject at the beginning of every sentence, and to follow it and all subordinate nouns with *all* their descriptive, qualifying, and exceptive clauses, so that even Hegel's prose has sometimes a soufflé lightness compared at times to some of Bentham's soggy puddings. Yet even here are plenty of sentences and paragraphs of epigrammatic sprightliness.

In any case, after due patience and care, his meaning is never in doubt. As always, he once again emphatically lays down the fundamental proposition that "the sole proper all-comprehensive end should be the greatest happiness of the whole community." And he lays it down as a universal normative proposition or value judgment. On the other hand, beginning at the opposite end, he posits the fundamental descriptive data of the human mind to be pleasures and pains. He then must bind these remote elements together—the universal normative with the concrete descriptive-empirical, and this he does in an architecture of axioms. The structure of Utilitarianism arose on a series of intermediate propositions, the axioms related not directly to or from the universal greatest happiness principle, but indirectly by stages, through axioms related to the four fundamental subordinate principles of security, subsistence, abundance, and equality.

This essay is really a dictionary, for Bentham's next step was necessarily to break down and define the vocabulary of the four subordinate principles in terms of pleasures and pains, of concrete sense impressions, *i.e.,* by way of paraphrasis.[1]

Thus most of these pages are once again preoccupied with definitions of the fundamental abstractions of Utilitarianism. As Bentham saw it, until he had first begun defining them in *A Fragment on Government* in 1776, these had been mere floating fictions, but had ever since been tightly bound to the facts of human feeling, to genuine joy and suffering, *e.g.,* happiness, unhappiness, good, evil, end, means, remedy, law, rule, principle, proposition, sanction, title, right, natural right, obligation, property, possession, power, command.

It seemed to him here as always that to complete the dictionary was to complete the system, which was at once a "metaphysics" and a "logic," his idiosyncratic terms for the dictionary of abstractions and the structure of propositions arising therefrom. Moreover, because most of these terms were ultimates that could not be defined beyond their basic elements of pleasure and pain, almost any one of them, expanded far enough, could itself become the foundation of the entire edifice.

Once again he borrowed his favorite medical analogy: his axioms are axioms of mental pathology. In one of his key sentences he said, "Experience, observation, and experiment—these are the foundations of all well-grounded medical practice: experience, observation, and experiment—such are the foundations of all well-grounded legislative practice."[2]

---

[1] *Cf.* pp. 244*ff.*
[2] See p. 261.

These pages are offered as substitutes for selections from the great *Constitutional Code*. They form the metaphysics, the dictionary of the system, as that was largely intended as the logic, the structure of concrete propositions. The *Code* abounds with invention of administrative particulars, many of which have long since been incorporated, through Bentham's disciples like Southwood Smith and Kaye-Shuttleworth and later the Fabians, into the machinery of the modern welfare state. But it is just for this reason, that they are too particular, that they do not belong in this book, which is intended to be a compilation of Bentham's most important general principles and doctrines. Indeed the *Constitutional Code* as he published it was just another such mass of fragments as we have become thoroughly familiar with. It stands as Book II in volume IX of the Collected Edition; as Book I, Bentham's editor, after his death, threw together all the random scraps of preliminary definitions, rules, and principles he found strewn about. But the *Pannomial Fragments* are a coherent whole, intended by Bentham himself to be *the* general introduction to the whole massive work, Books I and II included. Thus they are offered here.

Pannomial Fragments

(Vol. III, pp. 211ff.)

CHAPTER I. GENERAL OBSERVATIONS. By a Pannomion, under-stand on this occasion an all-comprehensive collection of law,—that is to say, of *rules* expressive of the will or wills of some person or persons belonging to the community, or say society in question, with whose will in so far as known, or guessed at, all other members of that same com-munity in question, whether from habit or otherwise, are regarded as disposed to act in compliance.

In the formation of such a work, the sole proper all-comprehensive end should be the greatest happiness of the whole community, governors and governed together,—the *greatest happiness principle* should be the fundamental principle.

The next specific principle is the *happiness-numeration principle*.

Rule: In case of collision and contest, happiness of each party being equal, prefer the happiness of the greater to that of the lesser number.

Maximizing universal security;—securing the existence of, and sufficiency of, the matter of subsistence for all the members of the community—maximizing the quantity of the matter of abundance in all its shapes;—securing the nearest approximation to absolute equality in the distribution of the matter of abundance, and the other modifications of the matter of property; that is to say, the nearest approximation consistent with uni-versal security, as above, for subsistence and maximization of the matter of abundance:—by these denominations, or for shortness, by the several words *security, subsistence, abundance,* and *equality,* may be characterized the several specific ends, which in the character of means stand next in subordination to the all embracing end—the greatest happiness of the greatest number of the individuals belonging to the community in question.

The following are the branches of the pannomion, to which the ends immediately subordinate to the greatest happiness principle respectively correspond:—

To constitutional law, the axioms and principles applying to equality.

243

To penal law, the axioms and principles applying to security; viz. as to—1. Person; 2. Reputation; 3. Property; 4. Condition in life.

The principle presiding over that branch of the *penal code*, which is employed in the endeavour to arrest, or apply remedy to offences considered as being and being intended to be productive of suffering to one party, without producing enjoyment, otherwise than from the contemplation of such suffering, to the other, is *the positive-pain-preventing principle.*

Rule: Let not any one produce pain on the part of any other, for no other purpose than the pleasure derived from the contemplation of that same pain.

The persons for the regulation of whose conduct the *positive-pain-preventing principle* applies are—

1. The subject citizens, taken at large.

2. The sovereign, in respect of the quantity, and thence the quality of the subsequentially preventive, or say punitive, remedy applied by him against any offence.

To civil law, more particularly, apply the axioms relating to security as to property. Sole principle—*the disappointment-preventing principle.*

Rule applying to the aggregate, composed of the several sources of positive good or happiness, elements of prosperity, objects as they thus are of general desire: Among a number of persons, competitors actually or eventually possible, for the benefit or source of happiness in question, exceptions excepted, give it to that one in whose breast the greatest quantity of pain or disappointment will have place, in the event of his not having the thing thenceforward in his possession, or say, at his command.

The exception is when, by any different disposition, happiness in greater quantity, probability taken into account, will be produced.

Of any such exception the existence ought not to be assumed: if it exist, the proof of its existence lies upon him by whom its existence is asserted.

To political economy apply the axioms and principles relating to subsistence and abundance. To political economy—that is to say, to those portions of the penal and civil codes in the rationale of which considerations suggested by the art and science of political economy are applicable and have place: considerations over and above and independent of the sensations produced by loss and gain.

By axioms of moral and political pathology, understand so many general propositions, by each of which statement is made of the pleasure or pain (chiefly of the pain) produced by the several sorts of evils, which are the result of human agency on the part of the several individuals respectively affected by them; to wit, by means of the influence exercised by them on the quantity or degree in which the benefits expressed by the fore-mentioned all important words, are by the respective parties, agents and patients, enjoyed, or the opposite burthens constituted by the absence of them endured.

Of these propositions, it will be observed that they divide themselves into *groups*;—one group being relative to security, another to subsistence, a third to abundance, the fourth and last to equality: the first bringing to view the enjoyment derived from the undisturbed possession of security at large—security in the most comprehensive application made of the word, contrasted with the enjoyment producible by the breach of it,— the second group bringing to view the subject of subsistence:—the third group bringing to view the subject of abundance,—and the fourth group bringing to view the subject of equality, and stating the evil consequence of any legislative arrangement by which a defalcation from the maximum of practicable equality is effected.

In each of the axioms, the antagonizing, or say competing, interests of two parties are conjointly brought to view:—in those which relate to security, these parties are, the maleficent agent, or say wrongdoer, and the patient wronged:—in those which relate to subsistence, abundance, and equality, they are the parties whose interest stands in competition, no blame being supposed to have place on either side. By the legislator, preference should be given to that interest by preference to which the happiness of the greatest number will be most augmented.

To the first of the three stages of the progress made in society by the good or evil flowing from a human act, belong the effects of which indication is given in and announced by these same four groups of axioms.

The principles which form the groundwork of the here proposed system, correspond to the above-mentioned *specific* ends, immediately *subordinate* to the all-comprehensive *end,* expressed for shortness by the *greatest-happiness principle,*—and have their foundation in *observations* on the pathology of the human mind as expressed in the above-mentioned *propositions,* to which, in consideration of their supposed incontrovertibility and extensive applicability, have been given, for distinction sake, the name of axioms.

As to these principles, the names by which expression is given to them have for their object and purpose *conciseness*—the conveying, by means of these several compound substantives, a conception of the several groups of pathological effects in a manner more concise, and thence more commodious, than by a repetition made each time of the several groups of axioms to which they correspond, and which they are employed to recall to mind.

Correspondent to the axioms having reference to security, will be found the principles following:—

1. Principle correspondent to security, and the axioms thereto belonging, is the *security-providing principle*.

Of the security-providing principle, the following modifications may be brought to view, corresponding to the several *objects* respecting which security requires to be afforded:—

I. The objects for, or say in respect of which security is endeavoured, are these—

1. Person: the person of individuals on the occasion of which body and mind require to be distinguished.

2. Reputation: the reputation of individuals or classes, or say the degree of estimation in which they are respectively held.

3. Property: the masses of the matter of wealth respectively belonging to them, and possessed by them in the shape of capital, or in the shape of income.

4. Power: the portions of power respectively belonging to them, for whose sake soever, or say to whose benefit soever exerciseable, whether for the sake and benefit of the individual power-holder himself—or for the sake of other persons, one or more, in any number; in which case the power is styled a *trust,* and the power-holder a *trustee,* and the person or persons for whose benefit it is exercised, or designed to be exercised, entitled *benefitee,* and the person or persons by whom the trust was created a *trustor.*

5. Rank: or say factitious reputation or estimation,—the source of factitious reputation or estimation put into the possession of the individual by a series of delusions operating on the imagination.

6. Condition in life, in so far as beneficial: the aggregate benefits included in it will be found composed of the above objects, two or more of them.

N. B. The four last-mentioned objects may, for conciseness sake, be spoken of as so many modifications of the matter of prosperity.

7. Miscellaneous rights: including exemptions from burthensome obligations.

8. The maleficent acts, or say offences, against which the endeavour is used to apply the appropriate punitive and other remedies.

9. The contingently maleficent agents, against whose maleficent acts the endeavour will be used to employ the several remedial applications. These may be—

1. External, or say foreign governments and subjects, considered as liable to become adversaries. Code in which provision is made against evil from that source, the Constitutional. Ch. &c. Defensive Force—sub-departments of the administration department, those of the army and the navy ministers.

2. Internal; viz. fellow-citizens; as distinguished into—1. Fellow-citizens at large, or say non-functionaries; 2. Functionaries considered in respect of the evil producible by them in such their several capacities.

3. The several classes of persons *to whom,* by the several arrangements employed, the security is endeavoured to be afforded. These may be distinguished into—(1) Citizens of the state in question . . . (2) Foreigners with reference to the state in question;—governments and subjects as above included.

A modification of the security-providing principle, applying to security in respect of all modifications of the matter of property, is the disappointment-preventing principle. The use of it is to convey intimation of the reason for whatever arrangements come to be made for affording security in respect of property and the other modifications of the matter of prosperity, considered with a view to the interest of the individual possessor. In the aggregate of these are contained all the security-requiring objects, as above, with the exception of *person.*

II. Subsistence-securing principle: correspondent subordinate end in view—subsistence. The use of it is to convey intimation of the reason for whatever arrangements come to be made for the purpose of securing, for the use of the community in question, a sufficient quantity of the matter of subsistence.

III. Abundance-maximizing principle: the use of it is to convey intimation of the reasons for whatever arrangements may come to be made in contemplation of their conduciveness to the accomplishment of that end.

IV. Equality-maximizing, or say, more properly, inequality-minimizing principle: the use of it is to convey intimation of the reasons for whatever arrangement come to be made, in contemplation of their conduciveness to this end.

CHAPTER II.   CONSIDERANDA.   . . . But what is a law, and what are laws themselves? Before this is explained, must be brought to view that species of matter which on each occasion is occupied in passing judgment on the aptitude of the law in question, considered as a *means* employed in and for the attainment of that end. To this purpose comes the need of the ideas, expression to which is given by the two mutually and intimately connected words *rule* and *principle.*

Correspondent to every rule you may have a principle: correspondent to every principle you may have a rule.

Of these two, a rule is the object which requires first to be taken into consideration and presented to view. Why? Because it is only by means of a rule that any moving force can be applied to the active faculty, or any guide to the intellectual—any mandate can be issued—any instruction given.

A *rule* is a *proposition*—an entire proposition: a *principle* is but a *term:* True it is, that by a principle instruction may be conveyed. Conveyed? Yes: but how? Not otherwise than through the medium of a proposition —the corresponding proposition—the proposition which it has the effect of presenting to the mind. Of presenting? Yes: and we may add, and of bringing back; for only in so far as the rule has been at the time in question, or some anterior time present to the mind, can any instruction, any clear idea be presented to the mind by a principle.

A principle, therefore, is as it were an abridgment of the corresponding rule:—in the compass of a single term, it serves to convey for some particular present use, to a mind already in possession of the rule, the essence of it: it is to the rule, what the essential oil is to the plant from which it is distilled.

So it does but answer this purpose, its uses are great and indisputable.

1. It saves words and thereby time.

2. By consisting of nothing more than a single term, and that term a noun-substantive, it presents an object which, by an apt assortment of other words, is upon occasion capable of being made up into another proposition.

So, it is true, may a rule—but only in a form comparatively embarrassing and inconvenient. This will appear by taking in hand any sentence in which a principle has place, and instead of the principle employing the corresponding rule.

Upon occasion, into any one sentence principles in any number may be inserted: and the greater the number, the stronger will be the impression of the embarrassment saved by the substitution of the principles to the rules.

A principle, as above, is no more than a single term; but that term may as well be composite, a compound of two or more words, as single. Of these words one must be a noun-substantive; the other may be either a noun-adjective or a participle; including under the appellation of a noun-adjective, a noun-substantive employed in that character, in the mode which is so happily in use in the English language, and which gives it, in comparison with every language in which this mode is not in use, a most eminently and incontestably useful advantage.

By an *axiom* is meant a sort of rule of which by certain properties, the combination of which is peculiar to it, the usefulness is pre-eminent in comparison with other rules. These properties are—

1. Incontestableness.

2. Comprehensiveness.

3. Clearness.

As to axioms, the axioms that belong to this subject are axioms of mental pathology. The facts they are enunciative of, are facts enunciative of certain sensations, as being produced by certain events or states of things operating as their efficient causes.

By a *reason* for any act, is conveyed the idea of its supposed addition, actual or probable, to the greatest happiness. This effect may be produced either—1. Immediately; 2. Through an intervening chain of any number of links.

A *law* is a word employed in three different senses, which require to be distinguished: but in each of them it imports that the *will* to which it gives expression either emanates from the supreme authority in the state, or has that same authority for its support.

In one sense it denotes an entire command,—the whole matter of a command. Call this the *integral* sense, and the sort of law a *complete law.*

In the second sense it contains no more than a portion of a command; and the matter of the command may be to an indefinite extent voluminous, containing laws of the first-mentioned sort in any number: in this sense it has for its synonym the word enactment: call the law in this sense a *fractional* or *incomplete* law.

In the third sense it designates the aggregate body of the enactive paragraphs to which it happens to have received the token of their being expressive of the will of the person or persons invested with the supreme authority in the political state, or of some person who acts in this behalf, under, and by virtue of that same authority.

By *power of classification* a species of legislative power is exercised. Thus when an enactment to any effect has been framed, if by any proposition bearing the form of a command or a rule, enlargement or retrenchment is applied to the genus, or say class of objects which contribute to constitute the subject-matter of the command;—by this means, in a sort of indirect way, by and with the help of the other words which enter into the composition of the enactment, is produced the effect of a different enactment: one of the classes of which that same subject-matter is composed receives thereby *contraction* or enlargement, and a fresh classification is made thereby.

Note here—in the giving existence to an enactment, three distinguishable parts are capable of being taken—or say, functions are capable of being performed: viz. the *institutive,* the *constitutive,* and the *consummative;* and this whether by one and the same authority, or by so many different authorities: by exercise given to the power of classification in any instance, a different consummation as it were is given to the several enactments, in the matter of which, the generic words in question are any of them contained.

Of this same function—of this same power, exercise is made by any functionary, or set of functionaries, belonging to a department other than, and thence inferior to, the *legislative;* for in no other way can classes be filled up by individuals, and reality given to general ideas. Call this power, power of location, or say *locative* power. But what difference there is between this case and the preceeding consists in this: in the former case, by no other authority than the legislative can the power be exercised—the effect produced: in the latter case it is produced in virtue of a general authorization given by the legislative authority, and by that authority is never produced, unless it be in consequence of some extraordinary occurrence.

So much for particular laws, and small masses of particular laws. Now for the divisions of the all-comprehensive aggregate in which they are all of them at all times comprised.

The Pannomion may be considered as composed of two branches—the effective and the constitutive.*

[*It may also be considered as divided into substantive and adjective. The substantive branch of the law has for its business the giving direction and effect to human conduct;—the adjective has for its business the giving execution and effect to substantive law.]

In the effective branch may be considered as contained the portion of the matter which is more immediately occupied in giving direction to the conduct of the members of the community of all classes.

The constitutive is occupied in determining who those persons in particular are, by whom the powers belonging to the effective branch shall be exercised.

Considered with relation to its connexion with good and evil employed in the character of punishment and reward for the purpose of giving direction to human conduct, the Pannomion is distinguished and divided into two branches—the directive and the sanctionative.

By the directive part, indication is given of the course which it is the desire of the law-giver that upon the occasion in question the subject-citizens should pursue.

By the sanctionative part, information is given to them of the inducement which they will find for the pursuing of those same courses.

The matter of which this inducement is composed, is either the matter of good as above, or the matter of evil. Where and in so far as it is of the matter of good, *remunerative* is the name that may be given to the law: where and in so far as it is the matter of *evil,* penal is the name commonly given to the law—*punitive,* a name that may be given to it.

These two branches of a law are addressed to different descriptions of persons:—the *directive* to persons at large—the *sanctionative* to the members of the official establishment.

By the sanctionative, provision is made of the inducement, to which the legislator trusts for the compliance he seeks and expects to find on the part of those to whom the directive branch of the law is addressed. This inducement is the eventual expectation of either good or evil in the mind of those to whom the directive branch of the law is addressed:— if it be *good,* the law in that branch of it is styled a *remunerative* law: if evil a *penal* law.

The persons to whom a remunerative law is addressed are those functionaries belonging to the administrative department, by whom disposal is made of the money, or whatever else the matter of good employed consists of, directing them eventually to bestow the article in question on the person in question in the event of his having complied with the directive law in question, and thereby rendered the service desired at his hands.

The persons to whom a penal law is addressed, are the official persons belonging to the judiciary department, presided over and directed by the judges.

Of the matter to which it may be convenient to give insertion in the civil code, and to which accordingly insertion is given in it, there are two different sorts: one of which may be styled the *directive* as above—the other the expositive.

To the directive belongs that sort of matter, of which, under that name, mention has been already made—the directive, without the addition of the sanctionative, and in particular the punitive.

Not that, without the addition of the sanctionative, the directive could in general without absurdity be trusted to. Of a correspondent eventual punishment, including, where applicable, satisfaction, to be administered in case of non-compliance, the existence must all along thereby be assumed. But in relation to punishment, this is the whole of that which naturally here finds its place:—in the penal code will be inserted all denunciation of extra punishment, together with what belongs to the mode in which the application made of the matter of punishment is brought about;—leaving to the civil code, the direction of the mode in which satisfaction, and in particular that branch of it which consists in the allotment of compensation for wrong, shall be administered.

The expositive matter belongs in common to, constitutes and forms part and parcel of, the directive part of the matter of the civil code, and the penal code.

Among the words and locutions, of which exposition is given in it, may be seen this or that word, in the exposition of which a prodigious quantity of matter is employed.

Take, for instance, the word *title* or the word *right*, when employed as synonymous with and equivalent to it. Exposition of it is alike necessary to the completion of any enactment belonging either to the civil or the penal code.

Take, in the first place, the *civil*. The principal part of it is occupied in the declaration of to what person or persons each subject-matter of property, each object of general desire, shall belong, in such sort as to be styled his or their own—who he is or they are, to whom it belongs— or say, who have title to it. Now, then, be the subject-matter what it may—who is it that has *title* to it? Who but he in whose favour some one in the list of completely collative events or states of things has place; no event or state of things having, with relation to that same title, an ablative effect, having at the same time place in the disfavour of that same individual.

So much for the portion in question—the portion of the matter of the civil code.

But not less necessary is reference made in the penal code to that same matter.

Take, for instance, in offences severally considered, offences affecting property,—the offence of *theft*. To the conveying of an accurate conception of the nature of this offence, mention of title is indispensable. Why? Answer: Because, when it is under the persuasion of his having a title to the thing in question, where it is under this persuasion that the man took it,—by no one will he be regarded as having committed the offence thus denominated: thence so it is, that in any well-adapted definition of this offence, averment of the non-existence of any such persuasion must be contained.

Not that in the idea of the offence it is necessary that the idea of any portion of that same matter in particular—the idea, for example, of any one collative event more than another—should have place.

Merely expositive, and mixed: of the one sort or the other will be found to be every particle of the matter which will with most convenience be aggregated to the matter of the civil code.

Constitutive of the mixed matter will be—1. Matter of general concernment; 2. Matter of particular concernment.

CHAPTER III. EXPOSITIONS. Only with reference to language can the attribute denoted by the word universal be with propriety attributed to the subject of *law*.

In each country, at each point of time, it is matter of accident whether a law to a given effect is in force; though, consideration had of the general effect, and not of the particular tenor, in no inconsiderable quantity, masses of the matter of law might be found, such as are not likely to be wanting in any country that has the use of letters. A mass of the matter of language expressive of law might be found, of which the equivalent cannot be wanting, in any country, among any assemblage of human beings, in the presence of each other, for any considerable length of time. This may be styled the language of universal law.

Follows the exposition of some of these terms, the use of which exposition upon this occasion is not so much to teach as to fix their import:—

1. *Obligation.*—Obligations may exist without rights;—rights cannot exist without obligations.

Obligation—a fictitious entity, is the product of a law—a real entity.

A law, when entire, is a command; but a command supposes eventual punishment; for without eventual punishment, or the apprehension of it, obedience would be an effect without a cause.

Reward—eventual reward, is not capable of securing obedience to will signified,—is not capable of giving to will the effect of a command:— apprehension of the abstraction of reward already in possession or expectancy may do it. Yes: but though *reward* alone be the word employed in the description of the case, the operation signified is of the nature of punishment;—the effect of it not enjoyment, but suffering.

Obligation has place, when the desire on the part of the superior, the obliger, being signified to the obligee, he understands at the same time, that in the event of his failing to comply with such desire, evil will befal him, and that to an amount greater than that of any evil which he could sustain in compliance with that desire.

2. *Right.*—Otherwise than from the idea of obligation, no clear idea can be attached to the word *right*.

The efficient causes of right are two:—

1. Absence of correspondent obligation. You have a *right* to perform whatever you are not under obligation to abstain from the performance of. Such is the right which every human being has in a state of nature.

2. The second efficient cause of right is, presence of correspondent obligation. This obligation is the obligation imposed upon other persons at large, to abstain from disturbing you in the exercise of the first-mentioned sort of right. The first-mentioned right may be termed a naked kind of right;—this second-mentioned right, a vested or established right.

The word right, is the name of a fictitious entity: one of those objects, the existence of which is feigned for the purpose of discourse, by a fiction so necessary, that without it human discourse could not be carried on.

A man is said to have it, to hold it, to possess it, to acquire it, to lose it. It is thus spoken of as if it were a portion of matter such as a man may take into his hand, keep it for a time and let it go again. According to a phrase more common in law language than in ordinary language, a man is even spoken of as being invested with it. Vestment is clothing: invested with it makes it an article of clothing, and is as much as to say is clothed with it.

To the substantive word are frequently prefixed, as adjuncts and attributives, not only the word political, but the word natural and the word moral: and thus rights are distinguished into natural, moral, and political.

From this mode of speech, much confusion of ideas has been the result.

The only one of the three cases in which the word right has any determinate and intelligible meaning is that in which it has the adjunct political attached to it: in this case, when a man is said to have a right (mentioning it), the existence of a certain matter of fact is asserted; namely, of a disposition on the part of those by whom the powers of government are exercised, to cause him, to possess and so far as depends upon them to have the faculty of enjoying, the benefit to which he has a right. If, then, the fact thus asserted be true, the case is, that amongst them they are prepared on occasion to render him this service: and to this service on the part of the subordinate functionaries to whose province the matter belongs, he has, if so it be, a right; the supreme functionaries being always prepared to do what depends upon them to cause this same service to be rendered by those same subordinate functionaries.

Now, in the case of alleged natural rights, no such matter of fact has place—nor any matter of fact other than what would have place supposing no such natural right to have place. In this case, no functionaries have place—or, if they have, no such disposition on their part, as above, has place; for if it have, it is the case of a political right, and not of a merely natural right. A man is never the better for having such natural right: admit that he has it, his condition is not in any respect different from what it would be if he had it not.

If I say a man has a right to this coat or to this piece of land, meaning a right in the political sense of the word,—what I assert is a matter of fact; namely, the existence of the disposition in question as above.

If I say a man has a natural right to the coat or the land—all that it can mean, if it mean any thing and mean true, is, that I am of opinion he ought to have a political right to it; that by the appropriate services rendered upon occasion to him by the appropriate functionaries of government, he ought to be protected and secured in the use of it: he ought to be so—that is to say, the idea of his being so is pleasing to me—the idea of the opposite result displeasing. . . .

It is not the rights of man which causes government to be established:

—on the contrary, it is the non-existence of those rights. What is true is, that from the beginning of things it has always been desirable that rights should exist—and *that* because they do not exist; since, so long as there are no rights, there can only be misery upon the earth—no sources of political happiness, no security for person, for abundance, for subsistence, for equality:—for where is the equality between the famished savage who has caught some game, and the still more famishing savage who is dying because he has not caught any?

Law supposes government: to establish a law, is to exercise an act of government. A law is a declaration of will—of a will conceived and manifested by an individual, or individuals, to whom the other individuals in the society to which such will has respect are generally disposed to obey.

Now government supposes the disposition to obedience:—the faculty of governing on the one part has for its sole efficient cause, and for its sole measure, the disposition to obey on the other part.

This disposition may have had for its cause either *habit* or *convention:* a convention announces the will of one moment, which the will of any other moment may revoke;—habit is the result of a system of conduct of which the commencement is lost in the abyss of time. A convention, whether it have ever yet been realized or not, is at least a conceivable and possible cause of this disposition to obedience, from which government, and what is called political society, and the only real laws, result. Habit of obedience is the cause, a little less sure—the foundation, a little less solid, of this useful, social, disposition, and happily the most common.

The true rampart, the only rampart, against a tyrannical government has always been, and still is, the faculty of allowing this disposition to obedience—without which there is no government—either to subsist or to cease. The existence of this faculty is as notorious as its power is efficacious.

Shall this habit of obedience be continued unbroken, or shall it be discontinued upon a certain occasion? Is there more to be gained than to be lost in point of happiness, by its discontinuance? Of the two masses of evil—intensity, duration, certainty, all included—which appears to be the greatest, that to which one believes one's self exposed from continued obedience, or that to which one believes one's self exposed by its discontinuance? . . .

It is an affair of calculation; and this calculation each one must make for himself according to circumstances. It is also a calculation that no one can fail to make, either ill or well, whatever may be the language he employs, or whosoever he may be.

But this calculation is not sufficiently rapid for those who choose for their amusement the destruction and reconstruction of governments. Rights of men strongly asserted, but ill-defined, never proved; rights of men, of which every violation is an act of oppression—rights ready to be violated at every moment—rights which the government violates every time it does anything which displeases you—right of insurrection ready to be exercised the first moment that oppression occurs;—this is the only remedy which suits those who would make equality to flourish at any rate, by taking the power of governing for themselves, and leaving obedience for all others.

It is the weakness of the understanding which has given birth to these pretended natural rights; it is the force of the passions which has led to their adoption, when, desirous of leading men to pursue a certain line of conduct which general utility does not furnish sufficient motives to induce them to pursue, or when, having such motives to induce them to pursue, or when, having such motives, a man knows not how to produce and develope them, yet wishes that there were laws to constrain men to pursue this conduct, or what comes to the same thing, that they would believe that there were such laws,—it has been found the shortest and easiest method to imagine laws to this effect. . . .

Two passions have laid claim to the giving birth to the declarations of rights—to the substitution, of the declaration of particular rights to the preparation of real laws—vanity and tyranny: vanity, which believes it can lull the world asleep, by being the first to do what all the world has always had before its eyes—tyranny, glad of finding a pretext for punishing all opposition, by directing against it the force of public hatred. Rights, there you have them always before your eyes: to deny their existence, is either to exhibit the most notorious bad faith or the most stupid blindness; the first a vice which renders you deserving of the indignation of all men—the other a weakness which consigns you to their contempt.

It is because without rights there can be no happiness, that it is at any rate determined to have rights: but rights cannot be created without creating obligations: it is that we may have rights, that we submit to obligations; and in respect to obligations, not to those alone which are strictly necessary for the establishment of the rights of which we feel the want, but also obligations such as those which may result from all the acts of authority exercised by government, which the general habit of obedience allows it to exercise.

The end of all these acts of authority should be to produce the greatest possible happiness to the community in question.

This is the true, and the only true end of the laws. Still, of the operations by which it is possible to conduct men towards this end, the effect—the constant, necessary, and most extensive effect, is to produce evil as well as good; to produce evil, that good may be produced, since upon no other conditions can it be produced.

The mystic tree of good and evil already so interesting, is not the only one of its kind: life, society, the law, resemble it, and yield fruits equally mixed. Upon the same bough are two sorts of fruits, of which the flavour is opposite—the one sweet and the other bitter.

The sweet fruits are *benefits* of all kinds—the bitter and thorny fruits are burthens. The benefits are *rights,* which under certain circumstances are called *powers*—the burthens are *obligations—duties.*

These products, so opposed in their nature, are simultaneous in their production, and inseparable in their existence. The law cannot confer a benefit, without at the same time imposing a burthen somewhere;—it cannot create a right, without at the same time creating an obligation—and if that right be of any value, even a numerous train of obligations. . . .

Rights are, then, the fruits of the law, and of the law alone. There are no rights without law—no rights contrary to the law—no rights anterior to the law. Before the existence of laws there may be reasons for wishing that there were laws—and doubtless such reasons cannot be wanting, and those of the strongest kind;—but a reason for wishing that we possessed a right, does not constitute a right. To confound the existence of a reason for wishing that we possessed a right, with the existence of the right itself, is to confound the existence of a want with the means of relieving it. It is the same as if one should say, *everybody is subject to hunger, therefore everybody has something to eat.*

There are no other than legal rights;—no natural rights—no rights of man, anterior or superior to those created by the laws. The assertion of such rights, absurd in logic, is pernicious in morals. A right without a law is an effect without a cause. We may feign a law, in order to speak of this fiction—in order to feign a right as having been created; but fiction is not truth.

We may feign laws of nature—rights of nature, in order to show the nullity of real laws, as contrary to these imaginary rights; and it is with this view that recourse is had to this fiction:—but the effect of these nullities can only be null.

3. *Possession.*—"Better," says a maxim of the old Roman, called civil law—"better (meaning in comparison with that of any other person,) is the condition of the possessor"—better his condition, that is to say, better the ground and reason which a person in his situation is able to make for the enjoyment of the thing, than any that can be made by any one else.

Of the propriety and reasonableness of this notion, scarcely by any one who hears of it, how far soever from being learned, can a sort of feeling fail of being entertained—by no one, even of the most learned, has expression, it is believed, been ever given to it. This omission, the greatest happiness principle, and that alone, can supply. In the case of loss of the possession, he who has the possession would feel a pain of privation—or say, regret, more acute—than a man of the same turn of mind, whose expectation of obtaining it was no stronger than the possessor's expectation of keeping it, would, in the event of his failing to obtain possession of it.

Of so many hundred millions of persons, each of whom, in case of his having had possession of the thing and then lost it, would upon the losing of it have felt pain in a certain shape proportioned to the value of the thing, not one feels pain in any shape at the thoughts of not having it: not one of them but might, in the shape in question, feel pain in any quantity more or less considerable, if after having the thing in possession, he were, without receiving or expecting any equivalent for it, to cease to have it.

The horse you have bred, and still keep in your stable, is yours. How is it constituted such—constituted by law? Answer: The naked right—the right of making use of it, the law has left you in possession of;—to wit, by the negative act of forbearing to inhibit you from using it: the established right, the law has conferred upon you by the order given to the judge to punish every person who shall disturb or have disturbed you in the use of it.

The horse which was yours, but by the gift you have made of it is become the horse of a friend of yours,—how has it been constituted such—constituted by law? Answer: By a *blank* left as it were in the command to the judge,—that blank being left to be filled up by you in favour of this friend of yours, or any other person to whom it may happen to be your wish to transfer the horse, either gratuitously or for a price.

So long as the law in question has this blank in it, it is an incompleted, an imperfect law—it waits an act on your part to render it a perfect one. The law in its completed state is the result of two functions, into which the legislative function in this case is divided—the initiative to it, and the consummative. By the legislator, the initiative is exercised—by you, the consummative.

In the same way in which, according to this example, rights and powers are given to individual persons, they may be and are given to classes of persons. On classes of persons, the correspondent obligations not only may, but must be imposed: in short, exceptions excepted, they must be imposed on all persons of all classes:—for supposing but a single person excepted from the obligation, your right is not entire,—it is shared by you with the person so excepted. If, for example, in transferring the horse to your friend, you kept yourself from being included in the obligation to abstain from the use of the horse—if, in a word, you kept yourself excepted from the obligation imposed on other persons in general, the horse is not your friend's alone, any more than yours; but, in the language of English law, you and he are joint tenants of the horse.

4. *Power.*—In common speech, the word power is used in two senses;—to wit, the above sense, which may be called the proper and legal sense—and another sense more ample, which may be styled the popular sense.

In the strictly legal sense, which is used in the penal and civil branches of law—in the popular sense, which is used in the constitutional branch.

In both cases, the fruit of the exercise of the power is looked to, and that fruit is compliance: on the part of the person subject to power, compliance with the wishes expressed, or presumed to be entertained, by the person by whom the power is possessed. For convenience of discourse, say in one word the *power-holder.*

The force of the remunerative sanction, it has above been observed, is not sufficient to constitute an obligation; it is, however, in a certain sense, sufficient, as everybody knows, to constitute power: the effect of power is produced, in so far as, by the will declared or presumed of him who in this sense is the power-holder, compliance is produced.

Power may be defined to be the faculty of giving determination either to the state of the passive faculties, or to that of the active faculties, of the subject in relation to and over which it is exercised;—say the correlative subject.

Power is either coercive or allocative.

Coercive power is either restrictive or compulsive.

Of the correlative subject, the passive faculties are either insensitive or sensitive.

If merely insensitive, it belongs to the class of inanimate beings, and is referred to the still more general denomination of things.

If sensitive, to the class of animals.

If the animals of the class in question are considered as belonging to the class of reasonable beings, the correlative subject is a person—including human beings of both sexes and all ages.

If considered as irrational, it has hitherto by lawyers been confounded with inanimate beings, and comprehended under the denomination of things.

In so far as the power is exercised with effect, the possessor of the power—say the power-holder—may, relation had to the correlative subject, be termed the *director*—the correlative subject the *directee.*

5. *Command.*—An instrument which as above has been mentioned as necessary to the generation of the fictitious entities, called a right and a power, is, as has been seen, a command. But a command is a discourse, expressive of the wish of a certain person, who, supposing his power independent of that of any other person, and to a certain extent sufficiently amply in respect of the subject-matters—to wit, persons, things moveable and immoveable, and acts of persons, and times—is a legislator;—say a legislator in the singular: for simplicity sake, the case of a division of the legislative power among divers persons or classes of persons, may on this occasion be put aside.

6. *Quasi Commands.*—Now then comes a doubt, and with it a question:—in the state of things you have hitherto been supposing, the law in question is of that sort called statute law: and in the case of statute law the print of a command is sufficiently visible. But obligations are created—rights established, not only by statute law, but by another species of law called common law: Where in this case is the command?—where is the person by whom it has been issued?—where, in a word, is the legislator? The judge is not a legislator. Far from claiming so to be, he would not so much as admit himself to be so: he puts aside, if not the function, at any rate the name.

Hitherto we have been in the region of realities: we are now of necessity transported into the region of fictions. In the domain of common law, everything is fiction but the power exercised by the judge.

On each occasion the judge does, it is true, issue a command:—this command is his decree; but this decree he on every occasion confesses he would not on any occasion have the power of issuing with effect, were it not for a command, general in its extent, and in such sort general as to include and give authority to this individual decree of his.

To be what it is, a command, general or individual, must be the command of some person. Who in this case is this person? Answer: Not any legislator; for if it were, the law would be a statute law. A person being necessary, and no real one to be found, hence comes the necessity of a fictitious one. The fictitious one, this fictitious person, is called the common law—or more generally, that he may be confounded with the real person in whose image he is made, *the law.*

To warrant the individual decree which he is about to pronounce, the judge comes out with some general proposition, saying, in words or in effect, *thus saith* THE LAW. On the occasion of the issuing of this sham law, the pretext always is, that it is but a copy of a proposition, equally general, delivered on some former occasion by some other judge or train of successive judges.

In this proposition there may be or may not be a grain of truth, but whether there be or be not, the individual decree has in both cases alike the effect of a law—of a real law—issued by a legislator avowing himself such, and acknowledged as such.

A command being the generic name of the really existing instrument of power called *a law,* let a *quasi command* be the name of that counterfeit instrument feigned to answer the purpose of it, to produce the effects of it, for the purpose of enabling the judge to produce, in the way of exacting compliance, the effect of a law. . . .

CHAPTER IV.   AXIOMS.

1. *Axioms of Mental Pathology—a necessary ground for all legislative arrangements.* By an axiom of mental pathology, considered as a ground for a legislative arrangement, understand a proposition expressive of the consequences in respect of pleasure or pain, or both, found by experience to result from certain sorts of occurrences, and in particular from such in which human agency bears a part: in other words, expressive of the connexion between such occurrences as are continually taking place, or liable to take place, and the pleasures and pains which are respectively the results of them.

Practical uses of these observations, two:—1. With regard to pleasures, the learning how to leave them undisturbed, and protected against disturbance—(for as to the giving increase to them by the power of the legislator to anything beyond a very inconsiderable amount, it is neither needful nor possible); 2. With regard to pains, the learning how on each occasion to minimize the amount of them in respect of magnitude and number—number of the individuals suffering under them—magnitude of the suffering in the case of each individual.

Arithmetic and medicine—these are the branches of art and science to which, in so far as the maximum of happiness is the object of his endeavours, the legislator must look for his means of operation:—the pains or losses of pleasure produced by a maleficent act correspond to the symptoms produced by a disease.

Experience, observation, and experiment—these are the foundations of all well-grounded medical practice: experience, observation, and experiment—such are the foundations of all well-grounded legislative practice.

In the case of both functionaries, the subject-matter of operation and the plan of operation is accordingly the same—the points of difference these:—In the case of the medical curator, the only individual who is the subject-matter of the operations performed by him, is the individual whose sufferings are in question, to whom relief is to be administered. In the case of the legislator, there are no limits to the description of the persons to whom it may happen to be the subject-matter of the operations performed by him.

By the medical curator, no power is possessed other than that which is given either by the patient himself, or in case of his inability, by those to whose management it happens to him to be subject:—by the legislatorial curator, power is possessed applicable to all persons, without exception, within his field of service; each person being considered in his opposite capacities,—namely, that of a person *by whom* pleasure or pain, or both, may be experienced, and that of a person *at whose hands* pleasure or pain, or both, may be experienced.

Axioms of *corporal* pathology may be styled those most extensively applicable positions, or say propositions, by which statement is made of the several sorts of occurrences by which pleasure or pain are or have place in the human body:—as also, the results observed to follow from the performance of such operations as have been performed, and the application made of such subject-matters as have been applied for the purpose of giving increase to the aggregate of pleasure, or causing termination, alleviation, or prevention, to have place in regard to pain.

Axioms of *mental* pathology may be styled those most commonly applicable propositions by which statement is made of the several occurrences by which pleasure or pain is made to have place in the human mind:—as also, the results observed to follow from the performance of such operations as have been performed, and the application of such subject matters as have been applied for the purpose of effecting the augmentation of the aggregate of the pleasures, or the diminution of the aggregate of the pains, by the termination, alleviation, or prevention of them respectively, when individually considered.

Security—subsistence—abundance—equality—*i.e.* minimization of inequality:—by these appellatives, denomination has been given to the particular ends which stand next in order to the universal end, the greatest happiness of the greatest number. This being admitted, these are the objects which will be in view in the formation of the several axioms of pathology which present themselves as suitable to the purpose of serving as guides to the practice of the legislatorial curator. . . .

2. *Axioms applicable to Security for Person.*

Axioms forming the ground for such legislative arrangements as have for their object and their justification, the affording security for person against such maleficent acts, to which it stands exposed.

1. The pleasure derivable by any person from the contemplation of pain suffered by another, is in no instance so great as the pain so suffered.

2. Not even when the pain so suffered has been the result of an act done by the person in question, for no other purpose than that of producing it.

Hence, one reason for endeavouring to give security against pain of body or mind, resulting from human agency, whether from design or inattention. . . .

Axiom: In no case is there any reason for believing that the pleasure of antipathy gratified is so great as the pain suffered by him at whose expense, as above, the pleasure is reaped.

Offences to which the axiom applies are—1. Offences affecting body; 2. Offences affecting the mind other than those belonging to the other classes; 3. Offences affecting reputation—the reputation of the sufferer—other than those by which the reputation of the evil doer is increased; 4. Offences affecting the condition in life of the sufferer, other than those by which the reputation of the evil doer is increased or expected to be increased.

For justification of the legislative arrangements necessary to afford security against maleficent acts affecting the person, what it is necessary to show is, that by them pain will not be produced in such quantity as will cause it to outweigh the pleasure that would have been produced by the maleficent acts so prevented.

For this purpose, in order to complete the demonstration and render it objection proof, in certain cases, it will be necessary to take into account not only the evil of the first order, but the evil of the second order likewise.

First, then, considering the matter on the footing of the effects of the first order on both sides,—Axioms bearing reference to the effects of the first order on both sides, are the following:—

Axioms serving as grounds and reasons for the provision made by the legislator for general security;—to wit, against the evils respectively produced by the several classes and genera of offences.

Case 1. An offence affecting person, or say corporal vexation, in any one of its several shapes—offender's motive, ill-will or spite—the enjoyment of the offender will not be so great as the evil of the first order, consisting in the suffering experienced by the party vexed.

Case 2. So if the offence be an offence productive of mental vexation—and the motive the same.

Case 3. So if the offence be an offence affecting reputation.

Case 4. So, exceptions excepted, in the case of every other class or genus of offences, the motive being ill-will or spite, as above.

Case 5. Exception are among offences affecting person and reputation jointly, the offences having for the motive sexual desire; to wit—1. Sexual seduction, allurative, or say enticitive; 2. Sexual seduction compulsory; 3. Rape; 4. Vexatious lascivious contrectation.

In any of these cases, what may happen is—that the enjoyment of the offender may be equal or more than equal to the suffering of the party wronged; in either of which cases the evil of the first order has no place. But to all other persons, the suffering of the one party will present itself as being to an indefinite degree greater than the enjoyment of the offender and proportioned to the apparent excess will be the actual alarm on the part and on behalf of persons exposed to the like wrong from the same cause: and thence, so far as regards alarm, will be the evil of the second order. . . .

Axiom: The pleasure of antipathy or revenge produced in the breast of the evil-doer by the contemplation of a pain of disappointment produced in the breast of the sufferer, is not in any case so great in magnitude as that same pain.

To this axiom corresponds, as being thereon grounded, a fundamental principle entitled the *disappointment-preventing principle.*

Operation necessary for the establishment and continuance of security,— Fixation of the text of the laws.

For leading expectation, the law need only be exhibited, provided that it be clear, and not too vast for comprehension. But that it may be exhibited, it is necessary that it exist. The greatest and most extensive cause of regret respecting English law, is,—that as respects a large portion, it has no existence. Instead of laws, it cannot even be said that we possess shadows of law:—shadows imply substances by which they are formed;— all that we possess is a *phantom,* conjured up by each one at his pleasure, to fill the place of the law. It is of these phantoms that *common law, unwritten, judge-made* law, is composed.

A discussion upon a point of unwritten or common law has been defined *a competition of opposite analogies.* In giving this definition, the most severe and well-deserved censure was passed both upon this species of law, and upon the carelessness of the legislators who have tolerated its pernicious existence—who have allowed the security of their fellow-citizens to remain without foundation, tossed about by the interminable and always shifting competition of opposite analogies,—who have left it upon a quicksand, when they might have placed it upon a rock.

3. *Axioms pathological, applicable to Subsistence.*

Axiom 1. Though to each individual his own subsistence be, by the nature of man, rendered the chief object of his care, and during his infancy an object of care to the author of his existence, yet a considerable portion of the aggregate number of the members of the community there will always be, in whose instance a subsistence cannot have place (without the legislator's care) without provision made by the legislator to that effect.

2. For the subsistence of all, and accordingly of these, provision will to a certain degree have been made by the provision for security in all its shapes, and for security of property in particular: as also for abundance; for abundance, because of the abundance possessed by some is composed a stock, a fund, out of which matter is capable of being taken applicable to the purpose of affording, whether immediate or through exchange, subsistence to others. But for the subordinate end to the purpose here in question, the utmost of what can be done for these two other subordinate ends, taken together, will not of itself be sufficient.

Of the nonpossession of the matter of subsistence in such quantity as is necessary to the support of life, death is the consequence: and such natural death is preceded by a course of suffering much greater than what is attendant on the most afflictive violent deaths employed for the purpose of punishment.

Rather than continue to labour under this affliction, individuals who are experiencing it will naturally and necessarily, in proportion as they find opportunity, do what depends upon them towards obtaining, at the charge of others, the means of rescuing themselves from it: and in proportion as endeavours to this purpose are employed, or believed to be intended to be employed, security for property is certainly diminished—security for person probably diminished on the part of all others.

By the coercive authority of the legislator provision cannot be made for the indigent, otherwise than by defalcation from the mass of the matter of abundance possessed by the relatively opulent, nor yet, without a correspondent defalcation more or less considerable, from security for property on their part.

In every habitual part of the earth, people, so soon as they behold themselves and their eventual offspring secured against death for want of the matter of subsistence, which security cannot be afforded otherwise than by correspondent defalcation from the matter of abundance in the hands of the relatively opulent, will continue to effect addition to the number of its inhabitants. But this augmentation thus produced will proceed with much greater rapidity than any addition that can be made to the quantity of the matter of subsistence possessed, as above, by the indigent, by defalcation made at the expense of security for property, as well as from the matter of abundance, by correspondent defalcation from the matter of abundance in the hands of the relatively opulent.

The consequence is, that sooner or later, on every habitable part of the earth's surface, the community will be composed of three classes of inhabitants:—1. Those by whom, with the addition of more or less of the matter of abundance, the matter of subsistence is possessed in a quantity sufficient for the preservation of life and health;—2. Those who, being in a state in which they are perishing for want of the matter of subsistence, are on their way to speedy death;—3. Those who to save themselves from impending death, are occupied in waging war upon the rest, providing the means of subsistence for themselves at the expense of the security of all, and the matter of subsistence and abundance in the possession of all.

So long as by arrangements taken for the purpose by government, the thus redundant part of the population can be cleared off by being conveyed from the habitable part of the globe in question to some other part, these two classes of quickly perishing individuals may be prevented from receiving formation, or if formed, from receiving increase. But in no one part of the habitable globe can this be done by government without expense, nor the matter of expense be obtained without defalcation made from security, and suffering from loss, by forced contribution as above; and sooner or later, in proportion as property and security for property establishes itself, the whole surface of the habitable globe cannot but be fully peopled, in such sort, that from no one spot to any other could human creatures be transplanted in a living and about to live state.

Human benevolence can, therefore, hardly be better employed than in a quiet solution of these difficulties, and in the reconciliation of a provision for the otherwise perishing indigent, with this continual tendency to an increase in the demand for such provision.

4. *Axioms applying to Abundance.*

1. Included in the mass of the matter of abundance, is the mass of the matter of subsistence. The matter of wealth is at once the matter of subsistence and the matter of abundance: the sole difference is the quantity;—it is less in the case of subsistence—greater in the case of abundance.

2. If of two persons, one has the minimum of subsistence without addition,—and the other, that same minimum with an addition,—the former has the matter of subsistence, the latter the matter of abundance:—understand, in comparison with him who has nothing beyond the minimum of the matter of subsistence,—the term abundance being a comparative, a relative term.

3. The matter of subsistence being, in the instance of each individual, necessary to existence, and existence necessary to happiness,—suppose a quantity of the matter of wealth sufficient for the subsistence of 10,000 persons, at the disposition of the legislator;—more happiness will be producible, by giving to each one of the 10,000 a particle of the matter of subsistence, than by giving to 5000 of them a portion of the matter of

abundance composed of two particles of the matter of subsistence, and then giving none to the remaining 5000: since, on that supposition, the 5000 thus left destitute would soon die through a lingering death.

4. But suppose that, after giving existence to the 10,000, and to each of them a particle of the matter of subsistence, the legislator have at his disposal a quantity of the matter of wealth sufficient for the subsistence of other 10,000 persons, and that he have the option—of either giving existence to an additional number of persons to that same amount, with a minimum of the matter of subsistence to each,—or instead, without making any addition to the first 10,000, of giving an addition to the quantity of wealth possessed by them,—a greater addition to the aggregate quantity of happiness would be made by dividing among the first 10,000 the whole additional quantity of wealth, than by making any addition to the number of persons brought into existence. For, supposing the whole 10,000 having each of them the minimum of the matter of subsistence on any given day,—the next day, in consequence of some accident, they might cease to have it, and in consequence cease to have existence: whereas, if of this same 10,000 some had, in addition to his minimum of the matter of subsistence, particles one or more of the matter of abundance, here would be a correspondent mass of the matter of wealth, capable of being by the legislator so disposed of as to be made to constitute the matter of subsistence to those who, otherwise being without subsistence, would soon be without existence.

5. Not that, as between the matter of subsistence, and the matter of abundance, the identity is other than virtual—identity with reference to the purpose here in question, to wit, the effect on happiness;—and this virtuality depends upon the facility of obtaining one of the sorts of matter necessary to subsistence, in exchange for matter neither necessary, nor so much as contributing to subsistence—potatoes, for example, in exchange for coin; but so far as is necessary to the guidance of the legislator's practice, this virtual identity always has had, and is likely always to have place.

6. Thus it is that the matter of abundance, as contradistinguished from the matter of subsistence, is contributory to happiness, in three distinguishable ways or capacities:—1. As contributing in a direct way to enjoyment, in a degree over and above what could be contributed by the mere matter of subsistence; 2. As contributing in an indirect way to security, to wit, by its capacity of serving, in the way of exchange, for the obtainment of the efficient instruments of security in any of these shapes; 3. As eventually contributing, in the same indirect way, to subsistence.

5. *Axioms applying to Equality, in respect of wealth.*

I. Case or state of things the first.—The quantities of wealth in question, considered as being in a quiescent state, actually in the hands of the two parties in question: neither entering into, nor going out of the hands of either.

1. *Caeteris paribus,*—to every particle of the matter of wealth corresponds a particle of the matter of happiness. Accordingly, thence,

2. So far as depends upon wealth,—of two persons having unequal fortunes, he who has most wealth must by a legislator be regarded as having most happiness.

3. But the quantity of happiness will not go on increasing in anything near the same proportion as the quantity of wealth:—ten thousand times the quantity of wealth will not bring with it ten thousand times the quantity of happiness. It will even be matter of doubt, whether ten thousand times the wealth will in general bring with it twice the happiness. Thus it is, that,

4. The effect of wealth in the production of happiness goes on diminishing, as the quantity by which the wealth of one man exceeds that of another goes on increasing: in other words, the quantity of happiness produced by a particle of wealth (each particle being of the same magnitude) will be less and less at every particle; the second will produce less than the first, the third than the second, and so on. . . .

On consideration of what is stated above, it will be found that the plan of distribution applied to the matter of wealth, which is most favourable to universality of subsistence, and thence, in other words, to the maximization of happiness, is that in which, while the fortune of the richest—of him whose situation is at the top of the scale, is greatest, the degrees between the fortune of the least rich and that of the most rich are more numerous,—in other words, the gradation most regular and insensible.

The larger the fortunes of the richest are, the smaller will be the number of those whose fortunes approach near to that high level: the smaller, therefore, the number of those from whose masses of property the largest defalcation could by possibility be made:—and, moreover, the larger those masses, the greater would be the difficulty which the legislator would experience as to the obtaining at their charge such defalcation as the nature of the case would not exclude the possibility of making.

Thus, for example, it would, in case of over population, be easier in England, or even in Ireland, to ward off famine for a time, than it would be in British India.

Equality requires, that though it be at the expense of all the other members of the community, the income of those whose income is composed of the wages of labour be maximized. Reason: Of these are composed the vast majority of the whole number of the members of the community.

Exceptions excepted, equality requires that the profits of stock be minimized. Reason: Because the net profit of stock is composed of the mass, or say portion remaining to the employer of the stock, after deduction made of the wages of the labour applied to it.

Exception will be—if this supposed case be really exemplified—where the possessors of the wages of labour are so many, and the possessors of the profits of stock so few, that by a small addition to the one, no sensible defalcation will be made from the other.

6. *Axioms relating to Power, Rank, and Reputation.*

By axioms relating to power, understand self-serving power, exempt from the obligation by which it is converted into trust.

As between individual and individual, the pleasure to the superior, to the power-holder from the possession and exercise of the power, is not so great as the pain experienced by the party subjected.

Therefore, only when converted into extra-benefiting by appropriate obligation, can it be conducive to greatest happiness.

The same observations will equally apply to rank, and factitious estimation produced by rank.

So also to extra reputation, or say estimation, unless when acquired by service rendered to others.

The principle corresponding to these axioms, as to equality, is *the inequality-minimizing principle.*

Chrestomathia

A Note on *Chrestomathia*

Chrestomathia, from the Greek, conducive to useful learning: this is Bentham's textbook of education, and it sprang, like almost everything else he ever wrote, from his passionate absorption in law and politics. Education, for him, was government, the government of the non-adult. He first became interested in the 1790's when he planned Panopticon Hill Villages for paupers, orphans, and the unemployed; and designed free schools for all, adults and children alike. The Bell and Lancastrian systems, whereby the pupils taught each other, fascinated him, and he planned to use their methods.

Nothing came of his plans then, but some fifteen years later he took them up again. In a new flush of practical enthusiasm, with Panopticon dead beyond resurrection, with, however, a large amount of unused capital that came from his reimbursement, Bentham launched a new scheme in 1815: a "Chrestomathic" or Utilitarian School for "the middling classes." For centuries the education offered in the conventional public schools had been strictly classical, and so it was to remain throughout the nineteenth century. But he had himself suffered through long years of Greek and Latin declensions and was convinced of their futility and total irrelevance to the obviously emerging technical needs of an industrial civilization.

But just what subjects were relevant? What should the curriculum be? That was the problem he set out to solve. Characteristically, he could answer in only one way, by first making an "exhaustive bifurcation,"
270

that is, a completely exhaustive survey of the entire field of art and science, of every conceivable subject of human interest from algebra to zoology. He was delighted. At last he had a good practical reason for doing something he had wanted to do ever since "that wonderful year" 1768, when he had first discovered the great French *Encyclopédie*. It had been prefaced with D'Alembert's Encyclopedical Tree, a chart of all human knowledge, modeled after Sir Francis Bacon's earlier example. Even then Bentham had been dissatisfied with it, for it was both illogical and incomplete. But until 1815, he had never found sufficient practical incentive to undertake so ambitious a project, the invention of a better alternative.

He also offered a Tree, but one whose central trunk was "eudaemonics," or the art-and-science of well-being. Every branch and twig of human knowledge found its place in the whole organism by its distance from well-being. His was a very symmetrical tree, designed of course on the exhaustively bifurcative system *per genus et differentiam*.

These following selections are from the appendix describing his method and object, and because they describe equally well the method and object of his entire life's work, are extremely important. It must never be forgotten that for Bentham there was no fundamental difference between art and science: all arts and all sciences are branches of the universal art of eudaemonics and the science of ontology. Arts are more nearly concerned with practice, and science with theory, but they continually overlap and intermingle.

Here Bentham explores one of his favorite metaphors, the map. All his life he tried to offer complete maps of the successive territories he surveyed; he saw himself as a cartographer, and his aim was completeness, all-comprehensiveness, a goal of the highest importance to him. Completeness meant mastery, and mastery was what he sought. And for whom did he seek it? Again, as always, the legislator. "Exercising dominion over almost every branch of art and science, . . . the legislator, on pain of acting blindfold, has need of an insight,—the more clear, correct, and extensive the better,—into the matter of every branch of art and science." [1]

No more than Panopticon was Bentham's school ever built, though he offered his backyard for the purpose. Having learned from Panopticon, he knew better than to undertake such a scheme alone, but all the same, the Committee was unable to raise enough money. It was perhaps just as well. The trampling of hundreds of feet through his beautiful, carefully tended flowerbeds must surely have shattered the equanimity of even this most benevolent of philosophers.

[1] See p. 278 below.

Chrestomathia

Appendix, Section X

(Vol. VIII, pp. 98ff.)

Section X. *Uses of a Synoptic Encyclopedical Table or Diagram.* By the name of an *Encyclopedical Sketch,* two perfectly different, however nearly related, objects may, with equal propriety, be designated, and under that common appellative thereby comprehended. The one is, a *continued discourse,* expressed in the forms of ordinary language: the other is a *Systematic Table* or *Diagram,* so constructed as to be in some degree *emblematic.* In the continued discourse, the relations in question are expressed at length in words and words alone: in the emblematic diagram some *image* is employed, by reason of which, while by their respective names, the objects in question are presented to the eye, all of them in the same place, and at the same time, certain relations*

[*Pleading for his quondam instructor, the poet *Archias,* "Between art and art," (says *Cicero,*) there exists throughout the whole assemblage of them, *commune vinculum,* a common tie—True; and that tie is . . . viz. their common *object—well-being*—by which they are constituted so many branches of the universal art, *Eudaemonics.* Between art and art?—Yes; and moreover between *science* and *science:* and of these the common tie is their common *subject,* viz. *substance:* and by this common tie it is that they are constituted so many branches of the universal *science, ontology—particular* as well as *general* ontology included. . . . But, between *art,* taken in its whole extent, and *science,* taken in its whole extent, there runs throughout that all-pervading and most intimate connexion. . . . For the arts he was speaking of, the Orator might thus, in virtue of this connexion, supposing him aware of it, and supposing it to have been suitable to his purpose and to the occasion, have found two, viz. the two above-mentioned common ties.

Not that, in any part of the field, any such conception, as it is in the power of any of the words in question to convey, of those *general* ideas, of which they are respectively the names, can serve in the place of ideas derived from the perception of individuals, of the correspondent individual objects respectively contained in them. No; it is only through *individual* objects, that any clear and adequate ideas are presented and lodged in the mind: and it is the opposite notion, that constituted the all-pervading error

272

of the class of philosophers called the *Schoolmen* or *School-Logicians,* and gave, to little less than the whole mass of knowledge or supposed knowledge of those times, the character of a nutshell without a kernel, or a skull without brains.

But what it is in the power of these words to do is—to afford so many ready *receptacles,* as it were, or *boxes,* in which the *individual ideas,*—in proportion as they are drawn forth from the *individual objects* which are their *sources,*—may be lodged and deposited, in such manner as to take hold of the memory, and there to remain, in readiness to be, at any time, called up for use.]

which they bear to one another, are at the same time held up to view. As to the image, that of a *tree,* with its trunk and branches, is that which, in the earliest example known*

[*the Tree of Porphyriaus]

was thus employed; nor does it appear that the nature of the case affords any object better adapted to this purpose.

To the form of a *continued discourse* the advantage attached is, that the quantity of explanation given by it is not restricted: but with this advantage is connected a disadvantage, viz. that, if it be of a certain length, it is only in succession that the several parts of it are presented to, and can be taken cognizance of by, the eye; so that, unless it be under the constantly repeated trouble and embarrassment, of turning backwards and forwards, leaf after leaf, or that of a constant strain upon the memory, or both, no comparison of part to part can be made.

In the *systematic diagram,* the advantage is, that, for the purpose of uninterrupted and universal comparison, continued to any length, after the objects with their several relations have been respectively explained, each of them, at whatever length may have been deemed requisite, in and by the continued discourse, the whole assemblage of them is, or at least, as above mentioned, may be so brought together, as to be kept under the eye at once, forming as it were so many parts of one and the same picture.

Thus it is, that to this form two perfectly distinguishable, howsoever closely connected, advantages, both of them of a practical nature, are attached: in the first place, of the whole matter taken together, *conception* is facilitated and expedited; in the next place, *comparison*—reciprocal comparison—the articles being capable of being run over for all purposes, in all directions, and in all imaginable orders of succession, without interruption, and with that *rapidity* which is proverbial as being among the characters of *thought.*

To set against these advantages, no disadvantage has place, except that to the quantity of matter, to which *this* form is capable of being given, there are limits which apply not to the other. But, within these limits, here, as in a *map* or an assortment of maps, it is seldom that, be the purpose what it may, within the quantity of space capable of being thus employed, a quantity of matter sufficient for the purpose will not be capable of being displayed.

Anterior to the time of Bacon, were the profit worth the trouble, Encyclopedical Sketches might, even in the *tabular* form, it is believed, be found, and in both forms in no inconsiderable abundance. But, by the true lights, shed upon the field of *thought and action,* and thence upon the field of *art and science,* by that resplendent genius, all those false lights have been extinguished.

Of the two above-distinguished forms, of which an Encyclopedical Sketch is susceptible, the only one, however, of which the works of Bacon afford an exemplification, is that of a continued discourse, the *purely verbal* form.

In like manner, in no other than the purely verbal form, and that, too, wrought in a looser texture, may be seen the Encyclopedical Sketch prefixed by *Ephraim Chambers* to his Dictionary of Arts and Sciences.

With the two Encyclopedical Sketches of *Bacon* and *Chambers* before him, *D'Alembert* prefixed to the French *Encyclopedia* his Encyclopedical Sketch, in the *purely verbal* form, taken, as he says, chiefly from Bacon: and, moreover—and for the first time reckoning from the days of Bacon—that correspondent sketch, in the form of a *systematic diagram.* . . .

This diagram is exhibited by him in the character of the principal object; and it is in the character of an *Explanation* of that principal object, that the continued and purely verbal discourse attached to it, is delivered by him.

Notwithstanding the imperfections above held up to view, to which others might have been added, signal was the service which, in the estimation of the author's collaborators, among whom were numbered almost all the men of any literary eminence whom France at that time afforded, was rendered by the instrument so constructed. . . . In it they beheld, nor with other eyes has it been beholden (it is believed) in that or other countries, by their contemporaries or their successors, a sort of *novum organum* in miniature: a sort of instrument, which every man, to whose lot it has fallen, to labour, upon a scale of any considerable extent, in any part of the field of art and science, ought to have constantly in his hands and before his eyes.

To what instruction soever may have been extractible from that diagram, whether any and what addition has been afforded, by the remarks herein above made on it, together with the subjoined sample of another, executed upon a plan considerably different, the reader will judge.

A Table of this sort may be considered as an instrument in the hand of *Analogy*.

Scarce will the *art* be found, from which, through the medium of *Analogy*, assistance may not, in some shape or other, be borrowed by some *other* art, not to say by *every* other.

By *Analogy*, scarce will the article of *knowledge* be found, by which, in some shape or other, *light* may not be received from some other, not to say every other.

Conception, retention, combination, generalization, analysis, distribution, comparison, methodization, invention—for all or any of these purposes, with an Encyclopedical tree in his hand, suited to the particular object which he has in view, skipping backwards and forwards, with the rapidity of thought, from twig to twig, hunting out and pursuing whatsoever analogies it appears to afford, the eye of the artist or of the man of science may, at pleasure, make its profit, of the labour expended on this field.

Yes, true it is that, no otherwise than through individual objects, can any clear ideas be imbibed, from the names of those ideal aggregates or bundles, of different sorts and sizes, into which, by the associating and dividing power of those appellations, they are collected and distributed. But, from a comparatively small number of individual objects, may be obtained very instructive and practically serviceable ideas, of very extensive aggregates. Many years ago, forty thousand, or thereabouts, was supposed to be the number of *species* of plants at that time more or less known: forty thousand, the number of those ideal aggregates, designated by the name of *species:* millions of millions the number of the individuals at each moment designated by those same specific names. Yet from any one of those individuals may be abstracted a tolerably adequate idea of the species in which it is considered as contained; and how small is the number of species necessary to plant in the mind the prodigiously extensive idea designated by the word *plant!*

By attention, applying itself all along with still closer and closer grasp, by this faculty it is that advances, fresh and fresh advances, all of them so many conquests, are continually made in the field of art and science. Each laborious and inventive adventurer proceeds on in the wilderness, as far as his inclination and the force of his mind will carry him. Sooner or later, the same man or another, more frequently another, makes a road, whereby, to succeeding travellers, the quantity of labour necessary to the reaching of that farthest point is more or less reduced. By successive labourers of this pioneering class, the road is made gradually smoother and smoother. Where one ends, another begins; and hence it is that the veriest pigmy is at present able to look down, from a point, which, by his utmost exertions, the giant of anterior times could never reach.

That, of the branches of Art and Science, which, by the denominations here employed are thus endeavoured to be brought to view, the distinctness is, in a multitude of instances, far from corresponding to the distinctness of the denominations themselves, is but too true, and present to view an imperfection no less undeniable than it is believed to be irremediable. In this tract, approximation is, throughout, the utmost that can be hoped for. But, unless and until some other scheme of distribution shall have been found, such as shall be exempt from, or at least in a less degree exposed to, this imputation of indistinctness, than that which is here submitted, the imperfection, so long as the work has any use, will not afford any sufficient reason for leaving it unattempted. That no scheme will be found altogether exempt from the imperfection, may be asserted with full assurance; and, if any scheme less tinctured with it than the present one is, could on this occasion, and by these eyes have been found, *that* and not *this* would have been the scheme in *this* place brought to view.

Let it not at any rate be said, that, by reason of this indistinctness, it is no more than upon a par with those other Encyclopedical Sketches, in the hope of superseding which it has been framed. Between the degree, and even the species of indistinctness, which has place in the two cases, wide indeed (it is believed) will be seen to be the difference. In *this* sketch (to borrow a phrase from Scottish history) in this sketch, may here and there be found (it is true) a small proportion of *debateable land,* concerning which it may be dubious to which of two contiguous districts it may with most propriety be said to belong: but in *those* cases, many are the instances, in which the whole of the territory, which is represented as belonging exclusively to one of two districts, may, with equal propriety, be said to belong to either or to both.

Section XI. *The Mode of Division should, as far as may be, be exhaustive —why?*

If, of a sketch of the kind in question, the utility is by any person recognised, to satisfy him of the utility of its being rendered *exhaustive,* not many words can, it is supposed, by necessary. To be *exhaustive,* the parts which, at each partition or division so made, are the results of the operation, must, if put together again, be equal to the whole; and thus, and in this sense, *exhaust* (to use the word employed by logicians) the contents of the whole. It is only in so far as the divisions which it contains are, in this sense, respectively *exhaustive,* that the information, contained in a work which is composed of them, can be *complete*—can be what it appears to *undertake* for being, can be what it *might* be, and what, if it might, it *ought* to be. This being the case, if it be *not* exhaustive, every proposition, in which the exhaustiveness and completeness of the division is assumed, will, in so far as the assumption is proceeded upon, be, *pro tanto*, erroneous and incorrect; and, if received and acted upon, delusive: and, in whatsoever state of the division the incompleteness has place, the consequence is, that, in every sub-division, the original imperfection is repeated, and the correspondent part of the work tainted with it.

But it is only by means of a system of division, carried on in the thus *declaredly* exhaustive mode, that any assurance can be afforded or obtained, that the survey taken of the field of *thought and action*, and therein of the field of *science and art*, or of whatsoever portion of that field is proposed to be comprehended, in the survey, is complete; any assurance, that, in the course of the progress made through it, a number of parts, in unlimited abundance each to an unlimited extent, may not have been omitted.

It is only in this way, that, even supposing the whole to have been actually embraced and comprehended in the survey, it can, in the mind that has embraced it, wear the aspect and character of a *whole:* instead of that of a regular *tree,* the form in which it presents itself will be no other than that of a confused heap of unconnected fragments,—each of them, in respect of *form* and *quantity,* boundless and indeterminate.

In the body of this work, intimation was given of what presented itself as the chief use, derivable from an insight, more or less extensive into those foreign languages, ancient and modern, in which the vernacular language has its roots. It consists (it was said) in *this,* viz. that, to an eye thus instructed, in the whole field of the language, there being no *hard words,* there shall be no absolutely *dark spots;* nothing that shall have the effect of casting a damp upon the mind, by presenting to it the idea of its ignorance, and thence of its weakness.

Correspondent to the sort of consciousness of power so obtainable in the field of language, is that which, by means of a set of *systematic sketches,* —and, in particular, by means of a set of *systematic* and *tabular diagrams,*—always supposing the mode pursued to be exhaustive, may be obtained and exercised over the field of *art and science.* No parts in it, from which through the medium of these appropriate denominations (the relations of which, as well those to one another, as to the matter of the body or branch of art and science, are determined and brought to view) ideas, more or less clear, *correct,* and *complete,* are not radiated to the surveying eye: in a word, no absolutely *dark spots:* no words that do not contribute their share towards the production of so desirable an effect, as that of substituting the exhilarating perception of mental strength, to the humiliating consciousness of ignorance and weakness.

Desirable as this property will, it is hoped, be acknowledged to be, with reference to the purpose at present in question,—a purpose will now be mentioned, to which it must be acknowledged not to be applicable.

Relations of *logical identity and diversity,* and relations of *practical dependence,* as between branch and branch, both these sets of *relations* have already been mentioned, as capable of being, with good effect, brought to view in the form of a *synoptic Table.* But, for the exhibition of relations thus different, neither can any one Table, nor any number of Tables, upon this same plan, be made to serve. In the plan, of division and correspondent distribution, pursued in the view given of the *logical* relations as above explained, *exhaustiveness* will indeed always be an essential feature. But where the relations to be exhibited are the *practical* sort of relations just spoken of, viz. those of *dependence,* or say, of *subservience,* (whether the subservience be mutual or but unilateral), the nature of the subject admits not of any such regularity and all-comprehensiveness. From branches of art and science, the most remote from one another in the logical tree, one and the same art may be seen looking for assistance. *Natural History, Anatomy, Chemistry, Architecture, Political History, Ethics*—all these, not to mention any more, the *Painter,* not to speak of the *Poet,* may have occasion to summon to his aid.

Exercising dominion over almost every branch of art and science, sometimes in furtherance of the interests of the professors of that particular branch, more frequently and more necessarily in furtherance of the interests of the whole community, the legislator, on pain of acting blindfold, has need of an insight,—the more clear, correct, and extensive the better,—into the matter of every such branch of art and science. For his use, therefore, to the Table of *logical relations,* exhibited upon an exhaustive plan, a Table of relations of *dependence* or *subservience,* as above explained, constructed upon a plan in which *particularity* and *copiousness* should be the ruling objects, would be an essential accompaniment.

Section XII. *Test of All-comprehensiveness in a Division how constructed—Additional Advantage, Distinctness and Instructiveness. Bifurcation why necessary.*

A problem is here proposed, and undertaken to be solved. A logical aggregate of any kind, as designated by any appropriate name, being given, required to divide it into a number of parts, each in like manner designated by a distinctive name, in such sort, that, in the sum of these parts, shall be contained the same individuals, and all the individuals which, and no other individuals than those which are contained in the whole.

Such is the problem, the solution of which is requisite for the present purpose. In other words, the solution of it consists in securing to the *parts,* into which the sort of *whole* in question is to be divided, the *property* of *all-comprehensiveness.*

For the accomplishing of this solution, what has been found necessary, is, the construction of an *instrument,* such as, being employed in the divisional operation in question, and thereby in the conformation of the parts, which are the results of it, shall serve as a *test,* in such sort, as to demonstrate, if such be really the case, that the division thus effected is in fact an all-comprehensive one: call it accordingly, *the test of all-comprehensiveness.*

An instrument of this sort has accordingly been constructed; and, on turning to the Encyclopaedical Table, will be seen to have, in every part of it, been explicitly or implicitly employed. It consists in what may be called the *contradictory formula:* the essence of which consists in the sign of *negation,* employed or employable in the designation of some one in each pair of branches, and *not* in that of the other. . . .

In and by the word *pair,* as applied to the branches thus produced, what is already implied is, that, by the instrument in question, it is only in the way of *bisection* that the problem can be solved. But in this mode, it will be seen, that every desirable purpose may be accomplished: that it cannot by any other mode; and that on any occasion at pleasure, by division into two parts, division into any other number of parts may, if there be any use in it, be accomplished. . . .*

[*Caution, *to prevent that misconception, by which* Aristotle, *after bewildering himself, kept the thinking part of the world bewildered for little less than two thousand years . . . and which by* Bacon *and* Locke, *has scarcely ever yet been done away.*

Lest, to the instrument here employed, viz. the *contradictory formula,*—employed as here in the character of a *test* of, and *security* for *all-comprehensiveness* and *distinctness,* in a logical division,—any extraordinary powers, beyond those which really beong to it, should be ascribed—lest, by being employed in the composition of propositions wearing on the face of them the form of *demonstration,* a degree of conclusiveness, independent of *observation* and *experiment,* and superior to anything which by means of those instruments of knowledge can be produced, should be supposed to be attainable,—this caution is subjoined:—a caution, which, however, to those who by an adequate conception of, and a sufficient attention to, the discoveries made in the region of mind by Bacon and Locke, have learnt to recognise the emptiness of the Aristotelian philosophy, will at the utmost be no more than a *memento.*

Yet, upon *observation* made of individual *perceptions,* and upon the correctness with which it has been made, and the judgments grounded on it deduced, will depend, in every instance, the truth of whatsoever propositions of a *general* nature can, upon that part of the field of thought and action, to which these same individual perceptions and judgments appertain, be framed and delivered.

By general words, a truth, in so far as ascertained by individual observation, may indeed be *expressed:* but, it is not by stringing together general words, be they what they may, or in what number they may, that truth can be *proved:* i.e. that sufficient ground for regarding any one of these propositions as true—any of the properties in question as really appertaining to the subject in question—can be afforded.

Of the formulary, here proposed in the character of a *test of all-comprehensiveness* in the division to which it is applied, what then is the real function and use?—*Answer.* To point the attention of the reader to the individual matters of fact, on which the possession of this property depends: to point the attention to them, viz. by the means of a pointed form of words, by which the existence of them in all the individual subjects in question is asserted in explicit terms.

That all living *bodies* . . . that all *living bodies,* other than those that are *sensitive,* are *insensitive,*—this, for example, is what can be neither denied nor doubted of.—Why? Because the assertion thus brought to view has, in truth, for its subject, nothing more than the import of certain words, compared with certain others:—words, the import of which is on both sides fixed by universal usage.

But that all the *living bodies,* which are call *animals,* are *sensitive,* i.e. possess the property of sensation,—of this proposition the truth depends upon individual observation: viz. partly upon the observation, that bodies, which at first view have been supposed to possess sensation, have upon further observation and experiment been found to give further indications of that property; partly upon the observation, that,—in whatever instance body has been found or supposed to be possessed of that same property,—*animal,* and not *plant,* has, of these two correspondently extensive names of classes, been the name to which it has been wont to be referred, as well as the name by which, in common language, it has been wont to be designated.

Of these two observations, the first is an observation relative to the *nature of things;* and the field it belongs to is that of *Natural History:* the other is an observation relative to the *import of words:* i.e. relative to the usage which, among that portion of the human species, by which the language in question has been employed, has obtained in respect of the *things,* or real objects, for the designation of which the *words* in question have been wont to be employed; and the *field* it belongs to is that of *language.*

It was by fancying that everything could be done, by putting together a parcel of phrases, expressive of the respective imports of certain *words,* mostly of certain *general* words, without any such trouble as that of applying *experiment* or observation to *individual things,*—that, for little less than two thousand years, the followers of Aristotle kept *art* and *science* nearly at a stand. . . .

It is from such truth as there is in the included *particular*—yes and even *individual*—propositions, that whatever truth there is in any more general one is originally perceived,—not *vice versa.* A general proposition is but an aggregate of individual ones: it can only be in so far as the individual propositions contained in it are true, that in the general proposition by which those individuals are contained any truth can be to be found.

The case is—that all *perceptions* are not only particular but *individual.* In so far as it goes beyond actually existing individuals on which the actual observation has been made, every general proposition,—how well warranted soever the *induction* is by which it has been formed,—how useful soever it is when applied to practice,—and how truly soever the sensation it produces in the mind is different from that produced in the same receptacle by any one of the individual observations of which it contains the assertion,—is still but a figment—the mere figment of the imagination.

Hence—once more, and for the last time—it is only in the character of a *provisional* test that this *general* formulary is presented. In *observation* and *experiment*—observation and experiment having for their subjects *individual* objects—in these are the only *original,* and in case of dispute or doubt, the only *definitive* tests to be found.

To give to mere assertion the appearance, and for that purpose the *name* of *demonstration,* is a contrivance, invented and brought forward, probably without seeing the hollowness of it, by *Aristotle,* and which, down to the present day, either from inability or from unwillingness, to recognise the hollowness of it, polemical writers have not yet prevailed upon themselves to abstain from the use of. The proposition which a man stands engaged to support, is in its nature a self-contradictory one, and thereby a mere heap of nonsense,—expressive neither of truth nor even so much as of falsehood? —Nothing will serve him but he must give a *demonstration* of it. The more palpable the absence of all genuine instruments of persuasion, the more urgent the demand for fallacious ones.]

On the Art of Invention

A Note on *On the Art of Invention*

Few and fragmentary as these pages are, they are nevertheless of the highest importance; for Bentham understood the art of invention as *the* motive power of civilization; the inventor therefore as among the most valuable of men; himself as one of the most prolific and inspired of social inventors; and these concise instructions as his most mature reflections on his own working methods. These of course he, as the first of the Utilitarians, wished to share with all who might prosper by them.

It is impossible to date these fragments exactly, but the style is late Benthamese, filled with tightly packed clauses and murmurs about interest-begotten prejudices, etc., which seem to place them some time after 1818, probably in the 1820's. He was then in his seventies and became each year ever more zealous to summarize the wisdom of a lifetime. These notes are such a summary.

Bentham pursued most of his major themes throughout his entire adult life, now picking one up, now dropping it, as he saw for the moment new purpose and significance elsewhere; but his thoughts on the art of invention rather pursued him, and these from earliest childhood on. "What is genius?" his father had demanded of his precocious but "raw" infant son some sixty years before, and the small child stood dumbly humiliated before his father's teasing friends.[1] Unable then to answer, the abashed boy stored the grating question in the front of his mind, until at last he discovered the Latin root: "genius" from GIGNO, meaning "to invent, to

[1] X, 27.

create." The genius, then, is the creative inventor, and the more fertile his creative imagination, the greater his genius.

The discovery had a powerful effect on Bentham. He asked himself, "Have I a *genius* for anything? What can *I* produce?" Then another question followed. "What of all earthly pursuits is the most important?" Legislation was the answer Helvétius gave. "Have I a genius for legislation?" Again and again he put the question to himself. "And have I indeed a genius for legislation? I gave myself the answer, fearfully and tremblingly—Yes!"[2]

Thereafter Bentham never doubted his own prodigious gifts, though until a few garrulous slips of old age to the ever-pandering Bowring, he was always modest and reserved about them. They enabled him to die as he had lived, a most happy man, secure in the comfortable knowledge of his creative contributions to the public welfare. "Someone," he said in his last days [as we have seen, p. 36 above], "must have been the most benevolent man who ever lived. If someone, why not I?"

Mementos 5 and 6 were the most important, for he considered analogy the key to invention—the exhaustive matching of things alike in some respects to test their similarities in others. In this way, in this MS as well as in most others, he traced and emphasized the correspondence between his own field of legislation and related branches of medicine, mathematics, architecture, and chemistry.

The Fabians have often been called "latter-day Benthamites" and with good reason, for they alone among his myriad judges and commentators have seen the fundamental significance of creative invention in the body of his thought. Graham Wallas, Beatrice and Sidney Webb were all great admirers and imitators of this side of Utilitarianism.

[2] *Ibid.*

On the Art of Invention

(Vol. VIII, 275–9, Ch. X, LOGIC, written 1811–1831)

Section I. *Of Invention in General.*

To *teach,* to *learn,* and to *invent,*—these are so many processes or operations, applicable alike to every branch of art or science.

To practice is a sort of operation exclusively applicable to arts; not applicable to any branch of discipline, otherwise than in so far as some portion of art is contained in it; between *teaching* and invention a sort of reciprocality is, moreover, observable; among the subjects of the art of *teaching,* may be the art of invention; among the subjects of the art of *invention* may be the art of teaching.

As between these two,—first, in the order of existence, must have come the art of *invention;* since whatsoever comes to be taught, must first have been invented before it could have been taught.

Of this chapter, the object is to afford such helps as, by the powers of an individual mind,—of the individual mind in question, are capable of being given to invention,—understand, of course, to invention in so far as it is useful,—to invention, in every quarter of the field of thought and action to which it can be applied.

A chapter which takes this for its subject, may be compared to the work of the handicraft, who, having to make a utensil or instrument of new construction, finds occasion, in the first place, to contrive and fabricate one or more of the tools, or other instruments, which he has to employ in making it.

Invention supposes art. The inventor of any branch of an art is the first individual by whom it is practised; or, if between conception and actual practice, there be a difference, insomuch as that of the art which a man was the first to practise, not he himself, but some other individual had been the first to conceive, the first individual by whom it had been conceived.

A *new art,* or a *new mode* of practising an art already invented; either of these may the invention have had for its *subjects.* Of this distinction,

284

the indication may, for clearness' sake, be in this or that instance not altogether without its use; although, in many instances, to draw the line between the two cases may be found a matter of such difficulty that, in those instances, the distinction may be seen to be rather a nominal, or verbal, than a real one; the words not finding an individual case to which they can be applied with truth.

Among the *helps* capable of being given to invention, some will be seen alike applicable to all arts; others to no other than this or that particular species of art.

Inventions applicable to all arts are thereby applicable to all *sciences*. Of this proposition, the truth depends upon, and follows from that of a proposition already brought to view, viz. that, between art and science, there exists throughout the whole field of thought and action, a constant conjunction: for every science a correspondent art, and for every art a correspondent science.

Section II. *Helps applicable to Arts in General without Exception or Distinction.*

In this view, a few rules present themselves as capable of being found, to some minds in the way of original instruction, to all minds in the way of memento or reminiscence, not altogether without their use; in some instances, by affording positive helps, in others by the indication of certain obstacles, the force of which will be to be encountered, which, in any tract of the field of invention, the labourer will find standing in his way, and opposing his progress; obstacles, of the existence, and force, and operation of which it concerns him to be well apprized, lest, when the time comes, they find him unprepared.

Memento 1. Whatever be the art which, or in which, you think to invent, keep steadily in view the particular end at which it aims, the effect the production of which it has for its object. Keep your eyes fixed upon the end. In two Latin words, *Respice finem.*

Memento 2. Beware of *intellectual servility.* In other words, take reason not custom for your guide: the reason of the thing, including the *nature* of the *effect* meant to be produced, not confining yourself to the pursuing of the *practice,* to the performance of those operations, and those only, by which alone the effect is as yet wont to be produced. *Sit non mos sed Ratio dux.*

Memento 3. Be on your guard against the confederated enemies of all good, and thereby of all new good: viz. 1. Indigenous intellectual weakness. 2. Sinister interest. 3. Interest-begotten prejudice. 4. Adoptive prejudice. When they cannot oppose by force these will oppose by discouragement, discouraging by opinion and advice.

Memento 4. In relation to every part of your subject, and every object

connected with it, render your ideas as clear as possible. *Lux undique fiat.*
Memento 5. For means and instruments, employ analogy. *Analogias undique indagato.*

Memento 6. In your look-out for analogies, for surveying that quarter of the field of thought and action to which the art in question belongs, employ the logical ladders, the ladders made of nests of aggregates placed in logical sub-alternation. *In analogiarum indagatione scalis logicis utere.*

Memento 7. Inquire and learn whatsoever, for the production of the effect in question, has been already in use or in prospect. *Jam acta et tentata discite.*

Memento 8. In such your survey of existing inventions, look out in preference for the latest of all, not looking backwards but for some special reason. *Postrema exquirito.*

Memento 9. *Quodlibet cum quolibet.* To everything forget not to apply anything. Suppose that of an indefinite multitude of objects, which in consideration of certain properties or qualities, in respect of which they are found or supposed to agree, and certain others, in respect of which they have been found or supposed to disagree, having all of them been placed in one or other of two classes, some article belonging to the one class has, with success, (*i.e.* with some new effect, which either has been found to be, or affords a prospect of being found to be, advantageous), been applied, no matter in what manner, nor to what purpose in particular, to some article belonging to the other class; in like manner, frame a general resolution not to be departed from in any instance, but for some special cause, (applying to that instance), to apply to each article belonging to the one class every article belonging to the other.

The sort of special cause here in question will be one of these two, viz. 1. Apparently preponderant probability of not producing any new result at all. 2. Apparently preponderant probability that the new result, if any, will, instead of proving preponderantly advantageous, prove preponderantly disadvantageous.

N.B.—Among physical arts and sciences, the branch of art and science to which this rule or memento is in a particular degree applicable, is the Chemical, including, in so far as they belong to it, the several subordinate and practical branches of art and science which come under its department, e.g. cookery, pharmacy, agriculture, architecture, in so far as concerns *materials.*

Memento 10. In taking a survey of practice, distinguish in it as many distinguishable points as the nature of the case appears to afford, and on each of these points, try its utility and propriety, by its relation to the end.

Examples.—The field of medical practice is a field in which many examples, indicative of the utility of this rule, might be collected. In the comparatively ancient system of pharmacy may be found medicines, in the composition of which there were drugs, to the amount of twenty or thirty different sorts, of which, by comparatively recent observation, experience, and experiment, all but two or three have been found either wholly inoperative, or unconducive to the end.

In every part of the field of practice in which the practice has not yet been thus directed, and its several distinguishable parts or points confronted with the proper end, uninfluencing circumstances, and even obstructive circumstances, i.e. obstacles, may be seen confounded with promotive causes, and the result, be it what it may, ascribed without distinction to their conjunct agency; and, in this way, the character of promotive causes ascribed to uninfluencing and even to obstructive causes.

Of this mode of confusion, examples will naturally be to be found in abundance in the system of government established in every country, and in particular in that branch which regards constitutional law. Of whatsoever degree of prosperity the state may be supposed to be in the enjoyment of, as many abuses and inperfections as in the theory or practice of it have place, will by all those who profit by them, be of course placed more or less confidently and explicitly upon the list of promotive causes.

On the subject of each of these mementos, a few observations present themselves as capable of having their use. In the course of them it will, it is believed, be seen that of all of them, howsoever at first view the contrary might in some instances be supposed, there is not one that is not in a manner, more or less pointed, applicable to every track which, in the field of thought and action, it is in the power of art and invention, not excepting science, to take.

The *two first mementos* demand a joint consideration.

The end? It may be asked, exists there any man, who, be the art what it may, in the practice of it, ever omits so much as for a moment either to keep his eyes fixed upon the end, or to keep a look-out for the fittest and most promising means?

Oh, yes; with the exception of the inventive few, who are few indeed, every man. The end, yes, of the end, he is not altogether unregardful: but as to *means*, the *means* which he sees pursued by others, by all those from whose discourse and practice his notions on the subject have been derived, these are the means which, from first to last, he has been in the habit of regarding as not only conducive to the end, but, if not the only ones that are so in any degree, at any rate those which are so in a higher degree than any others which the nature of the case admits of.

Let reason be fruitful, custom barren: such indeed is the advice which on this subject has been delivered. Delivered? but by whom?—by Bacon; by the man whose mind was of almost all minds the most unlike to others. In regard to fruitfulness, how stands the matter as between Reason and Custom in the world at large? Reason breeds like a pole-cat; Custom like a doe-rabbit.

Third Memento.

[There is here in the MS—"N.B. Invention is the offspring of genius"; a dictum the influence of which it was probably intended to examine. The paragraph following is headed, "Indigenous intellectual weakness"; and, at the end of it, there is a memorandum, "Go on with the three remaining natural enemies of genius."—Bowring's note.]

The more *stupid* a man is, especially if in his mind, *stupidity* be, as it is not unapt to be, accompanied by *self-conceit*, the more improbable it will appear to him, that to the invention in question, be it what it may, any such characters as those of *useful* and *meritorious,* would be found to belong to it. So difficult as the art is in its *present* state, so great the expense which, in the articles of genius and industry, it must have cost to the men of former times to bring the art up to its present mark in the scale of perfection, so great the multitudes that for so many ages must have been occupied in the endeavour to give to it every degree of perfection of which it is susceptible,—is it in any degree—is it preponderantly probable that, by the man in question (who in his exterior has probably nothing to distinguish him to his advantage, and whose weaknesses, whatever they may be, being indicated by Envy and Jealousy, are laid open to general observation), so important an addition to the art should really have been made. Such are the observations by which the consideration is diverted from modern invention.

Fourth Memento. Clarification of ideas.—If the subject be of the physical class, render the images, which you form of it in your mind, as correct and complete as possible.

If the subject be of the psychical class, in so far as the words employed in discoursing of it are names of fictitious entities, take the only course by which it is possible for a man to give perfect clearness to the ideas of which they serve to constitute the signs, viz. by searching out the real entities in which these names of fictitious entities have their source.

On some subjects, in some instances, without the use of words, a man may exercise invention, drawing his materials and instruments from the stock of ideas already laid up in his own mind.

But unless, by the actual survey of sensible works, the results and fruits of inventions already executed, it is only through the medium of words, that for his assistance in the exercise of invention, he can make any use of the inventions, or practices, or works of others. Here, then, are so many collections of signs of ideas, from which, according to the degree of attention bestowed on the consideration of them, and the degree of discernment with which that attention is accompanied, the ideas which he obtains from those words will be more or less clear, ambiguous, or obscure.

In so far as the words are such as to be themselves direct representatives of clear ideas, so much the better: but even where this is in but a small degree, or not in any degree, the case, still it will frequently happen, that by the reflections and comparisons of which in his mind they are productive, they may render to him more or less assistance towards the formation of other ideas, such as shall, in a greater or less degree, be clearer than those by which they were themselves suggested.

Fifth and Sixth Mementos. The mode and use of applying these *subalternation scales* are as follows, viz.:

I. Application in the *descending line.*

With the exception of such words as are names of individual objects, take any one of the material words that present themselves as belonging to the subject, not being the name of an individual alone, this word will be name of a *sort* of objects, the name, (say), of an aggregate. If the aggregate be the denomination of a *genus*, think of the several species which, by their respective names, present themselves as being contained under it. Whatsoever is predicated of the genus, will, in so far as it is truly predicated, be, with equal truth, predicable of all these several species.

II. Application in the *ascending line.*

In like manner look out for the name of the next superior genus; with reference to which, the genus in question is but a species, and observe, try, or conjecture, whether that which beyond doubt, has been found predicable with truth of the whole of this species, be, or promise to be, with like truth predicable of the whole, or any other part of the aggregate, designated by the name of that genus.

It is in the instance of the physical department of the field of thought and action, and more particularly to the chemical district of that department, that the applicability of this memento is most conspicuous. Upon every subject, try, or at least, think of trying, every operation; to every subject in the character of a menstruum, apply every subject in the character of a solvent, and so on.

It is to the extent in which application has been made of this memento, that chemical science is indebted for the prodigious progress which, within the compass of the present generation, has been made in it.

It is by the ideal decomposition, performed by the separate consideration of the several distinguishable operations, which respectively constitute the component parts of various mechanical arts, and thence, by the division of labour, that the great improvements, made within the last half century in manufactures, have been effected.

Seventh and Eighth Mementos. Inventions of the physical stamp, are those, in regard to which, the importance of these mementos is, generally speaking, at its highest pitch.

Discovery, practice, publication,—by these words are designated so many periods, which, in the career of invention, may, to the purpose here in question, be distinguished with practical advantage.

To the purpose of the discovery, that, generally speaking, it cannot but be of advantage to a person of an inventive turn, to be apprized of, and acquainted with whatsoever has been already invented, or thought of, in the same line, is obvious enough.

But so far as mere *discovery* is concerned, any inconvenience, which it can happen to a man to incur, from a want of acquaintance with anything that has already been discovered by others, is, in this case, but inconsiderable, in comparison with what is liable to have place. In the first place, so far, indeed, as for want of being pre-acquainted, with this or that discovery which has already been made by this or that other person, he fails of making this or that discovery, which, had it happened to him to have been acquainted with the existing discovery in question, he would have made: so far, here is so much lost to the individual in question, and to the world at large.

In the next place, in so far as after the discovery has been made by himself, it happens to him to learn that this same discovery has already been made by some one else; in this case, what is but natural enough is, that in proportion to what appears to be the degree of importance of the discovery, uneasiness in the shape of a pain of disappointment, should be experienced by him.

But in such a track as that of invention, no step that has ever been taken, no step, be the ulterior result of it what it may, is ever lost. Of every step, present pleasure is the accompaniment, from every step the mind derives increase of vigour; of that which is an instrument of future security and future pleasure.

Ninth Memento. Quodlibet cum quolibet.—A mechanical help will be found in the facility of confrontation. For this purpose, in so far as writing, i.e. manuscript is employed, let it be on one side only of the paper.

Reason.—Propositions, which are on different sides of the same plane, cannot invariably be confronted with each other. While that which is on page 2 is hunting for the terms of that which is on page 1, and what is intended to be compared with it, are either forgotten or become dubious. If such is liable to be the case with the smallest members of a discourse, how much more is it with those that are larger and longer, with complex sentences and whole paragraphs.

So in printing, nothing could be more incongruous than at the back of a table intended for a synoptic one, to print anything that may require to be confronted with any part of the matter of it.

Logical Arrangements, or Instruments of Invention and Discovery Employed by Jeremy Bentham

(Vol. III, pp. 285ff.)

Logical arrangements, which have served as so many *nova organa,* or instruments of invention or discovery to Jeremy Bentham, in the composition of his several works.

To enable himself to take a commanding view (says Bolingbroke) of the field of law and legislation, there are two principal vantage grounds, on which it is necessary for a man to mount, viz. *history* and *metaphysics.*

The observation is Lord Bolingbroke's, and it has been quoted from him by Hume, or some other author of the first eminence.

To that one of the two vantage grounds which is offered by history, the road is smooth and flowery; and of those who have ascended to it, and taken post upon it, there has been no want.

To that which belongs to the region of metaphysics, the road is rugged, and full of thorns. Few are they who have attempted to gain this height; and of those few, still fewer who have succeeded in reaching it, and placing themselves in any such station as hath afforded them any clear and extensive view of the regions stretched out at their feet.

In the following sketch, an enumeration is given of the several monticules which, in the course of his travels on the vantage ground of metaphysics—to call it by the name given to it by Bolingbroke—or, as some would say, of logic—were descried by the mind of the author, and on which, from time to time, it has taken its station, for the purpose of the surveys it has, for different purposes, had occasion to take of that extensive field which is occupied below, in common by ethics or morals, law, and legislation.

If their position merely be regarded—the post they occupy in the intellectual regions—these objects may, according to the figure of speech employed by Bolingbroke, be considered merely as so many stations or resting-places in that more arduous one of his two vantage grounds.

If the purposes and uses to which they have been applied be the object of regard, there will be a convenience in changing the figure, and considering them, with Lord Bacon, as so many engines or instruments, by the aid of which the different works that have been undertaken have been either accomplished, or at least laboured at and attempted.

In most instances, the instrument thus employed by the author was constructed by himself alone,—no part having been borrowed from any other hand;—in other instances, the instrument was found by him, in part at least, ready made; but either enlarged by himself, or applied to uses to which it had not been observed by him to have been applied by any one else. As often as the hand from which he thus received it could be determined and recollected, mention has been made of it.

New ideas derived from Logic. I. Division of entities into real and fictitious; or say, division of nouns-substantive into name of real entities, and names of fictitious entities:—

By the division and distinction thus brought to view, great is the light thrown upon the whole field of logic, and thereby over the whole field of art and science, more especially the psychical, and thence the ethical or moral branch of science.

It is for want of a clear conception of this distinction that many an empty name is considered as the representative of a correspondent reality:—in a word, that mere *fictions* are in abundance regarded as *realities.*

D'Alembert is the author in whose works the notion of this distinction was first observed by me:—*être fictif* is the expression employed by him for the designation of the sort of object, for the designation of which the appellation *fictitious entity* has ever since been employed.

In speaking of the faculties of the mind, the same distinction will also be found occasionally brought to view in the philosophical works of Voltaire.

By attention to this distinction it is, that I was enabled to discover and bring to view, in the case of a numerous class of words, their incapacity of being expounded by a definition in the ordinary form, viz. the form *per genus et differentiam,* which form of definition it has, with how little success and benefit soever hitherto, perhaps universally been the practice to bestow upon them and at the same time to bring to view the only instructive and useful exposition of which the words of this class are susceptible, viz. the exposition by *paraphrasis*—the only form of exposition by which the import attached to them is capable of being fixed, and at the same time placed in a clear and determinate point of view.

See, in particular, the class of political, including legal, fictitious entities, in respect to which, by indication of the relation which the import of the word in question bears in common to the fundamental ideas of pain and pleasure, a distinct and fixed meaning is thus given to a numerous tribe of words, of which, till that time, the meaning had been floating in the clouds, and blown about by every blast of doctrine:—words to the which, in the mind of many a writer, no assignable ideas, no fixed, no real import, had been annexed.

II. Division of entities, real and fictitious together, into physical and psychical:—

By means of this arrangement, considerable has been the light thrown upon the field of psychical entities, and the origin and affirmation of language: the connexion between the nomenclature of psychical and that of physical entities has been clearly pointed out. There is no name of a psychical entity, which is not also the name of a physical entity, in which capacity alone it must have continued to have been employed, long before it was transferred to the field of psychical entities, and made to serve in the character of a name of a psychical, and that most commonly a fictitious entity.

III. Relations between the import of the word *happiness*, and that of the words *pleasure* and *pain:*—

Sole positive element of happiness, alias *felicity*, alias *well-being*—pleasures, and those determinate ones: sole negative element of happiness, exemption from pains, and those equally determinate ones.

Determinate import thereby given to the word *utility*, a word necessarily employed for conciseness sake, in lieu of a phrase more or less protracted, in which the presence of pleasures and the absence of pains would be brought to view.

An action may be considered and spoken of as *useful*, as conducive to general utility, in proportion to the *value* of any pleasures which it is its tendency to produce, or of any pains which it is its tendency to avert.

Whether there ever were a time at which the word happiness failed of presenting to my mind the character of an aggregate, or compound, of which pleasures, and the exemption from corresponding pains, were the sole elements, is more than at present I can recollect. The satisfaction I remember to have experienced at the observation of this interpretation, as given to it in the first place by Helvétius, and afterward by Hartley, affords some presumption of its being at the first of these times new to me. But perhaps the cause of that satisfaction was not the novelty of the notion in relation to my own conceptions, but the circumstance of seeing the confirmation given to them in these works.

IV. Elements or dimensions of value in regard to pleasures and pains.—

It was from Beccaria's little treatise on crimes and punishments that I drew, as I well remember, the first hint of this principle, by which the precision and clearness and incontestableness of mathematical calculation are introduced for the first time into the field of morals—a field to which in its own nature they are applicable with a propriety no less incontestable, and when once brought to view, manifest, than that of physics, including its most elevated quarter, the field of mathematics.

The elements or dimensions of value, in regard to pleasures and pains, are—1. Intensity; 2. Duration: these belong to it whether considered as past or as future; and of these two taken together, its magnitude is composed. To these come to be added, but in the case only in which it is considered as not yet past—3. The certainty or probability of its arrival; 4. Its proximity, propinquity, or remoteness.

Thus far it is considered as confined to the breast of a single individual: if considered as seated, or capable of being seated, in a number of different breasts, it is then considered as existing under a fifth dimension, viz. Extent,—which extent has for its measure the number of the individuals who are considered as being thus affected;—the greater that number, the more extensive it is; the less, the less extensive.

Two other conceivable elements of value remain still to be ascribed to it, viz. 6. Fecundity; 7. Purity. Of these elements, neither, it is true, can be considered as belonging to the value of a pleasure or a pain when considered by itself: in both instances, it is considered inasmuch as it is capable of being accompanied or followed by sensations of the same or a different kind. If by sensations of the same kind, *i.e.* if, being a pain, by a pain—or being a pleasure, by a pleasure, it be considered as accompanied or followed, it may, in proportion to the number of such concomitant or consequent sensations, be termed *fruitful* or *unfruitful,* prolific or unprolific:—if by sensations of an opposite kind, it may, in proportion to the number of such concomitant or consequent sensations, be termed *impure,* in proportion to the number of those which it escapes or fails being accompanied with, *pure.*

For bringing to view in a concise form these elements, seven in number, the following memoriter verses, awkward as verses of that class naturally are, may for the present serve:—

> *Intense, long, sure, not distant, fruitful, pure,*
> Such marks in pleasures and in pains endure.
> Such pleasures seek, if *private* be thy end;
> If it be *public,* wide let them *extend.*
> Such *pains* avoid, whichever be thy view;
> If *pains* must come, let them *extend* to few.

[For a complete discussion see *Intd. to Morals and Legislation,* Chapter IV.—
M.P.M.]

Less awkward verses I cannot but suppose may one day be found, and
substituted to these with advantage, by some person who is more in use
to dress up language in the garb of poetry.

V. Extension of the use made of the word *matter,* from the field of
physics to the whole field of *psychics,* or *psychology,* including *ethics* and
politics:—

1. In the higher, or more general quarter of them; viz. in the phrases
matter of good, matter of evil.

2. In the department of *law* in general, and of *penal* law in particular,—*matter of satisfaction* or *compensation, matter of punishment, matter
of reward;* matter of punishment being neither more nor less than the
matter of evil applied to a particular purpose;—matter of reward, the
matter of *good* applied to *one* particular purpose;—matter of satisfaction,
the matter of good applied to *another* particular purpose.

3. In political economy— matter of wealth and its modifications; viz.
the matter of *subsistence,* and the matter of *opulence* or *abundance;* each
of these being neither more nor less than so many modifications of the
matter of *wealth;* and in so far as, through the medium of exchange,
interconvertibility as between them has place, with no other difference
than what corresponds to the difference in the purposes to which that
common matter comes to be applied.

Correctness, completeness, and consistency of the views taken of these
large portions of the field of thought and action,—conciseness in the
sketches made or to be made of them:—such are the desirable effects
which this locution presented itself as capable of contributing in large
proportion to the production of.

By this means, for the first time, were brought to view several analogies,
which have a clearer, as well as a more comprehensive view of all these
objects, having thereby been given, than in the nature of the case could,
or can have been given by any other means.

The matter of *good,* as to one-half of it—one of the two modifications
of which it is composed—viz. the negative—being the same thing as the
matter of *evil;* one and the same object—viz. pain—having by its presence
the effect of evil, by its absence or removal the effect of good;—the matter of good being, in its positive modification, composed of pleasures,
and their respective causes—in its negative modification, or form of
exemptions, *i.e.* exemptions from pain, and their respective causes.

In like manner, the matter of *evil* being as to one-half of it—as to one
of the two portions of which it is composed, viz. the negative—the same

thing as the matter of good; one and the same object—viz. pleasure—having by its presence the effect of good, by its *absence,* when considered as the result of loss, the effect of *evil:* the matter of evil being, in its positive form, composed of pains, and their respective causes—in its negative form, of losses corresponding to the different species of pleasures capable of being acquired and possessed, or lost, and their respective causes.

From this correspondency and interconvertibility, a practical result—in the hands of whosoever is able and willing to turn the observation to advantage—is the prevention of excess and waste in the application of both these portions.

A position which by this means is placed in the clearest and strongest point of view, is—that by whatsoever is done in any shape, in and by the exercise of the powers of government, is so much certain evil done, that good may come.

Though the matter of reward, and the matter of satisfaction (viz. for injuries sustained) are in themselves so much of the matter of good, yet it is only by coercion, and that in a quantity proportioned to the extent to which that coercion is applied, that the matter of good thus applied can be extracted.

That when, on the score of and in compensation for injury sustained, the matter of good is, in the character of matter of satisfaction, extracted from the author of the injury, it operates, in and by the whole amount of it, in the character of punishment, on the person from whom it is extracted: and whatsoever may be the quantity of punishment inflicted in this shape, in that same proportion is the demand for punishment satisfied; and whatsoever may be the amount of it in this shape, by so much less is the demand, if any, that remains for it in any other. . . .

VI. Good and evil of the first, second, and third orders, *i.e.* effects similar or opposite, producible in society by the operation of one and the same act at different stages of its progress:—effect in some cases homogeneous with reference to each other, in other cases heterogeneous, are produced in the way of good and evil by the influence of one and the same act in the course of its progress in and through society.

1. In the case of delinquency,—effects in the way of good and evil producible by an offence.

In the first stage comes a portion of the matter of good; viz. the advantage, whether in the shape of pleasure or of exemption from pain, the prospect of which was, in the character of a motive or inducement, the cause of the commission of the pernicious act.

At the next stage comes, in some cases, an effect of an opposite nature—a portion of the matter of evil; viz. if the pernicious act be of the number of those by which a determinate suffering is produced in the breast of an assignable individual or individuals;—here we have one portion of the matter of evil—call this portion *the evil of the first order.*

An ulterior, and in every respect perfectly distinct lot of evil, produced in some cases from the same cause, has been termed *the evil of the second order.* It consists partly of the alarm produced in other breasts by the apprehension of finding themselves among the sufferers from other pernicious acts, that appear likely to be produced by the individual offence in question, in the event of its having been found in its issue favourable to the offender.

Of the mass of evil capable of being produced by an act of delinquency, or at any rate by a multitude of acts of delinquency of the same nature, that portion which comes in at the third and last stage of its progress, is of a sort which, under any tolerably well-established government, is rarely, to any considerable extent, exemplified. It is that which has place, in so far as such being the effects of the alarm produced by the apprehension of continually recurring repetitions of the species of injury in question, the mischief has, from the passive and sensitive faculties of the persons thus threatened, extended itself to their active faculties, compelling them, as it were, to render themselves, by their own inactivity, instruments of their own ruin.

In that modification of delinquency and injury which is composed of acts of the predatory class, may be seen the clearest and strongest exemplification of this case.

In Asia and Africa, many are the instances in which spots, which though situated within the demesne of regular governments, and at one time kept accordingly in regular cultivation, have successively been to such a degree infested by the predatory incursions of neighbouring tribes, as to have at length been abandoned by their inhabitants, and left in a state of perfect desolation.

Under any European government instances are scarcely to be met with where, in its progress over the community, the evil produced by private delinquency has made so great an advance as to have arrived at this third stage.

Unfortunately, of evil, which, having been the result of the misconduct of the rulers themselves, has extended itself so far as to make its appearance in the character of an evil of the third order, examples are by no means rare. . . .

Extensive and important are the practical inferences that present themselves as following from this theory.

In the case of evil, the evil of the first order is next to nothing in comparison with the evil of the second order—not to speak of a stage of evil so unfrequently exemplified as the evil of the third order.

Of the four classes into which the whole mass of delinquency may be divided,—viz. offences against persons individually assignable—offences against a man's own welfare—offences prejudicial to a particular class of persons—offences prejudicial to the whole community at large,—in the second of these classes, viz. offences against a man's self, the principal element of the evil of the second order, viz. the alarm, is altogether wanting.

VII. Springs of actions,—appetites—desires—motives—interests.

Explanation of these psychical fictitious entities of the pathematic class, by that connexion which is common to them with pleasures and pains in the several shapes of which they are susceptible.

VIII. Sanctions or sources of obligation and inducement, five in number, viz.—

1. The physical sanction.
2. The moral or popular sanction.
3. The political, including the legal sanction.
4. The religious sanction.
5. The sanction of sympathy, limited in its application to a particular class of cases.

In so far as the word *sanction* is employed, what is thereby brought to view is, not the species of pleasure or pain by the prospect of which the influence on human will is exercised, and the effect produced, but only the *source* whence the pleasure and pain in question is expected to flow. . . .

That, in comparison with the several other moral forces to which the name of sanction has here been given, the force here termed the sympathetic sanction is in general very weak, is not to be denied: but, for the omitting it from the list of sanctions, this weakness, were it greater than it is, would not afford any sufficient warrant. Of itself, *i.e.* without assistance from any of the other sanctions, it is every now and then seen productive of very considerable effects. It is to the force of this sanction that the principle of utility (understand of general utility) stands indebted for whatsoever reception it meets with, other than that which it may happen to any other articles in the list of sanctions to be instrumental in procuring for it. Under the guidance of the principle of utility it operates in alliance with the several other sanctions: under the same guidance it may not unfrequently be seen operating in opposition to them, and checking them in those sinister courses of maleficence into which, in opposition to the dictates of general utility, they are all of them more or less apt to be led by the political sanction, whether under its own guidance, or under the guidance of the religious sanction. Equally steady and efficient in its action with any of those self-regarding sanctions it cannot be said to be; but a force, howsoever weak and unsteady, is still not the less force: and were it not for the operation of this sanction, no small portion of the good, physical and moral, which has place in human affairs, would be an effect without a cause.

In exact proportion to the efficiency of this principle would be the error committed by him who, on the occasion of any calculation made of the result of the moral forces on the sum or balance of which an effect depends, the production or prevention of which had become the object of human endeavour, should leave out of his calculation the operation of this cause.

Origin of the Theory of the Five Sanctions. In speaking of law, viz. the internal law of any political state (*internal,* I say, in contradistinction to *international*), Blackstone, by whom it is, by an appellative not very appropriate, termed *municipal,* after Puffendorf and others, divides it into four parts, one of which he terms the sanction, or sanctionative part. The sanction or sanctions of law is accordingly an expression of not unfrequent occurrence. So likewise the sanction or sanctions of religion: and accordingly this or that portion is spoken of as being confirmed by, or having received, the sanction of law or the sanction of religion. But as to that which, as above, is here termed the popular or moral sanction, I have no recollection, general or particular, of ever having seen it employed. To the sanction termed *political,* and employed in contradistinction to the legal sanction, viz. in so far as the whole of anything stands distinguished from a part of it, the same observation may also be extended.

In fine, so may it to the physical and the sympathetic: for, in relation to all these several sources of action, two things have, as above, and it is hoped not unsatisfactorily, been shown,—viz. that they are each of them distinct from all the rest, and that they are all of them what they are here termed sources of action; viz. motives, or sets of motives, derived in each of these five instances from so many different sources: to which may be added, that each of them is, according to circumstances, susceptible of such a degree of force as may prove sufficient, perhaps even the weakest of them, to enable it to overpower any one or more of the rest, *i.e.* to give determination to human conduct, even while all those others are operating in opposition to it.

[The list of sanctions was afterward enlarged by Bentham to 14.—M.P.M.]

IX. Conditions requisite for the accomplishment of any object, in so far as depends upon human means:—

Qualifications, both of them necessary, and together sufficient, on the part of the agent or agents in question, for the due accomplishment of any object whatsoever, and in particular for the due discharge of every political obligation, and thence for the due execution of every public trust,—appropriate *will,* and appropriate *power.*

Power is either power *ab extra,* or power *ab intra.* Power *ab extra* is correspondent to, and its efficiency proportionate to the extent and degree of compliance on the part of those over whom it is considered as being said to be exercised. Power *ab intra* will be in proportion to the degree of relative or appropriate knowledge, and the degree of appropriate active talent, on the part of him by whom the exercise of it comes to be made.

In so far as operation or co-operation towards the accomplishment of the object is considered as matter of duty or moral obligation, to possess the appropriate will or inclination is to possess the virtue of *probity—* relative probity: and when put in contrast and contradistinction with this requisite state of the will, appropriate knowledge has been termed intelligence.

Wisdom, probity, and power,—of these three, on attending Blackstone's lectures, and afterwards reading them when in print, under the name of Commentaries on the Laws of England, I observed the concurrent existence laid down by him as conditions necessary to, and at the same time sufficient to insure, in any given political community, the existence of good government.

With reference to government in the highest stations,—and in these alone, are these conditions and qualifications brought to view by Blackstone,—neither by him is anything done to show the relation borne to each other, as above, by these associated fictitious entities, or towards satisfying the reader that the division thus exhibited is of the *exhaustive* kind.

With the help of such amendments as seemed requisite, the enumeration and division appeared to me capable of being, with equal propriety and utility, applied in the political line to all subordinate stations; in the next place, to the accomplishment of any object whatsoever in the ascending or more comprehensive line.

X. Obligation and Right:—

Explanation of these moral, including political, fictitious entities, and of their relation to one another, by showing how they are constituted by the expectation of eventual good and evil, *i.e.* of pleasures and pains, or both, as the case may be, to be administered by the force of one or more of the five sanctions, as above, viz. the physical, the popular, or moral; the political, including the legal; the religious, and the sympathetic.

Of either the word obligation or the word right, if regarded as flowing from any other source, the sound is mere sound, without import or notion by which real existence in any shape is attributed to the things thus signified, or no better than an effusion of *ipse dixitism.*

XI. Proper Ends of the distributive branch of law:—

Ends or purposes, the fulfilment or accomplishment of which this branch of law ought to have for its principal objects,—*security, subsistence, abundance,* and *equality.*

In the mention made of security, a tacit but necessary reference is made to the several classes of injuries against individuals other than the man himself, to which every individual stands exposed. Security is security against mischief—against evil from whatever quarter it may happen to it to come, and against whatsoever of a man's possessions, or vulnerable part of a man's frame, it may happen to it to be directed or to strike.

On this occasion the great difficulty consists in tracing the lines of distinction by which these several factitious entities are separated from each other. Subsistence and abundance have one and the same matter— the matter of wealth: of security, that same matter is itself a main instrument and means whereby all other instrument of security may be obtained.

In the case both of subsistence and abundance, over the relation they bear to security there is some obscurity. Security has several branches— as many branches as there are distinguishable objects exposed to deterioration or destruction; and in the list of these objects are comprised that matter, the matter of wealth, which is common to subsistence and abundance—security against mischief to human life, person, reputation, property (*i.e.* the matter of wealth, considered as lodged in the hands of the individuals, or assemblages of individuals in question) and condition in life. Security is again divisible into as many branches as there are different sorts of offences, or pernicious acts, by which, *pro tanto,* security is destroyed or endangered.

All these objects are, with relation to each other, so many antagonizing forces. In some instances, by the measure by which one is attained, so are one or more of the others: in other instances, one cannot be attained, or endeavoured to be attained, but by the relinquishment, or, *pro tanto,* the sacrifice of one or more of the others.

Equality, in particular, finds in each of the other three a rival and an antagonist—and in security and subsistence, rivals and antagonists, of which the claims are of a superior order, and to which, on pain of universal destruction, in which itself will be involved, it must be obliged to yield. In a word, it is not equality itself, but only a tendency towards equality, after all the others are provided for, that, on the part of the ruling and other members of the community, is the proper object of endeavour.

At the same time, in proportion as the subject is inquired into, it will be found that in all good systems of law, and even in all systems, the very worst not excepted, more or less regard is paid to equality; that in the aggregate of the body of laws in every state, all these others are constantly aimed at, are the objects of constant care, solicitude, and active operation; and that in fact the laws have no other objects or ends in view, but which, short as it is, are comprehended in this list; and that in all bodies of law, the great and constant difficulty is on each occasion, in so far as the competition has place, to decide to which of them the greatest portion of favour is due,—for which, in preference to the rest, provision is to be made.

These things considered, of the ends of objects of the distributive branch of the law, how with propriety could any list, more or less ample, differently composed, have been given?

XII. Formation of an uniform and mutually correspondent set of terms, for the several modifications of which the creation, extinction, and transfer of subjects of possession, whether considered as sources of benefit or as sources of burthen, are susceptible:—and thence of a mutually connected and correspondent cluster of offences, consisting of the several possible modes of dealing as above with such subjects of possession, in the case in which they are considered as wrongful, and as such prohibited by statute law, or considered and treated as prohibited by judiciary *alias* judge-made law.

1. *Collation;* 2. *Ablation.* In the case, and at the point of time, at which the subject-matter is for the first time brought into existence, collation has place without ablation: if it be already in existence, then collation and ablation have place together, and of their union *translation* is the result: in so far as ablation has place without collation, then not translation, but *extinction,* is the result.

Performed in favour of the collator himself, collation is *self-collation:*—if regarded as wrongful, it is *wrongful* self-collation; or in one word, *usurpation* is the name by which it has been, and at any time may be, designated.

Performed by the ablator himself, ablation is *abdication:*—if by the laws regarded or treated as wrongful,—wrongful abdication is accordingly the name by which it may be designated.

XIII. *Division of offences,*—by which is meant all such acts as on the score of their reputed mischievousness are fit or have been or are likely to be regarded as fit to be,—viz. by the application of punishment—converted into offences,—from the consideration of the person or persons, with reference to whom, in the first instance, they are regarded as being or likely to be mischievous, into offences against others—*i.e.* regarded as prejudicial to others, and offences against a man's self—*i.e.* regarded as prejudicial to a man's self.

Division of offences regarded as prejudicial to others, into offences against assignable individuals, *alias* private offences—offences against the unassignable individuals belonging to this or that class, or this or that local district, *alias* semi-public offences—and offences against the unassignable individuals of whom is composed the population of the whole political state.

From the distinction thus brought to view have been deduced diverse conclusions of no inconsiderable importance with reference to practice:— offences so far as the mischief, if any, which they have for their result is confined to the author of the offence, are no fit objects of controul by punishment and penal laws.

Of the offence which in this case is regarded as mischievous—the mischief, if any, being by the supposition confined to the offender himself— the consequence is, that no sooner is it felt,—viz. by him the offender,— than by the whole amount of it, it operates upon him in the character of so much punishment.

Division of offences into *positive* and *negative;* or rather observation made, that in the nature of the case, for every offence committed by a positive act, there is room for a correspondent offence committed by a negative. The case of a positive offence, that where the mischief of the offence, as above, has for its cause a positive act—an act of *commission:* the case of a negative offence, that in which the mischief has for its cause a negative act—an act of *omission:* an act which consists in a man's omitting to do that which it was in his power to do towards the prevention of a mischief, which for want of such positive and preventive act on his part, either actually did take place, or at any rate would have taken place, but for some preventive obstacle, in the application of which he had not any share.

The principle of division here brought to view, extends itself over the whole field of delinquency—be the positive act what it may—the opposite negative act is alike conceivable—is alike capable of being exemplified. If in the case of the positive act any mischief seem to flow, the correspondent negative act can never be altogether unproductive of the like consequence.

As to the difference between the mischief of the one end and of the other, it consists altogether of the mischief of the second order; for as to the mischief of the first order, if it have place in both cases, it is exactly the same in both cases. But in the case of the negative offence, the mischief of the second order—the alarm and the danger—is next to nothing. On the part of the offender, all endeavours to prevent the mischief, which in the instance in question was actually produced were wanting. True; but it follows not that he will at any time employ any exertions in the endeavour to produce a similar mischief.

In respect of punishment, cases there are in which, under the laws perhaps of all civilized nations, the negative act is put exactly upon the same footing as the positive act. In these cases, for example, viz. when one person having another in his power, keeps him without sustenance till he dies—by a mother or nurse, a new-born child—a jailor, one or more of his prisoners. In respect of punishment, the negative course of conduct, of which in these cases loss of life is the result, is commonly put upon a footing little if any thing different from that which has place where the mischief has for its cause a positive act. So in case of a design hostile to the person or power of the sovereign, or this or that member of the sovereignty in a state, the negative offence, which in the case of a person by whom the existence of the design is known, is committed by omission to give information of it to the competent authorities, is commonly punished, not perhaps with exactly the same punishment as that which is appointed for him by whom an active part is taken in that same design, but yet with some other punishment which does not fall much short of it.

Wheresoever the obligation, considered as imposed by the law, is of a positive nature, the only sort of offence which the nature of the case renders possible is of the *negative kind:* and in this whole class of cases, the concomitancy of the two forms of delinquency fails. The sort of offence commissible by non-payment of taxes may serve by way of example. But in every other case, little has been the notice as yet taken of it.

XIV. Ends of Political Economy:—

These are the same as those of the distributive branch of law. Wherein, then, lies the difference? Answer? In so far as political economy is the object, so it is, that to two of those objects, viz. subsistence and abundance, a more particular and direct attention is paid, than either to security or to equality.

By distributive law, is declared what on the many occasions as shall happen to have been taken into view, shall be each man's own. By political economy, is endeavoured to be ascertained how far, and for what particular purposes, chiefly for the general purposes of abundance and subsistence (*i.e.* security for subsistence), the use which otherwise under distributive law each man might make of his own, shall, for the more effectual fulfilment of these several ends, be directed and restricted.

XV. Limits applied to the quantity and productions of Industry, by the quantity of the necessary instruments of production which at the place in question—at the time in question, are in existence.

These instruments are—

1. The aggregate mass of existing capital.

2. The aggregate mass of capacity for labour.

That no end can be successfully pursued to any point beyond the productive power of the aggregate mass of *means* of all sorts necessary to the pursuit and attainment of it, is a self-evident, not to say an identical proposition: any proposition inconsistent with it would be a contradiction in terms.

Yet from this theoretical aphorism, follow divers practical inferences, which though they will scarcely be found to admit of denial, have found great difficulty in obtaining assent.

[The last sheet is dated from Ford Abbey, October 21, 1814; and at its foot Bentham wrote, "Go on"; but no further traces have been found.—M.P.M.]

Parliamentary Reform Catechism

A Note on *Parliamentary Reform Catechism*

"The loom being set," Bentham once wrote, "I can at pleasure take up the thread and spin it wherever it is broken."[1] And so he did, on subject after subject, time and time again. Perhaps nowhere is this more clear than in his writings on parliamentary reform and democracy. By 1790 he had become a democrat. He drew two maps, a republican one for France and the United States, and a constitutional democratic one for England. Each country had different problems and circumstances; therefore each required different solutions, but of one thing he was sure, that some measure of democracy was good for them all.

But his conversion did not last long. When the French began to confiscate property, when the guillotine knives began to fall, Bentham, like almost everyone else in England, was horror-stricken. He rushed to join a reactionary patriotic society, but was intercepted by the more level-headed Romilly who warned him away from what seemed to Romilly a nest of crackpots. Bentham reconsidered, turned around, and marched home. For many years thereafter, he ignored politics, now totally caught up in Panopticon, the Poor Laws, and his many economic projects, designed to save the war economy from bankruptcy. During the French Wars he tried for many years to be a good, dedicated patriot.

By 1809, however, his patriotism had begun to turn sour and he had lost patience with the intransigently conservative, sinecure-ridden English government. He then took up the threads of three long, unfinished, and

[1] Box. 169, p. 141, University College Collection, London.

still unpublished essays that he had begun in 1790, "On the Efficient Cause and Measure of Constitutional Liberty," "Influence," and "Parliamentary Reform." These reappeared in new, much longer versions in 1809 as "Sinecures" and "Influence"; nor has either of these been published. In these essays he called for moderate parliamentary reform, proposing nothing new, but merely joining a swelling chorus of voices that had never been entirely silenced since the Duke of Richmond's days in the 1770's and 1780's.

But by 1817, the year of our selections, his "Introduction to the Catechism of Parliamentary Reform," Bentham was furiously outraged and unable to contain his fury. What had once been merely an intransigent sinecure-ridden oligarchy had turned for him into a terrifying, sickeningly corrupt military despotism. His standard medical metaphors were put to hard use. The country was poisoned to the depths; only the most radical surgery could now save it; and that knife-thrust was radical parliamentary reform, that is, virtually universal suffrage. This was the farthest limit of his political program, and one of his most exuberant flights of full-blown, purple rhetoric.

As for the *Catechism* itself, it is a much tamer thing, only one-eighth as long and not angry at all. It was written in 1809, before he had drunk the cup of disgust to the bottom. The Napoleonic War was still raging and therefore, as practical politics, reform of the mildest kind was virtually out of the question, and radical reform impossible. Nor had Bentham spun the threads in his own mind so far. It took several years of post-war hunger, unemployment, riots, and massacre to make him a complete radical. But he was at no time a revolutionary; at no time did he preach republicanism for England. He rejoiced in it for the United States; he recommended it for every new-formed or revolutionary state, but for his own government, he was content to make the most of tradition, fully aware that the deep-rooted constitutional customs had a hallowed sanctity that no new-founded statutes could replace.

Bentham's 1817 plan was therefore offered to the public in the shape of a violently rhetorical introduction to a mild catechism in the question-and-answer form. It sounds best read aloud in a voice of doom. Both documents, alone or taken together, are exceptions to the cliché that his later style is unreadable.

His radical plan was very simple. "Secresy, universality, equality, and annuality," he said, "—behold in them the four cardinal points of the constitutional compass: secresy is the polar star." [2] And secresy was also the cardinal point wherein his plan differed from the historically conven-

[2] III, p. 562.

tional ones. He had no desire to be original; quite the reverse. His object was to join a growing movement, to avoid all dissension, to make it expand as far, wide, and fast as possible. The spirit of anarchy must be crushed. All the same, secresy was of the first importance to him, a foundation stone rather than a polar star, without which the whole structure of guarantees must collapse. In three other less fundamental ways his plan also differed: in calling for freedom of suffrage, the exclusion of placemen, and constant attendance.

All the same, in fundamentals, Bentham was already a moderate democrat by 1790. What had led to his conversion? For it is a well-known fact that he began his career as the good stiff-necked Tory his father had trained him to be. He reversed the normal colors of the political spectrum. Most men turn from red to blue. After a fit of youthful radicalism they settle into a conservative middle and old age. Bentham turned from blue to red; the older he got, the more radical he became. The usual explanation for his change is his new friendship after 1805 with James Mill, father of John Stuart Mill and a persuasive democrat. But at most Mill reawakened his interest; almost all of his ideas were already contained in the 1790 essays, especially the important distinction between will and understanding and the influence between them; the demand for appropriate knowledge, inclination, and power in the elected representative; and the idea of political power as a trust held by the trustees of the people.

First he had to become interested in politics and there Lord Shelburne's friendship was decisive. He had been Prime Minister at the time of the Peace Treaty with America; he was one of the nation's most prominent Whigs and far outdid most of them in his radicalism; he had many seats at his disposal, and Bentham even thought for one glorious—if mistaken—moment that Shelburne planned to offer him one.

When the French Revolution broke out, Lord Shelburne's home became a radical center for propaganda and visiting revolutionaries. He set a small army, including Bentham, to work preparing model constitutions and legal systems for the French. Bentham wrote thousands of pages on parliamentary tactics, judicial codes, and jury trials. All helped him, all more or less forced him, to take a perspective of the entire structure of British government, and to his disgust, he found most of it weak and rotting. Therefore when he finished his French reforms, he turned to English.

He looked at the age-old, much revered jury system and wondered, if it is taken for granted by everybody that any random group of twelve men can be expected to follow often the most intricate chains of argument and subtle points of law, why should they not be able to perform so simple a choice as "Yes" or "No" on a ballot? Why should they not all vote?

He had long ceased to be frightened, as he once had been, by "the people." He had been terrified by the Gordon Riots, and then charged the masses with too much "zeal." He was soon to be frightened again, but in 1790, as in 1817, he rejoiced in the American experiment—"that newly created nation, one of the most enlightened, if not the most enlightened, at this day on the globe."[3] "Among the rebels," he said, "everything breathes contentment and unanimity."[4]

By 1817 it was not an excess of "zeal" in the people that he deplored, but an excess of torpidity. He wanted to make them angry and they refused to become so; too harried by their oppressors to throw off a national pall of lethargy. All of Bentham's humanitarian feelings rose up in him, and his "Introduction" is at times almost a howl of despair.

[3] I, p. 154, 1789.
[4] Stark, I, 194.

Parliamentary Reform Catechism

(Vol. III, pp. 435–57, 1817)

Introduction

Section I. History of the Ensuing Tract—Alarming State of the Country and the Constitution.

The following little tract was written as long ago as in the year 1809. It was offered at the time to one of the time-serving daily prints, in which other papers on the same subject had already found admittance. No name was sent with it: and, the weathercock being at that time upon the turn, insertion was declined.

From that time to the present, despair of use kept this, together with so many other papers, upon the shelf. In a state of things, such as the present, if in any, they possess a chance of finding readers.—Sad condition of human nature!—until the cup of calamity, mixed up by misrule, has been drunk to the very dregs, never has the man a chance of being heard, who would keep it from men's lips.

For a long time past had the necessity,—and not only the necessity, but supposing it attainable, the undangerousness,—of a Parliamentary Reform, and that a radical one, presented itself to my mind, if not in a light as yet sufficiently clear for communication, at any rate in the strongest colours. Long had this sole possible remedy against the otherwise mortal disease of misrule, been regarded by me as the country's only hope. . . .

Drawn on, in the road to that gulf, from those times down to the present,—the country, if my eyes do not deceive me, is already at the very brink:—reform or convulsion, such is the alternative. How faint soever the hope of its being attainable,—I for one, under the disease under which I see the country lingering, cannot discover any other than this one possible remedy. Of the composition of it—such as in my conception it must be, to be productive of any effect—some conception was and is now endeavoured to be given in the ensuing little tract. On the subject of the necessity, more than a few introductory pages cannot at this time, and in this place, be spared. To give any adequate conception of it, would require a much larger work.

For the destruction of everything by which the constitution of this country has ever been distinguished to its advantage, no additional measures need be employed: let but the principles already avowed continue to be avowed—let but the course of action, dictated by those principles, be persevered in—the consummation is effected.

Gagging Bills—suspension of the Habeas Corpus Act—interdiction of all communication between man and man for any such purpose as that of complaint or remedy—all these have already become precedent—all these are in preparation—all these are regarded as things of course.

The pit is already dug: one after another, or all together, the securities called *English liberties* will be cast into it. With the sacred name of reform on their lips, and nothing better than riot or pillage in their hearts, let but a dozen or a score of obscure desperadoes concert mischief in a garret or an ale-house, fear will be pretended—prudence and wisdom mimicked—honest cowards will be made to acquiesce and co-operate by feigned cowardice.—for the transgression of the dozen or the score, the million will be punished, and from the subjects of a disguised despotism will be made such under a despotism in form, to which disguise is no longer necessary:—such is the state of things, for which it is time for every man to prepare himself.

As for the *Habeas Corpus Act,* better the statute-book were rid of it. Standing or lying as it does, up one day, down another—it serves but to swell the list of sham-securities, with which, to keep up the delusion, the pages of our law books are defiled. When no man has need of it, then it is that it stands: comes a time when it might be of use, and then it is suspended.

Section II. Most Prominent Present Grievance, Garrisoning France.

The plains, or heights, or whatsoever they are, of *Waterloo*—will one day be pointed to by the historian as the grave—not only of French, but of English liberties. Not of France alone, but of Britain with her, was the conquest consummated in the Netherlands. Whatsoever has been done and is doing in France, will soon be done in Britain. Reader, would you wish to know the lot designed for you? Look to France, there you may behold it. . . .

There they are—our fifty thousand men, with the conqueror of French and English liberties—the protector of the Bourbons—the worthy vanquisher and successor to Bonaparte at the head of them: there they are—and, until every idea of good government—every idea of anything better than the most absolute despotism—has been weeded out by the Bourbons, as ever it had been by Bonaparte,—there it is that the whole of them, or whatsoever part may be deemed sufficient for the purpose, are destined to continue.

There they are, and for what is it that they were planted there?—For security? For the security of Britons? for the security of Frenchmen? for the security of Germans? for the security of Netherlanders? for the security of any other race of men under the sun? Impossible. . . .

Once more:—For what, then, is it that France has been, is now, and by the blessing of God is destined to be forever, garrisoned? Is it for security?—is it for the keeping out anarchy?—is it for the keeping out *bad* government? Alas! no: to any such object, never, never has any real fear attached itself: the healing—the moderately monarchical—constitution, on which, at their entrance, the despots set their perfidious foot, would that have been bad government? No: it was not for keeping out *bad*—it was for keeping out *good* government. Under whatsoever form it might have been established—constitutional monarchy, or upon the model of the American United States, democracy—*there* was the real object of terror to all the newly re-christianized crowned heads,—and to their loyal and correspondently pious,—coroneted, and not yet coroneted advisors.

There they are—but happily with the Atlantic between us and them—the never-sufficiently-accursed United States. There they are—living, and (oh, horror!) flourishing—and so flourishing! flourishing under a government so essentially *illegitimate!* Oh what a reproach to legitimacy! Oh what a reproach, a never-to-be-expunged reproach, to our own Matchless Constitution—matchless in rotten boroughs and sinecures! Oh! had they but one neck—these miscreants! Ten times, twenty times, any number of times, the blood spilt at Waterloo, would be well spent in cutting it. There they are, with their prosperity the effect: there they are, with their good government—their matchless good government—the cause of it. . . .

Here then is *one* use, for the fifty thousand Britons, who, in France, with the hundred thousand men of other nations, are preying at one and the same time upon the vitals of France and Britain. Here is one use—behold now another.

The other use—need it here be mentioned? Exists there that reader, who has not already told it to himself? Yes, it is to return to all plans of reform, to all petitions for reform—to all groans—to all complaints—to all cries for mercy—the proper, and properly, and already proposed answer, the bayonet. The bayonet? Yes: by the blessing of God, the bayonet. But is it altogether so sure, that, should matters come to the push, the direction that will be prescribed by legitimacy is exactly the direction in which the bayonets will move? The men by whom they will be to be pushed, of what class are they? Are they of the blood royal? —are they of the peerage? Are they not of the swinish multitude?—are they not as perfect swine as we are? Is it possible they should ever forget it? And when, in a direction that is not pleasing to him, the swine is driven, is he not apt to retrograde?

An army in France necessary for the security of Britain? Yes! if an army in China is so too;—not otherwise.

Propose anything good; the answer is at hand:—wild, theoretical, visionary, Utopian, impracticable, dangerous, destructive, ruinous, anarchical, subversive of all governments—there you have it. Well, but in America there it *is:* and no such evil consequences—nothing but what is good, results from it. Aha! and so the United States government is your government, is it?—You are a republican then, are you?—what you want is, to subvert this constitution of ours; the envy of nations! the pride of ages!—matchless in rotten boroughs and sinecures!—Very well: begin and set up your republic, and, in the meantime, you, who are so ready to talk of *feelings,* think what *yours* will be, when, after a few nights lodging in the Tower, the knife of the hangman, after having rubbed off its rust upon the Spenceans, is doing its office in your bowels.

Propose anything that would put any power into the hands of those of whose obedience all power is composed: you propose *democracy;* and if any such epithet as *democratical* is applicable to it, there you have a reason, and that a conclusive one, for casting it out without further thought: casting it off as if it were a viper, and trampling upon it: and for this reason—for there needs no other—is eternity to be given to everything that is corrupt and mischievous.

What, according to these men, is the use of the constitution? To make the *people* happy? Make them happy!—curse on the swinish multitude! What then? Why, to make the *one* man happy, the one object of legitimate idolatry,—with the small number of *others* to whom it accords with his high pleasure to impart any of the means of happiness.

Now, by this bugbear word *democracy,* are the people of this country to be frightened out of their senses?—frightened by Gwelphs any more than by Stuarts, into passive obedience and non-resistance.

Section III. Causes of the Above and All Other Mischiefs:—Particular Interests Monarchical and Aristocratical, Adverse to the Universal—Their Ascendancy.

Goaded to the task by the groans of all around me, of late,—with an attention, which the nature of the objects that were continually forcing themselves upon all eyes and upon all ears, rendered more and more painful to me,—I have been looking more closely than ever into the constitution;—I mean the present state of it;—and, in as few words as possible, of this most appalling of all examinations, what follows is the result.

As early as the year 1809, and I forget how much earlier, it had seemed to me (it has been already hinted), that in the principle which, by those in whose hands the fate of the country rested, had not only been acted upon but avowed, the road to national ruin might be but too clearly traced. This principle was—that in the hands of the trustees of the people, the substance of the people was a fund, out of which, without breach of trust, and without just reproach in any shape—*fortunes*—as the phrase is— by those who, without exposing themselves to punishment, could contrive to lay their hands on the means, might be—nay—and, it being matter of necessity, at any price, and to an amount absolutely unlimited, ought to be—*made*.

In this principle I saw the two domineering interests—the monarchical and the aristocratical—which in our mixed constitution—(for such at least it was at one time)—antagonizing with the every now and then struggling, but always vainly and feebly struggling, democratical: completely agreed, and without concert, because without need of concert, co-operating with each other,—in the dissemination, and in the inculcation of it: the party out of power as well as the party in power inculcating it in theory; the party in power, by theory and practice.

That, on the part of both these interests, this principle, together with the practice that belonged to it, was but too natural—was abundantly evident: that, for its adoption, it had any such plea as that of necessity, was a notion which, when once taken in hand, vanished at the slightest touch.

Power, money, factitious dignity—by an attractive force, the existence of which, and the omnipotence, is as indisputable as that by which the course of the heavenly bodies is determined—*each* of these elements of the *matter of good*—that precious matter, the whole mass of which, in so far as at the hands of the monarch it is sought by a member of either of the two other branches of the efficient sovereignty, operates in the character of *matter of corruptive influence*—attracts and draws to it the *two others:* the greater the quantity a man has of any one of them, the greater the facility he finds in his endeavours to obtain for himself the two others; each in a quantity proportioned to his desires:—those desires, which in human nature have no bounds.

The more he has of any one of them, the more therefore it is his *wish* to have of *that* and all of them. But the more he has of any one of them, the more is it *right* also that he should have of them? All of them at the expense of the people,—the poor people, at whose expense whatsoever is enjoyed by their rulers is enjoyed? Oh gross, oh flagitious absurdity! The more? No: but on the contrary the less. Whatsoever be the quantity of the *matter of reward*, which, in any shape whatsoever, may be necessary to obtain at a man's hands, the requisite service, the more he has of it in any *one* shape,—the less the need he has of it in any *other* shape.

In the case of the poorest individual,—in the character of a *guardian,* by any man has any such immoral notion ever been started, as that, in the substance of his *ward,* any proper source of enrichment to himself is to be found? Power, over a single individual and his little property, a sufficient payment for the labour: and power over twenty millions, and their property, together with all that mass of patronage,—lucrative of necessity, a great part of it,—shall it not be sufficient? Those who either have no property, or have it not in sufficient quantity for their maintenance,—such men must indeed, either be paid or not employed:—but, among men who not only have property, but have it in sufficiency, is it supposed that there can ever be a deficiency in the number of those, in whom the *pleasure* of possessing such power will be sufficient compensation for all the *pain* attached to the exercise of it? Look at the county magistracy: see we not there—not only an example, but a host of examples? Yes: and in those examples a host of proofs.

Unfortunately—in the breasts of all who have *power, merit* being, as they all agree and certify—to one another and to the people, infinite—so must be the *reward.*

Of the demand for the matter of reward—viz. money, power, and factitious dignity—(these are its principal shapes)—the infinity and absolute irresistibility being thus established, then and thereupon comes the demand for the supply—and that supply a proportionable one. Here, however, to a first view, comes somewhat of a difficulty. From the body of the people—how habitually soever blind and passive—money in *infinite* quantity cannot be demanded all at once: they would become desperate; they would rise: better (they would say to themselves), better be shot or hanged at once, then starved.

A set of drains must therefore be established and set to work: drains, by and through which, by degrees—those degrees ever in the eyes of the devourers but too slow—under colour either of *use,* or what is so much better, of *necessity*—money may be drawn out of the pockets of the blinded, deluded, unsuspicious, uninquisitive, and ever too patient people:—1. Wars: 2. Distant and proportionably burthensome dependencies all over the habitable globe—(and note, that, in prosecution of these views, every such dependency, without exception, has been made a source of net expense—net expense, the amount of which is destined to perpetual and unlimited increase): 3. Penal colonies: 4. Claims of universal dominion over the universal water-way of nations, with a determination to destroy the shipping of all nations by whom those claims shall be contested: 5. Annexation of "*Hanover* to *Hampshire*": and that to the end that not a hostile gun may be fired anywhere on the continent, but that we may be in readiness to interfere, subsidizing one of the contending parties, and helping to oppress the other! 6. Splendour of the crown; that effulgence, with the increase of which—and in exact proportion to that increase—will increase the respect, and with it the submission, and with it the happiness of the people: 7. Erection of *Hanover* into a kingdom for that purpose, and that the Hanoverians may the less grudge the increase of taxes that will be necessitated by the increase of *dignity*. Here, though not yet a complete one, is a list of these productive drains:—and are they not efficient ones? . . .

In regard to all these drains of money, and all these sources of merit and reward,—the great misfortune is this: For every shilling which, by means of any one of these drains, unless it be the last, the men of merit—and all placemen without exception are *ex officio* men of merit,—for every shilling which the men of merit thus put into their pockets, some score, or some dozen at least, must come out of the pockets of the poor people. A man who sets his neighbour's house on fire, that he may roast an egg for himself,—is the emblem by which a certain sort of man is pictured by Lord Bacon. Would you see a man of this sort, you need not look far, so you look high enough—for these five-and-twenty years or thereabouts—to go no further back—has this poor nation been kept on fire, lest the emblematic eggs in sufficient quantity should be wanting to its rulers. . . .

Money, power, factitious dignity—among the *modifications* of the *matter of good*—among the *good things* of this wicked world—those, as it is the *interest,* so has it ever been the study,—as it has been the study, so has it been the endeavour—of the monarch—as it has been, so will it, and where the monarch is a human being, so must it be everywhere—to draw to himself in the greatest quantity possible. And here we have one *partial,* one *separate,* one *sinister* interest, the *monarchical*—the interest of the ruling *one*—with which the *universal,* the *democratical* interest has to antagonize, and to which that all-comprehensive interest has all along been,—and unless the only possible remedy—even parliamentary reform, and that a radical one, should be applied,—is destined to be for ever made a sacrifice:—a sacrifice? Yes:, and by the blessing of God upon the legitimate and pious labours of his vicegerent and the express image of his person here upon earth, a still unresisting sacrifice. Omnipresence, immortality, impeccability—equal as he is to God, as touching all these *"attributes"* (ask Blackstone else . . .) who is there that, without adding impiety to disloyalty, can repine at seeing anything or everything he might otherwise call his own, included in the sacrifice?

Meantime the money, which, in an endless and boundless stream, is thus to keep flowing into the monarchical coffers—this one thing needful cannot find its way into those sacred receptacles without instruments and conduit-pipes. Upon and out of the pockets of the people it cannot be raised, but through the forms of parliament:—not but through the forms of parliament, nor therefore without the concurrence of the richest men in the country, in their various situations—in the situation of peers, great landholding, and as yet uncoroneted commoners, styled *country gentle-men,*—and others. In those men is the chief *property* of the country, and with it—(for in the language of the aristocratic school, *property* and *virtue* are synonymous terms)—the virtue of the country. And here we have another partial, separate, and sinister interest—the *aristocratical* interest—with which the democratical interest has also to antagonize:—another overbearing, and essentially and immutably hostile interest,—against which, and under which, the universal interest has to struggle, and as far as possible to defend itself. . . .

Extinguish monarchy?—suppress, extirpate the peerage?—Oh, not I indeed: nothing would I extinguish; nothing would I extirpate: *uti pos-sidetis*—that which you have, continue to have—and God bless you with it:—this, in all matters of reform,—this, in so far as is not inconsistent with the very essence of the reform, is—and so long as I have had any, has ever been with me a ruling principle. Leaving, with all my heart, the full benefit of it to monarchy and aristocracy—to the *ruling few,* my aim, my wishes, confine themselves to the securing, if it be possible, a participation in that same benefit to *democracy*—to the *subject-many*—to the poor suffering and starving people.

Monarchy a property! Not it indeed. Monarchy is a trust: is it not, Prince Regent?—have you not said it is? Peerage a property? Not it in-deed. Peerage is a trust: is it not my Lord anybody? If it is not, what business have you to be what you are, and where you are?

Ascendency! ascendency—that is what is sufficient: this, therefore, is all that should be asked for. . . .

In this state of things, C——r-General [Corruptor-General.—M.P.M.] being the proper style and title of the head-manager of the concern, taken by himself,—add the aristocracy—the corrupted and corrupting aristocracy—C——-General & Co. is the proper firm of the partnership. As to the business of it, it consists but too plainly, like that of the Bank of England, in draining the contents of all pockets into its own; and the more intolerable the indigence thus produced, the more craving the de-mand for that corruptive supply, by the hope of which men are engaged to concur in the continually repeated measures, from which the indigence receives its continually repeated aggravation.

Now of this almost universal corruption, what is the effect? A mere *moral* spot?—a mere *ideal* imperfection? Alas! no: but a somewhat more palpable and sensible one. What the real, the sensible mischief consists in is—the *sacrifice* made, as above, of the interest and comfort of the *subject-many*, to the overgrown felicity of the *ruling few:* the effect of the corruption being—to engage all whom it has corrupted to bear their respective parts in the perpetual accomplishment of their perpetual sacrifice. Is not this sufficiently intelligible? Well, if *that* expression be not, perhaps *this* may be: viz. that the *subject-many* long have been, and, but for the only remedy, may with but too much reason forever expect to be, continually more and more grievously oppressed, that the *ruling few* may be more and more profusely pampered.

Now suppose an army of Frenchmen garrisoning England, as an army of Englishmen (oh! pretenceless and inhuman tyranny!) are garrisoning France. In that case, what would the description of our condition be? What but that the dominion we were groaning under was the dominion of a set of men whose interest was opposite to our own, by whom that oppositeness was understood and felt, and by whom our interest was made a continual sacrifice to that separate and hostile interest. Well: *that,* and but too indisputably, is it not the description—the too just description—of the dominion under which we live?

Discarding the case of *public*—of *national*—subjection under a foreign yoke, take the case of *private*—of *domestic subjection:*—take the case of *negro* slavery. The description of the case, is it not still the same? The slaveholder, it may be said—for it is continually said—has an interest in common with that of his slaves. True: and so has the mail-coach contractor in common with that of his horses. While working them, and so long as they appear able to work, he accordingly allows them food. Yet, somehow or other, notwithstanding this community of interest, so it is, that but too often negro as well as horse are worked to the very death. How happens this? How but because, in the same breast with the conjunct interest, is lodged a separate and sinister interest, which is too strong for it. Even so is it in the case of C_____r-General and Co., under whose management the condition of the poor people is day by day approaching nearer and nearer to the condition of the negro and the horse.

"I can have no interest but that of my people," says the royal parrot—I can have no interest but that of my people: with these words in his mouth, he gives the touch of the sceptre to a bill for establishing a nest of sinecures.

Under the constitution as it stands—under the administration as it is carried on—in what state, as towards the one and the other, are the affections of the people? Take the answer from Lord Castlereagh. . . . In the year just ended [1816], 53,000 were the number of firelocks "indispensably necessary to aid the civil power in the discharge of its duty":

in other words, to keep the people from the endeavour to substitute a better to the government as it stands. Now, indeed, at this season of forced retrenchment, 5000 is the number of men to be struck off from the desired complement of 53,000. Struck off! Why? because they are regarded as superfluous? Oh no: for of those means of coercion which require no money, boundless is the supply which at this very moment is providing. Why, then? Even because,—as under the most perfectly undisguised despotism, so under a disguised one,—in so far as supplies cannot be had,— the revenue having, in the compass of a single year, fallen off, for example, by any such amount as that of one-sixth,—retrenchment must be made. In this time not only of peace but of triumph—no pretender in existence—France, instead of a cause of fear, an object of compassion— three-and-fifty thousand mean necessary to be kept up to prevent a second revolution! In the same year of the last century, as this is of the present one, our great-grandfathers—what would they have said to such a number? —our great-grandfathers, in whose days, a Pretender continually threatening from abroad, and at home a strong party, even after a defeat, were still strong enough to keep on foot matter for another rebellion, which in twenty-eight years from that time, actually broke out! In the same year of the last, as this is of the present century, what was the whole number demanded and provided for this same service? Answer: 16,000, and no more; not so much as *one-third* of the number actually in demand, as above. Walpole, then in opposition, opposing even that number on the ground of alleged excess.

Well then: by a standing army it is that we are governed: and a standing army—a standing army of the magnitude which has been seen:—this, then is the sort of instrument, without which, it is said, we could not be governed; and by which—so long as the constitution, in the form into which it has been moulded, lasts,—it is the intention of those that govern us that we shall be governed. And this is that constitution—that Matchless Constitution—in the praises of which, those whose opulence or power have been produced by, or are dependent, on, the abuses of it, never tire. And in this Constitution we have a Parliament:—and in this Parliament a House of Commons:—and in this House of Commons a mask for a military government of its own erection:—and this mask so transparent an one! and, under this military government, so long as the mask remains—under this military government are we to lie down, now and for ever, prostrate and contented.

Well: the *United States*—the seat of *representative democracy,* alias anarchy—what *plots,* real or pretended, have they, or have they ever had, in their bosom? What *standing army* is it that they have? On the subject of these concerns, which are the concerns of every man, what laws have they to prevent each man from communicating with every other?—on pain of death, to prevent every man who is *not,* from speaking his mind to any one who is a *soldier?*

Oh! but the fault, whatever it is, it is always the fault of the people:—behaving continually worse and worse, they must continually be treated with more and more just severity:—the sinners for their own sins—the non-sinners for the sins of the sinners—so long as any of them are left alive.

No: at this time—at any time, on the part of the people, any extensive discontent, that has ever manifested itself, never has it been the fault of the people. Discontent? No: patience—too much patience—in *that* has been their fault—their only fault: a sad fault *that:*—and, unhappily, under every government but an adequately representative government—under which alone the concerns which are those of every man, are left without restraint to the discourse of every man—an incurable one. The people? What interest have they in being governed badly?—in having their universal interest sacrificed to any separate and adverse interest? But the men by whom they have been governed—the interest which these men have had in governing badly—in governing as they have governed—this interest has here been made manifest, or nothing can be.

Section IV. Sole Remedy in Principle—Democratic Ascendency.

Such being the disease, behold now the remedy—the only remedy: he for whose nerves it is too strong, let him, as soon as the irritation pains him,—take warning and shut his eyes against; let him shut his eyes, and prepare his neck for a yoke, the pressure of which will continue on the increase, till either convulsion breaks it, or existence sinks under it. This remedy—two words, viz. *democratical ascendency,* will, in principle, suffice for the expression of it. Taking this for the general description of the *end—parliamentary reform* will next make its appearance in the character of a *means:* parliamentary reform *in general* as a proposed means: *radical* parliamentary reform, as the only means, by which either that immediate end, or the ultimate end—political salvation, can, in the nature of the case, be accomplished.

Without any outward and visible change in the forms of the constitution,—by the means already indicated, by the mere instrumentality of the ever-increasing mass of the matter of good operating in the hands of the crown in the character of matter of corruptive influence,—have the two separate, partial, and sinister interests,—viz. the *monarchical* and the *aristocratical,*—obtained over the *democratical* interest (which is no other than the *universal* interest,) not only an *ascendency*—but an ascendency so complete, that, under the outside show of a mixed and limited monarchy, a monarchy virtually and substantially absolute is the result.

Without any outward and visible change in the forms of the constitution—though waste already committed cannot be caused *not* to have been committed—though past misrule cannot be caused not to have reigned—yet may the plague be stayed. To the democratical, to the universal interest, *give*—one might almost say, restore—that ascendency which by the confederated, partial, and sinister interest has been so deplorably abused, and so long as it continues, will continue to be abused:—thus you have the remedy: *this* is what parliamentary reform will do, if it does anything: *this* is what parliamentary reform means, if it means anything. . . .

Now in this change—for unless the plague continues and spreads, a change there must be—in this change, is there any *innovation*? No: in substance there is not so much as an *innovation*. The one thing needful is—that the *power of the purse* should be actually and effectively in the hands of the real representatives, the freely chosen deputies of the body of the people: the *power of the purse, that* being the power by the exercise of which, for the defence of the people against Stuart tyranny, all other needful powers were acquired. Now, at various periods in the history of this country, this all-productive power was actually in the hands of the people: witness statute after statute: witness in one reign, viz. the splendid and unhappily conquering reign of Edward III, and at thirty-two years interval, two statutes, by each of which the annual holding of a parliament —and in those days parliaments annually holden were annually changed— was declared to be the legitimate state and condition of the government. . . .

Ascendency? Yes; ascendency it must be: nothing less will serve.

Talk of *mixture:* yes, this *may* serve, and *must* serve: but then, the intrinsically noxious ingredients—the ingredients which must be kept in, though for no better reason than that we are used to them—and being so used to them, could not bear—(for who is there that could bear?)—to part with them—these ingredients, of which the greatest praise would be that they were inoperative, must not be in any such proportion of force, as to destroy, or materially to impair, the efficiency of the only essentially useful one.

Talk of *balance:* never will it do: leave that to Mother Goose and Mother Blackstone. Balance! Balance! Politicians upon roses—to whom, to save the toil of thinking—on questions most wide in extent, and most high in importance—an allusion—an emblem—an anything—so as it has been accepted by others, is accepted as conclusive evidence—what mean ye by this your *balance*? Know ye not, that in a machine of any kind, when force *balance* each other, the machine is at a stand? Well, and in the machine of government, immobility—the perpetual absence of all motion—is that the thing which is wanted? Know ye not that—since an emblem you must have—since you can neither talk, nor attempt to think, but in hieroglyphics—know you not that, as in the case of the body *natural*, so in the case of the body *politic*, when motion ceases, the body dies?

So much for the *balance:* now for the *mixture*—the mixture to which, as such, such virtue is wont to be ascribed. Here is a form of government, in which the power is divided among three interests:—the interest of the great body of the people—of the *many:*—and two separate interests—the interest of the *one* and the interest of the *few*—both of which are adverse to it:—two separate and narrow interests, neither of which is kept on foot—but at the expense, to the loss, and by the sacrifice, of the broader interest. This form of government (say you) has its advantages. Its advantage?—compared with what?—compared with those forms of government, in which the people have no power at all, or in which, if they have any, they have not so much? Oh yes: with any such form of government for an object of comparison, its *excellence* is unquestionable. But, compare it with a form of government in which the interest of the people is the only interest that is looked to—in which neither a single man, with a separate and adverse interest of his own, nor a knot of men with a separate and adverse interest of their own, are to be found—where no interest is kept up at the expense, to the loss, by the sacrifice, of the universal interest to it,—where is *then* the *excellence*?

Nay, but (says somebody), in the form of government in question, what the *supreme*—the *universal* power is—is a compound—a mixture of the three *powers* corresponding to the three *interests:* what the *excellence* produced by it is in, is—not any one of the three ingredients taken by itself: no—it is the *mixture.* Take away any one of the three masses of power, the mixture is changed: the excellence is diminished:—take away any two of them, mixture has place no longer:—the excellence vanishes.

Good—this notion about *mixture:* Oh yes, good enough, so long as the respective natures of the several interests are kept out of sight. Look at them, and then see whether it be possible that, taking the power of the people for the *simple* substance,—by the adding to it either or both of the two other powers, and thus making a *mixture*,—any such quality as *excellence*, with reference to what belongs to the *simple* substance taken by itself, can be produced.

A form of government, in which the interest of the whole is the only interest provided for—in which the only power is a power having for its object the support of that interest,—in this form of government behold the *simple* substance. To this simple substance add, separately or conjunctively, a power employed in the support of the interest of one *single* person, and a power employed in the support of the interest of a comparatively *small knot* of persons,—in either of these cases you have a mixture:—well: compared, then, with the *simple* substance, when and where can be the advantage of this *mixture*?

What—what could man ever find to say in behalf of *monarchy,* but that monarchy is *legitimacy*?—or in behalf of *aristocracy,* but that *property is virtue*?

Fair questions these:—should any man feel disposed to answer them, let the answers be so too: and let them not—Oh! let them not! be either imprisonment or death! . . .

Balance? equality? No: I cannot say *equality,* when what I mean is *ascendency.* Palsied would be this hand—motionless this pen—if, for the first time in a life, already of some length, it were to attempt deception. Ascendency—this I do mean, nothing less: more I do not mean—indeed I do not. The monarch may, for aught I know, plunge his hangman's knife in my bowels; but I am not for "cashiering kings." The one thing needful and sufficient for the purpose—this I would have if I could: this I would have if I could, whatever were its name. More than this—not being in my view needful for the purpose—more I would not have if I could. For any more than for myself—for any more than myself—no title have I to speak. In speaking thus for myself, I speak what I should expect to find the sense—so long as it were the quiet sense—of a vast majority of the people—in two at least of the three kingdoms—high and low, rich and poor together. But, should the only remedy be refused, oppression continue, and exasperation rise against it, then it is not quiet sense that will speak, but exasperation: and, as to what exasperation may say or do, who is there that can undertake to measure it?

Section V. Remedy in Detail: Radical Parliamentary Reform: Elementary Arrangements in This Edition of It—Their Necessity.

Immediate cause of the mischief—on the part of the men acting as representatives of the people, coupled with adequate *power* a sinister *interest,* productive of a constant sacrifice made of the interest of the people.

Causes of the above cause,—in the breasts of these same agents,—*undue independence,* coupled with undue *dependence:* independence as towards their principles; dependence as towards the C_____r-General, by whose co_____tive influence the above-mentioned sacrifice is produced.

Here, in the above elements—here, in a nutshell, may be seen the mischief and its causes:—against this mischief, revolution apart, behold in *Parliamentary Reform* the name of the only possible remedy. In these elements, when developed, may be seen—what *radical* reform is—what the sort of reform termed *moderate* is; thence, what and where the difference.

The reform sketched out in the ensuing plan being of the *radical* kind,—

the advantages, by the consideration of which the several elementary arrangements contained in it were suggested, will there be found. But, on the present occasion, what is required is—from all the several arrangements in question, to show—this having been the result of the inquiry—that while, by *radical* reform, a remedy, and that an adequate one, would be applied,—by *moderate* reform, no remedy would be applied, or next to none. In brief, the *undue independence* would remain, and with it the *undue dependence*.

Thus far in generals: now for development:—

First point to be considered—*situations,* in and to both which, to be effectual, the remedy must apply itself. These are—

1. Situation of *parliamentary electors.*
2. Situation of *parliamentary representatives.*

1. First, as to the situation of *parliamentary electors.*

Take for the description of the *ultimate* end, *advancement of the universal interest.*

In the description of this end is included—*comprehension* of all distinguishable *particular interests:* viz. in such sort, that such of them, between which no repugnancy has place, may be provided for in conjunction, and *without defalcation:*—while, in regard to such of them, between which any such repugnancy has place, such defalcations, and such alone, shall be made, as, when taken all together, shall leave in the state of a *maximum* whatsoever residuum of comfort and security may be the result:— with exception to as *small* an extent as possible, interests *all* to be *advanced:* without *any* exception, all to be *considered.*

1. In the character of a means, in this same description is moreover included—if it be not rather the same thing in other words—*virtual universality of suffrage.*

2. In this same description is moreover included—if it be not the same thing again in other words—*practical equality of representation* or *suffrage.*

Applied to the name of the quality *universality,* the use of the adjunct *virtual* is—by the limitation of which it gives intimation, to distinguish it from *unlimited* universality of suffrage: *unlimited,* or *absolute,* being the *degree* of *universality,* which, but for the application of some limitative adjunct, would, according to the correct import of the word, be to be understood. Of absolute universality, if admitted, the effect would be— to admit to the exercise of the franchise in question persons of various descriptions, none of whom would be capable of exercising it to the advantage either of others or of themselves. *Idiots,* and *infants* in leading-strings, may serve for examples.

By *virtually* universal suffrage, what I mean is—that which remain of absolutely universal suffrage, when from the number of individuals designated by the word *universal,* all such *defalcations* shall have been made, as, by specific considerations, shall have been shown to be productive, each of them of a *benefit* in some special shape: that benefit being at the same time *preponderant* over every inconvenience, if any such there be, resulting from the limitation thus applied:—a limitation, viz. to the operation of the principle, by which the comprehension of all interests, as far as practicable, is prescribed.

If, in the instance of any *one* individual of the whole body of the people, it be right that the faculty of contributing to the choice of a representative to the choice of a person, by whom, in the representative assembly, his interest shall be advocated, be possessed and exercised,—how can it be otherwise than right, in the instance of any one *other* such person? In this question, viz. in the impossibility of finding an answer to it, unless it be in the case, and to the extent, of the several defalcations above alluded to,—will, it is believed, be found contained the substance of the argument in support of *universality of suffrage.*

If, in the instance of any one individual, it *be right* that he should possess a *share,* of a certain degree of *magnitude,* in the choice of a person, to form one in the aggregate body of the representatives of the people,—how can it be right that, in the instance of any other individual, the share should be either *less* or *greater*? In this question is contained the substance of the argument in support of *practical equality of representation.*

That which *universality of suffrage* has for its limit is—need of defalcation for divers special causes or reasons: to give intimation of this limit is the use of the adjunct *virtual.* That which *equality of representation* has for its limit is—in the first place, the inconvenience, which in the shape of *delay, vexation,* and *expense,* could not fail to be the result of any endeavour, employed at any assignable point of time, to give existence to *absolute* equality; in the next place, the impossibility, resulting from the diversities of which, in respect of increase and decrease, the quantity of the population is everywhere susceptible; viz. the impossibility of keeping on foot—for any length of time, any such absolute equality,—supposing it to have, in the first instance, been established.

3. In the same description is, moreover, included *freedom of suffrage: freedom,* to which, in the present instance, may be considered as equivalent terms—*genuineness* and *non-spuriousness.*

To say that a suffrage ought to be *free,* what is it but to say—that the *will* expressed by it ought to be the very will of the person by whom it is so expressed?—the will of that person and of that person only; his *self-formed* will,—the product of his own *judgment, self-formed* or *derivative* as the case may be,—not produced by the knowledge or belief of the existence of any *will* or *wish* considered as entertained by any other person, at whose hands the voter entertains an eventual expectation of receiving *good* or *evil*, in any shape: good or evil, according as, by him the said voter, the wishes of such other person, in relation to the matter in question, shall or shall not have been conformed to?

In so far as, in the instance of any voter, the vote which is given is, according to this explanation, and in this sense, not *free*, it is manifestly *not genuine:* it is *spurious:*—under the guise and disguise of the expression of the will of the *voter*, it is the will—not of the voter, but of some *other* person. In so far as it is given as and for the will of the voter, the giving it, is it any thing better than an act of *imposture*?

3 or 4. *Secresy of suffrage.* Short reason, its necessity to secure *freedom; i.e.* to secure *genuineness*—to prevent *spuriousness.* . . .

True it is, that it is only on the supposition, that on the part of the majority of the voters there exists, in the breast of each, either from self-formed or from derivative judgment, a practically adequate conception of the course dictated by his share in the universal interest,—true it is, that only in so far as this supposition is in conformity to fact, will the freedom in question, supposing it secured, be subservient to the great ends proposed: but, of the propriety of a supposition to this effect, proof sufficient for practice has already, it is presumed, been afforded. Nor as yet is the subject closed.

Freedom of suffrage being taken for the *end,*—it will soon (it is hoped) be generally seen and recognised, how essential, in every instance, to the accomplishment of this *end, secresy of suffrage* is in the character of a *means.*

In what different ways freedom of suffrage is *capable* of being taken away,—to what extent, and by the influence of what descriptions of persons it actually and constantly *is* taken away,—these are among the topics, under which the state of the case will presently be brought to view.

So much as to the situation of *elector:* now as to the situation of *representative.*

For the purpose of this part of the argument, the situation of elector must be supposed to have been properly marked out and established: and, for the marking out and establishment of it, the fulfilment of the above condition—the investing of the suffrage with the above-mentioned desirable qualities—viz. virtual universality, practical equality, freedom, and secresy, must be regarded as effected.

1. *Due dependence—i.e. dependence as towards constituents;* 2. *Due independence—i.e. independence as towards every other person:*—these, together with *universal constancy of attendance,* present themselves as occupying

in relation to this situation—as occupying, and on the same line—the first rank, in the scale of *ends* and *means*.

1. Dependence as towards constituents.—Understand dependence to this effect, viz. that, in the event of a man's becoming, in the eyes of the acting majority of his constituents, to a certain degree deficient in respect of any of the elements of appropriate aptitude (viz. appropriate probity, appropriate intellectual aptitude, or appropriate active talent),—it may, before he has had time, by means of such deficiency, to produce, in any considerable quantity, any irremediable mischief,—be in the power of his constituents, by means of a fresh election, to remove him from his seat.

2. Independence.—Understand as towards all other persons at large, but more particularly as towards C_____r-General and Co., by whose influence alone, the nature of the case considered, *dependence*, as towards himself, can ever,—in the instance of any proportion approaching to a majority of the whole population of the House,—have place. . . .

Such being the *primary* or *principal* securities, follow now two *secondary* or *instrumental* ones.

3. *Impermanence* of the situation; viz. to the degree in which it is secured by *annuality* of *re-election:*—by the annual recurrence of the elective process.

In two distinguishable ways does this species of instrumental security contribute to the two principal ones: 1. In proportion to the *short-livedness* of the power, diminishes, both to purchasers, and thence to sellers, the *venal* value of it;—the profit capable of being reaped by C_____r-General and Co. by corrupting the representative in question, and engaging him to betray his trust: 2. The profit to C_____r, and thence, in the shape of money or money's worth, the price which he will be willing to pay, and thence the corruptible representative be able to receive. In the same proportion, moreover, increases the power of the *antiseptic*—the corruption-opposing—remedy, placed in the hands of his constituents: the sooner the time for re-election comes, the earlier will that remedy be applicable. . . .

4. *Exclusion* of *placemen* from the faculty of *voting* in the House.

The mischief, against which *impermanence* of the situation is calculated to operate as a security, is *contingent* receipt of the matter of corruption: he who to his *seat* in the House adds the possession of any other office, with benefit in a pecuniary or any other shape annexed to it,—every such man is *actually* harbouring in his bosom a correspondent portion of that pestilential matter, and is actually under the dominion of its baneful influence. . . .

5. *Universal constancy of attendance.*

Be the place what it will, in which, if at all, the function, be it what it may, must be performed,—that function cannot be performed by a man who is not *there*. A maxim to this effect seems not to be very open to dispute. . . .

The Book of Fallacies

A Note on *The Book of Fallacies*

On some future day, when these incomplete sketches of political fallacies were to have been polished and perfected, Bentham hoped that in Parliament, ". . . instead of, Order! Order! a voice shall be heard, followed, if need be, by voices in scores, crying aloud, 'Stale! Stale! Fallacy of Authority! Fallacy of distrust!' " [1]

The Book of Fallacies was a fundamental part of his logic of the will; without it, the structure remained incomplete. Finally by 1820 he had worked up enough MS for Dumont to make a book in French; and in 1824 an English version appeared, based on the French text. Like the rest of his system of "logic," he defined fallacies in a unique, Utilitarian way: a mistake or false opinion *per se* was merely an error, but when it led to bad actions or consequences, it became a fallacy. The whole logical edifice was covered by the roof of "reason," that is, in his definition, its contribution to the greatest happiness of the greatest number. So far he had considered direct reason only, that is, the logic of the will as substantive and adjective law (civil, penal, and constitutional law; and the law of procedure and evidence). Now at last he came to consider the less direct means to reason, by showing the irrelevance of deceptive arguments.

He was angry when he wrote these pages, still carried along by the tide of furious rhetoric against corruption and sinister interest that he had un-

[1] II, p. 487.

leashed in *Catechism of Parliamentary Reform.* He saw fallacies as evil poisoned weapons in the tyrannical warfare of official despotism against a helpless and easily duped people. He insisted once again as he had throughout his life that words cut deeper than knives. To him, ideas are powerful weapons. Ideology was the fundamental cause of war; and abuse of language was the fundamental source of ideology. The first step toward progress, toward the advance of civilization, was peace; and the first step toward peace was the neutralization of language, the constant public exposure of emotive, deceptive eulogistic and dyslogistic words and phrases, of fallacies.

Bentham was always addicted to metaphor and analogy; hitherto, up to about 1817, his favorites had always been medical, but now he switched to warfare. Fallacies were poisoned weapons but they were also obstructive barricades against good government. He declared himself the enemy of government so long as it was the enemy of the people, and damn the consequences. He half expected to be thrown into jail and was ready to go. Of course, it was never in question; economic and political tensions eased in the 1820's, and in any case Bentham was far too eminent and ancient for such treatment. It would have been a heavy embarrassment for an already harassed government.

In *The Fallacies* Bentham once again emphasized a distinction he had been making since 1790—the influence of will on will *vs.* the influence of the understanding on the understanding. He insisted over and over again that effective Utilitarian politics must begin in free, unbiased judgment, that is, of the understanding on the understanding. Obviously, almost every opinion a man holds, he holds on trust from authority of some kind. On very few issues has he the expertise to judge wholly for himself. This Bentham saw was necessarily so. What he demanded, however, was that a man choose to act only after rational assessment of alternatives, *i.e.* not of will on will, but of will on understanding. These terms he had first borrowed from Blackstone's *Commentaries* and, as they were part of the common universe of discourse, he used them too.

But also in *The Fallacies,* Bentham introduced a new principle—the principle of universal self-interest, that at all times and all places, except on extraordinary occasions, every man pursues his own interest—such as he perceives it to be, which, of course, might be wholly different from his genuine self-interest. In his old age, there seemed to him no other mode of accounting for the reactionary ferocity of government, other than that a tremendously powerful and corrupt oligarchy was fanatically determined to hold on to its own privileges.

These pages were heavily edited, first by Dumont and then his English translator. They lack the fiery, whimsical pungency of Bentham's own disordered pages, but these have not been published; and it seemed proper to include some examples from this important last stage in the logic of the will.

The Book of Fallacies

(Vol. II, pp. 379 ff.)

INTRODUCTION. SECTION I. A FALLACY WHAT.

By the name of *fallacy*, it is common to designate any argument employed, or topic suggested, for the purpose, or with a probability, of producing the effect of deception,—of causing some erroneous opinion to be entertained by any person to whose mind such argument may have been presented.

SECTION II. FALLACIES, BY WHOM TREATED OF HERETOFORE.

The earliest author extant, in whose works any mention is made on the subject of *fallacies,* is Aristotle; by whom, in the course or rather on the occasion of his treatise on logic, not only is this subject started, but a list of the species of argument to which this denomination is applicable, is undertaken to be given. Upon the principle of the exhaustive method at so early a period employed by that astonishing genius, and, in comparison of what it might and ought to have been, so little turned to account since, *two* is the number of parts into which the whole mass is distributed,—fallacies in the diction, fallacies not in the diction: and thirteen (whereof in the diction six, not in the diction seven) is the number of the articles distributed between those two parts.

As from Aristotle down to Locke, on the subject of the origination of our ideas (deceptious and undeceptious included,)—so from Aristotle down to this present day, on the subject of the forms, of which such ideas or combinations of ideas as are employable in the character of instruments of deception, are susceptible,—all is a blank.

To do something in the way of filling up this blank, is the object of the present work. . . .

SECTION III.   RELATION OF FALLACIES TO VULGAR ERRORS.

Error—*vulgar error,* is an appellation given to an opinion which, being considered as false, is considered in itself only, and not with a view to any consequences, of any kind, of which it may be productive.

It is termed *vulgar* with reference to the persons by whom it is supposed to be entertained: and this either in respect of their multitude, simply, or in respect of the lowness of the station occupied by them, or the greater part of them, in the scale of respectability, in the scale of intelligence.

Fallacy is an appellation applied not exclusively to an opinion or to propositions enunciative of supposed opinions, but to discourse in any shape considered as having a tendency, with or without design, to cause any erroneous opinion to be embraced, or even, through the medium of erroneous opinion already entertained, to cause any pernicious course of action to be engaged or persevered in.

Thus, to believe that they who lived in early or old times were, because they lived in those times, wiser or better than those who live in later or modern times, is vulgar error: the employing that vulgar error in the endeavour to cause pernicious practices and institutions to be retained, is fallacy.

By those by whom the term *fallacy* has been employed—at any rate, by those by whom it was originally employed—deception has been considered not merely as a consequence more or less probable, but as a consequence the production of which was aimed at on the part at least of some of the utterers. . . .

That in the use of these instruments, such a thing as deception was the object of the set of men mentioned by Aristotle under the name of sophists, is altogether out of doubt. On every occasion on which they are mentioned by him, this intention of deceiving is either directly asserted or assumed.

SECTION IV.   POLITICAL FALLACIES THE SUBJECT OF THIS WORK.

The present work confines itself to the examination and exposure of only one class of fallacies, which class is determined by the nature of the occasion in which they are employed.

The occasion here in question is that of the formation of a decision procuring the adoption or rejection of some measure of *government:*

including under the notion of a measure of government, a measure of legislation as well as of administration—two operations so intimately connected, that the drawing of a boundary line between them will in some instances be matter of no small difficulty, but for the distinguishing of which on the present occasion, and for the purpose of the present work, there will not be any need.

Under the name of a *Treatise on Political Fallacies,* this work will possess the character, and, in so far as the character answers the design of it, have the effect of a treatise on *the art of government;*—having for its practical object and tendency, in the first place, the facilitating the introduction of such features of good government as remain to be introduced; in the next place giving them perpetuation—perpetuation, not by means of legislative clauses aiming directly at that object (an aim of which the inutility and mischievousness will come to be fully laid open to view in the course of this work), but by means of that instrument, viz. *reason,* by which alone the endeavour can be productive of any useful effect.

Employed in this endeavour, there are two ways in which this instrument may be applied: one, the more direct, by showing, on the occasion of each proposed measure, in what way, by what probable consequences it tends to promote the accomplishment of the end or object which it professes to have particularly in view: the other, the less direct, by pointing out the irrelevancy, and thus anticipating and destroying the persuasive force, of such deceptious arguments as have been in use, or appear likely to be employed in the endeavour to oppose it, and to dissuade men from concurring in the establishment of it.

Of these two different but harmonizing modes of applying this same instrument to its several purposes, the *more direct* is that of which a sample has, ever since the year 1802, been before the public, in that collection of unfinished papers on legislation, published at Paris in the French language, and which had the advantage of passing through the hands of Mr. Dumont, but for whose labours it would scarcely, in the author's lifetime at least, have seen the light. To exhibit the *less direct,* but in its application the more extensive mode, is the business of the present work.

To give existence to good argument was the object in that instance: to provide for the exposure of bad ones is the object in the present instance— to provide for the exposure of their real nature, and thence for the destruction of their pernicious force.

Sophistry is a hydra, of which, if all the necks could be exposed, the force would be destroyed. In this work they have been diligently looked out for, and in the course of it the principal and most active of them have been brought to view.

SECTION V.   DIVISION OR CLASSIFICATION OF FALLACIES.

So numerous are the instruments of persuasion which in the character of fallacies the present work will bring to view, that, for enabling the mind to obtain any tolerably satisfactory command over it, a set of divisions deduced from some source or other appeared to be altogether indispensable.

To frame these divisions with perfect logical accuracy will be an undertaking of no small difficulty—an undertaking requiring more time than either the author or editor has been able to bestow upon it. . . .

Mr. Dumont, who some few years since published in French a translation, or rather a *redaction,* of a considerable portion of the present work, divided the fallacies into three classes, according to the particular or special object to which the fallacies of each class appeared more immediately applicable. Some he supposed destined to repress discussion altogether—others to postpone it—others to perplex, when discussion could no longer be avoided. The first class he called fallacies of *authority,* the second fallacies of *delay,* and the third fallacies of *confusion:* he has also added to the name of each fallacy the Latin affix which points out the faculty or affection to which it is chiefly addressed.

The present editor has preferred this arrangement to that pursued by the author [Bentham had divided fallacies into "ins," "outs," and "either side," broken down into eleven subdivisions.—M.P.M.] and with some little variation he has adopted it in this work. [The selections in this book are taken from Part IV, Fallacies of Confusion.—M.P.M.] . . .

In the arrangement thus made, imperfections will be found, the removal of which, should the removal of them be practicable, and at the same time worth the trouble, must be left to some experter hand. The classes themselves are not in every instance sufficiently distinct from each other; the articles ranged under them respectively not appertaining with a degree of propriety sufficiently exclusive to the heads under which they are placed. Still, imperfect as it is, the arrangement will, it is hoped, be found by the reflecting reader not altogether without its use.

SECTION VI.   NOMENCLATURE OF POLITICAL FALLACIES.

Between the business of classification and that of nomenclature, the connexion is most intimate. To the work of classification no expression can be given but by means of nomenclature: no name other than what in the language of grammarians is called a *proper* name—no name more extensive in its application than is the name of an individual, can be applied; but a class if marked out, and as far as the work of the mind is creation, *created.*

Still, however, the two operations remain not the less distinguishable: for of the class marked out, a description may be given, of any length and degree of complication: the description given may be such as to occupy entire sentences in any number. But a name, properly so called, consists either of no more than one word, and that one a noun-substantive, or at most of no more than a substantive with its adjunct; or, if of words more than one, they must be in such sort linked together as to form in conjunction no more than a sort of compound word, occupying the place of a noun-substantive in the composition of a sentence.

Without prodigious circumlocution and inconvenience, a class of objects, however well marked out by description, cannot be designated, unless we substitute for the words constituting the description, a word, or very small cluster of words, so connected as to constitute a name. In this case, nomenclature is to description what, in algebraical operation, the substitution of a single letter of the alphabet for a line of any length, composed of numerical figures or letters of the alphabet or both together, is to the continuing and repeating at each step the complicated matter of that same line.

The class being marked out, whether by description or denomination, an operation that will remain to be performed is, if no name be as yet given to it, the finding for it and giving to it a name: if a name has been given to it, the sitting in judgment on such name, for the purpose of determining whether it presents as adequate a conception of the object as can be wished, or whether some other may not be devised by which that conception may be presented in a manner more adequate.

Blessed be he for evermore, in whatsoever robe arrayed, to whose creative genius we are indebted for the first conception of those too-short-lived vehicles, by which, as in a nutshell, intimation is conveyed to us of the essential character of those awful volumes, which, at the touch of the sceptre, become the rules of our conduct, and the arbiters of our destiny:—"The Alien Act," "The Turnpike Act," "The Middlesex Waterworks Bill," &c. &c!

How advantageous a substitute in some cases—how useful an additament in all cases, would they not make to those authoritative masses of words called *titles,* by which so large a proportion of sound and so small a proportion of instruction are at so large an expense of attention granted to us:—"An Act to explain and amend an Act entitled An Act to explain and amend," &c. &c.!

In two, three, four, or at the outside half a dozen words, information without pretension is given, which frequently when pretended is not given, but darkness and confusion given instead of it, in twice, thrice, four times, or half a dozen times as many lines.

Rouleaus of commodious and significative appellatives are thus issued day by day throughout the session from an invisible though not an unlicensed mint; but no sooner has the last newspaper that appeared the last day of the session made its way to the most distant of its stages, than all this learning, all this circulating medium, is as completely lost to the world and buried in oblivion as a French assignat.

So many yearly strings of words, not one of which is to be found in the works of Dryden, with whom the art of coining words fit to be used became numbered among the lost arts, and the art of giving birth to new ideas among the prohibited ones! So many words, not one of which would have found toleration from the orthodoxy of Charles Fox!

Let the workshop of invention be shut up for ever, rather than that the tympanum of taste should be grated by a new sound! Rigorous decree!—more rigorous if obedience or execution kept pace with design, than even the continent-blockading and commerce-crushing decrees proclaimed by Buonaparte.

So necessary is it, that when a thing is talked of, there should be a name to call it by—so conducive, not to say necessary, to the prevalence of reason, of common sense, and moral honesty, that instruments of deception should be talked of, and well talked of, and talked out of fashion—in a word, talked down,—that, without any other licence than the old one granted by Horace, and which, notwithstanding the acknowledged goodness of the authority, men are so strangely backward to make use of,—the author had, under the spur of necessity, struck out for each of these instruments of deception a separate barbarism, such as the tools which he had at command would enable him to produce: the objections, however, of a class of readers, who, under the denomination of *men of taste,* attach much more importance to the manner than to the matter of a composition, have induced the editor to suppress for the present some of these characteristic appellations, and to substitute for them a less expressive periphrasis. . . .

PART IV.   FALLACIES OF CONFUSION, THE OBJECT OF WHICH IS, TO PERPLEX, WHEN DISCUSSION CAN NO LONGER BE AVOIDED.

Chapter I.   Question-Begging Appellatives—(*ad judicium.*)

Petitio principii, or begging the question, is a fallacy very well known even to those who are not conversant with the principles of logic. In answer to a given question, the party who employs the fallacy contents himself by simply affirming the point in debate. Why does opium occasion sleep? Because it is soporiferous.

Begging the question is one of the fallacies enumerated by Aristotle; but Aristotle has not pointed out (what it will be the object of this chapter to expose) the mode of using the fallacy with the greatest effect, and least risk of detection,—namely, by the employment of a single appellative.

Exposition and Exposure.—Among the appellatives employed for the designation of objects belonging to the field of moral science, there are some by which the object is presented singly, unaccompanied by any sentiment of approbation or disapprobation attached to—as, *desire, labour, disposition, character, habit,* &c. With reference to the two sorts of appellatives which will come immediately to be mentioned, appellatives of this sort may be termed *neutral.*

There are others, by means of which, in addition to the principal object, the idea of general approbation as habitually attached to that object is presented—as, *industry, honour, piety, generosity, gratitude,* &c. These are termed *eulogistic* or laudatory.

Others there are, again, by means of which, in addition to the principal object, the idea of general disapprobation, as habitually attached to that object, is presented—as, *lust, avarice, luxury, covetousness, prodigality,* &c. These may be termed *dyslogistic* or vituperative. [See the nature of these denominations amply illustrated in *Springs-of-Action Table,* in Vol. I.—M.P.M.]

Among pains, pleasures, desires, emotions, motives, affections, propensities, dispositions, and other moral entities, some, but very far from all, are furnished with appellatives of all three sorts:—some, with none but eulogistic; others, and in a greater number, with none but those of the dyslogistic cast. By appellatives, I mean here, of course, *single-worded* appellatives; for by words, take but enough of them, anything may be expressed.

Originally, all terms expressive of any of these objects were (it seems reasonable to think) neutral. By degrees they acquired, some of them an eulogistic, some a dyslogistic, cast. This change extended itself, as the *moral sense* (if so loose and delusive a term may on this occasion be employed) advanced in growth.

But to return. As to the mode of employing this fallacy, it neither requires nor so much as admits of being taught: a man falls into it but too naturally of himself; and the more naturally and freely, the less he finds himself under the restraint of any such sense as that of shame. The great difficulty is to unlearn it: in the case of this, as of so many other fallacies, by teaching it, the humble endeavour here is, to unteach it.

In speaking of the *conduct,* the *behaviour,* the *intention,* the *motive,* the *disposition* of this or that man,—if he be one who is indifferent to you, of whom you care not whether he be well or ill thought of, you employ the *neutral* term:—if a man whom, on the occasion and for the purpose in question, it is your object to recommend to favour, especially a man of your own party, you employ the *eulogistic* term:—if he be a man whom it is your object to consign to aversion or contempt, you employ the *dyslogistic* term.

To the proposition of which it is the leading term, every such eulogistic or dyslogistic appellative, secretly, as it were, and in general insensibly, slips in another proposition of which that same leading term is the subject, and an assertion of approbation or disapprobation the predicate. The person, act, or thing in question, is *or* deserves to be, or is *and* deserves to be, an object of general approbation; or the person, act, or thing in question, is or deserves to be, or is and deserves to be, an object of general disapprobation.

The proposition thus asserted is commonly a proposition that requires to be proved. But in the case where the use of the term thus employed is fallacious, the proposition is one that is not true, and cannot be proved: and where the person by whom the fallacy is employed is conscious of its deceptive tendency, the object in the employment thus given to the appellative is, by means of the artifice, to cause that to be taken for true, which is not so.

By appropriate eulogistic and dyslogistic terms, so many arguments are made, by which, taking them altogether, misrule, in all its several departments, finds its justifying arguments, and these in but too many eyes, conclusive. Take, for instance, the following eulogistic terms:—

1. In the war department,—*honour* and *glory.*

2. In international affairs,—*honour, glory,* and *dignity.*

3. In the financial department, *liberality.* It being always at the expense of unwilling contributors that this *virtue* (for among the *virtues* it has its place in *Aristotle*) is exercised—for *liberality, depredation* may, in perhaps every case, and without any impropriety, be substituted.

4. In the higher parts of all official departments, *dignity—dignity,* though not in itself depredation, operates as often as the word is used, as a pretence for, and thence as a cause of depredation. Wherever you see dignity, be sure that money is requisite for the *support* of it: and that, in so far as the dignitary's own money is regarded as insufficient, public money, raised by taxes imposed on all other individuals, on the principle of *liberality,* must be found for the supply of it.

Exercised at a man's own expense, liberality may be, or may not be, according to circumstances, a virtue:—exercised at the expense of the public, it never can be anything better than vice. Exercised at a man's own expense, whether it be accompanied with prudence or no—whether it be accompanied or not with beneficence, it is at any rate disinterestedness: —exercised at the expense of the public, it is pure selfishness: it is, in a word, depredation: money or money's worth is taken from the public to purchase, for the use of the liberal man, respect, affection, gratitude, with its eventual fruits in the shape of services of all sorts—in a word, reputation, power.

When you have a practice or measure to condemn, find out some more general appellative, within the import of which the obnoxious practice or measure in question cannot be denied to be included, and to which you, or those whose interests and prejudices you have espoused, have contrived to annex a certain degree of unpopularity, in so much that the name of it has contracted a dyslogistic quality—has become a bad name.

Take, for example, *improvement* and *innovation:* under its own name to pass censure on any improvement might be too bold: applied to such an object, any expressions of censure you could employ might lose their force; employing them, you would seem to be running on in the track of self-contradiction and nonsense.

But improvement means something new, and so does *innovation.* Happily for your purpose, *innovation* has contracted a bad sense; it means something which is new and bad at the same time. Improvement, it is true, in indicating something new, indicates something good at the same time; and therefore, if the thing in question be good as well as new, innovation is not a proper term for it. However, as the idea of *novelty* was the only idea originally attached to the term innovation, and the only one which is directly expressed in the etymology of it, you may still venture to employ the word innovation, since no man can readily and immediately convict your appellation of being an improper one upon the face of it.

With the appellation thus chosen for the purpose of passing condemnation on the measure, he by whom it has been brought to view in the character of an improvement, is not (it is true) very likely to be well satisfied: but of this you could not have had any expectation. What you want is a pretence which your own partisans can lay hold of, for the purpose of deducing from it a colourable warrant for passing upon the improvement that censure which you are determined, and they, if not determined, are disposed and intend to pass on it.

Of this instrument of deception, the potency is most deplorable. It is but of late years that so much as the nature of it has in any way been laid before the public: and now that it has been laid before the public, the need there is of its being opposed with effect, and the extreme difficulty of opposing it with effect are at the same time and in equal degree manifest. In every part of the field of thought and discourse, the effect of language depends upon the principle of association—upon the association formed between words, and those ideas of which, in that way, they have become the signs. But in no small part of the field of discourse, one or other of the two censorial and reciprocally correspondent and opposite affections—the amicable and the hostile—that by which approbation, and that by which disapprobation, is expressed—are associated with the word in question by a tie little less strong than that by which the object in question, be it person or thing—be the thing a real or fictitious entity—be it operation or quality, is associated with that same articulate audible sign and its visible representations.

To diminish the effect of this instrument of deception (for to do it away completely, to render all minds, without exception, at all times insensible to it, seems scarcely possible) must, at any rate, be a work of time. But in proportion as its effect on the understanding, and through that channel on the temper and conduct of mankind, is diminished, the good effect of the exposure will become manifest.

By such of these passion-kindling appellatives as are of the eulogistic cast, comparatively speaking, no bad effect is produced: but by those which are of the dyslogistic, prodigious is the mischievous effect produced, considered in a moral point of view. By a single word or two of this complexion, what hostility has been produced! how intense the feeling of it! how wide the range of it! how full of mischief, in all imaginable shapes, the effects!

CHAPTER II.   IMPOSTOR TERMS—(*ad judicium.*)

Exposition.—The fallacy which consists in the employment of impostor terms, in some respects resembles that which has been exposed in the preceding chapter; but it is applied chiefly to the defence of things, which under their proper name are manifestly indefensible. Instead, therefore, of speaking of such things under their proper name, the sophist has recourse to some appellative, which, along with the indefensible object, includes some other—generally an object of favour; or at once substitutes an object of approbation for an object of censure. For instance, persecutors in matters of religion have no such word as persecution in their vocabulary: *zeal* is the word by which they characterize all their actions.

In the employment of this fallacy, two things are requisite:—

1. A fact or circumstance, which, under its proper name, and seen in its true colours, would be an object of censure, and which, therefore, it is necessary to disguise:—*(res tegenda.)*

2. The appellative which the sophist employs to conceal what would be deemed offensive, or even to bespeak a degree of favour for it by the aid of some happier accessary:—*(tegumen.)*

Exposure.—Example: *Influence of the Crown.*—The sinister influence of the crown is an object which, if expressed by any peculiar and distinctive appellation, would, comparatively speaking, find perhaps but few defenders; but which, so long as no other denomination is employed for the designation of it than the generic term influence, will rarely meet with indiscriminating reprobation.

Corruption,—the term which, in the eyes of those to whom this species of influence is an object of disapprobation, is the appropriate and only single-worded term capable of being employed for the expression of it—is a term of the *dyslogistic* cast. This, then, by any person whose meaning it is not to join in the condemnation passed on the practice or state of things which is designated, is one that cannot possibly be employed. In speaking of this practice and state of things, he is therefore obliged to go upon the look-out, and find some term, which, at the same time that its claim to the capacity of presenting to view the object in question cannot be contested, shall be of the eulogistic or at least of the neutral cast: and to one or other of these classes belongs the term *influence.*

Under the term *influence,* when the crown is considered as the possessor of it, are included two species of influence: the one of them such, that the removal of it could not, without an utter reprobation of the monarchical form of government, be by any person considered as desirable, nor, without the utter destruction of monarchical government, be considered as possible;—the other such—that in the opinion of many persons, the complete destruction or removal of it would, if possible, be desirable,—and that, though consistently with the continuance of the monarchical government, the complete removal of it would not be practicable, yet the diminution of it to such a degree as that the remainder should not be productive of any practically pernicious effects would not be impracticable.

Influence of *will on will*—influence of *understanding on understanding:* in this may be seen the distinction on which the utility or noxiousness of the sort of influence in question depends.

In the influence of understanding on understanding, may be seen that influence to which, by whomsoever exercised, on whomsoever exercised, and on what occasion soever exercised, the freest range ought to be left—left, although, as for instance, exercised by the crown, and on the representatives of the people. Not that to this influence it may not happen to be productive of mischief of any amount; but that because without this influence scarce any good could be accomplished, and because, when it

left free, disorder cannot present itself without leaving the door open
least for the entrance of the remedy.

~he influence of understanding on understanding is, in a word, no other
than the influence of human reason—a guide which, like other guides, is
liable to miss its way, or dishonestly to recommend a wrong course, but
which is the only guide of which the nature of the case is susceptible.

Under the British constitution, to the crown belongs either the sole
management, or a principal and leading part of the management of the
public business: and it is only by the influence of understanding on understanding, or by the influence of will on will, that by any person or persons, except by physical force immediately applied, anything can be done.

To the execution of the ordinary mass of duties belonging to the crown,
the influence of will on will, so long as the persons on whom it is exercised are the proper persons, is necessary. On all persons to whom it
belongs to the crown to give *orders,* this species of influence is necessary;
for it is only in virtue of this species of influence that *orders,* considered
as delivered from a superordinate to a subordinate—considered in a word
as *orders,* in contradistinction to mere suggestions, or arguments operating
by the influence of understanding on understanding,—can be productive
of any effect.

Thus far, then, in the case of influence of will on will, as well as in
the case of influence of understanding on understanding, no rational and
consistent objection can be made to the use of influence. In either case,
its title to the epithet *legitimate* influence is above dispute.

The case, among others, in which the title of the influence of the crown
is open to dispute—the case in which the epithet *sinister,* or any other
mark of disapprobation, may be bestowed upon it (bestowed upon the
bare possession, and without need of reference to the particular use and
application which on any particular occasion may happen to be made of
it),—is that where, being of that sort which is exercised by will on will,
the person on whom the occasion in question it is exercised, is either a
member of parliament, or a person possessed of an electoral vote with
reference to a seat in parliament.

The ground on which this species of influence thus exercised is, by
those by whom it is spoken of with disapprobation, represented as *sinister,* and deserving of that disapprobation, is simply this:—viz. that in so
far as this influence is efficient, the will professed to be pronounced is
not in truth the will of him whose will it professes to be, but the will of
him in whom the influence originates, and from whom it proceeds: in so
much, that if, for example, every member of parliament without exception
were in each house under the dominion of the influence of the crown,
and in every individual instance that influence were effectual,—the mon-

archy, instead of being the limited sort of monarchy it professes to be, would be in effect an absolute one—in form alone a limited one; nor so much as in form a limited one any longer than it happened to be the pleasure of the monarch that it should continue to be so.

The functions attached to the situation of a member of parliament may be included, most or all of them, under three denominations—the legislative, the judicial, and the inquisitorial: the legislative, in virtue of which, in each House, each member that pleases takes a part in the making of laws; the judicial, which, whether penal cases or cases non-penal be considered, is not exercised to any considerable extent but by the House of Lords; and the inquisitorial, the exercise of which is performed by an inquiry into facts, with a view to the exercise either of legislative authority, or of judicial authority, or both, whichever the case may be found to require. To the exercise of either branch may be referred what is done, when, on the ground of some defect either in point of moral or intellectual fitness, or both, application is made by either house for the removal of any member or members of the executive branch of the official establishment—any servant or servants of the crown.

But, for argument's sake, suppose the above-mentioned extreme case to be realized, all these functions are equally nugatory. Whatever law is acceptable to the crown, will be not only introduced but carried; no law that is not acceptable to the crown, will be so much as introduced: every judgment that is acceptable to the crown will be pronounced; no judgment that is not acceptable to the crown will be pronounced: every inquiry that is acceptable to the crown will be made; no inquiry that is not acceptable to the crown will be made: and in particular, let, on the part of the servants of the crown, any or all of them, misconduct in every imaginable shape be ever so enormous, no application that is not acceptable to the crown will ever be made for their removal; that is, no such application will ever be made at all; for in this state of things, supposing it, in the instance of any servant of the crown, to be the pleasure of the crown to remove him, he will be removed of course; nor can any such application be productive of anything better than needless loss of time.

Raised to the pitch supposed in this extreme case, there are not, it is supposed, many men in the country, by whom the influence of the crown, of that sort which is exercised by the will of the crown on the wills of members of parliament, would not be really regarded as coming under the denomination of sinister influence; not so much as a single one by whom its title to that denomination would be openly denied.

But among members of parliament, many there are on whom, beyond possibility of denial, this sort of influence—influence of will on will—is exerted: since no man can be in possession of any desirable situation from which he is removable, without its being exerted on him; say rather, without its exerting itself on him; for to the production of the full effect of influence, no act, no express intimation of will on the part of any person, is in any such situation necessary.

Here, then, comes the grand question in dispute. In some opinions, of that sort of influence of will on will, exercising itself from the crown on a member of parliament, or at any rate on a member of the House of Commons, composed of the elected representatives of the people, not any the least particle is necessary—not any the least particle is in any way beneficial—not any the least particle, in so far as it is operative, can be other than pernicious.

In the language of those by whom this opinion is held, every particle of such influence is sinister influence, corrupt or corruptive influence, or, in one word, corruption.

Others there are, in whose opinion, or at any rate, if not in their opinion, in whose language, of that influence thus actually exercising itself, the whole, or some part at any rate, is not only innoxious but beneficial, and not only beneficial but—to the maintenance of the constitution in a good and healthful state—absolutely necessary: and to this number must naturally be supposed to belong all those on whom this obnoxious species of influence is actually exercising itself.

Chapter III.   Vague Generalities—*(ad judicium.)*

Exposition.—Vague generalities comprehend a numerous class of fallacies, resorted to by those who, in preference to the most particular and determinate terms and expressions which the nature of the case in question admits of, employ others more general and indeterminate.

An expression is vague and ambiguous when it designates, by one and the same appellative, an object which may be good or bad, according to circumstances; and if, in the course of an inquiry touching the qualities of such an object, such an expression is employed without a recognition of this distinction, the expression operates as a fallacy.

Take, for instance, the terms, *government, laws, morals, religion.* The *genus* comprehended in each of these terms may be divided into two species—the *good* and *bad;* for no one can deny that there have been and still are in the world, bad governments, bad laws, bad systems of morals, and bad religions. The bare circumstance, therefore, of a man's attacking government or law, morals or religion, does not of itself afford the slightest presumption that he is engaged in anything blameable: if his attack is only directed against that which is bad in each, his efforts may be productive of good to any extent.

This essential distinction the defender of abuse takes care to keep out of sight, and boldly imputes to his antagonist an intention to subvert all governments, laws, morals or religion.

But it is in the way of insinuation, rather than in the form of direct assertion, that the argument is in this case most commonly brought to bear. Propose anything with a view to the improvement of the existing practice in relation to government at large, to the law, or to religion, he will treat you with an oration on the utility and necessity of government, of law, or of religion. To what end? To the end that of your own accord you may draw the inference which it is his desire you should draw, even that what is proposed has in its tendency something which is prejudicial to one or other or all of these objects of general regard. Of the truth of the intimation thus conveyed, had it been made in the form of a direct assertion or averment, some proof might naturally have been looked for: by a direct assertion, a sort of notice is given to the hearer or reader to prepare himself for something in the shape of proof; but when nothing is asserted, nothing is on the one hand offered, nothing on the other expected, to be proved.

1. *Order. Exposure.*—Among the several cloudy appellatives which have been commonly employed as cloaks for misgovernment, there is none more conspicuous in this atmosphere of illusion than the word *Order.*

The word *order* is in a peculiar degree adapted to the purpose of a cloak for *tyranny*—the word *order* is more extensive than law, or even than government.

But, what is still more material, the word *order* is of the eulogistic cast; whereas the words *government* and *law,* howsoever the things signified may have been taken in the lump for subjects of praise, the complexion of the signs themselves is still tolerably neutral: just as is the case with the words *constitution* and *institutions.*

Thus, whether the measure or arrangement be a mere transitory measure or a permanent law—if it be a tyrannical one, be it ever so tyrannical, in the word *order* you have a term not only wide enough, but in every respect better adapted than any other which the language can supply, to serve as a cloak for it. Suppose any number of men, by a speedy death or a lingering one, destroyed for meeting one another for the purpose of obtaining a remedy for the abuses by which they are suffering—what nobody can deny is, that by their destruction, *order* is maintained; for the *worst* order is as truly *order* as the *best*. Accordingly, a clearance of this sort having been effected, suppose in the House of Commons a Lord Castlereagh, or in the House of Lords a Lord Sidmouth, to stand up and insist, that by a measure so undeniably prudential order was maintained, with what truth could they be contradicted? And who is there that would have the boldness to assert that order ought not to be maintained?

To the word *order,* add the word *good,* the strength of the checks, if any there were, that were thus applied to tyranny, would be but little if at all increased. By the word *good,* no other idea is brought to view than that of the sentiment of approbation, as attached by the person by whom it is employed to the object designated by the substantive to which this adjunct is applied. Order is any arrangement which exists with reference to the object in question;—good order is that order, be it what it may, which it is my wish to be thought to approve of.

Take the state of things under *Nero,* under *Caligula:* with as indisputable propriety might the word *order* be applied to it, as to the state of things at present in Great Britain or the American United States.

What in the eyes of Bonaparte was good order? That which it had been his pleasure to establish.

By the adjunct *social,* the subject *order* is perhaps rendered somewhat the less fit for the use of tyrants, but not much. Among the purposes to which the word *social* is employed, is indeed that of bringing to view a state of things favourable to the happiness of society: but a purpose to which it is also employed, is that of bringing to view a state of things no otherwise considered than as having place in society. By the war which in the Roman history bears the name of the social war, no great addition to the happiness of society was ever supposed to be made; yet it was not the less a social one.

As often as any measure is brought forward having for its object the making any the slightest defalcation from the amount of the sacrifice made of the interest of the many to the interest of the few, *social* is the adjunct by which the *order* of things to which it is pronounced hostile, is designated.

By a defalcation made from any part of the mass of factitious delay, vexation, and expense, out of which, and in proportion to which, lawyers' profit is made to flow—by any defalcation made from the mass of needless and worse than useless emolument to office, with or without service or pretence of service—by any addition endeavoured to be made to the quantity, or improvement in the quality of service rendered, or time bestowed in service rendered in return for such emolument—by every endeavour that has for its object the persuading the people to place their fate at the disposal of any other agents than those in whose hands breach of trust is certain, due fulfillment of it morally and physically impossible,—*social order* is said to be endangered, and threatened to be destroyed.

Proportioned to the degree of clearness with which the only true and justifiable end of government is held up to view in any discourse that meets the public eye, is the danger and inconvenience to which those rulers are exposed, who, for their own particular interest, have been engaged in an habitual departure from that only legitimate and defensible course. Hence it is, that, when compared with the words *order, maintenance of order,* the use even of such words as *happiness, welfare, wellbeing,* is not altogether free from danger, wide-extending and comparatively indeterminate as the import of them is: to the single word *happiness,* substitute the phrase *greatest happiness of the greatest number,* the description of the end becomes more determinate and even instructive, the danger and inconvenience to misgovernment and its authors and its instruments still more alarming and distressing; for then, for a rule whereby to measure the goodness or badness of a government, men are referred to so simple and universally apprehensible a standard as the numeration table. By the pointing men's attentions to this end, and the clearness of the light thus cast upon it, the importance of such words as the word *order,* which by their obscurity substitute to the offensive light the useful and agreeable darkness, is more and more intimately felt.

2. *Establishment.* In the same way, again, *Establishment* is a word in use, to protect the bad parts of establishments, by charging those who wish to remove or alter them, with the wish to subvert all establishments, or all good establishments.

3. *Matchless Constitution.* The constitution has some good points; it has some bad ones: it gives facility, and, until reform—radical reform—shall have been accomplished, security and continual increase to waste, depredation, oppression, and corruption in every department, and in every variety of shape.

Now, in their own name respectively, waste, depredation, oppression, corruption, cannot be toasted: gentlemen would not cry, Waste for ever! Depredation for ever! Oppression for ever! Corruption for ever! But the constitution for ever! this a man may cry, and does cry, and makes a merit of it.

Of this instrument of rhetoric, the use is at least as old as Aristotle. As old as Aristotle is even the receipt for making it; for Aristotle has himself given it: and of how much longer standing the use of it may have been, may baffle the sagacity of a Mitford to determine. How sweet are gall and honey! How white are soot and snow!

Matchless Constitution! there's your sheet-anchor! there's your true standard!—rally round the constitution;—that is, rally round waste, rally round depredation, rally round oppression, rally round corruption, rally round election terrorism, rally round imposture—imposture on the hustings, imposture in Honourable House, imposture in every judicatory.

Connected with this toasting and this boasting, is a theory, such as a Westminster or Eton boy on the sixth form, aye, or his grandmother, might be ashamed of. For among those who are loudest in crying out theory (as often as any attempt is made at reasoning, any appeal made to the universally known and indisputable principles of human nature), always may some silly sentimental theory be found.

The constitution,—why must it not be looked into?—why is it, that under pain of being *ipso facto* anarchist convict, we must never presume to look at it otherwise than with shut eyes? Because it was the work of our ancestors,—of ancestors, of legislators, few of whom could so much as read, and those few had nothing before them that was worth the reading. First theoretical supposition, *wisdom of barbarian ancestors.*

When from their ordinary occupation, their order of the day, the cutting of one another's throats, or those of Welchmen, Scotchmen, or Irishmen, they could steal now and then a holiday, how did they employ it? In cutting Frenchmen's throats in order to get their money: this was active virtue:—leaving Frenchmen's throats uncut, was indolence, slumber, inglorious ease. Second theoretical supposition, *virtue of barbarian ancestors.*

Thus fraught with habitual wisdom and habitual virtue, they sat down and devised; and setting before them the best ends, and pursuing those best ends by the best means, they framed—in outline at any rate—they planned and executed our Matchless Constitution—the constitution as it stands: and may it for ever stand!

Planned and executed? On what occasion? on none. At what place? at none. By whom? by nobody.

At no time? Oh yes, says everything-as-it-should-be Blackstone. Oh yes, says Whig after Whig, after the charming commentator; anno Domini 1660, then it is that it was in its perfection, about fourteen years before James the Second mounted the throne with a design to govern in politics as they do in Morocco, and in religion as they do at Rome; to govern without parliament, or in spite of parliament: a state of things for which, at this same era of perfection, a preparation was made by a parliament, which being brought into as proper a state of corruption as if Lord Castlereagh had had the management of it, was kept on foot for several years together, and would have been kept a-foot till the whole system of despotism had been settled, but for the sham popish plot by which the fortunate calumny and subornation of the Whigs defeated the bigotry and tyranny of the Tories.

What, then, says the only true theory—that theory which is uniformly confirmed by all experience?

On no occasion, in no place, at no time, by no person possessing any adequate power, has any such end in view as the establishing the greatest happiness of the greatest number, been hitherto entertained: on no occasion, on the part of any such person, has there been any endeavour, any wish for any happiness other than his own and that of his own connexions, or any care about the happiness or security of the subject-many, any further than his own has been regarded as involved in it.

Among men of all classes, from the beginning of those times of which we have any account in history—among all men of all classes, an universal struggle and contention on the part of each individual for his own security and the means and instruments of his own happiness—for money, for power, for reputation natural and factitious, for constant ease, and incidental vengeance. In the course of this struggle, under favourable circumstances connected with geographical situation, this and that little security has been caught at, obtained, and retained by the subject many, against the conjoined tyranny of the monarch and his aristocracy. No plan pursued by anybody at any time—the good established, as well as the bad remaining, the result of an universal scramble, carried on in the storm of contending passions under favour of opportunity—at each period, some advantages which former periods had lost, others, which they had not gained.

But the only regular and constant means of security being the influence exercised by the will of the people on the body which in the same breath admit themselves and deny themselves to be their agents, and that influence having against it and above it the corruptive and counter-influence of the ruling few, the servants of the monarchy and the members of the aristocracy—and the quantity of the corruptive matter by which that corruptive influence operates, being every day on the increase; hence it is, that while all names remain unchanged, the whole state of things grows every day worse and worse, and so will continue to do, till even the forms of parliament are regarded as a useless incumbrance, and pure despotism, unless arrested by radical reform, takes up the sceptre without disguise.

While the matter of waste and corruption is continually accumulating—while the *avalanche* composed of it is continually rolling on—that things should continue long in their present state seems absolutely impossible. Three states of things contend for the ultimate result:—despotic monarchy undisguised by form; representative democracy under the form of monarchy; representative democracy under its own form.

In this, as in every country, the government has been as favourable to the interests of the ruling few, and thence as unfavourable to the general interests of the subject-many,—or, in one word, as *bad*—as the subject-many have endured to see it,—have persuaded themselves to suffer it to be. No abuse has, except under a sense of necessity, been parted with—no remedy, except under the like pressure, applied. But under the influence of circumstances in a great degree peculiar to this country, at one time or another the ruling few have found themselves under the necessity of sacrificing this or that abuse—of instituting, or suffering to grow up, this or that remedy.

It is thus, that under favour of the contest between Whigs and Tories, the liberty of the press, the foundation of all other liberties, has been suffered to grow up and continue. But this liberty of the press is not the work of institution, it is not the work of law: what there is of it that exists, exists not by means but in spite, of law. It is all of it contrary to law: by law there is no more liberty of the press in England, than in Spain or Morocco. It is not the constitution of the government, it is not the force of the law; it is the weakness of the law we have to thank for it. It is not the Whigs that we have to thank for it, any more than the Tories. The Tories—that is, the supporters of monarchy—would destroy it, simply assured of their never being in a condition to have need of it: the Whigs would with equal readiness destroy it, or concur in destroying it, could they possess that same comfortable assurance. But it has never been in their power; and to that impotence is it that we are indebted for their zeal for the liberty of the press and the support they have given to the people in the exercise of it. Without this arm they could not fight their battles; without this for a trumpet, they could not call the people to their aid.

Such corruption was not, in the head of any original framer of the constitution, the work of design: but were this said without explanation, an opinion that would naturally be supposed to be implied in it, is, that the constitution was originally in some one head, the whole, or the chief part of it, the work of design. The evil consequence of a notion pronouncing it the work of design would be, that, such a design being infinitely beyond the wisdom and virtue of any man in the present times, a planner would be looked out for in the most distant age that could be found;—thus the ancestor-wisdom fallacy would be the ruling principle, and the search would be fruitless and endless. But the non-existence of any determinate design in the formation of the constitution may be proved from *history*. The House of Commons is the characteristic and vital principle. Anno 1265, the man by whom the first *germ* was planted was Simon de Montfort, Earl of Leicester, a foreigner and a rebel. In this first call to the people, there was no better nor steadier design than that of obtaining momentary support for rebellion. The practice of seeing and hearing deputies from the lower orders before money was attempted to be taken out of their pockets, having thus sprung up in the next reign Edward the First saw his convenience in conforming to it. From this time till Henry the Sixth's, instances in which laws were enacted by kings, sometimes without consulting Commons—sometimes without consulting them or Lords, are not worth looking out. Henry the Sixth's was the first reign in which the House of Commons had really a part in legislation: till then, they had no part in the penning of any laws; no law was penned till after they were dissolved. Here, then, so late as about 1450 (between 1422 and 1461), the House of Commons, as a branch of the legislature, was an innovation: till then (anno 1450), *constitution* (if the House of Commons be a part of it), there was none. Parliament? Yes: consisting of king and lords, *legislators;* deputies of commons, *petitioners.* Even of this aristocratical parliament, the existence was precarious: indigence or weakness produced its occasional reproduction; more prudence and good fortune would have sufficed for throwing it into disuse and oblivion: like the obsolete legislative bodies of France and Spain, it would have been reduced to a possibility All this while, and down to the time when the re assembling of parliaments was imperfectly secured by indeterminate laws, occasioned by the temporary nature of pecuniary supplies, and the constant cravings of royal paupers, had the constitution been a tree, and both Houses branches, either or both might have been lopped off, and the tree remain a tree still.

After the bloody reigns of Henry the Eighth and Mary, and the too short reign of Edward the Sixth, comes that of Elizabeth, who openly made a merit of her wish to govern without parliament: members presuming to think for themselves, and to speak as they thought, were sent to prison for repentence. After the short parliaments produced in the times of James the First and Charles the First by profusion and distress, came the first long parliament. Where is now the constitution? Where the design?—the wisdom? The king having tried to govern without lords or commons, failed: the commons having extorted from the king's momentary despair, the act which converted them into a perpetual aristocracy, tried to govern without king or lords, and succeeded. In the time of Charles the Second, no design but the king's design of arbitrary government executed by the instrumentality of seventeen years long parliament. As yet, for the benefit of the people, no feasible design but in the seat of supreme power: and *there,* conception of any such design scarce in human nature.

The circumstance to which the cry of Matchless Constitution is in a great degree indebted for its pernicious efficiency, is—that there was a time in which the assertion contained in it was incontrovertibly true: till the American colonies threw off the yoke, and became independent states; no political state possessed of a constitution equalling it or approaching it in goodness, was anywhere to be found.

But from this its goodness in a comparative state, no well-grounded argument could at any time be afforded against any addition that could at any time be made to its intrinsic goodness. Persons happier than myself are not to be found anywhere: in this observation, supposing it true, what reason is there for my forbearing to make myself as much happier than I am at present, as I can make myself?

This pre-eminence is therefore nothing to the purpose; for of the pains taken in this way to hold it up to view, the design can be no other than to prevent it from being ever greater than it is.

But another misfortune is, that it is every day growing less and less: so that while men keep on vaunting this spurious substitute to positive goodness, sooner or later it will vanish altogether.

The supposition always is that, it is the same one day as another. But never for two days together has this been true. Since the Revolution took place, never, for two days together, has it been the same: every day it has been worse than the preceding; for by every day, in some way or other, addition has been made to the quantity of the matter of corruption—to that matter by which the effect of the only efficient cause of good government, the influence of the people, has been lessened.

A pure despotism may continue in the same state from the beginning to the end of time: by the same names, the same things may be always signified. But a mixed monarchy, such as the English, never can continue the same: the names may continue in use for any length of time; but by the same names, the same state of things is never for two days together signified. The quantity of the matter of corruption in the hands of the monarch being every day greater and greater, the practice in the application of it to its purpose, and thence the skill with which the application is made of it on the one hand, and the patience and indifference with which the application of it is witnessed, being every day greater and greater, the comparative quantity of the influence of the people, and of the security it affords, is every day growing less and less.

While the same names continue, no difference in the things signified is ever perceived, but by the very few, who having no interest in being themselves deceived, nor in deceiving others, turn their attention to the means of political improvement. Hence it was, that with a stupid indifference or acquiescence the Roman people sat still, while their constitution, a bad and confused mixture of aristocracy and democracy, was converted into a pure despotism.

With the title of representatives of the people, the people behold a set of men meeting in the House of Commons, originating the laws by which they are taxed, and concurring in all the other laws by which they are oppressed. Only in proportion as these their nominal representatives are chosen by the free suffrages of the people, and, in case of their betraying the people, are removable by them, can such representatives be of any use. But except in a small number of instances—too small to be on any one occasion soever capable of producing any visible effect— neither are these pretended representatives ever removable by them, nor have they ever been chosen by them. If, instead of a House of Commons and a House of Lords, there were two Houses of Lords and no House of Commons, the ultimate effect would be just the same. If it depended on the vote of a reflecting man, whether, instead of the present House of Commons, there should be another House of Lords, his vote would be for the affirmative: the existing delusion would be completely dissipated, and the real state of the nation be visible to all eyes; and a deal of time and trouble which is now expended in those debates, which, for the purpose of keeping on foot the delusion, are still suffered, would be saved.

As to representation, no man can even now be found so insensible to shame, as to affirm that any real representation has place: but though there is no real representation, there is, it is said, a *virtual* one; and with this, those who think it worth their while to keep up the delusion, and those who are, or act and speak as if they were deluded, are satisfied. If those who are so well satisfied with a virtual representation, which is not real, would be satisfied with a like virtual receipt of taxes on the one part, and a virtual payment of taxes on the other, all would be well. But this unfortunately is not the case: the payment is but too real, while the falsity of the only ground on which the exaction of it is so much as pretended to be justified, is matter of such incontestable verity, and such universal notoriety, that the assertion of its existence is a cruel mockery.

4. *Balance of Power.* In general, those by whom this phrase has been used, have not known what they mean by it: it has had no determinate meaning in their minds. Should any man ever find for it any determinate meaning, it will be this—that of the three branches between which, in this constitution, the aggregate powers of government are divided, it depends upon the will of each to prevent the two others from doing anything—from giving effect to any proposed measure. How, by such arrangement, evil should be produced, is easy enough to say; for of this state of things one sure effect is—that whatsoever is in the judgment of any one of them contrary to its own sinister interest, will not be done;

on the other hand, notwithstanding the supposed security, whatsoever measure is by them all seen or supposed to be conducive to the aggregate interest of them all, will be carried into effect, how plainly soever it may be contrary to the universal interest of the people. No abuse, in the preservation of which they have each an interest, will ever, so long as they can help it, be removed—no improvement, in the prevention of which any one of them has an interest, will ever be made.

The fact is, that wherever on this occasion the word *balance* is employed, the sentence is mere nonsense. By the word *balance* in its original import, is meant a pair of scales. In an arithmetical account, by an ellipsis to which, harsh as it is, custom has given its sanction, it is employed to signify that sum by which the aggregate of the sums that stand on one side of an account, exceeds the aggregate of the sums that stand on the other side of that same account. To the idea which, on the sort of occasion in question, the word *balance* is employed to bring to view, this word corresponds not in any degree in either of these senses. To accord with the sort of conception which, if any, it seems designed to convey, the word should be, not balance, but equipoise. When two bodies are so connected, that whenever the one is in motion, the other is in motion likewise, and *that* in such sort, that in proportion as one rises the other falls, and yet at the moment in question no such motion has place, the two bodies may be said to be in *equipoise;* one weighs exactly as much as the other. But of the figure of speech here in question, the object is not to present a clear view of the matter, but to prevent any such view of it from being taken: to this purpose, therefore, the nonsensical expression serves better than any significant one. The ideas belonging to the subject are thrown into confusion—the mind's eye, in its endeavours to see into it is bewildered; and this is what is wanted.

It is by a series of simultaneous operations that the business of government is carried on—by a series of actions: action ceasing, the body-politic, like the body-natural, is at an end. By a balance, if anything, is meant a pair of scales with a weight in each: the scales being even, if the weights are uneven, that in which is the heaviest weight begins to move; it moves downward, and at the same time the other scale with the weight in it moves upwards. All the while this motion is going on, no equipoise has place—the two forces do not balance each other: if the wish is that they should balance each other, then into the scale which has in it the lighter weight, must be put such other weight as shall make it exactly equal to the heavier weight; or, what comes to the same thing, a correspondent weight taken from that scale which has in it the heavier weight.

The balance is now restored. The two scales hang even: neither of the two forces preponderates over the other. But with reference to the end in view, or which ought to be in view—the use to be derived from the machine—what is the consequence?—All motion is at an end.

In the case in question, instead of two, as in a common pair of scales, there are three forces, which are supposed, or said to be, antagonizing with one another. But were this all the difference, no conclusive objection to the metaphor could be derived from it; for, from one, and the same fulcrum or fixed point you might have three scales hanging with weights in them, if there were any use in it. In the expression, the image would be more complicated, but in substance it would be still the same.

Pre-eminently indeterminate, indistinct, and confused on every occasion, is the language in which, to the purpose in question, application is made to this image of a balance: and on every occasion, when thus steadily looked into, it will be found to be neither better nor worse than so much nonsense: nothing can it serve for the justification of—nothing can it serve for the explanation of.

The fallacy often assumes a more elaborate shape:—"The constitution is composed of three forces, which, antagonizing with each other, cause the business of government to be carried on in a course which is different from the course in which it would be carried on if directed solely by any one, and is that which results from the joint influence of them all, each one of them contributing in the same proportion to the production of it."

Composition and resolution of forces: this image, though not so familiar as the other, is free from the particular absurdity which attaches upon the other: but upon the whole, the matter will not be found much mended by it. In proportion as it is well conducted, the business of government is uniformly carried on in a direction tending to a certain end—the greatest happiness of the greatest number:—in proportion as they are well conducted, the operations of all the agents concerned, tend to that same end. In the case in question, here are three forces, each tending to a certain end: take any one of these forces; take the direction in which it acts; suppose that direction tending to the same exclusively legitimate end, and suppose it acting alone, undisturbed, and unopposed, the end will be obtained by it: add now another of these forces; suppose it acting exactly in the same direction, the same end will be attained with the same exactness, and attained so much the sooner; and so again, if you add the third. But that second force—if the direction in which it acts be supposed to be ever so little different from that exclusively legitimate direction in which the first force acts, the greater the difference, the further will the aggregate or compound force be from attaining the exact position of that legitimate end.

But in the case in question, how is it with the three forces? So far from their all tending to that end, the end they tend to is in each instance as opposite to that end as possible. True it is, that amongst these three several forces, that sort of relation really has place by which the sort of compromise in question is produced: a sort of direction which is not exactly the same as that which would be taken on the supposition that any one of the three acted alone, clear of the influence of both the others. But with all this complication, what is the direction taken by the machine? Not that which carries it to the only legitimate end, but that which carries it to an end not very widely distant from the exact opposite one.

In plain language, here are two bodies of men, and one individual more powerful than the two bodies put together—say three powers—each pursuing its own interest, each interest a little different from each of the two others, and not only different from, but opposite to, that of the greatest number of the people. Of the substance of the people, each gets to itself and devours as much as it can: each of them, were it alone, would be able to get more of that substance, and accordingly would get more of that substance, than it does at present; but in its endeavours to get that more, it would find itself counteracted by the two others; each, therefore, permits the two others to get their respective shares, and thus it is that harmony is preserved.

Balance of forces.—A case there is, in which this metaphor, this image, may be employed with propriety: this is the case of international law and international relations. Supposing it attainable, what is meant by a balance of forces, or a balance of power, is a legitimate object—an object, the effectuation of which is beneficial to all the parties interested. What is that object? It is, in one word, *rest*—rest, the absence of all hostile motion, together with the absence of all coercion exercised by one of the parties over another—that rest, which is the fruit of mutual and universal independence. Here then, as between nation and nation, that rest which is the result of well-balanced forces is peace and prosperity. But on the part of the several official authorities and persons by whose operations the business of government in its several departments is carried on, is it prosperity that rest has for its consequence? No: on the contrary, of universal rest, in the forces of the body-politic as in those of the body-natural, the consequence is death. No action on the part of the officers of government, no money collected in their hands—no money, no subsistence; no subsistence, no service;—no service, everything falls to pieces, anarchy takes the place of government, government gives place to anarchy.

The metaphor of the balance, though so far from being applicable to the purpose in question, is in itself plain enough: it presents an image. The metaphor of the composition of forces is far from being so: it presents not any image. To all but the comparatively few, to whom the principles of mechanics, together with those principles of geometry that are associated with them, are thus far familiar, they present no conception at all: the conversion of the two tracts described by two bodies meeting with one another at an angle formed by the two sides of a parallelogram, into the tract described by the diagonal of the parallelogram, is an operation never performed for any purpose of ordinary life, and incapable of being performed otherwise than by some elaborate mechanism constructed for this and no other purpose.

When the metaphor here in question is employed, the three forces in question—the three powers in question, are, according to the description given of them, the power of the Monarch, the power of the House of Lords, and the power of the People. Even according to this statement, no more than as to a third part of it would the interest of the people be promoted: as to two thirds, it would be sacrificed. For example: out of every £300 raised upon the whole people, one hundred would be raised for the sake, and applied to the use of the whole people; the two other thirds, for the sake and to the use of the two confederative powers—to wit, the monarch and the House of Lords.

Not very advantageous to the majority of the people, not very eminently conducive to good government, would be this state of things; in a prodigious degree, however, more conducive would it be, than is the real state of things. For, in the respect in question, what is this real state of things? The power described as above by the name of the power of the people, is, instead of being the power of the people, the power of the monarch, and the power of the House of Lords, together with that of the rest of the aristocracy under that other name.

5. *Glorious Revolution.* This is a Whig's cry, as often as it is a time to look bold, and make the people believe that he had rather be hanged than not stand by them. What? a revolution for the people? No: but, what is so much better, a revolution for the Whigs—a revolution of 1688. There is your revolution—the only one that should ever be thought of without horror. A revolution for discarding kings? No: only a revolution for changing them. There would be some use in changing them—there would be something to be got by it. When their forefathers of 1688 changed James for William and Mary, William got a good slice of the cake, and they got the rest among them. If, instead of being changed, kings were discarded, what would the Whigs get by it? They would get nothing;—they would lose not a little: they would lose their seats, unless they really sat and did the business they were sent to do, and then they would lose their ease.

The real uses of this revolution were the putting an end to the tyranny, political and religious, of the Stuarts:—the political, governing without parliament, and forcing the people to pay taxes without even so much as the show of consenting to them by deputies chosen by themselves:—the religious, forcing men to join in a system of religion which they believed not to be true.

But the deficiencies of the revolution were, leaving the power of governing, and in particular that of taxing, in the hands of men whose interest it was to make the amount of the taxes excessive, and to exercise misrule to a great extent in a great variety of other ways.

So far as by security given to all, and thence, by check put to the power of the crown, the particular interest of the aristocratical leaders in the revolution promised to be served, such security was established, such check was applied. But where security could not be afforded to the whole community without trenching on the power of the ruling few, there it was denied. Freedom of election, as against the despotic power of the monarch, was established;—freedom of election, as against the disguised despotism of the aristocracy. Tories and Whigs together, remained excluded.

Last Epigrams and Sayings

A Note on *Last Epigrams and Sayings*

The gods on Bentham's Olympus were all secular, and he was loyal to them. They shaped his early style, and that remained with him until he died. There is much misunderstanding of this important point, for it is generally taken for granted that later Bentham is eccentrically jargonical and unreadable. Laski claimed that his obfuscations set back political science by fifty years. Augustine Birrell was overwhelmed by their crudity. "I felt," he said, "as though I had been asked to masticate an icthyosaurus." [1]

Few deny that his early style was lucid, terse, witty, epigrammatic, and straightforward—as well it might be, closely modeled as it was on two idols, Voltaire[2] and above all, Sir Francis Bacon. But then, it is said, he abandoned it in favor of monstrous, idiosyncratic, jaw-cracking neologisms. This is not true. Bentham abandoned nothing; he added, and continued to write in several styles, including others hitherto unacknowledged, for example, the letter-form or the dialogue, of which there are many specimens among his unpublished manuscripts.

Here among these last epigrams we have good examples. At the same time that he dashed off Baconian maxims, he took care to explain his jargonical method, or Nomography, the gist of which lies in the use of certain key functional verbs.

The themes of this last manuscript, no less than the styles, are the same

[1] Mack, p. 196.
[2] Whose *White Bull* Bentham translated as a young man.

mixture of old and new: some of them Bentham had emphasized ever since the 1770's, the years of his earliest practice pages and epigrams; others he developed with growing bitterness only in his old age. The word "calculate," for example, was always one of the fundamental terms of his vocabulary, along with others like "preponderance" and "Utilitarian." Old also was his relentless attack on the irrationality of English law, of "matchless constitution." Indeed, his whole life's work may be seen as an effort to create a rational, well-argued structure of law. His method from start to finish was the same nominalism and empiricism, learned initially as early as 1768 from Bacon and Locke. He would emphatically have insisted at any time that "when we come to data we come to real use."

But there were other new elements besides style; mood, for one thing. He had for decades been discreet, hoping to achieve his ends by quiet supplication. The years flew by, and he had nothing but failure upon failure to show for them. English law in 1820 was even more agonizingly tortuous, irrational, expensive, and dilatory than it had been in 1770. For one thing, there was much more of it. Gradually he became more and more angry and unrestrained, even demagogical, as he became ever more of a radical democrat. Keeping to his favorite medical metaphors, he felt that nothing less than an heroically stiff dose would cure the utterly prostrate victim, the British body politic. At the same time that he became ever more radical, he became ever more republican and anti-monarchical and personally vindictive. The caprices and inanities of the mad George III and the gluttonous George IV became rather an obsession; and he attributed the failure of Panopticon to George III's direct intervention, whether mistakenly or not we do not now know.

On the whole, though, Bentham's explosions were more high- than mean-spirited, churned out with impartial, exuberant zest, even gaiety. This became all the more true in the 1820's when the cause of law reform was at last seriously taken up by a platoon of parliamentary disciples—Lord Brougham, Daniel O'Connell, Sir Francis Burdett, Joseph Hume, and others. He died on June 6, 1832, having lived just long enough to rejoice in the passing of the great Reform Act of 1832.

Last Epigrams and Sayings
1831–32

(Vol. XI, pp. 71–74.)

To Lady Hannah Elice, October 24, 1831.

"The way to be comfortable is to make others comfortable.

The way to make others comfortable is to appear to love them.

The way to appear to love them—is to love them in reality.

Probatur ab experientia, per Jeremy Bentham, Queen's Square Place, Westminster. Born, 15th February, anno 1748—Written (this copy) 24th October, 1831."

From Bentham's Memorandum-Book, 1831.

"A child in arms—an Ourang Outang. Put a crown upon its head—put a sceptre in its paw. Blackstone's god it would be—all his attributes it would have: the good people of England would bow down and worship it, and tax themselves a million a-year to feed it."

"Arithmetical, algebraical, and musical notation are a portion of the quasi-universal written language; while the correspondent spoken exists in all its varieties. . . ."

"Unapt words in use:—1. *Integrity*—vice *integrality.* 2. *Calculate*—ambiguous, as between *likely* to produce the effect and *designed* to do so."

"A member of the aristocracy looks upon himself as the richer by every pleasure he deprives the democracy of."

"Vague generality is the lurking-place of error and fallacy."

"*Nomography.*—Proposed addition to the number of auxiliary verbs.

By this denomination may be designated certain verbs, which, by being prefixed to the nouns-substantive which are employed in the names of the corresponding operations, perform, and, as will be seen, with considerable advantage, the service, or say functions of, and become synonymous to, the several verbs, which, by a single word, are each of them expressive of the same idea.

These are:—

1. To *make,* with its synonymes, perform, etc.
2. To *give,* with its synonymes, transmit, etc.
3. To *receive,* with its synonymes."

[It was Bentham's characteristic habit to use such compound verbs and nouns rather than active verbs as ordinarily used. He found them much more convenient for analysis and synthesis.—M.P.M.]

"You don't know the idea again, unless you see it clothed in the same words. The *verb-substantive,* as it is commonly called, call it rather the universally applicable verb, for it serves to predicate existence of whatever subject-matter it is applied to.

With the help of the appropriate substantive, it might supersede the use of all other verbs; and the simplicity of inflection, and facility of being learnt, might then be maximized. . . ."

"1831—February 16.—The day after arrival at the age of 83.

J. B.'s frame of mind.

J. B. the most ambitious of the ambitious. His empire—the empire he aspires to—extending to, and comprehending, the whole human race, in all places,—in all habitable places of the earth, at all future time.

J. B. the most philanthropic of the philanthropic: philanthropy the end and instrument of his ambition.

Limits it has no other than those of the earth."

"*Logic.*—Abstraction is one thing,—association another; relation comprehends both: the one the converse of the other; *relation* is the most abstract of all abstractions.

Each thing is,—the whole of it, what it is,—but we may consider the whole of it together, or any one or more parts of it at a time, as we please —thus we make,—thus we have abstracted,—abstract ideas. . . ."

"*Data* are the fruit of induction. When we come to *data,* we come to *real use.*"

"Proceeding by analysis, you take in hand a relatively large thing of any kind, in any number: you put them together, and so make them into a whole.

Proceeding—operating in the way of analysis, you do as you do by a cucumber, when you cut it into slips to be eaten, when it has been peppered, salted, and vinegared.

Proceeding in the way of synthesis, you do by them as you do by a number of gooseberries, when you make them into a pie; or of grains of millet, when you make them into a pudding."

"Wherever there is a word, there is a thing: so says the common notion—the result of the association of ideas.

Wherever there is a word, there is a thing: hence the almost universal practice of confounding *fictitious* entities with *real* ones—corresponding names of fictitious entities with *real* ones. Hence, common law, mind, soul, virtue, vice.

Identity of nomenclature is certificate of identity of nature: diversity of diversity:—how absurd, how inconsistent to make the certificate a false one!" . . .

"Civil Code.—Power of aggregation: power of disaggregation. These are, in an indirect form, branches of the power of legislation. When the exercise given to legislative power does not apply directly to individuals, individually considered, exercise given to the power of aggregation is necessary to bring the mandate and the obligation home to individuals."

"Under matchless constitution, the *end* aimed at is maximization of depredation and oppression:—oppression for the pleasure of it, and depredation for the profit of it.

For the compassing these ends, the means which are employed, and which, so long as matchless constitution continues, matchless constitution will continue to employ are these: Denial of justice to all but the ruling and influential few, and by the non-lawyers among these few, consent to purchase what is called justice of the lawyer tribe, that the profit upon the sale may give them a community of interest in the maintenance of the system of depredation and oppression."

"A *fixed* penalty is a *license* in *disguise*."

"A government in which the few exercise dominion over the many, does it not stand condemned by that very circumstance?"

"When interest closes the eyes, the whole force of reason cannot open them."

"England, is it not a nation in which laws are established without any ratiocinative articles: without reason assigned; without reason assignable; without reference to reason; without any regard to reason; in the very teeth of reason? Is not this a headless nation?"

"A many-headed Incubus is the aristocracy of England."

"Make public functionaries uneasy. High-pressure engine, nothing is to be done without it. Nothing to be done by the people for their own security, but by applying to their rulers the force of the engine."

[And following is the very last memorandum that Bentham's amanuensis and executor, John Bowring, found, probably written early in 1832.—M.P.M.]

"I have two *minds:* one of which is perpetually occupied in looking at, and examining the other,—thus studying human nature, partly with a view to my own happiness,—partly with a view to that of the human species."

Index

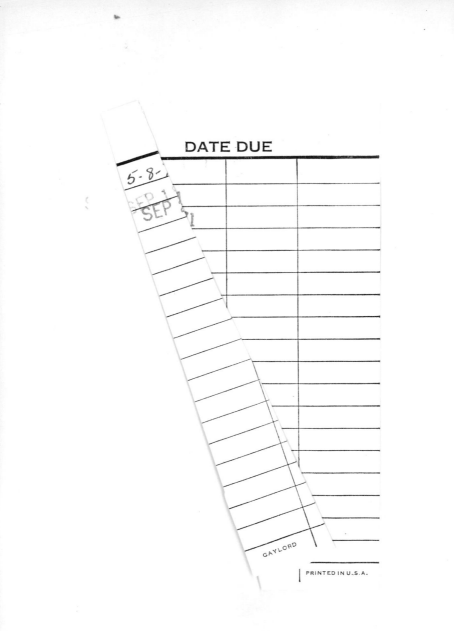

DATE DUE

5-8-

SEP

SEP